New York City Politics

New York City Politics

Governing Gotham

BRUCE F. BERG

RUTGERS UNIVERSITY PRESS

NEW BRUNSWICK, NEW JERSEY, AND LONDON

LIBRARY OF CONGRESS CATALOGING-IN-PUBLICATION DATA

Berg, Bruce F.
    New York City politics : governing Gotham / Bruce F. Berg.
        p. cm.
    Includes bibliographical references and index.
    ISBN 978-0-8135-4190-7 (hardcover : alk.paper) — ISBN 978-0-8135-4191-4
    (pbk. : alk. paper)
    1. New York (N.Y.)—Politics and government—1951–
    2. New York (N.Y.)—Economic policy.   3. New York (N.Y.)—Social policy.   I. Title
    JS1230.B47 2007
    320.9747'1—dc22   2007008413

A British Cataloging-in-Publication record for this book is available
from the British Library

Visit our Web site: http://rutgerspress.rutgers.edu

Manufactured in the United States of America

To Abbey

CONTENTS

ACKNOWLEDGMENTS

I became interested in urban politics while taking courses with David Caputo at Purdue University and with Bernard Ross and Wayne Hoffman at American University. I was fortunate to be a graduate student studying urban politics at the time of the New York City fiscal crisis. At that point, my study of urban politics and New York City politics became nearly synonymous. Teaching and living in New York City for three decades further strengthened my New York City chauvinism, both socially and scholarly.

I am greatly indebted to Fordham University and its Office of Research for providing me with the necessary release time to conduct the research for and initial writing of the manuscript. I have been assisted in this work by my colleagues at Fordham. Paul Kantor reviewed several early chapters of the manuscript and his comments were invaluable. David Lawrence also reviewed the introductory chapter and supplied helpful comments. Rich Fleisher and Jeff Cohen provided bibliographic help for the chapters on the city council and mayor, respectively. Jeanne Flavin provided editorial guidance with the manuscript prospectus. At Fordham, I was also aided by a group of graduate and undergraduate assistants including Alyssa Lugg, Samantha Lindsay, Joe Messina, and Nathan Powell. They provided research, bibliographic, and editorial assistance.

At Rutgers University Press, I am grateful to Marlie Wasserman for her decision to support the project, and Marilyn Campbell deserves thanks for her pre-publication assistance with formatting.

I am probably most indebted to my family. Throughout the project, they were a source of encouragement, criticism, and distraction. They also provided very substantive assistance as well. Jake Berg read the first draft of the first chapter and provided very positive feedback. Toward the end of the project, Jonah Berg provided technical assistance that saved a great deal of time in formatting the manuscript to the publisher's specifications. Finally, my wife, Abbey, proofread the manuscript, asked appropriate questions, and provided encouragement throughout the project.

New York City Politics

1

Introduction

At the beginning of the twenty-first century, the governance of American cities is influenced by a variety of forces. These forces include the fiscal needs of the cities' political systems and the constraints that affect the systems' ability to raise revenue; the cities' position in the American federal system; and the increasing racial and ethnic diversity of the cities' populations. No city illustrates the influence of these forces better than New York City.

Over the past several decades, the study of urban politics has produced a number of approaches to explain the behavior of urban political systems. Many of these approaches have succeeded in addressing some, but not all, of the above-mentioned forces. Moreover, few studies have attempted to address how the divergent yet at times overlapping nature of these forces affects a single urban political system. This work will examine how those critical forces—economic/fiscal, intergovernmental, and social—affect the governance of New York City.

The Governance of the City's Political System

Governance of the city's political system involves a complex set of functions around three broad themes: democratic accountability, the delivery of public goods and services, and the maintenance of civil harmony. These three themes incorporate the political system's goal of processing inputs and producing outputs while promoting system stability and survival (Easton 1965). First, the theme of democratic accountability concerns the extent to which the leaders of the political system respond to the demands of the people and are held accountable to the people. Democratic accountability depends on elections but also on the representative nature of the entire political system, including interest groups, political parties, and the executive branch of government. The second theme, the delivery of goods and services, concerns the ability of the political system to deliver those public goods and services vital to the city. This theme includes the delivery of those services that over time have been deemed critical to urban governments, such as police, fire, sanitation, public health, and education. The service delivery function also encompasses amenities such as parks, welfare, and social services that promote health and a level of well-being for all citizens regardless of income and that add to the city's overall quality of life. Over time, the service delivery responsibilities of urban political systems have more or less stabilized, but are still influenced by available resources and citizen demands.

The third theme, the maintenance of civil harmony, recognizes that there will be conflicts among those involved in the political system in regard to decisions concerning the delivery of public goods and services and the response to citizen demands. Political system decisions create winners and losers. The theme of civil harmony suggests that governance of the political system is best served when those active in the system remain committed to the process by which decisions are made, regardless of whether they win or lose those key decisions. Those in the political system promoting this theme cannot sit idly by and hope that commitment to the process emanates from the democratic procedures themselves. Commitment to civil harmony within a democratic process is achieved through a number of formal and informal mechanisms. First, civil harmony is advanced through an array of inclusive democratic procedures allowing all citizens to participate in the political decision-making process. These procedures must allow all to participate equally, however indirectly, in those decisions affecting the delivery of public goods and services. Second, civil harmony is advanced through the process's distributive decisions. There must be some minimal level of fairness in the distribution of public goods and services, such that even if the delivery of goods and services is not equal, it approaches equitability. A third way civil harmony is advanced is through the behavior of the leaders of the political system. Their behavior amid political conflict and reaction to political setbacks sets a tone and acts as a cue for their followers as well as for their political adversaries. Leaders help set the parameters for what is acceptable political behavior. Civil harmony is not synonymous with civil order, although a lack of civil harmony may result in a decline in civil order.

This book will examine how the social, economic, and intergovernmental forces affect the governance of the city. For the most part, the impact of these forces on city governance is divergent. First, each of the forces pulls the city in different directions through the constraints that they place on public decision makers. Occasionally, the impact of those forces overlaps and temporarily combines to pull the city in the same direction, but for the most part city decision makers find themselves conflicted when faced with the multiple forces. Second, while the forces present challenges for the governance of the city, the impact of the forces on city governance is by no means dysfunctional. In fact, in many instances the impact that the forces have on the city's political system enhances the themes of governance.

To understand political system governance, one must examine the key input and output institutions and actors, relevant behavior on the part of the decision makers, and the contextual environment within which New York City politics takes place. Understanding the formal as well as the informal political institutions and processes that formulate, legitimize, and implement public policy are critical to understanding governance. Interests groups, political parties, legislatures, executives, and bureaucrats all play key roles in New York City governance.

A Tale of Two Sports Venues

Most decisions made by New York City's political system lack controversy, lack visibility, and are supported by the citizenry indirectly through the electoral process or through their tacit consent. A smaller of number of decisions, given their impact, scope, and resulting conflict, raise issues of governance. It is through these decisions that one can observe most directly the impact of economic, social, and intergovernmental forces on the city. The Bloomberg administration's pursuit of two sports venue megaprojects illustrates these decisions.

Michael Bloomberg became mayor of New York City four months after the 2001 terrorist attacks on the World Trade Center. The first year of his administration was spent dealing with the economic impact of the attacks on the city, including their fiscal impact on the city's budget. Both of these challenges were exacerbated by an economic downturn that had begun in New York City in late 2000. The city and state were faced with the economic redevelopment of Lower Manhattan in the aftermath of the attacks. Although these conditions had the potential for increasing the level of political tension in the city, the political system under Mayor Bloomberg addressed them with a very low level of conflict. A cooperative city council assisted the mayor in controlling the city's budget and in raising city revenues via an 18 percent property tax increase. The Lower Manhattan Development Corporation (LMDC), an agency created jointly by the city and the state, took control of the cleanup and redevelopment of Lower Manhattan. And while the LMDC excluded the mayor and city officials from day-to-day oversight of the redevelopment, it also freed the mayor from having to oversee and take responsibility for the entire project. The low level of political conflict in the first year of the Bloomberg administration was attributed to the mood of cooperation in the post-9/11 era, the role of the state and federal governments in assisting the city in the immediate aftermath of the attacks, and the mayor's passive, nonconfrontational style in addressing potentially conflictual issues such as service delivery cuts. Regardless of the reasons behind the city's political peace in 2002, the lack of conflict allowed Mayor Bloomberg to look beyond Lower Manhattan during his first term and focus on the economic development potential of other parts of the city.

Freed from the day-to-day details of lower Manhattan's reconstruction, the Bloomberg administration addressed two proposed megaprojects during its first term. Both involved professional sports venues. The first project, which received far more attention than the second, was a proposed Olympic Stadium on Manhattan's Far West Side. The proposed stadium was part of the city's bid to host the 2012 Olympics. In addition, the stadium was connected to a proposed expansion of the Javits Convention Center, located immediately adjacent to the proposed Olympic Stadium site. Finally, the stadium was also linked to the city's attempt to lure one of New York's football teams, the New York Jets, back to New York City. Both the Jets and the Giants were sharing a stadium, initially built for the Giants, in East Rutherford, New Jersey, a suburb of New York City. The second project was a basketball arena proposed by Forest City Ratner developer Bruce Ratner. Ratner purchased the New Jersey Nets in 2004 with the intention of moving the team to Brooklyn after building an arena not far from Brooklyn's downtown. The Ratner project included housing, office, and commercial space spread among a number of towers surrounding the arena. Yet despite the imperative under which cities and elected officials operate to promote economic development and the quick fix that megaprojects provide these officials, the Olympic Stadium proposal failed to win approval in the political process at the city and state levels. Despite contrived lawsuits by project opponents, the basketball arena (at the time of this writing) appears to be on its way to realization.

New York City's Olympic Stadium

New York City's bid to land the 2012 Summer Olympics was initiated almost two years before Mayor Bloomberg took office. The effort was headed by Dan Doctoroff, who had also been in charge of New York City's failed attempt to get the 2008 Summer Olympics (Bondy 1999). Before taking over the nonprofit group NYC2012, "authorized by the city to compete for the games," Doctoroff had been a managing partner of a private equity investment firm (Cardwell 2001). Mayor Bloomberg's appointment of Doctoroff as one of his five deputy mayors, focusing on economic development, signaled his administration's support of the city's Olympic bid. And although Doctoroff's appointment as deputy mayor for economic development forced his resignation as formal head of NYC2012, Doctoroff noted that he would "continue as the city's main representative in furthering the plan" (Cardwell 2001). Early in his tenure as deputy mayor, Doctoroff admitted that if it was not for the city's Olympic bid, he would not be in city government (O'Keefe and Cyphers 2002).

A major piece of the city's bid for the Olympics was a new stadium. The rail yards on Manhattan's Far West Side had long been targeted as an attractive site. At the outset of his administration, Mayor Bloomberg was not fully committed to a stadium on Manhattan's West Side or anywhere else. Given the state of the city's economy in the aftermath of the terrorist attacks, Bloomberg halted preliminary plans for new stadiums for the New York Yankees and Mets (Saul 2002a). He was in favor of expanding the Jacob Javits Convention Center, the city's primary convention and trade show venue on Manhattan's West Side. There was consensus across the city's political system that the Javits Center was not large enough for the city to be competitive in attracting large conventions and trade shows and that the center, a state-controlled entity, should be expanded. By May 2002, however, the New York Jets had proposed a plan that would combine an expansion of the Javits Center, the Olympic Stadium, and a new stadium for the Jets (Bagli 2002). By October 2002, approximately ten months into the Bloomberg administration, the mayor articulated support for the stadium (Saul 2002b).

Over the next two and half years, Mayor Bloomberg became the stadium's strongest supporter. At the same time, the project mobilized considerable opposition. Community groups from the neighborhoods surrounding the stadium site (Hell's Kitchen, Chelsea, Clinton) opposed the plan not only because of the disruption that would be created from the stadium's construction but also the traffic congestion that would be produced on those days when the Jets played. Groups representing the East Side of Manhattan opposed the plan, realizing that the stadium's construction would deploy the Metropolitan Transit Authority's (MTA) infrastructure improvements to the Far West Side. East Side groups were hoping for the construction of the long-awaited Second Avenue Subway that would take pressure off the East Side's Lexington Avenue line. They feared that stadium approval would result in the MTA's concentration on extending the 7 train from Times Square to accommodate the new needs of the Far West Side. Groups from across the city opposed the stadium, arguing that the site was far more appropriate for needed housing and parkland. Many of the same groups focused on the price that the city and state would pay for the project. Even though the Jets had agreed to pay for the construction of the stadium itself, the city and state had agreed to pay for the platform over the rail yards on which the stadium would sit, and a retractable roof for the stadium that would make the building usable all year. The city's and state's contributions for the stadium were estimated at approximately $300 million each (Herbert 2005). The opposition was also focused on the Metropolitan Transit Authority. The MTA owned the land over which the stadium would be built. Opponents were concerned that the MTA would give the Jets the right to build on MTA property for a price far below market rates. Stadium opponents as well as transit advocates were angry that the MTA, an agency that had raised mass transit fares and reduced service, might be selling property rights at a loss (Herbert 2005).

The Regional Plan Association (RPA), a nonprofit group of business officials, also opposed the plan. RPA's analysis of the stadium argued, "the experience in North America is that stadiums, particularly football and dual use stadiums, have repelled commercial residential development, not attracted it" (Bagli 2004). Probably the most vociferous opponent to the Far West Side stadium plan was James Dolan, the head of Cablevision and the owner of Madison Square Garden. Dolan viewed the proposed stadium as competition with the Garden to be the city's premier sports and convention center. Between 2003 and mid-2005, Dolan spent millions of dollars in advertising and litigation to oppose the stadium

(*New York Times* 2005b). The stadium's supporters, including the construction and trade unions, countered with advertising of their own. Attempting to broaden the coalition supporting the stadium, early in 2005, Mayor Bloomberg and the owners of the New York Jets committed themselves to including businesses owned by minorities and women in the stadium construction project, including providing those minority- and women-owned businesses with consulting services that would make them more competitive in the construction bidding process (Rutenberg 2005). And after Mayor Bloomberg agreed to establish a task force led by Congressman Charles Rangel to "ensure that minorities, women and high school graduates" were included in the stadium construction, the Reverend Al Sharpton announced his support for the stadium (*New York Times* 2005a). As the 2005 election year approached, Democratic candidates for mayor, seeking to run against Mayor Bloomberg, came out in opposition to the proposed stadium. Possibly the most visible of the candidate opponents was City Council Speaker C. Gifford Miller. As City Council Speaker, on a council where Democrats outnumbered Republicans 48–3, Miller used the council and its role in the legislative and policymaking process to oppose the stadium.

While the Regional Plan Association's analysis questioned whether the proposed sports and convention center would "generate enough economic activity to justify its unprecedented cost," New York City's Independent Budget Office (IBO), an independent city agency, concluded that the project could be economically viable (Bagli 2004; NYC Independent Budget Office 2005). The IBO report concluded that over the proposed thirty-one-year financing of the sports and convention center, the project could generate over $200 million in revenue for the city, the state, and the Metropolitan Transit Authority (Independent Budget Office 2005). While this is not a great deal of money over a thirty-one-year period, the IBO report also noted that in order to break even, the convention center would only need to host fourteen conventions per year, in addition to the Jets games (IBO 2005). The project's proponents claimed that the sports and convention center would host many more conventions than that.

As summer 2005 approached, Mayor Bloomberg and the Olympics/Jets Stadium proponents pushed for a resolution. They believed that a firm commitment to build the stadium would help with the city's Olympic bid. The International Olympic Committee was scheduled to make a decision in July 2005. The decision-making body where the stadium issue would be resolved was the New York State Public Authorities Board, a state agency that would have to approve the $300 million state contribution to the stadium as well as the MTA's ability to sell property rights to the Jets at less than market rates. There were three voting members of the board, representatives of Governor Pataki, Speaker of the New York State Assembly Sheldon Silver (a Democrat who represented Lower Manhattan), and State Senate Majority Leader Joseph Bruno (an upstate Republican) (Bagli 2005b; Nielsen 2006). Governor Pataki, a stadium proponent, delayed a vote by the Public Authorities Board several times during Spring, 2005 in order to give Mayor

Bloomberg and the project's proponents a chance to convince Silver and Bruno to support the project (Bagli 2005b). Both Bruno and Silver agreed to support the stadium if the city first received the Olympic bid but refused to support the project prior to the city's receiving the bid (Stout and Bagli 2005). Mayor Bloomberg, on the contrary, insisted that a commitment by the city to build the stadium would be needed to land the bid (Bagli 2005c). On several occasions, however, Sheldon Silver had expressed "concerns that the office space to be built as part of a broader plan to transform the area around the stadium would compete with office space to be built in Lower Manhattan," Silver's district (Cooper and Bagli 2005).

On June 6, the state Public Authorities Control Board met and rejected the state's support of a stadium on Manhattan's Far West Side. State Assembly Speaker Silver and State Senate Majority Leader Bruno both opposed the project. Bruno's opposition to the stadium was attributed to traditional upstate-downstate antipathy. Silver explained his opposition, stating that he could not support the stadium because commercial redevelopment of the Far West Side, which was appended to the stadium plan, would hinder the redevelopment of Lower Manhattan (Bagli and Cooper 2005). In the aftermath of the West Side stadium rejection, the Bloomberg administration hastily entered into an agreement with the New York Mets. The Mets were preparing to build and pay for a new stadium in Queens, next to their existing stadium. According to the arrangement, the city would pay the additional cost of converting the stadium for Olympic use if the city received the 2012 Olympics bid (Zinser 2005). When London was awarded the 2012 Olympics, there was no need for the city to pursue any additional arrangement with the Mets.

Atlantic Yards Nets Arena

Similar to the New York Jets football team, the New Jersey Nets of the National Basketball Association played in New Jersey and in 2002–2003 were looking for a new arena. Rumors in mid-2003 had developer Bruce Ratner of Forest City Ratner building the Nets an arena in Brooklyn above the Long Island Railroad lines on Atlantic Avenue (Farrell 2003). By late 2003, Ratner had unveiled an entire complex for the Brooklyn Atlantic Yards designed by world-famous architect Frank Gehry. The complex included an arena for the Nets surrounded by office towers, apartment buildings, commercial space, and six acres of parkland. Some of the proposed towers were sixty stories tall, much taller than any other existing building in downtown Brooklyn (Cardwell 2005). The financing and construction of the project was contingent, in part, on Ratner's purchase of the Nets basketball franchise (Muschamp 2003). As originally designed, the twenty-one-acre project would be the "largest development in the city outside of Manhattan in the last 25 years" (Bagli 2005a). Also similar to the Jets stadium issue, the state and the MTA were major participants in the project. Some of the land on which the arena complex would be built was owned by the MTA.

Unlike the Jets/Olympic Stadium, which would have required at least $600 million of state and city financing, developer Bruce Ratner announced at a press conference that his project "will be almost exclusively privately financed" (quoted in Bagli 2003). The state and city each were expected to contribute approximately $100 million for "site preparation, new streets and utilities and environmental cleanup" (Bagli 2005a). Ratner was also relying on the state to condemn one block in the project area that housed approximately 100 residents (Bagli 2003). Early in 2005, the city and state signed a nonbinding memorandum of understanding approving Ratner's proposal to build the arena as well as over a dozen mixed-income residential buildings adjacent to the arena site. In another agreement promulgated at the same time as the memorandum of understanding, the state and city agreed that they "would arrange for (Ratner's) firm to obtain rights to build almost 1.9 million square feet of residential and commercial space in downtown Brooklyn, even if the MTA rejected the firm's bid" denying it the ability to build the arena (Hemel 2005). Since the project's sponsor was the Empire State Development Corporation, an agency of New York State, the project was exempt from the city's Uniform Land Use Review Process, a sometimes politically contentious but democratically transparent process (Confessore 2005c). The project would still have to go through an environmental review and be approved by state the Public Authorities Control Board, the same board that rejected the proposed Olympic/Jets Stadium (Bagli 2005a).

As in the case of the Far West Side stadium, the MTA was a major landholder in the Atlantic Yards. Forest City Ratner needed the MTA to make its land available, either through sale or lease (Bagli 2003). In September 2005, the MTA board voted to sell Forest City Ratner the rights to build above the Atlantic Avenue rail yards. Ratner was forced to double its initial bid, from 50 to 100 million dollars, in order get the MTA's approval. There was another firm that had offered the MTA more for the rights to build over the rail yards but the MTA termed the other bid "incomplete" (Colford 2005).

Similar to the Olympic/Jets Stadium, the Nets Arena project generated opposition. At the center of the opposition were several hundred individuals who would be displaced if the state condemned the property on which their residences stood. These individuals were supported in their opposition by community groups who feared that the Atlantic Yards project would change the character of the Brooklyn community (Green 2005). The opposition groups held rallies and developed alternate plans for the neighborhood, arguing that Ratner's proposal would be environmentally harmful to the neighborhood and would result in overdevelopment (Rutenberg and Brick 2005). Some members of the city council, especially those representing communities near or adjacent to the arena, opposed the project. They argued that at the very least, the project should be subject to the city's Uniform Land Use Review Process (ULURP) rather than being deliberated at the state level (New York City Council Press Conference 2005). C. Gifford Miller, Democratic Speaker of the City Council and candidate for mayor, supported the project. Contrasting his support for the Atlantic Yards project with his opposition to the Jets/Olympic Stadium, Miller noted the importance of the community involvement and the commitment by Forest City Ratner to build low-income housing (Confessore 2005a).

Ratner was able to deflate the opposition with a multifaceted strategy. First, he hired one of the city's leading public relations firms with Democratic Party connections. The firm assisted Forest City Ratner in recruiting local politicians to support the arena project. The public relations firm organized presentations for "community boards, businesses, block associations, and others" (Confessore 2005b). Second, Forest City Ratner hired a media consultant who produced promotional mailings that were sent to households in Brooklyn neighborhoods surrounding the project (Confessore 2005b). Third, Forest City Ratner reached out to select community groups in Brooklyn, especially those who had been addressing issues of unemployment among low-income Brooklynites.

The most significant blow to the opposition was the signing of an unprecedented legally binding Community Benefits Agreement between Forest City Ratner and a number of community groups. Among the agreement participants were groups who would have been expected to oppose the project, including the Association for Community Organizations for Reform Now (ACORN), a national grassroots advocacy organization for disadvantaged communities, as well as leading minority clerics in the Brooklyn community. The agreement covered the inclusion of low-income housing in the project, the use of minority contractors in the construction of the project, job training, and community use of the arena and its facilities (Rutenberg and Brick 2005; New York City Mayor's Office 2005). While the Agreement did not eliminate the opposition, it significantly weakened it (Kolben 2005). In 2006, the State Public Authorities Board approved the Atlantic Yards project.

Urban political systems make binding decisions on their citizens. As was illustrated in both the Olympic Stadium and Nets Arena cases, governance of an urban political system includes the processing of inputs (demands and supports) and the production of outputs (binding policy decisions) (Easton 1965). Scarce resources/supports limit the number of demands to which any political system can respond. Not every demand gets a positive response. Given the number and variety of demands that urban political systems receive, officials inside the system have considerable discretion in choosing which demands to respond to. They are not however entirely free to pick and choose as they please. Societal forces, both inside and outside the political system, influence the choices they make.

Governance of an urban political system, such as New York City, encompasses a complex set of functions. These include the maintenance of democratic accountability by which the demands enter the political system, the delivery of goods and services (outputs) based on decisions by political officials regarding the use of supports, and the fact that these sometimes highly charged political decisions occur amid varying levels of civil harmony.

The debates and decisions surrounding the Far West Side Olympic/Jets Stadium and the Atlantic Yards Nets Arena reflect the governance issues facing many urban political systems today. They reflect the demands being made upon urban political systems and the constraints under which these political systems must respond. Public officials want to expand their cities' tax bases and make their cities attractive for their constituents as well as those outside the city. They must do this, however, amid a context that imposes constraints. In both the arena and stadium debates, public officials wanted to respond positively to the demands being made, but they were influenced if not constrained by other political constituencies. Although these other constituencies shared the broad value of economic growth, they brought with them other values that inhibited, if not pro-hibited, the achievement of consensus on the particular issue at hand. These other values included ethnic, racial, as well as intergovernmental interests.

In both the Olympic/Jets Stadium case and the Nets Arena case, propo-nents sought to include minority groups in their coalitions. In the Nets Arena case, the inclusion of these groups, via the Community Benefits Agreement, appeared to be enough to marginalize the remaining opposition. In the Olympic/ Jets Stadium case, the inclusion of minority groups was not sufficient to reverse the balance of power against the stadium. Similarly, New York State played a major role in the decisions regarding both projects. Both projects were exempted from the city's land use process because of the state involvement. While this freed the projects from many local political forces, it tied the proj-ects to a small number of state officials, especially the Public Authorities Board. This board was responsible for rejecting the stadium project due to a combi-nation of upstate indifference, if not antipathy, toward the city, and concern about the Far West Side's possible competition with Lower Manhattan's recov-ery. The same board, however, supported the Nets Arena, although it could have just as easily rejected that project too. At the same time, the two projects' exemption from the local land use process angered local politicians and threat-ened civil harmony, especially the Atlantic Yards project, in which a number of local politicians, excluded from key decisions regarding the project, challenged its legitimacy.

The Economic City: The Need for a Positive Fiscal Balance

The city is a business center. In fact, the development of the modern city is pri-marily the result of economic behavior on the part of those seeking to manu-facture, buy, sell, or trade goods. New York City is no exception. Once a center of national economic activity, the city has now become a center of global financial activity as well. The lifeblood of a city is its employment base. Jobs bring people to the city in search of economic betterment. Job growth allows families and communities to expand in an environment of economic security. Without a healthy employment base, mobile residents will leave to look for economic security elsewhere and investors will take their capital to jurisdictions where there is a greater chance of receiving a positive return on their risk-taking.

As part of the urban milieu, political systems need a healthy employment base also. And political systems need money. The services that New York City's political system must deliver to its citizens (e.g., police, fire, transportation, education) and those that it would like to deliver (e.g., parks, libraries, cultural affairs), require significant inputs of labor and capital. Political systems raise most of the revenue to fund their programs and services by taxing the economic activities, and resulting wealth, of its citizens and businesses, who in turn benefit from these programs and services.

Despite the reliance on tax revenues to fund services, New York City government officials realize that raising the taxes of citizens and businesses will encourage those with high tax burdens to leave the city and move to jurisdictions where the tax bite is not as great. Charles Teibout's classic dictum that people will "vote with their feet" suggests that people locate in a particular jurisdiction because of the specific mix of taxes and services offered by that jurisdiction (Tiebout 1956). It is one of the ironies of urban fiscal policy that those who can afford to pay high taxes are most able to move to jurisdictions to escape those taxes, and those who cannot afford to pay higher taxes are immobile. A second irony of urban fiscal policy is that those who can afford to pay higher taxes usually do not demand or need as comprehensive a set of services from an urban political system as do low-income residents. Those in need of more comprehensive services (e.g., health, welfare, housing, education) cannot on their own fiscally support the tax base of political systems to pay for these services. As a result, cities need to find ways to create a positive fiscal flow without destroying their tax base.

In creating a positive fiscal flow, New York City, like other cities, has utilized several devices. First, as noted above, the city has raised taxes. This method of raising revenue has significant limitations. Many politicians perceive that at some undetermined level, raising taxes will encourage wealthier components of the population, both citizens and businesses, to relocate to jurisdictions with lower taxes. Thus, raising taxes might have a negative impact on a city's fiscal flow if taxpayers relocate when taxes are increased. Research on business relocation, however, suggests that while taxes might be a consideration in corporate decisions to relocate, they are rarely, if ever, the primary factor (Lund 1984).

A second method of creating a positive fiscal flow is through intergovernmental transfers. New York City has been, and remains, very dependent upon the state and federal levels of government for financial support. As a source of revenue, however, intergovernmental transfers have some significant drawbacks. New York City cannot control intergovernmental fiscal transfers. Receipt of funds from the state and federal levels are subject to politicized budgetary proceedings in Albany and Washington, respectively. The city's fiscal decision makers cannot depend on revenue sources that must traverse a scrutinizing, and sometimes hostile, budgetary process. An additional problem with intergovernmental fiscal transfers is that they are usually earmarked or dedicated for specific purposes. They lack the flexibility of locally raised tax revenues. On occasion, matching requirements or accompanying mandates may even require the city to divert some of its own resources to the funded function or service as a condition of receiving the money.

A third source of positive fiscal flow can be achieved through preventing the growth of services delivered by the city or by cutbacks in those services. Similar to taxes, though, limiting or cutting back on services creates problems. There may be an undetermined threshold below which if city service delivery falls, it will result in the exodus of those affluent taxpayers who can afford to move. During the later half of the twentieth century, the city's inability to address the problems with its schools was a significant factor in decisions made by many middle- and upper-middle-class parents to move out of the city to suburban jurisdictions to deal with their children's education. Tiebout's dictum holds here as well. Similarly, budget cuts on the city's capital stock that results in deferred maintenance on critical infrastructure elements (e.g., roads, tunnels, bridges, mass transit) may result in businesses leaving the city, or deciding not to move to the city.

Given the limitations associated with the three previously mentioned means of creating a positive revenue flow, urban political officials have found that expanding the tax base by attracting more jobs to the city and by promoting the development of underutilized real estate may be the most politically palatable method. Increased economic development within the city's boundaries expands the tax base without raising taxes. Assuming new economic activity can be attracted, this fourth strategy produces no large group of losers. Jobs are created and city revenues increase, enabling the city to deliver a higher level of services. As in the case of the sports venues, some neighborhoods may be unhappy with the location of economic activity, or certain types of business in their communities. In addition some indigenous businesses may be upset with new sources of competition. The appearance of a large Pathmark grocery store in East Harlem, funded in part by Black entrepreneurs, resulted in significant protests from the Hispanic bodega owners in the community (Pulley 1995). Compared to the other means of creating a positive fiscal balance, increasing the city's ability to raise revenue through the promotion of economic growth is less controversial while giving city officials more autonomy from other levels of government.

Independent of its direct effect on tax revenues, economic growth has become one of the metrics by which mayors and urban political regimes measure their success. In the postindustrial city, documented economic growth has become a critical public relations and campaign tool for incumbent mayors and city officials, while documented economic decline has become a political albatross. At one of Mayor Rudolph Giuliani's "town meetings" in June 1997, a resident of Queens queried the mayor on New York's high unemployment rate. The mayor deflected the question by noting the complexities of measuring unemployment and labor force participation, making clear that the measured level of unemployment was a statistic that was not necessarily controllable through city policies or mayoral leadership. Then he went on to discuss how under his administration, New York had gained 150,000 new jobs, while under the previous administration, the city had lost 300,000 jobs. The message was clear. The current administration was managing the city competently as reflected in private sector decisions to either expand their businesses or locate into the city. The previous administration had not been successful in managing city affairs and had lost the confidence of business, resulting in a job exodus (Giuliani 1997). Regardless of whether the goal of urban economic growth is to demonstrate administrative competence or create a positive fiscal flow for the city, or both, the dilemma for city officials is that they are very dependent upon private sector activities for their own political success.

Over the last several decades, approaches to the study of urban politics have emphasized the role that the economic growth imperative has played in urban political systems, sometimes to the exclusion of other forces. While these perspectives are incomplete in their understanding of urban politics, the overemphasis on economic forces is understandable. These approaches—regime theory, the growth engine perspective, and corporatism—that emphasized the primacy of economic development in urban politics replaced an outmoded perspective, pluralism, developed earlier in the twentieth century that failed to recognize the importance of economic forces, relative to others. While the economic growth imperative is important in understanding the governance of New York City, it is not the only contextual factor that affects the city's governance.

The Intergovernmental City

A second set of factors that has an impact on New York City politics is the city's position within the intergovernmental system of the United States. On two occasions in the last thirty-five years, New York City's government structure was either temporarily or permanently altered through intervention of the federal or state governments. Over the same time period, actions by both the state and federal governments have constantly affected the city's budget, tax base, and ability to raise its own revenue. In addition, there are few areas of public policy where the city can act alone without influence from the federal or state levels of government. For example, decisions made in Albany affect local issues such as rent control and the city's school system, in addition to the previously discussed stadium and arena. And since September 11, 2001, the city and the federal government have strengthened their relationship regarding the rebuilding of Lower Manhattan and the funding of counterterrorism activities.

The United States political system is a federal system whereby both the national and state governments share sovereign power. The local governments are not part of the federal system and therefore lack the legal status, established in the U.S. Constitution, of the two higher levels of government. In 1868, Judge John F. Dillon of the Iowa Supreme Court issued several decisions that became the foundation for the legal relationship between states and their local governments. In one of the decisions, Judge Dillon noted that "municipal corporations owe their origin to and derive their powers and rights wholly from the legislature" (Zimmerman 1992). Explicit in the wording and the intent of Dillon's Rule is the belief that local governments are creatures of the state and as such their powers can be limited by state action. Moreover, if there is any doubt whether a function or power to act lays in state or local government hands, Dillon's Rule suggests that the state has primacy. What Dillon's Rule makes clear is that the relationship between the city and the state is not based on the shared power principles of federalism. Local governments are not sovereign levels of government who share power with the state. New York State is a unitary, not a federal, system where all power emanates from the state level. At the same time, however, Dillon's Rule has rarely been used as a guide for day-to-day city-state relations. All recognize that the local governments, as the level of government closest to the people, play a significant role in delivering services and addressing public needs. Both politically and administratively, the state would find it burdensome to run the affairs of New York City or any local government from Albany. As a result, New York State, similar to other states, has employed the legal principal of home rule to grant local governments the limited powers to run themselves.

As creatures of the states, local governments formally have little or no relationship with the national government. While the city's relationship with the state is formal and longstanding, the most significant aspects of the city's relationship with the national government date back only to the middle of the last century. New York City's relationship with the federal government was the result of a combined effort by large cities in the mid-twentieth century to use their increased representation at the federal level to gain benefits that many large cities could not get at the state level, where they lacked equitable representation due to legislative malapportionment. During the late 1940s, the federal government began to pass legislation that targeted money directly to the cities. These new urban-oriented federal programs were conspicuous in that the federal funds went directly from Washington to the cities, bypassing the states. Those who designed the programs were aware of the anti-city feeling in many state capitals, and they wanted to protect the money from being controlled by state officials who might spend the money on nonurban areas.

The increased federal aid, combined with a steady stream of state aid, made the city more dependent on other levels of government. As noted earlier, intergovernmental revenues became a standard technique for creating a positive fiscal flow. The city, however, could not always control the amount of aid it was receiving on an annual basis, creating a great deal of uncertainty in the city's own budgetary process. In addition, the aid was frequently accompanied by requirements dictating how the intergovernmental aid was to be spent, taking discretion away from the city. At the extreme, both the state and the federal government have resorted to issuing mandates, regulations that require the city to act without accompanying intergovernmental assistance.

The Social City

New York City's political history is closely tied to the immigration of ethnic and racial groups, their political mobilization, and the ultimate elevation of their leaders to positions of political power. Since the nineteenth century, the political system has served as a mechanism for the articulation of ethnic and racial interests. It has also served as a playing field upon which ethnic conflict has been managed.

New York City has the status of a majority-minority city. Whites make up a minority of the city's population, even if the heterogeneous group of white New Yorkers can be grouped together. In addition, no single ethnic or racial group makes up a majority of New York City's population. The very high percentage of foreign-born individuals living in the city elevates the significance of race and ethnicity in the city even today. In addition, neighborhood settlement patterns in many parts of the city serve to heighten racial and ethnic identity. The extreme heterogeneity of New York City combined with the ethnic/immigrant enclaves serves to strengthen racial and ethnic identity.

Racial and ethnic groupings in New York City continue to be used as the political shorthand through which electoral coalitions are structured as well as the gauge by which service delivery equity is measured. Racial and ethnic group leaders serve as brokers representing the interests of their constituents to the larger political system and interpreting city politics for their members. Electoral politics in New York City, in part, is viewed as an exercise in coalition building among racial and ethnic groups. Given intergroup tensions in the city, the inclusion of some groups in one's coalition makes it difficult to include others. Edward Koch's mobilization of white ethnic support during his first term cost him minority support that had been instrumental in his initial election. Rudolph Giuliani's courting of the Hasidic community in his 1993 bid for mayor, as well as his criticism of Mayor Dinkins's handling of the 1991 Crown Heights riots, made it virtually impossible to mobilize the Black community on his behalf.

While race and ethnicity might not affect the same aspects of governance as the imperative for economic growth, those areas of public policy influenced by racial and ethnic politics in the city are certainly no less important. In New York City, electoral politics and many public policy issues including crime, education, and sanitation have been perennially defined in ethnic and racial terms, and this in turn has influenced electoral as well as broader governance decisions.

Contextual factors, whether social, economic, or intergovernmental, constrain the choices made by those governing the political system. Contextual factors rarely dictate or determine policy, but they frequently limit the choices made by those with the formal authority to govern the city. After examining the economic, social, and intergovernmental forces within which New York City politics takes place, this book will examine critical actors and institutions who participate in the governance of New York City's political system. These actors and institutions include interest groups, political parties, the mayor, the city council, and the municipal bureaucracy. In discussing the principal actors and institutions involved in governing the city, the primary focus will be on how these actors and institutions are constrained by the contextual forces.

Within the city's political system, the role of the mayor, the city council, and the municipal bureaucracy are critical to the formulation and implementation of public policy. The mayor is the primary agenda setter in the public policy arena as well as the chief executive. The city council is the formal policymaking body, but the council also plays an important representation function within the policymaking process. Critical to understanding the role of the formal institutions of city government and their role in policy making is understanding the recent New York City charter revision and its impact on those actors and institutions. The municipal bureaucracy implements policy, but uses its discretion as both policy implementers and policy experts to shape policy to fit the needs of clients, interested publics, as well as the concerns of the bureaucrats themselves.

Beyond the formal institutions of governance, New York City politics has a rich tradition and history of interest group involvement in public policymaking. In addition, despite the city's frequent appearance as a one party town, political parties have played a significant, although at times uneven, role in the governance of the city. Their most critical role is the structuring of the electoral process and electoral coalitions.

The Urban Crisis: Forgotten But Not Gone

Throughout the 1960s and 1970s, the literature on urban politics and the state of cities spoke of an urban crisis. The movement of the middle class out of the cities left a low-income population with social and economic needs. In addition, due to the middle-class exit, cities lost the tax base with which to finance an adequate response to the rising needs of the urban poor. These problems were exacerbated by crumbling infrastructure and the decline in low-skilled but well-paying manufacturing jobs in urban areas. The fact that the new urban poor were primarily minority and the exiting middle class primarily White added to the tension as well as the intransigence of the problem. Many of the nation's best and brightest minds debated the plight of the cities and possible solutions that could alleviate the economic and social distress. For the most part, their conclusions were based on the assumption that the roots of the urban crisis were systemic and not individual. Based on this assumption, the federal government, state governments and many nonprofit organizations formulated and implemented programs designed to solve pieces of the urban problem. Some programs experienced moderate success while others failed. At times it was difficult to assess whether the failures were due to poorly conceived programs or inadequately funded good ones.

The riots of the late 1960s ended much of the innovative attempts to deal with urban poverty and unrest. Due to the inability of the programs of the 1960s to solve the urban crisis and because public attention was drawn away from cities by the Vietnam War, an air of hopelessness and cynicism took over urban policy discussions. Whereas during the 1960s, the federal government was viewed as a source of policy innovation and leadership, the emerging view of the 1970s was that the federal level stifled local innovation. Slowly, the urban crisis slipped off the national agenda, leaving the states, the cities, and the private sector to deal with urban problems that were no longer labeled a crisis. By the early 1980s, the liberal agenda for the cities was a historical artifact of American social policy and the subject of criticism across the ideological spectrum. To the extent that the emerging conservative majority had an urban agenda, it was tied to the private sector and local governments' ability to foster economic growth with little help from the federal level. It also saw urban problems as having their roots much more in individual behavior than in systemic factors. Government programs were and would continue to be unsuccessful unless individuals wanted to abandon socially dysfunctional behaviors. The 1996 Personal Responsibility and Work Opportunity Reconciliation Act that significantly reformed the welfare system from an entitlement to a temporary grant, reflects this change in philosophy.

Almost forty years after the urban crisis began receiving national attention, some conditions in the city have changed and some new problems have arisen, but the urban crisis remains. A disproportionate number of the nation's poor still live in the cities. As in the sixties, the vast proportion of these individuals is minority. They are inadequately housed and schooled. The long-term impacts of these problems are seen daily in their poor health and inability to find adequate employment. Urban poverty has become a fact of life, not a condition to be erad-icated. Urban governments still have difficulty raising adequate revenue to deliver quality services to their populations. They are still highly dependent on intergov-ernmental revenues to balance their budgets even though the federal govern-ment gives them far less, as a percentage of own-source revenue, than it did thirty years ago. Despite continued aid the federal government is no longer looked to as the source of comprehensive solutions or the sole financier of comprehensive programs.

Cities, and especially New York City, are still places of great contrast. The very poor do not live that far from the very rich. In some cases, the social indica-tors suggest a worsening crisis. Some neighborhoods are void of any middle-class or social institutions to support community stability and development. Some of these neighborhoods have gone through waves of heroin and crack cocaine, fur-ther deteriorating the social fabric. Single-parent families headed by females have become the dominant family type in many of these communities. In con-trast, gentrification in some of the city's communities is "solving" the poverty problem by pushing low-income families out, to be replaced by the new urban upper middle class.

New York City Politics and Theories of Urban Politics

The study of urban politics is rich in theoretical perspectives offering varying explanations for the governance of urban political systems. Few, if any, of these theoretical perspectives assumes the status of a macro-theory, claiming or demonstrating an ability to explain all urban political phenomena. A number of the theoretical perspectives, however, appear to have mid-level status in that they attempt to explain a significant segment of the urban political milieu (e.g., the urban political economy).

One cannot test the accuracy or validity of a theory of urban governance based on the behavior of one urban political system even if that city is the largest or the most representative. Even if there were consensus that New York City was a typical urban political system with a context and governing structures and processes similar to other cities, verifying theory based on a sample of one would be problematic. No such attempt will be made. The heuristic value, however, of studying one political system and its environment is taken as a given. While the accuracy of the explanatory power of an approach cannot be validated based on a study of one city, the initial stages of theory construction or testing might be possible. Any number of popular theories of politics has been conceived in the study of one city (Stone 1989; Dahl 1961). Any theory construction emanating from this study of New York City politics and policy promises to be complex. The central thesis of this analysis is that the governance of the city's political system is significantly influenced by three forces: economic, social, and intergovernmental. As previously noted, although this perspective will at times appear to be a one-way deterministic model, this analysis will present a number of examples of actors and institutions within New York City politics attempting to influence those forces that constrain them.

Additionally, although one cannot validate theory based on a study of New York City alone, one may be able to call into question those theoretical perspectives that are unable to explain the governance of New York City. Given what many believe to be the place of New York City in the study of urban politics, a theoretical perspective that cannot explain New York City's political system and its governance should be called into question. Non–New Yorkers may view the above statement as just another example of New York City chauvinism, but the above statement can and should be made about any of the larger cities in the United States.

Any attempt to impose structure on a sample of events places one at risk of misinterpreting those events and drawing the incorrect conclusions as to their significance. In their study of organizations, Cohen and March (1972) developed a "garbage can model" of decision making to deal with "organized anarchies."

Organized anarchies are characterized in part as decision situations or organizations subject to ill-defined preferences and fluid participation in the decision-making process. The "garbage can model" was developed specifically to deal with situations in which it was apparent that organizational actors were not behaving rationally. These actors were not behaving in accordance with their self-interest as defined by those observing their behavior and with no apparent ordered structure influencing their behavior from outside the organization. Under those circumstances, Cohen and his colleagues found organizations to be "a collection of choices looking for problems, issues and feelings looking for decision situations in which they might be aired, solutions looking for issues to which they might be the answer, and decision makers looking for work" (Martin 1982, 21).

In the absence of structure being hypothesized in this analysis, New York City's political system might also be one of those organized anarchies. Joanne Martin points out in her critical analysis of the garbage can model that it is not so much a theory as it is a metaphor for situations that defy structural interpretation. Significant factors simply exist inside a garbage can interacting in a way that, while not necessarily random, continually affirms the null hypothesis as they relate to structural relationships among them. They cannot be explained adequately by one approach or theory. The universe of all decisions (e.g., public policies) will not be examined in this study. As a result, the author is open to criticism that the policies examined in this analysis will present an inaccurate interpretation of New York City politics through the skewed sample of decisions being examined; however, it is an interpretation that affirms the hypothesized structural relationships. The reader has been warned.

2

The Economic Development Imperative

As discussed in the previous chapter, the city's attempt to build sports venues reflects a commitment to promoting economic growth across the city, even though there is frequently disagreement over the ways in which economic growth is being pursued. The city's intent to promote economic growth and the diverse strategies it employs to do so have become institutionalized over the last two decades. This chapter will discuss several of the methods employed by the city to promote economic growth.

The Economic Development Imperative and Governance

New York City, similar to all political systems, needs revenue to fund the delivery of goods and services, a major component of governance. Through the creation of new employment and the enhancement of land to more productive uses, the city expands its taxable assets. The proposed conversion of the Hudson Rail Yards to an Olympic/football stadium and the conversion of Brooklyn's Atlantic Yards to a professional basketball arena and office/residential complex were supported by governing elites because they were viewed as economic development projects that would benefit the city's tax base as well as creating jobs and wealth for the citizens of the city.

Economic development, however, also affects the governance of the city through its relationship to the other governance functions of democratic accountability and, less directly, civil harmony. As the Hudson Rail Yards and Atlantic Yards projects illustrate, large economic development projects are controversial for a number of reasons. First, they have an impact on the community where they are located. Some will view the impact positively and will support the project. As in the case of the Olympic Stadium and the Nets Arena, however, some will view the impact negatively and will oppose the project. Second, given the investment of public resources to subsidize the development, some will oppose the project, arguing that it is a bad risk for the city, a poor investment of public resources. Third, as in the case of Madison Square Garden's opposition to the proposed Olympic Stadium, some will oppose a project because they believe it compromises their own competitive advantage.

The existence of opponents and proponents to economic development projects, together with the fact that such projects include an investment of the political system's resources, necessitates that decisions regarding such projects take place through a process that is democratically accountable. The lack of such a process in making decisions regarding political system support of the project will result in some calling the legitimacy of the decision into question.

New York City's Changing Economy

Over the past several decades, those governing the city have had to promote economic development amid a changing economy. Since the 1960s, the city has gone through three major economic changes. First, between 1970 and 2000, manufacturing employment in New York City declined from almost 18 percent of its employment base to 4 percent, today representing approximately 250,000 jobs (United States Department of Commerce 2002). The manufacturing job losses experienced by New York were similar to losses experienced by other Northeastern and Midwestern cities, as jobs left urban areas, the region, and the country. Some jobs simply disappeared as firms went out of business because they could not compete with businesses in other parts of the region, country, or world with lower production costs. Despite this national, if not global trend, there are still officials and groups in the city who advocate economic development programs that will retain and attract manufacturing employment.

The role of the federal government in the decline of manufacturing jobs in the city should not be understated. The growth of the interstate highway system, a federal program, made the cost of moving goods far less expensive than it once had been. This negatively affected the relative advantage of locating factories in the city. Due to the ability to move goods fast and for little cost, the necessity of keeping manufacturing centers close to consumer markets decreased. Goods could be delivered to people living in New York City without locating the factory there. In addition, new manufacturing technologies favored one-story facilities with loading docks and ample parking facilities instead of renovating old multistory urban factory buildings. These new factories required a great deal of land. Land quantity and cost considerations influenced manufacturing movement out of the city to the suburbs, on many occasions out of the region, and on some occasions out of the country. Furthermore, population shifts away from Northeastern and Midwestern urban centers created new consumer markets for manufacturing goods across the country as well as new labor markets to staff the new factories.

Second, at the same time the city was experiencing a decline in manufacturing jobs, it was experiencing an increase in service employment. The primary area of service employment increase was in consumer services and included jobs in private health and social services, education, and retail industries. Consumer services comprised 24 percent of the city's employment base in 1970 but increased to 42 percent by 2000 (United States Department of Commerce 2002). A secondary area of service industry growth was in the financial, investment, and real estate (FIRE) sector (Drennan 1991, 34). Consumer service jobs pay less than manufacturing jobs or FIRE sector jobs. In fact some consumer service jobs were part-time, offered no benefits, and in some cases even full-time employment in the consumer service industry paid a wage that placed a family at or near the poverty level. In the past the unskilled and uneducated had a chance of obtaining a decent-paying manufacturing job. As manufacturing jobs were replaced by low-level consumer service jobs, being employed did not necessarily keep one out of poverty.

Unlike retail services employment, FIRE industry jobs, open to skilled college-educated individuals, paid so well that even though they never comprised a large percentage of the city's employment base (14.2 percent in 2000), their contribution to the city's tax base was proportionally greater than many other larger sectors, enhancing the importance attached to the financial sector in the city (New York City Office of Management and Budget 2001; United States Department of Commerce, 2002).

During the 1980s and 1990s, New York City's producer services employment base began to take on more of an international orientation, the third change. Saskia Sassen (1991) hypothesizes that several factors contributed to New York City's transformation from a city merely oriented toward FIRE services to a "global city" economy centered on international producer services (Sassen 1991, 1). First, the decentralization of economic activity, especially manufacturing, on a global scale created a need for greater centralized management, planning, and control. Although the location of manufacturing and economic activity became decentralized throughout the prior decades, ownership was not decentralized. In addition, centralized control became necessary to deal with the increasing involvement of governments in the regulation of economic activity on a multinational scale. Second, as global economic activity became more decentralized, support services developed and were produced to assist the corporations in controlling their decentralized enterprises. These support services included telecommunications, computers, advertising, and legal and financial services. These new producer services needed to locate near clients. In fact, the global dispersion of clients and client locations made the creation of a centralized marketplace of producer services all the more important from a potential client's perspective (Sassen 1991, 107). In some cases producer service firms specializing in advertising, legal services, telecommunications, or finance combined to offer a joint service to a multinational firm. Sassen argues that while the dispersal of manufacturing and the development of decentralized information technologies could have rendered cities obsolete, a select number of cities, including New York City, evolved into centers of command for the global economy. In New York's case, the city became a center for finance and other specialized services purchased by global corporations and governments (Sassen 1997, 175).

Although New York City's central business district (CBD), defined as Manhattan south of Ninety-sixth Street, survived the thirty-year transition from a manufacturing-based economy to a global city, outerborough economic health did not fare as well. The manufacturing job losses that Manhattan suffered were compensated for by increases in the service sector and particularly the higher-paying FIRE sector. Not only did the outer boroughs not recover the manufacturing job losses they suffered in the 1970s and 1980s through gains in service jobs, but the service jobs they did attract were more in the lower paying consumer service sector than the producer service sector. Manhattan's CBD survived because it remained the center of business activity in the region, despite its changing economy. The outer boroughs lacked the characteristics of a central business district. In the past they had served the region more as residential centers than as manufacturing centers. They also lacked the housing stock to offer residences to the growing white-collar workforce in the FIRE sector who either located in Manhattan or moved to the suburbs. The appearance of poverty populations in the outer boroughs made them even less attractive (Savitch 1988, 40).

The increased mobility of capital and the attention that corporate moves have received has exacerbated the uncertainty for New York City's public decision makers, making them even more aware of the city's vulnerability and their consequent need to act affirmatively to promote economic growth. The city's relationship with business and promotion of economic development, however, was not new even though many of the mechanisms through which the present relationship manifests itself might be. As far back as the early 1800s, the promotion of economic growth was seen as synonymous with good government. Businessmen were seen as the likely group from which political leaders would be chosen, and politicians of the day understood that they were in office in part to promote the economic interests of their city. The "merchant entrepreneur" class stood atop the local economic and political hierarchy because the two sectors were seen as being synonymous (Kantor and Judd 1992, 67). Probably the most significant manifestation of overlap among political and economic leaders in the early eighteenth century was the building of the Erie Canal by New York State Governor DeWitt Clinton. By connecting New York City to newly emerging cities in the Midwest, including its farmers and trappers, the canal made New York City the principal Atlantic coast port (Lankevich and Furer 1984, 83). As the largest public works project of its era, the canal's impact on the New York City economy was felt for over a century, as the high point in tonnage carried on the canal was not reached until 1951 (Lankevich and Furer 1984, 87).

The Tools of Economic Development in New York City

New York City's political system has a number of tools at its disposal in the promotion of economic development. These policies include land use regulations, tax incentives, capital formation assistance, infrastructure improvements, employment assistance, energy cost reductions, and the provision of business services. It is beyond the range of this book to discuss all of these policies; however, three will be discussed. Land use regulations, tax incentives, and Business Improvement Districts (BIDs) reflect a range of strategies used by the city to promote economic growth. They differ in the degree of transparency in their promulgation, centralized decision making involved in their implementation, as well as the level of controversy surrounding their use.

Land Use Regulations

Urban land use regulation is one of the oldest, most often used means of promoting economic development. Often referred to as land use planning and zoning, land use regulations attempt to create a map as well as rules regarding the use of public and private land in a city, with the goal of constraining and coordinating private land use decisions and achieving a uniform, consistent vision of city land use. Comprehensive planning takes into account issues of housing, industrial and commercial needs, open space, and transportation. The principal tool of land use regulation is the zoning ordinance. Zoning is usually accomplished through a law by which districts or zones are established throughout the city for various types of urban land use. The goal of these zones is to minimize adjacent incompatible land uses and foster economic growth, the efficient use of land, and/or aesthetic considerations. Like most American cities, New York City has never attempted to implement a comprehensive land use plan. Land use decisions are made primarily through the real estate market and the decisions of private developers. The political system, through the use of planning and zoning, plays more of a reactive rather than a comprehensive planning role by enacting zoning ordinances that deal with pieces of the urban landscape, as well as frequently reacting to or coordinating with private land use decisions. As a result, land use planning is incremental and piecemeal.

As an economic development tool, land use regulation may be considered a necessary, but not sufficient, mechanism for promoting economic development. Land use regulations make land available for different types of productive uses, but by themselves, these regulations do not guarantee development. Other complementary tools would include infrastructure improvements including streets, utilities, and possibly mass transportation, as well as other amenities delivered by the city such as schools and parks (Angotti 2003). Entrepreneurial capital is also a necessary ingredient in most economic development projects.

New York City was one of the first cities to adopt a zoning ordinance, receiving the state legislature's permission to adopt the ordinance in 1916. The primary impetus for the zoning ordinance came from Fifth Avenue merchants concerned about the spread of the garment industry and factory loft buildings (Kwartler 1996, 1288). The zoning ordinance included varying restrictions on lot size, building height and density, and the height of the building allowed at the street lot line.

Over the past decades, New York City's land use regulation policies have promoted economic development in a number of ways. First, much of the land use regulation activity in which the city's political system has become involved is site specific. The zoning map allows certain types of land uses within certain zones of the city. If a developer is building within the regulations established for a given zone, they can build without having to go through the city's Uniform Land Use Review Process (ULURP). This is called building "as of right." If one wants to develop land within a zone that is not compatible with the current land use regulations for that area, one must go through ULURP and seek an amendment to the zoning map. Individual developers have frequently asked the city for permission to use land in a way that is incompatible with the current zoning ordinance.

The site-specific land use planning function exists within New York City's Department of City Planning (DCP). The director of the DCP is appointed by the mayor. The director also serves as the chair of the City Planning Commission. The Commission is comprised of thirteen members; seven, including the chair, appointed by the mayor; one each appointed by the five borough presidents; and one appointed by the Public Advocate (Kivelson 1991, 63). As part of ULURP, the city council has the final say on all land use decisions, given its ability to override mayoral vetoes. Table 2.1 displays the stages of ULURP. The ULURP applies to any site-specific land use that would change the city's land use plan. Legislated in 1975, and amended by the 1989 City Charter revision, the ULURP begins at the community level and then moves to the borough president's office. The process then moves to the City Planning Commission and next to the city council. The mayor can veto any city council decision on land use but the council can override with a two-thirds vote. Before any application can be reviewed at the community board level initiating the ULURP process, it must be certified by the Department of City Planning, which establishes rules and standards for land use applications. The process includes public hearings at several levels of government as well as the preparation of an environmental impact statement (Kivelson 1991, 66). Given the multiple stages of the process and the access of the public and their representatives throughout the process, ULURP may be the most democratically accountable aspect of the city's economic development policy.

How the site-specific ULURP process works can be illustrated by examining the Riverside South development in Manhattan. In May 1992, the City Planning Department certified Donald Trump's proposal for a three-billion-dollar, fifty-six-acre residential and commercial development on the site of the old Penn Rail Yards on Manhattan's Upper West Side. In the mid-eighties, Trump's original proposal for the area, Television City, would have included the world's tallest

TABLE 2.1

Uniform Land Use Review Process (ULURP)

Time Allowed	*Action Taken*
No time limit	Applicant files plan with Department of City Planning.
	Department of City Planning certifies plan as complete. Application is filed.
Within 60 Days	Community Board notifies public, holds public hearing, and makes recommendation to Borough President.
Within 30 Days	Borough President and Borough Board (members of City Council from the borough) submit recommendation to City Planning Commission or waive right to do so.
Within 60 Days	City Planning Commission holds hearing.
	Application is modified, approved, or disapproved.
Within 50 Days	City Council reviews application and holds public hearing. Council can approve, modify, or disapprove the application.
Within 5 Days	Mayor reviews application. Mayor accepts or vetoes the application.
Within 10 Days	Council can override the Mayor's veto by two-thirds vote.

building and a number of sixty- and seventy-story towers. Trump also wanted the New York State Urban Development Corporation to be involved in the project because it would have enabled the project to skirt much of the ULURP process, similar to the Nets arena project discussed in the last chapter (Savitch 1988, 68). The opposition of a large coalition of community groups, plus personal enmity between Mayor Koch and Donald Trump, killed the project.

The 1992 version, Riverside South, was a scaled-down version of Trump's original project. The new proposal included sixteen apartment buildings, none more than forty stories, with almost six thousand units and an office and studio building with over two million square feet of space. The project would run between Fifty-ninth Street and Seventy-second Street along the Hudson River and it was projected to add approximately ten thousand residents to the neighborhood (Lueck 1992). Despite its being scaled down, it would be the largest building project in the city's history. In order to prevent an outcome similar to the first proposal and to help successfully navigate the needed ULURP rezoning, Trump gained the support of a number of community and environmental groups including the Municipal Arts Society, the Natural Resources Defense Council, the Regional Plan Association, Friends of Riverside Park, and People for Westpride, a group of community activists who had opposed Trump's original project. In order to gain the support of many of these groups as well as prominent politicians,

Trump made a number of legally binding concessions, known as a restrictive declaration. The most significant concession was a twenty-two-acre waterfront park adjacent to the project and Riverside Park on Manhattan's West Side. The concessions also included a commitment of funds to renovate the Seventy-second Street IRT subway station in anticipation of greater crowding from the new residents and a commitment not to increase the sewage input of the waste treatment facility several miles north on the Hudson River. Later in the ULURP process, Trump also agreed to set aside 10 percent of the residential units for subsidized housing (Lueck 1992).

Even with the restrictive declaration there was still opposition to the project. The ULURP process for Riverside South began at the Community Board level. Due to the project's size and location, two community boards held hearings on the project and both voted overwhelmingly not to approve it. For the communities surrounding the proposed project, the concessions being proposed by Trump were insufficient. Many were surprised, and some felt betrayed, when at the next stage of the process Borough President Ruth Messinger and the Borough Board supported the project. Messinger, a long-time liberal politician from the West Side, had previously been critical of the project but claimed that Trump had made enough concessions to meet her objections (Lueck 1992). Messinger's approval of the project may have signaled to citywide participants in the process that the only opposition was in the immediate neighborhood. The City Planning Commission then unanimously approved the project. The city council and the mayor followed suit. Beyond the community level, city officials believed that the Riverside South proposal with the concessions was a sound deal for the city, not to mention the thousands of construction jobs that it would create (*New York Times* 1992; Prokesch 1992).

In 2004, the Swedish furniture chain Ikea used ULURP to rezone land on Brooklyn's Red Hook waterfront from manufacturing to commercial in order to build one of their stores. Responding to opposition from the community regarding potential traffic congestion, Ikea pledged to run weekend ferry service to and from Manhattan as well as shuttle busses from the nearest subway. Seeking to gain the support of nearby public housing residents, Ikea also promised to train local residents and hire from the community (Cardwell 2004). After the rezoning application was approved through ULURP, the opposition unsuccessfully contested the environmental impact statement filed by Ikea in state court (Cardwell 2005b; Son 2005). The vast majority of projects that seek approval through ULURP are much smaller in scale than Trump's Riverside South project or Ikea, and most do not produce the level of conflict or controversy of those projects.

A second type of zoning focuses on an entire community. This type of zoning differs significantly from site-specific zoning. Site-specific zoning is usually initiated by a private developer who seeks a change in the zoning map in order to increase the value of his land via economic development. Zoning that focuses on an entire community is usually initiated inside the political system in recognition of development activity and/or pressures in the community, or to make a community more conducive to economic development opportunities.

The Brooklyn communities of Williamsburg and Greenpoint are located along the East River adjacent to Lower Manhattan. Occupying the waterfront, much of the land in these two communities had been zoned for manufacturing and industry since the early 1900s. As manufacturing declined during the later half of the last century, factories closed down and warehouses emptied out. Given the location and the available vacant real estate, Williamsburg and Greenpoint began to experience the early stages of gentrification and development pressures in the 1990s. Partly in recognition of these pending changes and pressures, indigenous community groups together with the New York City Department of City Planning developed plans for the communities in 2001. These plans, known as 197-a plans, laid out broad principles regarding the desired transformation of the communities. The principles included saving some of the land for the remaining manufacturing activities, public access to the waterfront, ample parkland, and affordable housing (Angotti 2003). The principles articulated in the 197-a plans then had to be translated into block-by-block zoning changes on a map.

When the Bloomberg administration issued the zoning map for Williamsburg and Greenpoint in 2005, many residents of those two communities were angry. They saw the Bloomberg proposal as promoting luxury high-rise development along the waterfront, with little or no attempt to save remaining manufacturing jobs, promote affordable housing, or guarantee public access to the waterfront (Ferguson 2005). The communities feared that the administration's waterfront zoning proposals would result in additional development pressures further inland, ultimately changing the character of the entire community. The community activists opposing the zoning proposal were joined in their opposition by the Brooklyn Borough President, Marty Markowtiz, and key members of the city council, including those representing the Greenpoint-Williamsburg communities (Cardwell 2005a: Cardwell 2005c). With opposition from the city council, the Bloomberg administration was forced to compromise on its initial zoning proposal in order to assure council approval. The compromise included additional land zoned for parks, additional tax breaks and bonuses that would increase the percentage of affordable housing built by developers, and guaranteed public access to a waterfront esplanade after development had taken place (Cardwell 2005d). In addition the Bloomberg administration designated an additional thirteen blocks for manufacturing activity. In the initial plan these blocks had been designated for mixed residential/manufacturing use and many in the community feared that under that zoning designation, the manufacturing activities would have succumbed to residential development pressures, resulting in the loss of more manufacturing jobs (Angotti 2005).

In the aftermath of September 11, 2001, as the city's economy began to recover and the city began to experience residential real estate pressures, a number of communities, especially those in the outer boroughs, became concerned with overdevelopment. In some communities, such as parts of Staten Island, overdevelopment had strained available infrastructure including sewers, roads, and schools. In 2003 the Bloomberg administration responded to the demands of Staten Island communities and elected officials by forming a Staten Island Growth Management Task Force that developed new zoning regulations to control growth (New York City Mayor's Office 2003). Other parts of the city had not been rezoned since 1961, a time when growth was anticipated but the level of growth desired was less clear. In response to development pressures these communities began to push for down-zoning or contextual zoning, to control residential density and "to preserve neighborhood character" (Scott 2005). "Contextual zoning rules aim to ensure that the size and scale of new development is consistent with the existing neighborhood" (Angotti 2004). The Bloomberg administration responded by proposing a large number of community-based down-zoning ordinances, all of which were passed by the city council. These new ordinances protected low-density neighborhoods comprised of single family or semi-detached homes from having to deal with new apartment complexes or McMansions. At the same time down-zoning depressed development in some neighborhoods, critics of down-zoning were concerned that it would increase development pressures in other communities. They wondered whether a city could accommodate concerns about "out of scale development" through down-zoning at the same time it was attempting to respond to an affordable housing shortage (Scott 2005).

A third type of land use regulation deals with nuisances. In part, land use planning in the United States originated to keep unattractive and unhealthy land uses, such as factories, segregated in one part of the city. While nuisance zoning can be site specific, types of nuisances can be regulated through direct acts of the city council amending the zoning ordinance. In 1995, the city council passed, with Mayor Giuliani's enthusiastic support, an amended zoning ordinance restricting the location of adult entertainment businesses. The law defined an adult entertainment or book store as any establishment whose inventory of merchandise was at least 40 percent adult oriented (New York Times 1998). The law restricted the location of these businesses to manufacturing and commercial areas. They could not locate within five hundred feet of another adult entertainment business and they had to be at least five hundred feet away from homes, schools, and churches (Toy 1996). The law was upheld by the New York State Supreme Court when the owners of the adult businesses questioned the constitutionality of the law. After several appeals, in 1998, the U.S. Court of Appeals also upheld the city law regulating the location of adult bookstores and adult entertainment establishments (New York Times 1998).

The law was involved in the Times Square redevelopment effort sponsored by the city, the state, and a number of corporate partners. Many adult entertainment businesses in the Times Square area had been moved out of the area prior to the passage of the 1995 legislation. In some cases, the businesses lost their leases as the property changed hands and increased in value. In other cases, the city had stepped up enforcement of existing building and property permits in an attempt to shut down as many of the shops as possible. The 1995 law did not ban the presence of X-rated stores in the Time Square area, but it succeeded in significantly reducing the total number of these businesses and prevented them from clustering on one street or block.

Not all land use regulation is achieved through zoning. One such example is sidewalk cafes. In 2002, the city council and the Bloomberg administration streamlined the process for restaurants that wanted approval for creating sidewalk cafes. Prior to the reform, the process for getting approval took on average over a year and involved multiple agencies (New York City Mayor's Office 2003). The process was so cumbersome that many restaurants broke the law and created sidewalk cafes without going through the approval process. The fines the restaurants incurred when and if they got caught were viewed as an acceptable cost of doing business (Cardwell 2002a). Although sidewalk cafes add to the ambience of a community and enhance community economic development, some neighborhood residents contend that sidewalk cafes clog the sidewalks and cause unwanted noise (Cardwell 2002a). Due to the nuisance issues, several communities in Manhattan have come to view sidewalk cafes as an important land use question. Under the legislation passed by the council and signed by the mayor in early 2003, the new process would shorten the time needed to obtain a permit to fewer than 140 days. In addition, the city Department of Consumer Affairs (DCA) would be the sole agency involved in the licensing and enforcement process. The department would hold public hearings to allow communities input on whether the license should be granted. With DCA's recommendation, the city council would retain final authority over the licensing of sidewalk cafes. The new process also increased the fees that restaurants would pay the city for the licensing of the cafe, in effect, rent for the use of the sidewalk (Cardwell 2002b).

The advantage of ULURP and the city's land use planning and zoning policies is that they produce land use decisions over which consensus has been achieved. A process that must involve local community boards, borough boards chaired by the borough president, the City Planning Commission, the city council, and the mayor forces a proposal through a gauntlet of community, borough, and citywide interests. To make it through this process, the proposal sponsors must tailor the proposal to obtain the approval of majority interests in the city without mobilizing too strong an opposition. The disadvantage of this process is that it is incapable of producing a coordinated long-term growth strategy for the city that addresses land use and infrastructure goals and needs. As will be discussed later in this chapter, this type of comprehensive planning can only take place outside the confines of the city's land use planning process.

Despite the above examples that demonstrate how planning and zoning facilitate economic growth, economic development in the city has frequently

proceeded without planning and zoning or in complete violation of existing zoning regulations. During the 1960s and 1970s, lofts and warehouses zoned for
manufacturing in SoHo were occupied by artists taking advantage of the low
rents. SoHo had been a commercial center in the later part of the nineteenth
century but entered a prolonged decline as businesses moved uptown (Gold
1996, 1088). Although zoned for manufacturing, the building stock in SoHo was
incompatible with the needs of modern manufacturing technology. By the 1980s,
SoHo had become a fashionable neighborhood complete with galleries, restaurants, and boutiques. Transformation of the neighborhood was so sweeping that
many of the artists who served as the pioneers of SoHo found they could no
longer afford to remain.

What would explain the city not enforcing its own zoning ordinance in the
case of SoHo? First, SoHo was transformed during a period of city budget cutting.
The numbers of city building inspectors fell dramatically, making violators more
difficult to detect and apprehend. In some cases, creative interpretation of the
zoning laws defined the artists as manufacturers. Also, in the 1970s, zoning laws
were amended to allow certified artists to legally occupy SoHo's lofts through the
artists-residence program. Enforcement of the law, however, was left up to the
landlords, who had an interest in renting to whoever could afford to pay regardless of whether they were certified (Johnson 1996). Second, city officials were
aware of the fact that the zoning laws were being violated but chose to look
the other way. Regarding the enforcement of zoning laws in the face of massive
noncompliance, Joseph Rose, former Director of City Planning, noted that "when
the market says, this is stupid, we're not going to abide by it, it gets very difficult"
(Johnson 1996). If the real estate market is producing what city officials perceive
to be positive results, there is less of a need to enforce existing zoning laws, especially in an enforcement system that is primarily complaint-driven (Johnson
1996).

The Group of 35 Report

In early 2000, a group of thirty-five business executives along with a few govern-
ment, labor, and nonprofit executives were commissioned by Senator Charles
Schumer "to address the growing shortage of commercial office space in New
York City" (Group of 35, Preamble 2001, 1). The group included several members
of the Giuliani administration including the president of the city Economic
Development Corporation and the Deputy Mayor for Economic Development and
Finance (Group of 35, Group 2001). The executive director of the group was from
the Regional Plan Association, a nonprofit group supported by regional business
interests. The report was commissioned at a time when, due to high rents and low
office vacancy rates, many directly affected by economic development in New York
City were concerned that businesses would look outside the city to grow. What
made the report comprehensive was its focus on the entire city, and especially the
outer boroughs. It was also comprehensive because its recommendations noted

that in order to be successful in encouraging and managing future economic growth, a combination of tools, including land condemnation, zoning, tax incentives, and infrastructure improvements would have to be employed. The report noted that while office rents in the city were the highest they had been in two decades and office vacancy rates were the lowest they had been in two decades, the city's office space inventory had grown by only fifteen million square feet during the 1990s. This was twenty-nine million square feet less than in the office space growth of the 1980s and thirty-nine million square feet less than the 1970s (Schumer 2001). The report of the Group of 35, *Preparing for the Future: A Commercial Development Strategy for New York City*, was published in June 2001. To some extent the report was premised on the assumption that the economic growth the city was experiencing in 2000 would continue. Even if growth slowed or stopped, however, the report attempted to foresee a time when business would have to look beyond lower Manhattan and Midtown in order to expand. The report concluded that in order to prepare for future office growth, the city would have to mobilize and rezone land to create three new central business districts: downtown Brooklyn, Long Island City (in Queens), and the Far West Side of Manhattan. In addition, the report cited the need for the creation of five "ancillary business districts" including Harlem, Jamaica and Flushing (Queens), the "Hub" in the Bronx, and Staten Island (Schumer 2001). The report addressed the transportation and other infrastructure improvements that would be needed to make these new centers of business competitive. Finally the report argued that the city must develop the capacity to attract more of the emerging biotech industry as well as remain competitive in its ability to retain and attract information technology companies (Schumer 2001).

What allowed the members of the Group of 35 and its staff to produce a comprehensive analysis of New York's growth and future needs were the same characteristics that limited the probability of its being fully implemented. The report was divorced from any political process that might legitimize and lend authority to the report's conclusions. Such a process involving interests from communities, boroughs, the city, and the state would have limited the scope of the report and/or considerably delayed its publication as the various stakeholders attempted to insert their perspective in the final product. In the aftermath of the 2001 terrorist attacks, the city faced a very different economic development agenda than it did the year before. And although part of the Bloomberg administration's plan for the Far West Side of Manhattan included new office space as suggested by the Group of 35, it was that part of the far west side plan, and not the stadium, that earned the opposition of State Assembly Speaker Sheldon Silver, one of the three members of the state Public Authorities Board.

Tax Incentives

Land use regulations create an environment in which economic development takes place. Although they structure market decisions, on their own they may do little to promote decisions to invest in the city beyond those encouraged by the real estate market. In postindustrial America, cities have learned that relying on the market and the traditional city zoning functions are insufficient to make the city attractive for investment. The mobility of capital and the proliferation of possible places for capital investment have created a far more competitive investment environment than existed thirty years ago. As a result, cities have had to do more than create zones where development can take place. They have had to take a more active role in attracting economic development. For their part, investors and businesses have also realized that the investment environment offers them more opportunities than before. They have also become more aggressive in making demands on cities to gain concessions before moving capital into the city. One type of concession that is now frequently offered by cities to investors and businesses is the tax incentive. Tax incentives lower the overall tax obligation of the investor/developer, making it more lucrative to invest in the city. Tax incentives are a form of tax expenditure. That is, public policy is promulgated not through the allocation of funds from an annual budgetary process but through a program that commits public funding through tax forgiveness.

As early as the mid-1970s, New York City began to engage in the practice of offering businesses and investors tax incentives for locating, remaining, or expanding their businesses inside the city. Prior to that point, city officials had depended primarily upon state and federal money to subsidize large-scale urban development. Toward the end of the 1970s, most of the federal funding sources began to dry up and the state was forced to expend a great deal of funding on the city's fiscal crisis. In part, this induced the Koch administration to negotiate directly with private developers. Having just survived near-bankruptcy, the city could not offer private developers large capital subsidies up front to attract them to the city or to convince them to stay. The city could, however, offer developers and businesses tax breaks over a long term that would increase the profitability of the development by lowering the tax obligation. Tax incentives are far less visible than direct subsidies and do not show up in a budget document unless tax expenditures are examined.

New York City has offered tax incentives to businesses through two mechanisms. First, the city administers several programs in which standard, "as of right" tax incentives are offered to businesses that fall into a specific category or are engaged in a specific type of activity. These "as of right" incentives are created by the city or state legislature and signed into law by the mayor or governor, respectively. Second, through the city's Economic Development Corporation (formerly the Public Development Corporation), the city negotiates tax incentives with individual businesses (firm-specific) in order to convince them to locate in New York City or to remain in the city.

There are several types of as of right programs offering tax abatements to businesses. The Industrial and Commercial Incentive Program (ICIP), initiated in 1984 and administered by the Department of Finance, offers two types of tax abatements. Businesses in the city that are renovating, constructing, or physically improving industrial facilities are eligible to receive a twenty-five-year property tax exemption equal to the increase in the assessed value of the property due to the construction or renovation. In order to qualify for the abatement, the renovation or construction must have produced an expenditure of at least 10 percent of the assessed value of the facility. The business receives the full value of the exemption for the first sixteen years but the exemption declines by 10 percent in years seventeen though twenty-five (New York City Department of Finance 1996). In addition to the above exemption, those involved in new construction or renovation of industrial properties are eligible to receive a twelve-year property tax abatement. This abatement is based on the preexisting property taxes on the assessed value of the land and structures, for the tax years preceding the issuance of the building permit. This is done in recognition of the fact that while the property is being improved, it is probably not being productive. "The abatement is fifty percent for the first four years, declining by ten percent every other year for the remaining eight" (New York City Economic Development Corporation, ICIP 2003). To qualify the investment must equal at least 25 percent of the assessed value of the project (NYC Economic Development Corporation, ICIP 2003).

The ICIP also offers tax abatements for commercial renovation and construction projects; however, the eligibility requirements are more restrictive and not as lucrative as those for industrial construction or renovation. The standard incentive package for a commercial renovation is a twelve-year property tax exemption with a full exemption for the first eight years declining by 20 percent a year for the final four years. Similar to the industrial construction and renovation incentives, the exemption is based on "increases in the assessed value solely attributable to the improvements made" (NYC Economic Development Corporation, ICIP 2003). The minimum investment in order to be eligible for the exemption is 20 percent of the assessed value of the project (NYC Economic Development Corporation, ICIP 2003). In addition, when the program was amended in 1992, it offered increased benefits for commercial development in economically distressed areas of the outer boroughs and in Manhattan, north of Ninety-sixth Street. The structure of the commercial property tax abatements is similar to the industrial renovation abatements, but the length of the abatement is shorter.

Similar to the ICIP, many of the city's tax incentive and abatement programs offer more lucrative incentive and abatement packages for those businesses locating or expanding in the outer boroughs or north of Ninety-sixth Street in Manhattan. Businesses leasing space in these areas are exempt from paying the city's Commercial Rent and Occupancy Tax. Those businesses south of Ninety-sixth Street with annual rents lower than $200,000 are also exempt. Mayor Giuliani had expressed the desire to eliminate the Commercial Rent and Occupancy Tax entirely, but projected deficits for fiscal years late in his second term prevented this from happening (Herszenhorn 2000).

Other tax abatement programs are more place specific. Through the Lower Manhattan Revitalization Plan initiated in the mid-nineties, the city offered a range of property tax abatements, commercial rent tax reductions, and energy cost reductions to commercial and residential developments south of Chambers Street. The tax incentives and cost reductions were supposed to work in tandem with zoning changes in lower Manhattan with the purpose of changing the area into a twenty-four-hour community by converting outdated office buildings into housing. All renovations in the area, both residential and commercial, received a five-year property tax abatement equal to 50 percent in the first three years and scaled-down abatements in years four and five (NYC Economic Development Corporation, Lower Manhattan Economic Revitalization Plan 2003).

In another example of place-oriented tax incentives, late in his first term Mayor Giuliani initiated the New Commercial Expansion Program, which offered a package of incentives to businesses locating or expanding on eligible properties within designated areas in the outer boroughs or north of Ninety-sixth Street in Manhattan. Eighteen commercial areas were designated: Harlem in Manhattan, Long Island City and Jamaica in Queens, the West Shore and North Shore areas on Staten Island, the Red Hook and Brownsville sections of Brooklyn, and the Hunts Point and Fordham-Bathgath sections of the Bronx. Tax incentives included tax credits for hiring or relocating eligible employees, rent abatements for tenants signing new or expanded leases in eligible buildings, and energy discounts. In order to qualify, the economic activity had to be located on properties within the designated areas that fell under specific commercial or manufacturing zoning categories (New York City Department of Finance).

New York City's Economic Development Corporation, a city agency, negotiates with individual businesses that wish to locate or expand their operations in New York City, or are threatening to leave. Each negotiated firm-specific agreement is different. These negotiations take place through the auspices of the New York City Industrial Development Agency (IDA). The agency was created in 1974 as a corporate government agency for the purpose of attracting, promoting, retaining, and developing economically sound industries. The IDA Board of Directors has fifteen members. Eleven are appointed by the mayor and five are appointed on the recommendation of each of the borough presidents. There are four ex officio members of the board including the comptroller, who is the only elected official on the board (Good Jobs New York 2001). Through the IDA, businesses are attracted to New York City or are enticed to stay through the offering of exemptions from taxes, reductions in taxes, or tax credits. Since the agency has no employees, its functions are carried out through the Economic Development Corporation (New York City Comptroller's Office 1997). The tax incentives have included sales tax reductions, property tax abatements, and relief from the city's commercial rent tax, where applicable. In addition, in cooperation with Con Edison, the local public utility, the negotiated incentive packages have also included energy cost reductions. The EDC makes tax incentives available to businesses through job retention or expansion agreements. Implicit in each agreement is the expectation that the company will retain a certain level of employment in the city, or expand employment if that is part of the agreement. Businesses are required to report average annual employment to the EDC. As long as the company keeps its employment level within an agreed upon range or expands employment if that is part of the agreement, it will receive tax breaks over the life of the agreement. Businesses that fall below their threshold receive reduced benefits, while those surpassing the agreed upon employment level may be rewarded with increased benefits (NYC Comptroller's Office 1997).

The structure and extent of the incentive package is determined by a number of factors. First, the number and type of jobs at stake play a significant role in how aggressively the city seeks to keep or attract the business in question. In July 1997, the Swingline Stapler Company announced their intention to leave their Queens home and move their four hundred and fifty jobs to Nogales, Mexico. At a press conference the same week, Mayor Giuliani noted that although the city had made an attempt through the offering of tax incentives to keep Swingline in Queens, negotiations broke off. In emphasizing his mild disappointment that Swingline was leaving, the mayor pointed out that most of the Swingline jobs were low-paying jobs and that while negotiations between New York City and the Queens-based company had been unsuccessful, that same week the city had negotiated a deal with the Mercantile Exchange to keep over eight thousand jobs in the city (Giuliani 1997). The city has aggressively sought to attract and retain businesses with a large number of high-paying jobs over smaller businesses and those that have a large number of low-paid employees.

Given New York City's location in a tristate area, a second factor affecting negotiations between the city and businesses is the existence of an offer from an adjoining jurisdiction. In late March 1997, Standard and Poor, the nationally reputed bond rating agency and long time corporate resident of New York City, informed the city government that it was considering a move of its two thousand jobs to Jersey City, New Jersey. As a subsidiary of McGraw-Hill, the company's rationale for the considered move was to merge with the parent corporation's financial information services in a single complex. At the same time, however, Standard and Poor made it clear that a major factor in its considered move was whether New York City would grant the company tax breaks and other incentives to remain in Lower Manhattan (Bagli 1997b).

The fact that New Jersey, Connecticut, and some of their local governments have in the past attempted to lure businesses away from New York has exacerbated the city's negotiations with businesses threatening to leave. In 1991, New York, New Jersey, and Connecticut reached an agreement not to aggressively compete for companies located in each others' states. The agreement between New York and Connecticut appeared to collapse in 1994 when the Swiss Bank Corporation decided to move from New York City to Stamford, Connecticut. Connecticut claimed the Swiss Bank Corporation initiated the contact with

Connecticut officials. The Giuliani administration, however, retaliated by placing advertisements in several local Connecticut newspapers informing the taxpayers of Connecticut that the Swiss Bank Corp. move would cost them 120 million dollars, the dollar amount of the tax breaks and incentives Connecticut was giving the corporation. The New York City Deputy Mayor for Finance accused Connecticut of breaking the nonaggression pact (Lueck 1994a). In 1997, the city also accused New Jersey of breaking the pact when it offered Standard and Poor subsidies and tax incentives worth over $50 million to relocate to Jersey City. New Jersey claimed that Standard and Poor had initiated the discussion about relocating (Bagli 1997d).

A possible third factor affecting tax incentive negotiations between the city and businesses is the state of the real estate and labor market in the city at the time of the negotiation. Several weeks prior to the Standard and Poor threat, the Giuliani administration had negotiated a deal with ING Barings, a British-Dutch financial services company, to stay in the city rather than move to Connecticut. The company was looking for more space and informed the city of a ninety million dollar difference over fifteen years between relocating to an office complex in Stamford, Connecticut, and comparable space in Midtown Manhattan (Bagli 1997a). What was unique about the ING Barings agreement with the Giuliani administration was that the $3.4 million in sales tax exemptions and the additional $1.65 million in energy discounts received by the corporation were tied to job growth and not simply retention. ING Barings would get nothing if they maintained their current work force, but if they added almost nine hundred new jobs over the fifteen years, then they would receive tax exemptions and energy discounts (Bagli 1997c). The ING Barings deal, however, appeared to be tied more to the real estate market and economic climate in New York and not to the involvement of other competing governments. The lower office vacancy rates in Manhattan and the growing ease in retaining and attracting businesses in the mid-1990s encouraged the city's Economic Development Corporation and New York State to take a stronger negotiating position. Tax incentives and subsidies were only being offered if a corporation increased its employment in the city, not simply for staying in the city.

Not every mayoral administration adopts a similar tax incentive strategy. In the aftermath of the 1975 fiscal crisis, the Koch administration adopted an active strategy toward attracting and retaining business. The behavior of the Giuliani administration was similar and became even more aggressive as the city's fiscal position improved throughout the 1990s. The Dinkins administration started out with a conservative strategy of offering firm-specific tax incentive packages only to those businesses locating in the outer boroughs. As the city began to lose jobs, however, the Dinkins administration became more aggressive in offering tax break packages to firms regardless of where they were thinking of locating. Similar to the Dinkins administration, the early Bloomberg years appeared to be characterized by a conservative tax incentive strategy. In part this was due to the city's post-9/11 fiscal crisis in the early part of the Bloomberg administration. And as the New York City office and commercial real estate market began to recover from the recession of 2000–01 and the impact of terrorist attacks, the Bloomberg administration maintained a very low level of firm-specific tax incentive agreements with corporations, believing that offering tax breaks was not necessary given the economic climate and the low office vacancy rates.

New York State, which has broader taxing power than the city, frequently joins the city in offering businesses and developers tax incentives to remain or locate there. Through the Empire State Development Corporation (formerly the New York State Urban Development Corporation and the New York State Department of Economic Development), New York governors have sought to retain and lure businesses as aggressively as have New York City mayors.

The tax incentive strategy of pursuing economic growth has been criticized in several ways. Amid the interstate and interlocal competition for business, there are few advocates for the entire region. The Regional Plan Association has argued that the three states and their respective local governments are wasting valuable tax dollars fighting a "zero sum game" when the entire region could benefit from more cooperative attempts to attract business to the tri-state region (Bagli 1997d). Research on the effectiveness of tax incentives in inducing business moves has produced very mixed results. To some extent, however, the research has demonstrated that tax abatements create more of an incentive for intraregional business relocation than interregional relocation (Sternberg 1993). As a result, some have concluded that the tax abatement strategy creates no additional value for the New York metropolitan region as a whole. Tax incentives are more likely to induce a business to move from one side of the Hudson River to the other but are far less likely to be an influential factor in business decisions to move into the region. Regional Plan Association President, Claude Shostal, noted early in 1997 that "you could put that money into schools and transportation programs that would benefit everybody and the whole pie would grow. But it's difficult for elected officials not to play the game" (Bagli 1997d).

Other critics have questioned the benefits these corporate deals create for the low-income residents of the city. If the city and state are giving away valuable tax revenue to retain corporations in the city, what do the poor get? Tax revenue being used to subsidize corporations cannot be allocated to schools, police, or public hospitals. Moreover, many of the negotiated agreements between the city and corporations create conditions under which the city does not break even or profit from the retention of the corporation for years, if not decades. At the very least, the tax breaks given to large corporations shift the tax burden in the city to small and medium size companies, as well as other tax payers, who rarely, if ever, get similar benefits (Bagli 1999). As one reporter noted, "the owners of Madison Square Garden pay no property taxes. Not a penny since 1981. Down the street, the owner of Twin Donuts must pay his entire share" (Dwyer 1999). "Reducing taxes for one firm and not others in the same industry makes the playing field uneven by subsidizing one of several competitors" (Lynam 1999). In 1999, the city gave the accounting firm Ernst and Young a $20 million incentive package to build a new office tower. This could allow Ernst and Young to lower its fees, taking business away from some of its competitors (Lynam 1999).

A 1997 analysis of the Economic Development Corporation's job retention agreements by the New York City Comptroller found several problems. First, not every agreement resulted in stable or increased employment. Of the thirteen job retention/tax incentive agreements analyzed by the comptroller, five companies were below their agreed-upon employment base in at least one of the years of the agreement and four of the firms were below the base for all years of the agreement. A second and much more serious problem was the finding by the comptroller that the EDC did not adequately monitor the employment levels of the companies with whom it had agreements. The comptroller's study found that in all but two of the agreements analyzed, the companies were not in compliance with the reporting requirements. The companies were not accurately or adequately reporting their employment levels to the EDC and the EDC was not following up on the inaccurate or nonexistent reports. Moreover the comptroller found that the EDC was not verifying the information it received from the companies. Simply stated, the EDC did not know whether the companies were living up to their part of the negotiated agreement, but the companies were still getting their tax breaks (New York City Comptroller's Office 1997). As a result, New York City officials were unable to assess whether the program was successful or not.

A study by the Center for an Urban Future also found that many of the corporations who entered into firm-specific tax incentive agreements with the city never lived up to their end of the bargain because they were acquired by other companies, they were sold, they moved major parts of their business out of the city, or they went out of business (Center for an Urban Future 2001). Studies conducted to assess the impact of tax incentive strategies on business activity or job growth have also produced mixed results (Sternberg 1993, 10). While giving corporations money is obviously valuable to the corporation, its value to the greater public is in doubt. According to Ernest Sternberg, firm-specific tax incentive strategies may not only be bad economics for cities, but may also be bad politics. Negotiated agreements between the city and individual corporations, obscured from public scrutiny, are the new version of the back room deal. Which businesses receive favorable tax treatment from the city and which businesses are ignored is a function of bureaucratic/executive decision making that is not subject to public accountability. Frequently the terms of the agreements and the agreements themselves are not publicized. The lack of visibility of this aspect of city economic growth policy makes it conducive to favoritism and possibly corruption (Sternberg 1993, 17).

Sternberg's criticism was supported by a report conducted by the city's Independent Budget Office (IBO) in 2001 (New York City Independent Budget Office 2001). The subject of the IBO study was the 1993 city law that mandates that the Economic Development Corporation publicly report retention deals with corporations that provide "tax benefits, loans, and other financial arrangements with a value greater than $250,000" or are expected to save twenty-five or more jobs (NYC Independent Budget Office 2001, 1). The IBO study concluded that Economic Development Corporation compliance with the law in reporting business retention deals had several problems, including the understatement of the fiscal cost of the retention agreement to the city, overly optimistic estimates of the positive budgetary impacts of the agreements, and unreliable job retention and creation data (NYC Independent Budget Office 2001, 1). For example, the IBO study stated that in reporting the positive impact of a business retention deal, the EDC includes property tax revenues that the retained business will pay to the city. In response, the IBO argued that the EDC incorrectly assumed that the city would not receive property tax revenues if the business left. The IBO report claimed that while the business may leave, the land and the building cannot leave, and the property owner is still obligated to pay the real estate taxes (NYC Independent Budget Office 2001, 4). Similar to the criticism of the EDC by the comptroller, the IBO report also noted that employment data reported by the EDC was unreliable because it is data given to the EDC by the employer/business and never independently confirmed by the EDC (NYC Independent Budget Office 2001, 5).

Sternberg also argues that the tax incentive strategy concentrates only on those jobs that threaten to leave the city when businesses relocate, when in fact many more jobs are lost to the city when firms downsize or go out of business because they cannot compete in an emerging global market. Implicit in this critique is Sternberg's proposal that the city should be promoting economic growth by helping firms compete rather than attracting those who already do. Principle among Sternberg's recommendations is that the city invest in its human resources, expanding the skills of the workforce to make the city's businesses and overall business climate more competitive. Other critics have argued that since the majority of job growth comes from small businesses and new companies, many of the tax incentives the city is offering are not as valuable to these businesses that need capital or capital formation assistance (Smith, Ready and Judd 1992, 539).

In response to the critics it should be noted that the city's tax incentive strategy to achieve economic growth is neither single-minded in its goal, nor is it the only strategy the city employs. As previously discussed, some of the city tax incentive programs are targeted at distressed areas or particular types of economic growth. And although they do not receive the type of public or media attention of firm-specific tax incentive packages, the city has implemented a number of human resource and capital formation assistance programs as well as a wide array of other programs promoting economic growth and supporting indigenous businesses. Many critiques of the tax incentive strategy treat this element of economic development policy in isolation and not part of a larger package, as is clearly the case in New York City. Moreover, the city uses tax incentives for more than the promotion of commercial or industrial business activity. The city's Department of Finance annual report on tax expenditures calculated that the most expensive tax expenditures employed by the city are in the area of housing, with a great deal of the tax expenditure activity supporting the development of low- and moderate-income housing (New York City Department of Finance 2001; 2002). In 2001, the top five property tax expenditure programs, ranked in order of expense, were all housing related (NYC Department of Finance 2001). In 2002, four of the top five property tax expenditure programs were housing related (NYC Department of Finance 2002). Business and excise tax incentive programs in both 1998 and 1999, the last years for which data is available, accounted for just over four hundred million dollars. Most of this was as of right programs, not firm-specific agreements (NYC Department of Finance 2001; 2002).

In his earlier cited statement, Regional Plan Association President Shostal implied that the tax incentive strategy is being driven in part by a misperception on the part of government officials that tax incentives work. Yet the research on the impact of tax incentives on business behavior is far from conclusive. At the same time, however, the strategy is also being used as a defense mechanism. As seen from the examples above, New York City uses tax incentives to attract or retain businesses because many of its neighbors do. Given the level of intraregional competition that has occurred, and its visibility, city officials may have no choice but to offer these incentives in order to stay in the competition, even though much of the competition is founded on misperception and a lack of conclusive research results. And while businesses inside or outside the region may not see the tax incentives as significant factors in location or expansion decisions, those businesses already in the region are not going to discount programs that lower their tax burden and increase their profitability.

Business Improvement Districts (BIDs)

Another strategy that the city has adopted in promoting economic growth is the formation of business improvement districts (BIDs). "A Business Improvement District is a self initiated consortium of property owners who elect to make a collective contribution to the maintenance, development and promotion of their commercial districts" (Walsh 2002).

BIDs are assisted by the local government, which collects additional taxes from the property owners in the area and then disburses them back to BID organizations. BIDs represent a far more decentralized strategy than tax incentives because they rely on the initiative of community businesses to organize. BIDs are a community-wide as opposed to a citywide strategy to promote a positive business climate. BIDs see themselves as competing with all other businesses outside their boundaries, including those inside the city. In addition, with few exceptions, BIDs focus primarily on commercial/retail businesses, whereas firm-specific tax incentives have more of a corporate focus.

Under a 1980 state law and a subsequent city ordinance in 1982, property owners in a community could create a BID by a majority vote plus the approval of a service plan by the city council. BIDs sign a five-year contract with the city laying out what services it will deliver as well as capital projects. Four city representatives sit on the BID board representing the Department of Business Services, the comptroller, the borough president, and the city council (Lueck 1998). The City Department of Finance collects mandatory annual assessments from all property owners in the district and returns the money to the BID to spend on services. The BID assessment has the same legal status as taxes, carrying the same penalties for failure to pay (Lueck 1994b). Prior to the 1982 ordinance, state legislation in the late 1970s had created Special Assessment Districts (SADs) that had operated under principles similar to BIDs (New York City Council 1995, 6). Since the ordinance, the number of BIDs has grown from three to more than fifty at the end of 2005, with several BIDS in planning or awaiting approval (NYC Department of Small Business Services Website: Business Improvement Districts 2006). In New York City there are three types of BIDS. Some BIDS occupy the commercial areas of the central business district (CBD). In fact by 2002, there were no commercial areas of the CBD not covered by a BID. Other BIDS cover "mixed-use districts" including commercial and residential areas. These types of BIDS may be found inside or outside of the CBD (Walsh 2002). A third type of BID is the "main-street" BID. This BID covers areas outside the CBD and may include commercial strips along with residential areas (Walsh 2002).

Most BIDs provide four types of services for their members: sanitation, security, marketing and promotion, and capital improvements (Walsh 2002). A few of the larger BIDs also provide social services to a segment of the population within the district. BID sanitation programs supplement the City Department of Sanitation services by providing more frequent and more thorough sidewalk and gutter trash pickup. Most BIDs have also installed additional trash receptacles throughout the district. Where relevant, some BIDs also implement graffiti removal programs. In the area of security, many BIDs hire and train their own security force. The security forces are not armed and usually are trained to contact the police rather than attempt to apprehend individuals on their own when a crime is observed or suspected. Some BIDs have attempted to help their member merchants by cooperating with the City Department of Consumer Affairs in removing unlicensed vendors from the area. At the same time, however, BIDS have come into conflict with their own members when storefront displays or signs violate local zoning regulations.

The BIDs' primary reason for existence is to promote the businesses in the district and create a positive business climate that will enhance economic growth in the area. BIDs have developed a number of activities to promote their members including street fairs, concerts, festivals, newsletters and even web sites on the internet. In addition, the previously mentioned sanitation and security services are designed primarily to make the district a safer and more enjoyable place to shop and do business.

Within the political system, BIDS act as advocates for their communities and coalitions of property owners. Although they provide services to their members,

BIDs in New York City lobby the executive branch, and the city council if necessary, to obtain additional services such as sanitation, safety, and beautification.
When rezoning is necessary to improve the commercial profile of the district,
BIDs have pursued this as well (Walsh 2002). BIDs also lobby the executive
and legislative branches for needed capital improvements. The Fourteenth
Street–Union Square BID participated in the process that produced approximately one hundred million dollars in capital improvement to the area including
the renovation of Union Square Park, street reconstruction, the addition of street
lighting, and a massive reconstruction of the subway station at Union Square.
The infrastructure improvement allowed the BID to market itself more effectively
and attract new businesses (Walsh 2002).

While most BIDs are looking for commercial development, a few are seeking
a different type of development. After an aborted attempt at developing office
towers, the Times Square Business Improvement District turned its attention
toward creating an entertainment complex in the area, seeking entertainment/
tourism industry involvement. Quite different from both the Times Square BID,
the Alliance for Downtown New York, the BID for Lower Manhattan, was a major
participant in the conversion of the financial district into a residential community. The alliance was a key actor in the conversion of older vacant, office buildings into residential use as well as general sanitation and security improvements
in the financial district that increased the leasing of commercial space as well.
The Alliance for Downtown New York was also instrumental in promoting the
Information Technology District (ITD). In the mid-1990s, southern Manhattan
began to emerge as the home of a number of small high growth information technology companies. To further promote New York's "Silicon Alley," the Alliance
helped sponsor the building and establishment of the Information Technology
Center, a 400,000-square-foot building that offered its leasees satellite accessi-
bility, single and multi-mode fiber optics, video conferencing, and internet
access. The alliance also worked with landlords in the area to create facilities in
other buildings around Broad Street that would be conducive to information technology companies (Alliance for Downtown New York Information Technology
District 1997). After the September 11 attacks, the Alliance played a major role in
the recovery and rebuilding of Lower Manhattan. They assisted the Lower
Manhattan Development Corporation in providing a clearinghouse for information on economic development opportunities in Lower Manhattan and in promoting development as well. In November 2003, the Alliance initiated a free bus
service that connected the eastern and western sides of Lower Manhattan
(Alliance for Downtown 2003).

A 1995 study of BIDs by the city council produced a mixed set of conclusions
regarding their role. According to the study, over half the property owner members of BIDs thought they were not a good investment (New York City Council
1995, v.). The report further suggested that many BIDs were not accountable to
their members due to few or unpublicized meetings, and a lack of oversight by
any city agency or the city council. The report claimed few BIDs made any attempt

to survey member satisfaction with the services being delivered. The council report noted that it was virtually impossible to dissolve a BID once it had been created (New York City Council 1995, vi). BID budgets varied widely, but in three BIDs the managers were being paid higher salaries than the mayor. At the same time, however, a majority of BID members surveyed by the council study were satisfied with the sanitation services being provided, although a majority did not see positive results from the security services and many were unaware of the promotional activities of the BIDs (New York City Council 1995, xvi–xvii). The city council was not the only set of public officials concerned with BID performance. In 1996, Mayor Giuliani restricted the power of BIDs from borrowing money. Prior to that point, BIDS had been able to sell bonds for capital improvements with city approval. Only a few BIDs had taken advantage of this power, yet over $56 million had been borrowed by BIDS in the 1990s (Levy 1996). This action on the part of the Giuliani administration was motivated in part by a concern with the managerial capability of some BIDs and a desire to keep them out of debt through greater city control. It was also motivated by the fact that the city was rapidly approaching its own debt limit; and while the city is not responsible if BIDs default on their bonds, the BID debt is counted against the city's own debt limit by the state (Levy 1996).

During Mayor Giuliani's second term, he took a number of actions suggesting he no longer favored promoting BIDs as an economic development strategy. In 1998, the Giuliani administration issued new regulations regarding city control of BID activities. These regulations required BIDs to discuss all new initiatives with the Department of Business Services, the executive branch agency responsible for overseeing their activities. In issuing the regulations, the mayor noted that many of the BIDs had formed at a time when the city was not functioning as well as it was in the late 1990s, implying the city no longer needed BIDs to promote economic development (Lueck 1998). In 1999, primarily in response to publicized poor management in a small number of BIDs, the Giuliani administration froze the budgets of all BIDs, no longer allowing the members to raise their assessments (Pristin 2002a). This moratorium remained in place throughout the remainder of the Giuliani administration. In addition, although the law allows BIDs to form if 49.5 percent of the property owners support formation, both the Giuliani administration and the city council set a more stringent, informal standard of 70 percent approval in the late 1990s (Pristin 2002a). Finally, in early 2001, the Giuliani administration proposed but never implemented a policy that would have charged BIDs a fee for city administrative services that they did not previously have to pay (Pristin 2001).

The Bloomberg administration appeared to adopt a more positive position on the role of BIDs in the city's economy. Mayor Bloomberg appointed a former BID executive director as his Commissioner of Business Services (now Small Business Services), the agency that oversees BID activities. In addition, early in his administration, the mayor noted that BIDS would be valuable additions to communities in delivering services during times of budget scarcity (Pristin 2002a). The mayor explained the difference between his and his predecessor's position on BIDs as being a function of the economic climate and the fact that the city was going to have to depend more on public-private relationships than in the past. In May 2002, he proposed streamlining the process by which a local group could qualify as a BID in addition to providing "seed money" for BID development in moderate- and low-income neighborhoods (Pristin 2002b). Under the Giuliani administration and before, it could take up to two years for a community group to achieve BID status. The mayor also removed the informal moratorium Mayor Giuliani placed on BIDs increasing their assessments, and considered lifting the ban on BIDs issuing long-term debt. With approximately twenty BIDs applying for the ability to increase assessments, the city council also appeared to be developing a more cooperative attitude toward their activities. The chair of the council's committee on finance suggested that, partly as a result of the budget crisis, the BID applications would get a good reception (Pristin 2002b).

Interest Groups and Economic Development

While the need to promote economic development as a means to produce a positive fiscal flow has been internalized by officials inside the political system, it is also an interest pursued by an array of highly diverse groups. Developers, indigenous businesses of various types and sizes, unions, and neighborhoods have differing perspectives on what economic development means. These groups define economic development in the context of their own parochial interest and pursue it inside the political system.

In the case of the Jets/Olympic Stadium proposal, the Jets and the Bloomberg administration had a significantly different perspective on economic development than did the Dolan family and the activists representing the communities surrounding the Hudson Rail Yards. The community activists were not opposed to development of the rail yards, but they were seeking housing, parkland, and community services. The Dolan family, owners of Madison Square Garden were similarly not opposed to development of the rail yards but they did not support what they perceived as government-subsidized competition. In the mid-1990s a consortium of minority developers in Harlem proposed building a Pathmark supermarket on 125th Street. They were opposed by a number of small bodega owners in East Harlem who, similar to the Dolan family, saw the Pathmark as government-subsidized competition. The Pathmark developers prevailed. In the Williamsburg-Greenpoint section of Brooklyn, as in other parts of the city, the remaining manufacturing interests competed with residential developers for control of economic development along the waterfront. It is not uncommon to find those whose goal is economic development competing with each other within New York City's political system.

As a result of the diversity of economic development interests in the city, there is an inequality among these groups in their ability to produce favorable political outcomes. Although large-scale developers represent only one of many interests within the economic development arena of New York City, their ability to influence the political system surpasses that of most other economic development interests. In existence since 1896, The Real Estate Board of New York (REBNY) has served as an advocate for real estate interests. In 1916, REBNY supported the city's first zoning law. More recently, the organization advocated tax policies and other public programs that encouraged real estate development, including the elimination of rent regulations (Weiss 1995).

Due to its broadly defined interest in real estate development, both commercial as well as residential, REBNY's approximately six thousand members include not only landlords and property owners but also builders, brokers, managers, banks, financial service companies, utilities, architects, and contractors. Although developers constitute approximately 15 percent of the membership, they dominate the organization. REBNY's influence in city and state politics is not only the result of the wealth and prestige of its members but also of its highly expert and professional staff. Many of REBNY's staff served in the city and state government prior to joining the organization. This gives the organization a substantive as well as a procedural knowledge of real estate public policy and the workings of the city government (Bellush 1990).

In addition to having organizations to represent their interests, large-scale developers perennially rank among those groups who hire lobbyists to represent their interests in the city's political system. Affluent groups, such as developers, have the ability to purchase access and/or political skills by hiring the services of a lobbyist or lobbying firm. In many cases, the most sought after lobbyists are those who have served at high levels of the city government in the past or those individuals who are close associates of key decision makers inside the system. In either case, groups hiring the lobbyists are in effect purchasing the experience, knowledge, and access that the lobbyists possess because of their former position or friendships. According to a study conducted by the New York Public Interest Research Group (NYPIRG) in 1999, two of the top ten groups utilizing lobbyists, defined by money spent, were developers. The report noted that much of the money spent on lobbyists in New York City is linked to real estate development projects. Five of the top ten groups were business associations: the American Insurance Association; the Greater New York Hospital Association; Air Transport Association; the Neighborhood Business Association; and the National Association of Securities Dealers. Two were individual businesses: Home Depot and Kaufman Astoria Studies. And one was a not-for-profit institution, New York University (McCarthy 2001).

As illustrated in the conflict over the location of a Pathmark grocery store in East Harlem, a major division within the city's economic development/business community is between large and small retail enterprises. Smaller businesses are concerned that the political system subsidizes larger retail establishments, giving them an additional competitive edge through the offering of tax incentives, zoning concessions, and siting assistance. This has been a frequent concern of small neighborhood businesses when shopping centers or megastores have moved into the community. In 1998, a group of neighborhood merchants near Crotona Park in the Bronx decided not to resist the building of a Pathmark shopping center in their neighborhood. In fact, some of the merchants saw the development as a possible means of increased retail demand in the community. Their spokesperson however, expressed the concern that the new shopping center might receive assistance from the city, especially since the land on which the development would occur was city owned. The spokesperson noted, "These subsides have been very difficult to come by for the small scale store owner. If there's public money involved in the future, it shouldn't just run to the large chains. Small retailers should be offered the opportunity to grow their businesses too" (Halbfinger 1998). Many of the larger retail businesses are part of national chains. This gives them the corporate infrastructure to approach the political system and lobby for subsidies, in addition to being able to identify existing "as of right" public policies that can be utilized to their benefit.

The city's business community is also divided between those companies within the city's central business district (CBD) and those located in the outer boroughs or sections of Manhattan not considered part of the CBD. What characterizes the CBD is a significantly higher density of corporate and retail activity than in other parts of the city, as well as in relationship to residential land uses. The emergence of New York as a global city and the importance of the financial, investment, and real estate communities to the city's fiscal health have resulted in the city paying a great deal of attention to economic development of the central business district.

Outerborough businesses have complained that the CBD receives better police, sanitation, and snow removal services. As some city agencies responded to complaints that outer boroughs were being neglected, there were examples of contradictory city actions in the outer boroughs. In one instance, the City Planning Commission approved a revitalization plan for the Red Hook section of Brooklyn while another city agency simultaneously identified the same community as the site of a waste transfer station (Gonzalez 1999).

There is a subset of economic development interests whose focus is low-income areas of the city outside of the CBD. Their needs are very different from those business interests located in more middle-class areas or the CBD. Given the risks involved in investing or establishing a business in low-income areas, institutions and actors that typically provide capital are not always present. One group of actors who pursue development in low-income areas are community economic development organizations. They lobby public as well as private institutions to promote investment in their neighborhood. During the 1990s, community activists in the South Bronx were instrumental in getting a number of banks to open branches in the community and to dispense loans to small businesses. One group of activists in the Bronx, Community on the Move, used the 1977 federal Community Reinvestment Act to force banks to locate in low-income areas. The law required banks to provide services to low-income communities in cities where they do business, and gave community groups the ability to challenge bank mergers based on the banks' efforts in servicing low-income areas. Although the banks that moved into the South Bronx were initially resistant, several years later some of them expressed pleasant surprise at their profitability (Rohde 1997).

A second set of interests pursuing economic development in low-income neighborhoods are nonprofit groups. Nonprofit groups have a variety of goals ranging from advocacy to service delivery to self-help. Their funding sources include foundations, governments, and individuals. One such group, the Neighborhood Economic Development Advocacy Project, assisted Community on the Move in getting banks to locate in the South Bronx. In the mid-1990s the group collected and disseminated data on the imbalance of banking services in the city. Their study found that in Manhattan there was one bank branch for every 2,709 residents, while in the Bronx there was one branch for every 12,038 residents (Rohde 1997). Neighborhood Housing Services is another nonprofit group that attempts to deal with the shortage of development capital in low-income communities. The group runs the Storeworks program. It encourages indigenous businesses to take title of deserted buildings in low-income neighborhoods by giving them low purchase prices, low interest rates, and, when necessary, a subsidy from the city to pay for the difference between the purchase price and the renovation of the building. Storeworks seeks to find buyers who have a stake in the community and who will not attempt to turn a quick profit by selling the property once it has been renovated. In order to achieve this goal, the program favors those who will either reside or set up businesses in the building. The program is dependent upon the city's Department of Housing Preservation and Development, which sells properties to the group for one dollar. The city also provides a twenty-year real estate tax abatement. For the first ten years of the abatement, the property is taxed at its pre-rehabilitation value. In years eleven through twenty, the assessed value increases by one-tenth the difference between the pre-rehabilitation value and the post-rehabilitation value (Hevesi 1998).

Organized Labor and Economic Development

Organized labor has traditionally been viewed as one of the counterbalancing forces to the power of business in American politics. In New York City, however, labor unions, particularly private sector unions, have supported large-scale development proposals because these projects create jobs. New York City politics has played a significant role in the evolution of organized labor's political power. During the Depression, labor strength in the city manifested itself in Senator Robert Wagner's (D-NY) sponsorship of federal legislation that guaranteed the right of collective bargaining and created the National Labor Relations Board (Candaele and Wilentz 1995).

The evolution of organized labor's political power in New York City is closely related to the experience of organized labor at the national level, but they are not identical. New York City's loss of private sector unionized employment such as those in the manufacturing sector mirrors the decline at the national level. In New York City, however, this decline was paralleled by the emergence of public employee unions. As a result, the percentage of unionized workers in New York City never dipped as low as the nation overall. In the history of organized labor in the United States, the unionization of municipal and/or public employees occurred much later than the organization of private sector employees. Municipal employee unionization in New York City emerged after World War II. Shortly before the war, a major precedent was set when the Transport Workers Union was able to continue the enforcement of its contract after the city assumed control of public transportation. Municipal union membership increased throughout the 1950s. In 1958, under Mayor Wagner, unions representing government employees won the right to organize and to engage in collective bargaining. From that point on, municipal unions and their leaders have played a major role in city politics. During the mid-1960s, public employee union militancy became so fierce with strikes by the transport workers, social workers, and sanitation workers that New York State passed the Taylor Law that imposes heavy fines on municipal unions who strike (Candaele and Wilentz 1995).

Municipal union membership continued to grow throughout the 1960s and 1970s. The changing composition of municipal unions and the consequent change in policy focus created a division between city municipal unions and the more conservative private sector segments of organized labor representing the building and construction trades unions. The building trades unions became one of the major advocates of almost any large construction project. They supported the building of Westway and Donald Trump's proposal for Riverside South on Manhattan's West Side, over community opposition. In early 1999, the building trades unions supported the construction of a water filtration plant in Van Cortlandt Park in the Bronx over the opposition of community groups, the borough president, members of the New York State Assembly and Senate, as well as some environmental groups. The building trades unions have become one of the city's most vocal advocates for policies that promote economic growth. They were strong supporters of the Jets/Olympic Stadium. Municipal employee unions have been far less active in the promotion of economic growth.

Not In My Backyard (NIMBY)

Not In My Back Yard, or NIMBY, has been used to characterize a category of organized political activities, primarily in local politics, that seek to defend neighborhood or community interests against unwanted development or location of public facilities including landfills, megastores, homeless shelters, or stadiums. These developments are perceived to be a nuisance that would upset the neighborhood's character, status quo, and/or property values. NIMBY reflects the mobilization of neighborhood interests to prevent a nuisance from locating in the community. In many cases where NIMBY interests are mobilized, the project in question is one that benefits the larger political system even if more local, parochial interests view it as inimical to them.

In late 1997, Mayor Giuliani announced a plan to breathe new financial life into the Theater District. The goal of the plan was to strengthen the theater industry and insure that landmark theaters would continue to be used for legitimate theater by countering development pressures on theater owners. According to Joseph Rose, then Chair of the City Planning Commission, the plan would "preserve, strengthen and enhance the Broadway theaters and the theater districts" as well as "provide for the appropriate development of Eighth Avenue by mandating new design controls while allowing new developments to support theater preservation goals" (New York City Council Committee on Land Use 1998). The plan involved the use of air rights or development rights for twenty-five landmark theaters. Air rights, also known as unused development rights, are equal to the difference between the size of an existing building and the maximum that zoning rules would allow on the lot. Since the theaters were designated city landmarks, the owners of the buildings were prohibited from modifying the exterior of the building in any way, and prevented from developing the air rights, the space immediately above the landmark building. Current zoning law, however, did allow them to sell the air rights to the developers of property next to or across the street from the landmark. The Giuliani administration was proposing an expansion of the area where landmark theater air rights could be moved. The new zone would include the area between Fortieth and Fifty-seventh Streets and between the Avenue of the Americas and Eighth Avenue. Within this new expanded district, developers purchasing air rights from theater owners could use the air rights to increase the floor area of new buildings by up to 20 percent over what current zoning laws allowed without going through any type of public review. If developers submitted their plan to use the air rights to a public review, they could potentially increase the floor area of new buildings by 40 percent. Theater owners who sell their air rights under the proposed new guidelines would have to promise to continue to operate their buildings as theaters for at least twenty-five years (Dunlap 1998a; Lyman 1997).

The primary opposition to the theater subdistrict air rights plan came from the Hell's Kitchen and Clinton neighborhoods immediately to the west of the Theater District. In a letter to the *New York Times* in early 1998, Cynthia Cooper, a member of the Community Board that included Hell's Kitchen, wrote that "as the proposal stands, special residential protection in Hell's Kitchen will be stripped away to allow development of larger high rises. A neighborhood that houses a huge number of people involved in theater will be prey to real estate speculators and sudden price inflation" (Cooper 1998). Cooper's fear was that the development of air rights along Eighth Avenue would spur so much development that it would ultimately displace low- and middle-income residents and change the character of the neighborhood. The upzoning proposed by the plan would allow office towers and high rise residential buildings on the west side of Eighth Avenue. Residents feared that more intense land uses would add congestion to their neighborhood and ultimately result in escalating real estate prices, driving many of the residents out.

As part of the Uniform Land Use Review Process (ULURP), the Giuliani theater air rights proposal went before two Community Boards in Manhattan that included parts of the theater subdistrict as well as the neighboring communities. The proposal was rejected by both boards. When the Manhattan Borough Board met, the representatives of the affected neighborhoods came out in force. The board voted to oppose the plan, suggesting a modified plan with greater public review and a smaller geographic area where the air rights could be developed. Commenting on the defeat of the proposal in the borough board, Joseph Rose, Chairman of the City Planning Commission, stated that the borough board was "a forum that plays to the most reactionary and obstructionist elements of the Manhattan political spectrum" (Dunlap 1998b). When the proposal reached the City Planning Commission and the City Council Committee on Land Use Subcommittee on Zoning and Franchises, groups supporting the plan turned out. They included the Actors Equity Association, the International Alliance of Theatrical Stage Employees, the Alliance of Resident Theaters, the Theater Development Fund, the League of American Theaters and Producers, the Manhattan Theater Club, Playwrights Horizon, the United Scenic Artists Union, the Society of State Directors and Choreographers, and the Ushers and Doormen's Union (New York City Council Committee on Land Use 1998). The City Planning Commission voted to approve the proposal. The council approved the plan with some small modifications. The council removed eleven blocks on the west side of Eighth Avenue from the district where air rights could be used. This area abutted the more residential neighborhoods of Hell's Kitchen and Clinton (Dunlap 1998c). A group of residents who were not satisfied with the compromise sued to block the zoning change. In June 1999, the New York State Supreme Court ruled in favor of the residents, the Clinton Special District Coalition. The courts overturned the zoning change because no environmental impact statement and review was performed prior to approval (Newman 1999). In 2001, that ruling was overturned in favor of the air rights transfer. By that point, however, the city's economy was declining, so there was little pressure or impetus to build new towers in the area surrounding the theater district.

NIMBY interests face an uphill battle because they represent a narrow parochial view competing against a more citywide perspective. As a result, these interests are rarely successful unless they can find a procedural issue on which to base their claim or expand the scope of conflict to include other communities, as was the case in the theater subdistrict case. The one resource NIMBY groups have in their favor is an intensity of interest that encourages them to further their cause.

New York State's Role in New York City's Economic Development

In its efforts to promote economic growth, New York City frequently does not act alone. As in the case of the Olympic/Jets Stadium and the Nets Arena, New York State plays a significant role in many of the city's economic development projects. The state played a primary role in the building of Battery Park City in the 1970s and the redevelopment of Times Square in the 1990s. The state is the principal force behind the Lower Manhattan Development Corporation (LMDC), the agency with the responsibility for rebuilding of the area after the terrorist attacks. The LMDC is a subsidiary of the Empire State Development Corporation, a state agency. Governor Pataki appointed seven members of the eleven-person board, while Mayor Giuliani appointed four (Wyatt 2001). Louis Tomson, the first Executive Director of LMDC, was a long-time associate of Governor Pataki, serving in the Pataki administration overseeing the state's public authorities (Good Jobs New York 2002). As previously noted, while state control of Lower Manhattan's redevelopment through the LMDC deprives Mayor Bloomberg or any city officials of direct influence or control over the process or outcome, it frees the mayor of any direct responsibility as well. At the outset of his second term, however, Mayor Bloomberg appeared to be more enthusiastic about playing a major role in the redevelopment of Lower Manhattan.

The state has a significant interest in supporting the city's attempt to create and maintain a positive fiscal flow via economic growth. City success alleviates some pressure on the state to assist the city via state revenue; and given the importance of New York City for the rest of the state, an economically healthy city goes a long way toward creating an economically healthy state. New York State employs a number of different programmatic tools in promoting economic growth.

New York State, like most states, has developed an array of promotional programs and services in an attempt to make the state a more attractive business location. Under the Pataki administration, many of these programs were reorganized under the Empire State Development agency. While the agency administers some programs oriented toward business attraction, the agency also serves as the chief promoter of the state as a business friendly environment. In recognition of the global business environment, Empire State Development has offices in Canada, the United Kingdom, Germany, and Japan. These offices serve as promoters of New York State businesses abroad but they also serve as centers for attracting foreign investment to the state (Empire State Development 1997b). Most importantly, Empire State Development provides financial assistance to businesses in their acquisition of land, buildings, or machinery. The assistance may be in the form of a direct loan, an interest rate subsidy to reduce the cost of borrowing from the private sector, or a loan guarantee (Empire State Development 1997a). In a very small number of cases, the Empire State Development Corporation will negotiate a specific and unique package of subsidies or tax incentives with a business or industry for the purpose of attracting them or keeping them in New York State.

One of the most significant economic development programs administered by the state is the Empire Zone Program (formerly the Economic Development Zone Program). This program is modeled on the urban enterprise zone program that received a great deal of attention at the federal level during the Reagan administration but did not become law until President Clinton took office. Similar to the city's use of tax incentives, the principle behind the program is that the public sector can induce economic development and job creation in depressed urban areas by packaging an array of tax incentives that would bias the location and/or expansion decisions of businesses. What makes the program unique is that it involves little or no funding up front. The program contains no direct loans or subsidies to the private sector. Instead, the entire program is made up of tax expenditures, subsidizing businesses by alleviating their tax burden rather than handing them cash.

New York's Economic Zone Program began in 1986. By 2006, over seventy zones had been designated across the state, with eleven in New York City. In order to be eligible for Empire Zone status, certain criteria have to be met using federal census data, including: a poverty rate of at least 20 percent, an unemployment rate of at least 1.25 times the statewide rate, an area with a population of at least two thousand people but no larger than two square miles, and also with at least 25 percent vacant land, abandoned land, or land available for industrial or commercial redevelopment (New York State Empire Zones 2002a). Areas designated as Empire Zones can only maintain that status for fifteen years, with declining benefits in years eleven through fifteen. In addition, local governments must share with Empire State Development, the cost for administering the zone (New York State Comptroller's Office 1995). For those areas that qualify for Empire Zone status, the following tax incentives are available:

- A ten-year exemption from state sales tax on purchases of goods and services used predominantly in the zone;
- A refundable credit against business taxes equal to a percentage of the real property taxes paid based on increased employment in the zone;
- A Wage Tax Credit for five years, for full-time employees in new jobs equal to $1,500 for employees in specially targeted groups;
- Tax credits for businesses that create new jobs and/or make new investments in property or equipment;
- Utility rate savings (New York State Empire Zones 2002b).

Of the eleven Empire Zones in New York City, all are located outside the central business district with the exception of the Chinatown Empire Zone. That was added in 2006 in part as a result of the impact of the terrorist attacks on the economy of Lower Manhattan. Whether the Empire Zone Program has been successful in creating new jobs or in reinvigorating economically depressed areas has not yet been determined. An audit of three State Empire Zones located in the city by the state comptroller in 2004 concluded that many, if not a majority, of businesses receiving tax breaks through the Empire Zone program did not meet job creation goals (New York State Comptroller 2004a). According to the report, "only fifteen of the businesses in the East Harlem Empire Zone met or exceeded their targets for creating jobs" (Cooper 2004). In other Empire Zones in the city, many businesses taking part created no new jobs, or even lost jobs (New York State Comptroller 2004a). These findings were disputed by the Empire State Development Corporation (Cooper 2004). Some private groups monitoring the program believe that the Empire Zone program does little more than subsidize the movement of jobs within the state from one site to another, with no net growth (Hernandez 1996). A study by the New York State Comptroller's office in 1995 found that the State Department of Economic Development did not have access to information controlled by the State Department of Labor or the State Department of Taxation and Finance that was necessary to evaluate the program's effectiveness. In some cases, the lack of access was due to state laws regulating access (New York State Comptroller's Office 1995). These same data access issues were restated by the State Comptroller in 2004 (New York State Comptroller 2004b). As a result, there was the concern on the part of state auditors that businesses might be taking advantage of the tax incentives without creating new jobs (New York State Comptroller's Office 1995).

Conclusion

New York City's economic health and its ability to produce a positive fiscal flow has been and continues to be heavily dependent on macroeconomic trends and business cycles. The city's budget surpluses of the late 1990s can be attributed largely to the health of the stock market and the FIRE industries in the city. Similarly, the growth in business and corporate activity as well as the renewed health of the residential real estate industry in the mid- to late 1990s was more attributable to market trends than to governmental activity. Months before September 11, 2001, city officials began to track the impact of economic stagnation and decline on the city's employment base and the consequent decreasing ability of the city government to raise revenue (New York City Office of Management and Budget 2001). New York City's economic growth policies can complement these larger economic trends but there is little evidence that they can significantly influence or counter them. If New York City's economic growth elites were once in a position to influence economic development through the use of various tools such as those discussed in this chapter, the rise of the global economy has certainly decreased this influence. Economic development tools such as zoning, tax incentives, and the creation of BIDS place New York City in a position to take advantage of emerging economic trends but they have little direct impact on the trends themselves. Economic growth policy in New York City reacts and adapts to global, national, and regional changes.

The redevelopment of southern Manhattan in the mid- to late 1990s is an excellent example. Through zoning, tax incentives, and the activities of a BID, the city promoted and encouraged the redevelopment of Wall Street and its surrounding community into a twenty-four-hour neighborhood. Without a significant number of older vacant buildings, however, the redevelopment of this community could never have taken place. The buildings were not vacant because of city economic growth policy. Their design and structure, which was not conducive to the new information technologies, inhibited their usage as modern corporate centers. An oversupply of office space brought on by the building boom of the mid-1980s also contributed to their decline. Once the buildings became vacant, the city was in a position to promote the conversion of the community. Even then, the strategies the city used to promote the redevelopment of the area may have had little impact if it was not for that fact that in the mid- to late 1990s, downtown office space rented for 30 percent less than comparable space in Midtown (Oser 1997). The costs of residential space were also less than comparable space in more established residential neighborhoods in Manhattan. The zoning changes that lowered the square footage required per unit placed Lower Manhattan in a position to take advantage of the healthy real estate market. And tax incentives induced developers to move into Lower Manhattan and convert the buildings. The policy changes on their own, however, without the healthy market would have done little.

If the city's economic development promotion policies have only a minimal impact on economic growth relative to the power of market forces far beyond the control of city policymakers, then why has the city's political system become so oriented toward churning out programs designed to promote economic growth? First, as previously stated, although the research on business movement and expansion has demonstrated that government policy may not be a major factor in many corporate movement decisions, public officials appear to be driven more by the perception that economic growth promotion policy plays a major factor in much corporate decision making than the reality of its uncertain impact. Second, although the marginal returns of each additional program to promote economic growth may be minimal, there is always the possibility, however small, that a public program or decision will make a difference in some businesses' decision making.

Even in the face of contradictory evidence in the aggregate, a single case of a corporation choosing to stay or move in the city due to the existence of a tax abatement or zoning change reinforces public official perceptions that these programs are significant. In interstate metropolitan areas such as New York City's, the fact that neighboring jurisdictions are engaging in similar economic development promotion policies contributes to the perception of the policies' efficacy and necessity. Third, public officials may be held responsible for the economic health of the city, whether or not they are responsible or have the necessary authority or tools to have any impact at all. As a result, public officials will do whatever is within their means to bring about economic growth. If they are unsuccessful, at the very least they will have amassed a record of attempts at economic development promotion that allows them to demonstrate to the electorate that they have not sat on their hands.

A related issue in the assessment of the city's economic growth promotion policies is the extent to which the outer boroughs and northern Manhattan have been neglected at the expense of the central business district (CBD). A review of the policies and examples discussed in this chapter offers two conclusions regarding the city's treatment of the outer boroughs. First, although some economic growth promotion policies are targeted in the CBD, others are more evenly spread across the entire city. Taken as a whole, one cannot conclude that the outer boroughs have been neglected. With many of the city's "as of right" incentive programs, businesses receive a larger abatement if they locate or expand in the outer boroughs or north of Ninety-sixth Street in Manhattan. At the same time, however, the city's firm-specific tax incentive agreements favor the CBD. According to data produced by a watchdog group who tracks firm-specific tax incentive deals, only six of the sixty most lucrative agreements the city has promulgated in the last two decades have dealt with firms locating outside the CBD (Good Jobs New York 2006). And while the Bloomberg administration has promoted outerborough economic development through the creation of plans for Coney Island, Williamsburg/Greenpoint in Brooklyn, and the South Bronx, Mayor Bloomberg did spend the bulk of his first term promoting development on the Far West Side of Manhattan, technically within the CBD.

Second, since private market decisions drive city economic growth far more than city policies, there may be little that city growth promotion policies can offer the outer boroughs. Of course, as suggested by the Group of 35 Report, the city has never implemented, let alone developed, a citywide economic development strategy that would invest sufficient capital in a section of the outer boroughs to make it attractive to large-scale business expansion. The infrastructure, and especially the transportation improvements needed to make an outerborough area attractive enough to compete with the central business district, would be an expensive undertaking.

Over the past several decades, and certainly since the city's fiscal crisis of the 1970s, economic development has become an integral part of city governance in several ways. First, economic prosperity, including job creation, has become part of the electorate's expectations for the city's elected officials, especially the mayor. These expectations have held steady, if not increased, even in light of evidence that city officials may not be entirely responsible for the economic development successes or failures the city experiences. City officials have responded to these expectations by pursuing economic development with greater, but not complete transparency, as well as by changing the discourse of electoral politics to include evaluations of economic development performance. That the city still negotiates firm-specific tax incentives behind closed doors and that some large-scale economic development projects are exempted from ULURP, however, allows critics to question the democratic accountability of some of the city's economic development policies. Second, successful economic development contributes to the city's ability to deliver an acceptable level of public goods and services without raising taxes. Thus, not only does the public gauge the city's economic development success directly through measures such as job creation, but they also do it indirectly via the city's ability to address increasing demands on services without increasing taxes. Third, while successful economic development promotes civil harmony by allowing the city to deliver public goods and services, it also challenges civil harmony. Projects exempted from ULURP are deprived of legitimacy derived through local political processes. Debates over such projects can become divisive since opponents recognize that their access to procedures to stop the project may be limited, if not non-existent. In addition, specific neighborhoods and communities in the city may be asked to bear the burden of economic development through the siting of projects in their communities. While the occurrence of economic development in a neighborhood can appear attractive through the offering of amenities and access to jobs, these same projects may also increase traffic and potential environmental health hazards.

Despite the issues mentioned above, economic growth is by far the most palatable and least controversial means of creating a positive fiscal flow. Compared with the other means of city revenue growth, which include taxes, service reductions, or intergovernmental transfers, economic growth also creates the lowest short-term political costs for elected officials.

The most critical issue surrounding economic growth promotion policies is their effectiveness. Do they work? Information needed to answer this question is sketchy at best and unavailable at worst. The programs discussed in this chapter place New York City in a position to take advantage of market changes and to compete with neighboring jurisdictions that are attempting to take advantage of the same changes. It is not known whether these programs do in fact influence the movement of the marketplace in any way or how much they benefit the city's fiscal flow more than decentralized market changes would in the absence of these programs. The overall efficacy of economic growth promotion programs and their impact on the market may be irrelevant. What is clear is that city decision makers believe in the efficacy of these changes or at least believe it is necessary to engage in these activities because other jurisdictions are doing the same thing. While it may seem irrational that a major component of city politics is being driven more by perception than by reality and results, for city officials there may be little difference between the two.

3

The State and the City

In chapter one, the role of the state Public Authorities Board in rejecting the Jets/Olympic Stadium and approving the Nets basketball arena was discussed. In chapter two, the state's role in assisting the city with economic development was examined further. The state is involved in every aspect of city governance. Dillon's Rule, discussed in chapter one, gives the state the ability to intervene in, if not control, most of the activities of its local governments. State laws affect how the city raises revenue and delivers services. The state gives the city the ability to structure its political system but still mandates, regulates, and monitors how democratic accountability will be achieved. And finally, state policies influence the city's ability to maintain civil harmony.

The New York City Fiscal Crisis

There may be no better illustration of Dillon's Rule than New York State–New York City relations during and after the city's fiscal crisis of the mid-1970s. This work will not attempt to offer an in-depth analysis of the New York City fiscal crisis. There have been several studies (Bailey 1984; Shefter 1988) that have exhaustively examined the crisis and its implications for New York City politics and fiscal relations.

In the mid-1970s, New York City faced fiscal problems similar to many other U.S. cities. During the 1950s and 1960s, a large percentage of the city's middle class left for the suburbs, leaving a growing concentration of low-income residents, primarily minorities, who needed city services but did not significantly contribute to its tax base. This problem was exacerbated by state requirements that the city share substantially in the cost of services, primarily welfare and Medicaid, going to low-income New Yorkers. The resulting financial burden that New York State placed on the city was much greater than any other state placed on its cities. The problem was also exacerbated by the city's own fiscal practices.

With state permission, the city was selling short-term debt in anticipation of incoming tax revenues. City accountants, however, routinely overestimated incoming revenue, making it necessary for the city sell more short-term bonds to pay off those that had matured. In 1975, the banks, the financial agents selling city tax anticipation notes, informed the city that they would no longer sell city short-term bonds. Unable to sell bonds to meet it debt obligations and unable to raise the revenue on its own, the city faced defaulting on its debt and, in effect, declaring bankruptcy (United States Congressional Budget Office 1975; Robertson 1975).

As the legal guardian of the city, the state's role in assisting the city out of its crisis was never in doubt. Even if the state had allowed the city to default on its short-term bonds, the state would have been ultimately responsible for the delivery of basic services to its citizens in the city if budget cuts and public employee layoffs had caused major disruptions. On a less legal, but still compelling level, given the city's status within the state as a major source of tax revenue, the state could not allow conditions in the city to deteriorate to the point where the revenue flow of tax dollars from the city to Albany was seriously disrupted. In addition, relations between New York City and New York State have been, and will be, affected by the degree of upstate antipathy for the city. This upstate hostility toward the city is exacerbated by partisan differences between the city and upstate political constituencies. Upstate Republicans have their institutional base in the New York State Senate, which has had a Republican majority for many years and whose leadership is predominantly representative of upstate constituencies. The New York State Assembly is controlled by Democrats, with a majority of those from the city. Upstate Republicans have traditionally viewed New York City public officials as profligate tax and spend liberals who are constantly calling on the state for greater financial assistance for social programs and expansive government activities. Unlike the two houses of the state legislature, the governor's office has been very competitive on a partisan level.

The state's response to the city's fiscal crisis took on two different institutional forms. The first response was the creation of the Municipal Assistance Corporation (MAC) in June 1975. It was created to sell bonds to assist the city in meeting its debt obligations when city bonds were no longer marketable. When MAC bonds failed to solve the city's problems, the second response, the Emergency Financial Control Board (EFCB), was created to monitor and control the city's fiscal activities until a viable long-term financial plan could be developed that would allow the city to meet its obligations to its creditors as well as deliver services to its citizens. Unlike MAC, EFCB was not in the bond market. Its primary purpose was to act as the state's agent in overseeing city spending and revenue collection in order to regain the confidence of investors in MAC bonds. Its secondary purpose was to assuage State Senate Republicans, who were concerned about giving state money to the city or MAC (Bailey 1984).

The EFCB controlled city spending in a quasi-governmental fashion for almost a year, and the state legislature established procedures to reimpose the

EFCB on the city if specific fiscal criteria were violated. The EFCB had seven members: the governor, the mayor, the state and city comptrollers, and three additional members appointed by the governor with the approval of the State Senate. It was apparent from the inception of EFCB, and from Governor Hugh Carey's initial appointments, that these three outside appointees would be representatives of the financial community. There has been considerable discussion and debate over the role of the financial community in the fiscal crisis. Most are in agreement, however, that with three members on the EFCB, the banks were given a major say in city fiscal affairs. Mayor Abe Beame openly opposed the actions proposed by the state, but he was not in a position of strength. He was politically vulnerable given the fiscal plight of the city as well as his perceived role in the city's crisis. Eventually, Mayor Beame became the mouthpiece through which the EFCB controlled city finances. While this was clearly a case of politics as unusual, the EFCB's being able to speak through the mayor made their control of city finances look more like politics as usual in the eyes of New York City residents and the media (Bailey 1984).

Through its control over the city's finances, EFCB virtually ran New York City for over a year, acting as a shadow government. EFCB was responsible for developing a financial plan for the city that would produce a balanced budget. EFCB could not set specific budget priorities for the city, but it could audit any aspect of city government and had access to all city records. In addition, EFCB had control over all city revenue through the EFCB Fund. The EFCB had power over the disbursement of this money, not the mayor, other officials in the executive branch, or the city council (Bailey 1984, 13–46). Although EFCB did not overstep its legal authority, the powers that the state legislature gave it and the activities it undertook as a result created potential conflicts with the institutions of democratic governance in New York City. EFCB was not politically accountable to any set of voters even though four of its members were elected officials. Implicit in the legislation creating the EFCB was the assumption that the mayor was in control. In addition, EFCB needed the mayor in order to give their decisions an air of legitimacy. Although the actions of the EFCB compromised the normal process of city government, through EFCB, the mayor gained power relative to other city officials and, as a spokesperson for the board, the appearance of mayoral power and control was not diminished (Bailey 1984).

The role of the governor, Hugh Carey, in the city fiscal crisis cannot be understated. As the state's leading political official, the governor played a central role in assisting the city. As the state's chief executive, the governor had the power and the obligation to mold the state's response. In addition, as a Democrat from New York City, the governor had the ability to use his own informal political contacts, combined with his official status, to prevent a default on the city's debt. In addition, the governor led the city's successful effort to obtain aid, in the form of loan guarantees, from the federal government in dealing with the fiscal crisis (Ruby 1975).

The New York City fiscal crisis changed the legal and political landscape of New York State–New York City relations. The impact of the fiscal crisis on state-city relations can still be felt through the institutional mechanisms created by the state to monitor and control city fiscal activities. The Financial Control Board (the "Emergency" part of its name has been removed) still exists, and meets yearly to review the city's budget and four-year financial plan.

New York City–New York State Relations

New York State–New York City relations have many dimensions. These include the granting of home rule, the monitoring of city finances, state aid to the city, and state mandates imposed upon the city through the functional assignment of programmatic responsibilities between the two levels of government.

Home Rule

Home rule provisions give local governments the power to select a set of governmental structures and procedures, as well as deliver services to their residents, without state interference. Home rule gives local governments autonomy by delegating specific powers from the state level to the local level. Home rule messages have their origin either in the state constitution or through state legislative enactments. A home rule provision enacted through state legislation is perceived as being less secure, since legislatures have the power to retract or modify whatever powers they have granted through the home rule charter (Dye 1991, 270). It was through home rule legislation in the early part of the twentieth century that New York City received the power to draft its own charter and get it approved by city voters. Prior to that time the city charter had been a matter of state legislation. The extent to which state governments grant home rule to their local governments, however, and the powers granted within home rule charters, varies widely from state to state.

New York City's relationship with New York State regarding home rule has been neither consistent nor smooth. The city's status as an independent corporation was accepted by the state in the 1800s, in part because the city's incorporation predated the state's existence (Benjamin 1988, 115). As a result, the city acted with very little state intrusion. Several factors changed this relationship during the 1800s. First, as the city grew, the structure and function of city government expanded beyond the powers granted to the city in its charter. The city was then forced to go to the state to seek an expansion of its powers, consequently giving the state greater control of city government affairs. Second, as the demographics of the city changed because of immigration, those opposed to growing immigrant political power saw the state government as a way to wrest control from the immigrant-driven city political apparatus (Benjamin 1988). Third, the corruption of the city's Democratic Party political machine, Tammany Hall, served as an additional catalyst for state intervention. Finally, during the nineteenth century, the city developed into a Democratic Party stronghold, whereas the state government was dominated by the Republicans, exacerbating whatever differences already existed.

Regardless of the possible advantages of a vague home rule message, the disadvantages remain. In 1997, the future of the city's controversial rent control law was deliberated in the state legislature and not in the city council chambers. Throughout the recent history of New York City's school system, the city has had to go to the state every time it has wanted a restructuring. In 1996, the city needed state permission to give the chancellor more control at the expense of the community school boards. And in 2002, Mayor Bloomberg went to the state level to get the New York City School Board abolished and to have the school system placed under mayoral control.

Monitoring City Fiscal and Budgetary Practices

There are two entities at the state level that monitor the city's fiscal affairs on a regular basis: the Financial Control Board (FCB) and the State Comptroller. The relationship between the EFCB and the city was significantly different in the years following the crisis than during the crisis. In the midst of the city's fiscal crisis, the board ordered hundreds of millions of dollars in budget cuts that went well beyond those proposed by the Beame administration. It controlled the wages of city workers, demanded that thousands of city employees be laid off, and rejected a contract negotiated between the Board of Education and the teachers' union. The board was also instrumental in getting the state to take over the City University system and in making major changes in the city's Health and Hospitals Corporation (Finder 1986).

Once the immediate threat of default disappeared, the board moved city fiscal decisions in a desired direction more by threatening to use its powers than by actually using them. Formally, the "Emergency" was dropped from the Financial Control Board's name in 1978 when the life of the board was extended thirty years. In 1986, however, when the city made the last of its payments on the federal loans promulgated by the Ford administration and had balanced its budget according to Generally Accepted Accounting Principles for three consecutive years, the board placed its power in "sunset." That is, the board relinquished its power to annually reject or approve the city's budget and financial plans. The board continued to monitor the city's budgetary and fiscal decisions and retained the right to reimpose its control on the city if the city did not meet certain fiscal criteria including: failure to pay the interest or principal of any of its bonds when due; incurring an operating deficit of more than one hundred million dollars at the end of a fiscal year; and failure to balance the city's budget other than capital debt, if control needed to be re-imposed in the joint opinion of the state and city comptrollers, or if the city damaged its credit by violating state mandated budget and accounting practices (New York State Financial Control Board 2006; New York State Financial Control Board 1997). According to legislation amended in 1978, the board's powers will expire in 2008.

Although a member of the FCB, the State Comptroller has served as an independent monitor of all city operations. Comptrollers have differed in the way in which they have sought to exercise their monitoring function. Some have dealt exclusively with the city's fiscal operations while others have cast a much broader net, examining the fiscal implications of policy choices being made by the city. Two factors have played a role in the comptroller's choices. First, when the city's fiscal condition is weak (e.g., when projected deficits are high), comptrollers have tended to use their office to examine pressing fiscal issues and their long-term implications for city budgets. Arthur Leavitt, comptroller during the fiscal crisis, dealt with those issues having direct impact on the city's ability to pay off its debt. Later comptrollers were not subject to the same fiscal crisis immediacy and therefore had greater freedom to examine aspects of New York City government that were more indirectly connected to fiscal policy. For example, during the Giuliani administration, State Comptroller Carl McCall studied and issued reports on a wide range of city activities including the city's recycling policy, the Health and Hospitals Corporation's emergency preparedness program, and the New York City Police Department's and the city Department of Transportation's efforts to reduce fare evasions on the subway (New York State, New York State Comptroller's Office 1995, 1996a, 1996b).

A second factor influencing the behavior of state comptrollers in their monitoring of the city is partisanship. This is most evident when the state comptroller and the mayor are members of different political parties, and it is exacerbated even further when the state comptroller is seeking, or considering seeking, higher elected office. Some comptrollers have not been overly partisan. During the Koch and Dinkins administrations, for instance, Republican State Comptroller Edward Regan monitored city finances, yet rarely was accused of being partisan. Regan defined his role narrowly, and as a result, rarely used the comptroller's office to monitor areas of city government beyond those directly related to city fiscal activities. In addition, Regan had no aspirations, at least none publicly displayed, to advance his political career beyond the office of comptroller. As a result, he was rarely accused of being partisan in the exercise of his office. Arthur Levitt, Regan's predecessor, had defended the neutrality of the state comptroller's office in the early seventies when Governor Rockefeller pressured him to engage in fiscal examinations of city finances that would have embarrassed Mayor John Lindsay (New York Times 1997b).

Unlike the relationship between State Comptroller Regan and Mayors Koch and Dinkins, the relationship between Mayor Giuliani and State Comptroller McCall was particularly partisan and conflictual. On several occasions, Mayor Giuliani accused Comptroller McCall of using his office to promote a partisan agenda. In March 1997, Giuliani ordered city agencies to stop sharing various types of information with McCall's office. Aides to the mayor claimed that McCall was conducting audits of city agencies for the purpose of embarrassing the mayor's upcoming reelection efforts later that year. At issue in particular was the belief on the part of Giuliani and his aides that some of the comptroller's audits were designed to assess the accuracy of the Mayor's Management Report for the purpose of publicly discrediting the document (Levy 1997a). The Giuliani administration viewed McCall as more of a political adversary than a neutral fiscal monitor. McCall was a political ally and supporter of former Democratic Mayor David Dinkins. He was also viewed by many in New York City and New York State politics as an individual with political ambitions beyond the comptroller's office. Indeed, he later ran for governor.

On at least one occasion, Comptroller McCall sued Mayor Giuliani in order to obtain needed information (Toy 1997). The incident furthered the perspective of some that Giuliani would indiscriminately attack any of the city's fiscal monitors who were critical of his administration's performance, but the incident also damaged the neutrality and integrity of the state comptroller's office. McCall was accused of breaking with the nonpartisan legacy of state comptrollers (Nagourney 1997).

State Fiscal Assistance to New York City

Aside from the overall legal control that the state exercises over the city, the most important component of New York State–New York City relations is fiscal. New York State has a significant impact on New York City's routine fiscal affairs in three ways. First, the state gives the city a great deal of money on which the city has come to depend. Second, the state gives the city the legal authority to raise revenue by allowing it to use various types of taxes. And third, the state affects the city's fiscal position by manipulating the assignment of functional responsibilities between the two levels of government. Relative to other states' relationships with their local governments, New York State has a unique fiscal relationship with its local governments in general and with New York City in particular. New York State ranks forty-ninth among all states in taxes raised as a percentage of all state and local taxes. The state's low 39 percent is surpassed only by New Hampshire's 38 percent (Kolbert 1991). While New Hampshire's ranking is probably more a function of very low state tax rates, New York State's ranking is due more to high local tax rates, especially those in New York City. Yet it is also a function of the state's unwillingness to fund city programs and service delivery with state revenues. New York City performs services not undertaken by most large cities including a large municipal hospital and health care system and a large array of services to homeless individuals. At the same time, however, New York City ranks high among large cities with the percentage of state administered revenues in the city budget, and the city would rank first if state aid is measured on a per capita basis (Musselwhite 1988).

Although routine annual state aid to New York City dates back to the early 1900s, it was not until Governor Rockefeller's tenure in the 1960s that state aid to the city began to increase and establish a level of consistency and dependence that still exists today. Table 3.1 shows state and federal aid to New York City as a percentage of total city revenue. The data for this table comes from the New York

City Comptroller's Office. Unfortunately, the comptroller's office changed their method of calculating intergovernmental aid in the late 1970s. As a result, the data suffers from two problems. First, the percentages before 1978 and after 1977 cannot be compared due to revisions in the way aid was calculated. Second, after 1977, a significant percentage of intergovernmental aid coming from both the state and federal levels of government was not disaggregated. For the most part, the nondisaggregated aid represents unrestricted aid that both levels of government gave to the city. As the table displays, the percentage of nondisaggregated aid declines from 1978 to the present. The decline in nondisaggregated aid that took place during the early to mid-1980s coincides with the demise of federal revenue sharing, the one federal intergovernmental fiscal assistance program that gave unrestricted aid to state and local governments. This will be discussed in chapter four. Table 3.1 does show that by the late 1970s, the federal government was giving as much financial aid to the city as the state was giving. At that point, federal aid to the city declines significantly throughout the 1980s. And although state to city revenue as a percentage of total city revenue declined during the 1980s and leveled off during the 1990s, it still comprises approximately one fifth of all city revenue.

State financial assistance to the city has several important characteristics. First, only a small percentage of the funds are general purpose. New York State has a small program of general revenue sharing that gives the city unrestricted use of state funds. While unrestricted state aid to the city has grown steadily, it has never approached the dollar amounts of state education or social services aid to the city. Most of the funding is earmarked for specific policy areas. In fact, four policy areas—education, welfare, health, and transportation—account for most state aid to the city. Second, the majority of state fiscal assistance to the city is formula based; that is, a predetermined formula or set of variables is used to calculate the amount of aid the city receives. These funding formulas are established in the state legislature. The formula base of state money means that an extremely small percentage of state fiscal assistance is distributed according to the discretion of the governor or state bureaucrats on a project basis. The city rarely has to compete with other local governments for state funds on a project level. The competition for state funds takes place primarily in the state legislature where funding formulas and variable weightings that make up the formulas are determined (Green and Moore 1988).

The amount of state aid that New York City receives and the process and format by which it is received has created two highly significant issues in the city's relationship with the state. First, the city's budget and overall fiscal position is highly dependent upon decisions made during the state budgetary process. Second, given the city's increasing overall dependency on state funds over the last several decades, the issue of equity has become increasingly important in the discussion of state-local fiscal relations.

The city's budgetary process is not really complete until the state's budget decisions have been finalized. Final decisions at the state level are often not

TABLE 3.1

State and Federal Aid to New York City as a Percentage of New York City Income

Year	State aid	Federal aid	Not disaggregated
1970	26%	16%	
1971	26%	17%	
1972	26%	18%	
1973	24%	21%	
1974	25%	20%	
1975	24%	20%	
1976	24%	22%	
1977	22%	22%	
1978	18%	19%	8%
1979	17%	17%	8%
1980	17%	17%	6%
1981	17%	15%	6%
1982	18%	15%	5%
1983	17%	14%	6%
1984	17%	14%	6%
1985	18%	13%	5%
1986	19%	13%	4%
1987	18%	11%	3%
1988	19%	11%	3%
1989	19%	11%	3%
1990	20%	11%	3%
1991	20%	11%	3%
1992	19%	12%	3%
1993	19%	12%	2%
1994	19%	13%	2%
1995	20%	13%	2%
1996	19%	13%	2%
1997	18%	12%	2%
1998	18%	12%	2%
1999	18%	12%	2%
2000	19%	12%	2%
2001	19%	11%	2%
2002	20%	15%	1%
2003	19%	13%	2%
2004	19%	11%	1%
2005	17%	13%	0%

Source: Comprehensive Annual Financial Report of
the Comptroller (for the following years): 1969–1970,
1970–1971, 1971–1972, 1972–1973, 1973–1974, 1974–1975, 1975–1976,
1977, 1980, 1986, 1989, 1990,
1994, 2001, 2002, 2003, 2004, 2005.

made until after the city's formal budget process cycle is completed. This condition creates a great deal of uncertainty for the mayor, the city council, and city budget officials. As a result, city officials and those representing the city in Albany have become major participants in the state budgetary process. In addition, state budget analysts, both inside and outside of government, spend a considerable amount of time examining the impact of state budget decisions on the city.

City budget officials plan on a level of state aid when they construct the mayor's budget that is announced in January. And if the January state aid estimates are correct, the city is able to avoid making needless, and politically unpopular, decisions. In 1995, the January estimates of the mayor's budget office significantly overestimated what the state ultimately gave the city. The city received 670 million dollars less than requested primarily because the state cut less in Medicaid than initially anticipated. Each dollar cut by the state would have allowed the city to cut a similar amount since the state and city jointly match the federal portion of Medicaid funding. The mayor and the city council were faced with the task of making additional cuts on top of the eight hundred million dollars in cuts already made to city services before the state budget was finalized (Myers 1995).

Is New York City receiving its fair share of state revenues? A major problem in answering this question is defining what equity means in the context of state-local fiscal relations. While some have argued that the city should be receiving approximately what other localities in the state receive on a per capita basis, others have claimed that state-local fiscal assistance should reflect what the city's residents send to the state in the way of tax revenues. Still others base their argument for equity on a more subjective concept of need. According to this argument, given the city's large low-income and homeless population relative to other local governments, the city should receive more from the state than either a per capita or tax revenue return concept of equity would suggest.

A perennial complaint of New York City mayors is that the city has been shortchanged by the state through its distribution of aid to local governments. For several decades the city maintained that the state's distribution of school aid through the state's funding formulas did not take into consideration the city's growing school age population or the increasing percentage of foreign born or special needs students (New York Times 1997a). As of 1997, the city's school population comprised 37 percent of the state total, yet the city only received 34 percent of state educational comprehensive operating aid assistance. In addition, the percentage of students with special needs in the city school system was much higher than the state's overall percentage. This led some to argue that the city should receive more education aid than an amount proportional to the number of students in the city schools relative to the entire state. The politics of modifying the state's educational funding formulas are complex and favor the status quo. Any modification of the funding formulas must be approved by the state legislature. The upstate Republican-controlled State Senate has been reluctant to change the comprehensive operating aid formula in a way that would shift more school funds to the city. In fact, in the early 1990s the state legislature went so far as to consider counting each New York City student as 94 percent of a student in order to decrease the city's share of comprehensive state education aid relative to the rest of the state (Verhovek 1990).

There are also many variables within the funding formulas, and the distributional implications of manipulating a single variable are not always clear. Additional money for school transportation usually aids suburban and upstate school districts while money for bilingual education would send more money to the city (Vehovek 1990). The existence of these separate funds for education, however, has made it easier at times for upstate Republicans to cut pieces of the education budget that affect the city far more than their own constituencies. Funding cuts for special education or dropout prevention have affected the city far more than other local school systems in the state.

At the root of the state school aid controversy, however, is the fact that the state educational assistance funding formula and the overall distribution of state aid to local school systems do not take into consideration the differential ability of local governments to raise revenue for schools. In most states, local school funding is based on the property tax. As a result wealthy districts (e.g., those with high property values throughout the district) are able to raise more revenue than poorer school districts, sometimes even at lower tax rates. A wealthy school district such as Great Neck in Nassau County spends approximately twice per pupil than what New York City spends; yet Great Neck still receives substantial funding from the state, even though it is less than what the city receives. The state funding formula does not take into consideration differences in the local government's ability to raise revenue. In addition, the state formula has both a ceiling and a floor. So just as some low-income districts get less than they should because of the ceiling depressing the amount the formula gives them, the floor in the formula increases the amount that many wealthy districts get by giving them more than the formula would if left unencumbered (Goodnough 2000; Zernike 2001). In part, due to the ceiling and floor in the formula, in 2002 New York State had the country's largest gap in school funding between poor and affluent school districts. The per capita gap between what wealthy districts and poor districts got from the state was over $2,100, more than twice the national average (Winter 2002).

In 2000, the state gave the city approximately two thousand dollars less per pupil to New York City than it was giving to other urban school districts, and nine hundred dollars less than the average school district in the state (Perez-Pena and Goodnough 2001a; Wyatt 2001). At the same time, New York City spent less of its own revenue on its students than other urban school districts in the state. This was due in part to the fact that New York City, unlike some other cities in the state, had to support a range of social and other services that siphons off money from the schools (Perez-Pena and Goodnough 2001a).

New York State's funding of local public education has been the subject of at least two lawsuits in the past three decades. In the mid-1970s, a group of school districts, not including New York City, sued the state, arguing that the state's funding of education through local property taxes was discriminatory because it favored property-rich school districts that could raise more money per pupil with an equal or lower rate of taxation. The districts argued further that the state education aid formula exacerbated the already existing inequalities (Dionne 1982). Larger cities in the state including New York City later joined the suit agreeing with the plaintiff's argument, but adding that large cities had additional problems such as a concentration of disabled students and those with special needs. In 1982, after almost eight years of litigation, the New York Court of Appeals overturned the ruling of two lower courts in New York State, finding that the state's system of financing public schools was constitutional and that there was no "constitutional requirement that spending be equal among the districts" (Dionne 1982). While the court recognized the existence of inequalities among the schools districts' abilities to raise revenue, the court's decision stated that any attempt by the state to equalize educational opportunities across the state would "inevitably work the demise of local control of education" (quoted in Dionne 1982).

In 1993, a coalition of advocacy groups and parents from the city called the Campaign for Fiscal Equity filed suit in state court arguing that the state had failed to insure that students in low-income school districts receive an adequate education, as mandated by the state constitution. A prior interpretation of New York State's constitution gave individuals the right to a "sound, basic education" (Goodnough 1999b). Learning from the results of the 1982 suit, the plaintiffs in this suit did not challenge the equity of the funding formula or the property tax base by which local education revenues are raised. They challenged the adequacy of the financing. They also alleged, however, that the state was engaging in racial discrimination by giving less money proportionately to New York City, which had an overwhelmingly non-White school population. Given this charge, the plaintiffs alleged in the suit that the state was violating Title VI of the 1964 Civil Rights Act, which stated that "state agencies receiving federal money cannot discriminate on the basis of race" (Goodnough 1999b). After several years of the state attempting to have the suit dismissed, the litigation moved forward with a higher court's definition of what a "sound, basic education" should entail (Goodnough 1999b). The New York State Court of Appeals wrote in 1995 that, "a sound, basic education . . . should consist of the basic literacy, calculating and verbal skills necessary to enable children to eventually function productively as civic participants capable of voting and serving on a jury" (quoted in Goodnough 1999b). At the trial in October, 1999, the plaintiffs argued that the New York City school system performed poorly because it did not receive adequate funding from the state. Lawyers for the state argued that the funding the city received from the state was adequate to produce a "minimally adequate" education (Goodnough 1999c).

The state's lawyers argued further that the state gives the city's school system a great deal of money but that it is not always used wisely.

In January 2001, New York Supreme Court Judge Leland DeGrasse issued his ruling on the suit filed by the Campaign for Fiscal Equity. DeGrasse ruled that "the education provided New York City students is so deficient that it falls below the constitutional floor set by the education article or the New York Constitution. The court also finds that the state's actions are a substantial cause of this constitutional violation" (quoted in *New York Times* 2001). Judge DeGrasse also supported the plaintiffs' civil rights charges ruling that the state school funding formulas had a "disparate impact on minority public school children" (*New York Times* 2001). Judge DeGrasse's ruling was interpreted as mandating that the state had to provide funding to assist the city, in achieving a level of educational competency defined by the Court of Appeals in 1995 (Rothstein 2001). Less than a week after the ruling, Governor Pataki, arguing that the judge had overstepped his authority, announced that the state would appeal the ruling to the Appellate Division of the State Supreme Court (Perez-Pena and Goodnough 2001b).

In June 2002, the Appellate Division of the State Supreme Court overturned Judge DeGrasse's decision, ruling that the state was not obligated to provide more than a "middle school level education" and to prepare students for low-level employment (Perez-Pena 2002). According to the majority in this case, the state's constitutional mandate was to provide students in the state with a sixth- to eighth-grade education that would get them a minimum wage job. Disagreeing with Judge DeGrasse and the court's prior ruling on the meaning of a "sound, basic education," Justice Alfred Lerner, writing for the majority, stated that "the ability to function productively should be interpreted as the ability to get a job, and support oneself, and thereby not be a charge on the public fisc" (quoted in Perez-Pena 2002). The majority opinion also noted that the evidence presented in the case was unconvincing that the New York City schools offered an inadequate education and that poorly qualified teachers, overcrowded schools, and schools with outdated computers or no libraries produced an inadequate education (Perez-Pena 2002).

Unhappy with the decision of the 2002 Appellate Division of the State Supreme Court, the Campaign for Fiscal Equity appealed the decision to the New York Court of Appeals, the highest court in the state. Although not part of the original Campaign for Fiscal Equity coalition, early in 2003, Mayor Bloomberg announced that the city would file an additional brief in support of the Campaign for Fiscal Equity at the Court of Appeals level (Worth 2003). In June 2003, the Court of Appeals overturned the Appellate Division's 2002 ruling, agreeing with Justice DeGrasse's 2001 ruling. The court gave the governor until July 30, 2004, to conduct a study that would "ascertain the actual cost of providing a sound basic education in New York City," and reform the state's education funding system to provide the city with the necessary finances to provide a sound, basic education (Wolff and Wardenski 2003).

In the months that followed this decision, commissions appointed by Governor Pataki, the Campaign for Fiscal Equity, and the New York State Board of Regents all undertook studies to assess the cost of providing a sound basic education to city students. In February 2005, with still no plan by the state to respond to the lawsuit, the New York State Supreme Court that originally heard the case ordered the state to spend $5.6 billion on the city schools for operating expenses and $9.2 billion for new capital spending. Governor Pataki appealed the ruling (Medina 2006a: Rahimi 2005). In March 2006, the governor's appeal was rejected when the Appellate Division of New York Supreme Court ruled that the city schools were being underfunded by at least $4.7 billion a year as well as the $9.2 billion in capital funds over a five-year period (Medina 2006b). While the March 2006 ruling ordered the governor and legislature to take action, it did not tell them specifically what must be done and as a result did not provide immediate relief for the city (Medina 2006c). Nevertheless, several days after the ruling, as part of a state legislative budget agreement, both houses of the legislature authorized $11.2 billion in capital funds for school construction. Even though the state had not given the city the operating expenses ordered by the court, some viewed this action on the part of the state as the beginning of the lawsuit's resolution (Hakim and Medina 2006). Finally, in November 2006, the State Court of Appeals ordered the state to pay the city an additional $1.93 billion a year in operating costs for the city school system. This was considerably less than the $4.7 billion mandated by the Appellate Division of the Supreme Court (Herszenhorn 2006).

State Control Over City Taxes and Debt

The state also exercises a great deal of control over the city's ability to raise revenue. While the city has discretion to impose and regulate property taxes and a segment of the sales tax without direct state intervention, the city needs state approval to utilize most of its other revenue-raising instruments. This lack of autonomy for the city is significant because the city stands out among local governments in New York State in its dependence upon fiscal instruments other than the property tax. In 2004 and 2005, the property tax comprised less than one quarter of the city's total revenue stream, and this was only after the city raised the property tax by 18 percent in 2002. The city's use of sales and income taxes equaled or surpassed the amount of revenue raised by the property tax in those years (New York City Comptroller's Office 2005). Up until the mid-eighties, the city was the only local government in New York State to raise revenue via a personal income tax or a tax on real estate transfers. Along with a number of taxes on commercial activity employed by the city, all required the approval of the state legislature (Green and Moore 1988, 221). Not only must the city seek the state's permission to raise revenue, but it is the state that often dictates which taxing instrument will be used, imposing its revenue-raising preferences on the city. In the mid-eighties, the Koch administration wanted to use a real estate transaction tax to close a budget gap. The State Senate opposed the provision tax-ing cooperative apartment sales, and approved a tax on hotel rooms instead. The Senate preferred to tax nonresidents (Benjamin 1988, 127).

In 1999, in response to an issue raised in a State Senate election campaign in a New York suburb, the state abolished the city's tax on nonresidents who worked in the city, otherwise known as the commuter tax (*New York Times* 1999). The state had given the city the ability to levy the tax in the mid-1960s. The tax was a little less than half of 1 percent on taxable income earned in the city by those living outside of the city. This is equal to approximately $180 on a forty thousand dollar income. Although the state legislature and the governor only abolished the tax for New York State residents, suits by Connecticut and New Jersey following New York State's abolition resulted in the tax being abolished for their commuters as well. As a result, the city lost approximately four hundred million dollars of revenue in fiscal year 2000 and equivalent losses in future fis-cal years as well (Levy 1999).

Most major cities have a commuter tax, and in most cases the rate is higher than New York's was before it was abolished (Herszehorn 1999). Many see the commuter tax as fair in that those who work in the city but who do not live there are paying their fare share for the services they enjoy during their forty hours a week in the city. Opponents claim that those who work in the city support city revenues by locating their offices, buying lunch, and shopping in the city, all of which result in increased city revenues. The fact that the city, in 1999, had a budget surplus added additional weight to the opponents' case.

Although Mayor Giuliani had been a proponent of tax decreases throughout his administration, both he and City Council Speaker Peter Vallone lobbied unsuccessfully in Albany to keep the tax. Mayor Giuliani argued that the city should have the option of deciding which of its taxes to reduce or eliminate, even if state permission was needed (Levy 1999). Assessing the significance of the state action on the city budget, Robert Harding, Mayor Giuliani's budget director queried, "how is New York City going to manage its money if Albany, on a whim, can repeal a tax that is an important source of revenue. . . . We are being forced to move away from targeted tax cuts and meet somebody else's idea of how we should govern our city" (quoted in Goodnough 1999a). What surprised many, and certainly surprised Mayor Giuliani and Speaker Vallone, was that the commuter tax repeal was supported by Democratic Speaker of the State Assembly, Sheldon Silver, from Lower Manhattan. Being from New York City, as well as being a Democrat, many assumed that Silver would use his power as assembly speaker to stop the repeal. When questioned, however, about the impact of the repeal on the city's budget and his support of the repeal, Silver noted that Mayor Giuliani and Speaker Vallone should simply set aside some of their other proposed tax reductions to make up the difference (Goodnough 1999a).

In 2003, Mayor Bloomberg unsuccessfully sought permission from the state to allow the city to reinstate the commuter tax or something similar. The city, facing a budget deficit of over six billion dollars for fiscal year 2004, had already raised its property tax almost 20 percent, as well as cut services. In January 2003, it was still facing an over three billion dollar deficit and the mayor sought help from the state. In February 2003, Mayor Bloomberg spoke before New York State Assembly and Senate Joint Legislative Fiscal Committees. "Some say that taxing people who work in the five boroughs but who live elsewhere is unfair. I ask them to remember that the livelihoods, property values and standard of living of those who live in our neighboring states and counties are to a large extent a function of proximity to New York City. And when our police officers, firefighters and emergency medical technicians respond to calls, residency does not matter. . . . New York State taxes everyone that works in New York State whether they live in the state or not. New Jersey taxes everyone that works in New Jersey whether they live there or not. Yonkers taxes everyone that works in Yonkers whether they live there or not" (Bloomberg 2003).

The state and city have also feuded over the use of the sales tax. As of 1997, the state sales tax was 4 percent and the state allowed each local government to use an additional 3 percent sales tax to raise local revenue. The state gave New York City and several other local governments special permission to use a 4 percent sales tax. Both Mayors Giuliani and Bloomberg have wanted to eliminate the sales tax on clothing as a way to promote business in the city as well as raise revenue. In initially proposing the reduction Mayor Giuliani argued that because of the city's higher sales tax relative to its neighbors, the city was losing business. And although the elimination of the sales tax would mean lost revenue to both the city and the state, he argued that the additional business in the city because of the untaxed sales on clothing would create a net increase in revenue for the city through other taxes (Steinhauer 1997). The State Senate's Republican majority opposed the move by the city, fueled by the fears of Republicans from the city's suburbs that a sales tax elimination by the city would leave the suburbs and suburban merchants at a competitive disadvantage (Levy 1997b). Ultimately, as part of its fiscal year 1998 budget, the state agreed to eliminate its 4 percent tax on clothing items costing one hundred dollars or less beginning in December 1999. The provision allowed local governments in the state to eliminate their sales tax on clothing as well (Perez-Pena 1997a). The state sales tax on clothing was later reinstated and the city's ability to lower its own sales tax on clothing was restricted to one week in September before the opening of school and one week in January. In 2003, the state allowed the city to temporarily raise its sales tax to 4.125 percent in order to generate additional revenue for two years (New York City Council 2003).

In addition to controlling many of the tax instruments that the city uses, the state also has the power, by virtue of the state's constitution, to regulate the city's debt. According to a nineteenth-century provision in the state constitution, the city's debt ceiling is calculated as a percentage of its property tax base. The short-term borrowing that got the city into trouble, and was the source of the 1975 fiscal crisis, was not subject to constitutional or other state limits prior to the crisis. As previously discussed, city debt of all types came under the regulation of the Emergency Financial Control Board during the 1975 fiscal crisis and remains under FCB control even though the FCB formal control of city fiscal operations has been in sunset since 1986. In 1996, Mayor Giuliani lobbied the governor and state legislature to raise the city's debt ceiling, which was 10 percent of its property tax base. During the late 1980s and early 1990s, the property tax base of the city fell significantly while the amount of city debt continued to grow. City officials were concerned that the state-mandated debt ceiling would be violated. City officials also argued that basing the city's debt ceiling on the property tax base did not make sense because property taxes accounted for less than a quarter of the city's tax revenue. The state agreed with the city's position. In early 1997, the state legislature created the New York City Transitional Finance Authority, giving the city the ability to borrow up to 7.5 billion dollars beyond its debt limit for capital projects. The mayor was given control over the authority through his power to appoint three of the five members of the board. In addition, the legislature gave the city a great deal of discretion as to how the new debt could be used (Perez-Pena 1997b).

Another way in which the state has extended the city's capacity to incur debt is through the creation of special districts or public authorities. Special districts are usually single or limited purpose quasi-governmental units that are independent from general purpose governments such as New York City. They offer several advantages to a city or metropolitan area, but the primary one is the ability to incur debt for capital construction above and beyond state limits on local government debt. The other significant advantage of special districts or public authorities is their ability to cross jurisdictional boundaries in order to encompass the geographic scale of the service being delivered. Thus, in the case of a transportation authority or a port facility that crosses jurisdictional boundaries, a special district can provide balanced administration across those boundary lines, which general purpose local governments could not. The disadvantage of special districts is their lack of accountability to both the voters of the region and, in most cases, the elected officials of the relevant local governments. Special district officials are appointed, usually at the state level, and serve for fixed terms (Hallman 1977).

During Governor Rockefeller's administration, public authorities became a significant tool of the state's urban policy. And while the city did not have effective control over the public authorities, the city was the prime beneficiary both in terms of the authorities' focus as well as the more direct capital construction that took place without the city having to incur any additional debt. Two of the public authorities created by Rockefeller were the Urban Development Corporation (UDC) (now: Empire State Development Corporation—ESDC) and the MTA.

The New York State Empire State Development Corporation (ESDC) was formed in 1968 by the state legislature with the purpose of financing and constructing building projects throughout the state. The mandate given to the UDC was to stimulate the local economies of New York State through increased employment, improvement of the housing stock, and the construction of public facilities (Guttfreund 1995). Initially given the power to sell up to a billion dollars in tax-exempt bonds, this amount was later increased to two billion. In addition, the UDC was given the power to override local zoning and building ordinances as well as issue building permits. Within New York City, the UDC was responsible for a great deal of capital investment well beyond what the city, by itself, could have financed within its own debt limit. The UDC initiated and financed the Roosevelt Island new town project. In the late seventies, it assisted Donald Trump's development of the Grand Hyatt Hotel by purchasing building materials, allowing Trump to avoid paying a sales tax. Similar methods were used to assist the Mariott Corporation in building the Mariott Marquis Hotel in Times Square and the Rouse Corporation in building the South Street Seaport. The UDC took over the financing and construction of Battery Park City as well as the Javits Convention Center when both projects got bogged down due to debt problems. In early 1975, the UDC defaulted on its bonds. Although the default lasted only two months, it received considerable publicity, just prior to the city's fiscal crisis (Henderson 1994).

Similar to ESDC, the MTA was established by state legislation in 1968. The MTA Board of Directors has authority over the New York City Transit Authority, the Staten Island Rapid Transit Authority, the Long Island Rail Road, the Metro-North Commuter Railroad, the Metropolitan Suburban Bus Authority, and the Triborough Bridge and Tunnel Authority. The scope of its authority not only makes it a major focus for the infusion of capital into the metropolitan region and the city, but also a significant actor in terms of the region's infrastructure, and an agency that residents of the region depend upon on a daily basis. The MTA Board of Directors consists of a chairman, sixteen voting members, two non-voting members, and four nonvoting alternates that are all appointed by the governor with the advice and consent of the State Senate. Of the sixteen voting members, eleven are appointed with the recommendation of local officials. The mayor has four recommendations, the county executives of Nassau, Suffolk, Westchester, Dutchess, Orange, Putnam, and Rockland counties have one recommendation each. The representatives of the suburban counties on the MTA Board have only a quarter vote each. Of the remaining five voting members, three must reside within the city and two must live in the city or other counties within the MTA's operating region. The remaining nonvoting members and alternates represent the unions as well as transit users.

Another of the special districts affecting New York City is the Port Authority, formed by New York State and New Jersey. The Port Authority of New York and New Jersey is a bi-state special district established in 1921 to improve the port facilities and connecting transportation in and around New York. The Port Authority's impact upon New York City has primarily been through the development of infrastructure. In addition to administering the port facilities in New York and New Jersey, the Port Authority built the George Washington Bridge, the Lincoln Tunnel, and the bridges connecting New Jersey to Staten Island. The authority built the Verrazano-Narrows Bridge connecting Staten Island and Brooklyn as well as the Throgs Neck Bridge connecting Queens and the Bronx. By 1950, the authority administered the three largest airports in the New York metropolitan area. In the 1960s, the Port Authority took over many of the passenger rail links between New Jersey and New York. It was also responsible for building the World Trade Center in the 1970s (Doig 1995, 925). Throughout the middle of the twentieth century the Port Authority was viewed as a major and positive force in the development of the region. Free of direct political influence and having a professional staff, the agency was able to take a "long term perspective" on regional growth and infrastructure needs (Leone 2002).

The Port Authority is governed by twelve commissioners. The governors of New York and New Jersey each appoint six and retain the ability to veto the actions of the authority. The mayor has no formal input into decisions made by the authority. Most of the Port Authority's budget is obtained from revenues, such as tolls, it receives from the projects it has built or developed. It receives no direct tax revenue. Although the Port Authority has been an advocate for regional cooperation and regional economic development, it has never assumed a leadership position in the region. The leadership of the Port Authority has preferred to stay out of politics as much as possible, retaining their political neutrality. This neutrality is supported by the authority's state-oriented governing structure. The fact that the authority is not accountable to local politicians or voters, and does not receive local tax monies, lowers its political profile despite its impact on the metropolitan area (Berg and Kantor 1996, 40–41). To the extent that its activities have an impact on New York City, the Port Authority becomes one more manifestation of the state's control over the city.

In the past several decades, however, relations between the city and the Port Authority have not been good. Mayor Koch saw the Port Authority's ownership of the World Trade Center as depriving the city of millions of dollars of real estate tax revenue (Berg and Kantor 1996, 41). Mayor Giuliani was critical of the Port Authority throughout his tenure. In 1995, the Giuliani administration, through its Department of City Planning, issued a critical report on the role of the Port Authority (New York City Department of City Planning 1995). The report focused on the fact that the PATH trains, which take New Jersey commuters to and from Manhattan, were being subsidized by the Port Authority's other activities. As a result "revenue raised throughout the region is disproportionately devoted to subsidizing New Jersey commuters. These subsidies have increased dramatically over the years, with resulting inequities both in the level of subsidies provided to commuters in different parts of the region and in the allocation of resources between New York and New Jersey" (New York City Department of City Planning 1995, 1). The report was also critical of the Port Authority's administration of the metropolitan area's three major airports. While the report recognized that the authority had made some improvements at La Guardia Airport, it was very critical of the Port Authority's handling of Kennedy Airport, compared to its treatment of Newark Airport. The report cited data that passenger departures at Newark Airport had increased significantly but not at Kennedy. The report also noted that "air transportation employment had declined in Queens County while more than doubling in Essex County," New Jersey (NYC Department of City Planning 1995, 7). Several months after the Giuliani administration issued its report, Governor Pataki joined the criticism, stating that the Port Authority was poorly run and had over the years favored New Jersey (Fisher 1995).

In the aftermath of the September 11 attacks, much of the animus regarding the operations of the Port Authority dissipated. A number of Port Authority employees died in the attacks, including its executive director. Although the agency had sold the World Trade Center less than a year before the attack, it still owned the land on which the center was located. As a result, the Port Authority was a major actor in discussions on the redevelopment of Lower Manhattan. Early in his administration, Mayor Bloomberg signed a long-term agreement with the Port Authority for the continued operation of New York City's two airports.

State-City Division of Functional Responsibilities

New York State also exercises control over the city's fiscal health by influencing, if not at times controlling, the functional program or service delivery areas for which the city is responsible. These include program areas such as child welfare and education. In examining the functional division of responsibilities between the two levels of government, there are four possible ways that the status quo division of functional responsibilities has been changed. First, the state has assumed direct responsibility for programs or areas of service delivery previously controlled by the city, such as the city university system, thereby relieving the city of financial and administrative responsibility for the program. Second, the state has also created special authorities. Rather than assuming direct responsibility for the program on its own the state has, on occasion, created special authorities to assume responsibility for the financing and delivery of a service that the city would have to undertake in the special authority's absence. Third, the state has mandated that the city share in the cost of a program or area of service delivery being administered by the state, the city, or jointly. And fourth, the state can mandate that the city take on new responsibility for the delivery of a service or modify a current responsibility without regard to the fiscal consequences for the city of having to assume new functions.

New York City is unique in that not only has it performed functions that other large city governments have not undertaken, but it also delivers these services in such a comprehensive manner as to distinguish itself from those few municipal governments who have undertaken similar forms of service delivery. The two best examples of this practice are the City University system and the city's large municipal hospital system. The city's functional array separates it from other cities not only in quantity and quality, but in the financial burden this places on the city. As a result, from the city's perspective, the most helpful form of functional reassignment occurs when the state assumes the responsibility for the financing and administration of a function previously performed by the city. There are two examples of this in the city's recent history. In the wake of the 1975 fiscal crisis, the state assumed an increasing share of the cost of the City University (CUNY) system, beginning in 1978. This included total financing and control over CUNY's four-year colleges and increasing financial support of CUNY's community college system. Before the fiscal crisis, the state had paid for half the costs of the CUNY system (Green and Moore 1988, 237). While a merger with the State University (SUNY) system was rejected, the city's Board of Higher Education was replaced by a new Board of Trustees with a majority of appointees from the state level rather than from the city. During this same period, the state also assumed an increasing role in the financing and operation of the city court system, as it did with the local court systems across the state. By the early 1980s, all courts in the city were part of the state Unified Court System and operated under the supervision of the Chief Judge of the State Court of Appeals, who is the Chief Judge of the State (New York City Department of Citywide Administrative Services 1996). These takeovers occurred with little public controversy about the city's loss of control over these functions. Instead, city officials appeared to be far more supportive of the state relieving the city of the fiscal responsibility.

Another way in which the state has assumed functional responsibilities, otherwise undertaken by the city, is through the establishment of public authorities. As previously discussed, public authorities provide a means by which the state and the city can circumvent the limits on local and state debt in order to facilitate greater public capital investment within the city. In their capital financing and investment capacity, public authorities such as the MTA and the ESDC also take on functions that in their absence, the city would have to perform. Through the creation of the MTA, the state effectively assumed control over mass transportation financing and planning in the city and in the New York State portion of the metropolitan region. Although the city contributes funds to the MTA, it gets a great deal more in return through the MTA's ability to borrow. All of the major capital improvements to the city's subway system have been financed by the MTA either through federal and state grants or through debt financing. To the extent that mass transportation is a key infrastructure component in the city's attempts to promote economic development, the MTA performs a vital function beyond the daily movement of people from home to work.

The primary disadvantage to the city in the state assumption of functional responsibilities is the city's loss of control over the functions in question. With regard to the MTA, city officials have little control over fare increases or transit service quality issues. In 2005 when the Transit Workers Union went out on strike, Mayor Bloomberg was very vocal in his condemnation of the strike and its negative fiscal impact on the city, but he had no official role in the negotiations between the MTA and the union.

In one of the more controversial aspects of state-local functional assignment, New York State has mandated that its local governments share in the financing of Medicaid and Temporary Assistance to Needy Families (TANF), the two largest federal-state programs targeted to low-income families. With both the Medicaid program and Aid to Families with Dependent Children (AFDC) (changed to the Temporary Assistance to Needy Families in 1996), local governments in New York are required to pay up to one half of the federally required state matching funds. The state policy of mandating local participation evolved, in part, due to New York's tradition of upstate-downstate conflict. Fewer than ten states require their local government to pay any significant share of these costs, and no state comes close to placing the burden on its local governments that New York State does (Gold 1983). Every county in New York State must adhere to the cost-sharing mandate, but given the disproportionate number of residents living below the poverty line in the five counties that comprise the city relative to the rest of the state, the burden of this mandate falls most heavily on the city.

New York City's initial response to the Medicaid state funding arrangement was positive because the program provided federal funding for health care services that the city and state had been previously funding on their own. As a result, city officials viewed Medicaid as relief for the local tax financing of indigent health care. Within a few years, however, Medicaid eligibility expanded and health care costs increased dramatically making the dollar amount of the city's share of Medicaid financing far greater than the city's health care costs for indigent medical care delivery prior to Medicaid. Counties in New York State do have more leeway in tailoring their Medicaid and welfare programs to local needs but they, and the city in particular, pay a price for this additional flexibility.

Every mayor since Ed Koch has called on the state to relieve the city's unique burden. During the 1980s, Democratic Governors Carey and Cuomo placed Medicaid financing relief for the city on their agenda, but they were only minimally successful in getting the legislature to cooperate. There has been some minimal relief with regard to Medicaid but upstate antipathy and state fiscal problems have inhibited any major relief efforts. In 1983, the legislature passed Medicaid Overburden Legislation, in which the state agreed to finance the full cost of Medicaid expenses for certain categories of mental disability (Blum and Blank 1988). Also as part of this legislation, beginning in 1984, the state increased its share of Medicaid long-term care financing, lowering the city's percentage over three years from 25 percent to 10 percent (Green & Moore 1988, 237).

Realizing that the state was not going to take over the financing of Medicaid, Mayor Giuliani opted for a different tactic. Since the city was mandated to match state Medicaid spending on approximately a dollar for dollar basis, the mayor lobbied at the state level for cuts in the state's Medicaid program. For every dollar that the state reduced its own Medicaid expenditures, the city would save a dollar as well, regardless of its impact on Medicaid beneficiaries. Although Governor Pataki did cut some Medicaid spending, it never went as far as Mayor Giuliani desired (Steinhauer 2003).

Not all state-local functional assignment controversies originate in the legislative and executive branches. The courts have occasionally mandated that the city take on functional responsibilities. In the case of the homeless, the courts mandated that the state had the responsibility of sheltering the homeless, but the state was able to shift this responsibility to the local governments. The city was given this function with insufficient funding from the state. Eventually the federal government established some funding for homeless services, but it also was insufficient, leaving the city fiscally burdened with an additional responsibility. Not only did the state courts mandate that the city shelter the homeless, but at times the courts became directly involved in how the city carried out its mandate. In most cases, advocacy groups representing the homeless were behind much of the court activity. These groups used the courts, via litigation, to establish and later enforce mandates requiring the city to deliver services to homeless individuals and families. The city also attempted to use the courts to secure judicial approval for lowering standards in the shelters when budget constraints dictated a change in policy, but it was unsuccessful (Gruson 1982). As a result of the court mandates and the rise in the homeless population, city spending on the homeless increased from less than 10 million dollars in the early 1980s to more than 500 million in the early 1990s. And while the federal and state levels shared in the expense, especially for homeless families, the city bore the greatest share of the burden (Nix 1986).

The litigation that produced these mandates involved three significant court cases. In 1979, Robert Hayes, who later became counsel to the Coalition for the Homeless, filed suit on behalf of several homeless men seeking shelter from New York City. In the suit, *Callahan v. Carey*, Hayes claimed that the New York State Constitution included an implied right to shelter that the state and the city were obligated to provide. The 1938 state constitution did include a clause that the "aid, care and support of the needy are public concerns and shall be provided by the state," but this phrase had been ignored by prior courts (Blau 1992, 100). The state courts chose not to ignore the clause in the *Callahan* suit and ruled on behalf of Hayes and his homeless clients. After several years of legal maneuvering, the city entered into a consent decree with the Coalition for the Homeless, agreeing to provide safe and decent shelter to homeless men. Prior to the *Callahan* ruling, New York City's homeless policy consisted of an intake shelter on East Third Street that distributed vouchers to homeless men for the neighboring single room occupancy hotels. When the vouchers and the East Third Street Shelter's auditorium were filled, as they were increasingly in the late seventies, men were turned away (Goodwin 1983).

The consent decree in *Callahan* did not end the conflict between the city and Hayes's group. In the years following the initial suit, Hayes went back to court on numerous occasions to get the courts to enforce the 1981 consent decree and to pursue a comprehensive definition of safe and decent shelter that included clean bedding, adequate heat, a minimal amount of space per person, and health care (Tobier 1989). Hayes sought not only to force the city to make good on its new legal obligation to the homeless, but also to define this obligation in as comprehensive a way as possible to secure more services for his clients. In addition, since *Callahan* applied only to homeless men, Hayes and the Coalition for the Homeless filed subsequent suits to expand the right to shelter to other populations. In 1983, *Eldridge v. Koch* extended the consent decree to women and in 1986, *McCain v. Koch* applied the right to adequate shelter to families.

Political scientist Paul Peterson has suggested that higher levels of government should assume responsibility for redistributive programs, programs that take money from the haves and give to the have-nots. The rationale behind Peterson's argument is that taxpayers are much less likely or able to vote with their feet and move out of a national (or state) political system because the higher taxes are going to fund redistributive programs. The same taxpayers, however, would be much more likely to consider moving out of a state or local political system with relatively higher tax rates. At the same time Peterson is quick to note that the political incentives facing elected officials at all levels of government frequently encourage them to make dysfunctional choices by eschewing redistributive programs. Legislators at all levels seek to maximize their chances of getting reelected by taking credit for developmental programs that bring benefits to one's tax-paying constituents while avoiding responsibility for redistributive programs that might take benefits away from those constituents. Thus, according to Peterson, while it makes sense for the national level of government to finance and administer redistributive programs, legislators at the national level are just as likely as legislators at the state and local levels to avoid redistributive programs, passing them off on another level of government (Peterson 1995).

If higher levels of government had employed Peterson's economic logic, New York City would not be so burdened with the financing of redistributive programs including Medicaid, TANF, and services to the homeless. However, given the allocation of funding responsibilities for these programs, it appears as if Peterson's political incentive approach better explains the behavior of the various levels of government in dealing with the functional assignment of redistributive programs. Both the federal and state levels of government have sought to pass off these functions to lower levels of government. As the lowest level of government, New York City gets left holding the bag.

City Influence at the State Level

Given the state's far-reaching influence in city politics and government, the city and its officials have responded with a continuous effort to shape state policy. Over time, this effort has taken on both a formal institutional approach as well as a more ad hoc informal approach. The institutional approach involves the presence of representatives of the city government in Albany on a full-time basis as well as elected state officials who represent the city and its citizens. The informal ad hoc approach involves the frequent, but not necessarily routine, attempts by city officials to lobby for city interests at the state level. This is done either through communicating directly with state officials or by getting the city's position articulated through the media.

The mayor maintains an Office of State Legislative Affairs in Albany. On a day-to-day basis, the office represents the city throughout the entire state government but more importantly the office acts as the eyes and ears of the city in the state capital. The staff reviews legislation and comments on legislative proposals. They interact with state officials on routine matters and maintain constant contact with the mayor and city agencies as to when nonroutine matters regarding the city's relationship with the state might arise. The city council established a state legislative office in Albany in 1986 as well. Its mission overlaps with that of the mayor's Office of State Legislative Affairs. The city council's permanent office also performs a more focused role in conveying the council's perspective on state issues to the legislature. Given the vagueness of the city's home rule message and the resulting degree of influence that the state exercises over city affairs, the city council frequently passes resolutions calling on the state to act, and the state legislature on occasion seeks the input of the city council on various issues as well. This exchange takes place most often on issues of taxation or budget. The only two other city institutions to maintain a permanent office in Albany were the Board of Education, which is now defunct after its reorganization as a city agency, and the City University (CUNY) system. Given the amount of funding that the city Board of Education received from the state and the degree of administrative and substantive policy control that the state Education Department and Board of Regents exercises over the city educational system, a permanent office in Albany was understandable. After the reorganization of the city school system in 2002, the mayor's office took over the role of formally representing the school system at the state level. With regard to the city university, as previously noted, the state took over the CUNY system in the early 1980s. As a result CUNY is just as much a state agency as a city agency, if not more so.

The most permanent and formal representation New York City maintains at the state level is through its elected representatives in the state senate and the state assembly. Through the electoral ties to their constituents, these legislators represent the interests of the city in the state legislature. While they are not accountable in any way to officials elected at the city level, the common constituency these state legislators share with city officials and the resulting shared interest in responding to the desires of these citizens creates a common bond. In addition, state officials representing the city and elected city officials have for the most part shared party affiliation. New York City's success at the state level has been and remains tied to the Democratic Party. Given that the Democratic Party has only controlled the State Senate for two years since 1894, the city's interests are best represented at the state level when the city controls both the state assembly and the governor's office. State policymaking is frequently a function of negotiations between the governor, the Majority Leader of the State Senate, and the Speaker of the State Assembly. At a minimum, the Democratic Party needs to control the state assembly for the city to have any voice among the formal policy-making institutions at the state level. Since the Democrats took control of the state assembly in 1975, the speaker has been from New York City. As in the case of the 1999 abolition of the commuter tax, however, New York City's representatives in the state assembly may not always act in the interest of the city, as defined by the city's elected officials (Benjamin 1988, 137).

The recent history of city representation in the state law-making institutions is very much tied to the reapportionment revolution that came out of the U.S. Supreme Court cases of the early 1960s and the federal Voting Rights Act of 1965. Both before and after the reapportionment revolution, the primary tension behind legislative redistricting in New York State politics was a concern by upstate politicians to limit the influence of the city at the state level. Prior to 1966, Republican Party control of both houses of the state legislature allowed upstate Republicans to control what reapportionment took place. During this period, this goal was sometimes sublimated to a secondary goal on the part of incumbents to protect their seats by controlling the drawing of legislative district lines. Prior to reapportionment, the tradition in both houses of the New York State legislature had been to guarantee representation to counties before factor-ing in population. In the assembly this was done within a fixed number of seats, while in the senate new seats were added (Benjamin 1988, 129–130).

Ultimately, reapportionment brought on by cases in the U.S. Supreme Court dictated that population be the primary criterion for representation in the state assembly. This stabilized city influence at the state level by giving the Democrats control of the assembly. They have maintained control. By the time equitable representation was established, however, the city was losing population to the suburbs. As a result of the demographic changes, city success in the assembly is dependent upon Democratic seats in the suburbs and upstate even though the city remains the primary stronghold for Democratic seats in the assembly. Whereas in 1953, all but one Democratic senator and forty-eight of the fifty-two Democratic members of the assembly came from the city, by the eighties, New York City Democrats made up only 60 percent of the Democratic assembly and a little over 70 percent of Democrats in the senate (Benjamin 1988, 133–137). While the city needs the support of upstate Democrats to be successful in the assembly, upstate Republicans need the five or six Republican-held senate seats from the city in order to keep their majority in the senate.

While assembly Democrats cannot give the city everything it wants at the state level, they have the ability to block the most damaging legislation. This was clearly the case in the 1997 deliberations over city rent control regulations.

In responding to city need, however, the assembly Democrats' definition of city needs may be different than the mayor's. In 1997 and 1998, the assembly passed legislation damaging the city's ability to negotiate labor contracts with the Patrolman's Benevolent Association, the union representing the city police officers. The mayor campaigned against the legislation but the assembly and the state senate overrode the governor's veto. And as already noted, in 1999, the assembly, dominated by Democrats from the city, voted to abolish the commuter tax.

The governor's relationship with the city is also a significant factor in state-city relations. Political scientist Gerald Benjamin has argued that while most of New York's governors in the second half of the twentieth century have been from the city, they have not necessarily been of the city (Benjamin 1988, 112). By this, he means that New York City government has not proved to be an effective recruiting ground for governors. Governors who were from the city have not for the most part held office in New York City before becoming governor. Apparently, being so closely associated with the city is not an asset when seeking office at the state level. Mayor Ed Koch's failed gubernatorial attempt serves as an excellent example of this axiom. And in fact, no New York City mayor won election to a higher office in the twentieth century. More importantly, though, having a governor from the city does not appear to provide any guarantee that the city will be any more successful in lobbying the state. Governor Nelson Rockefeller may have explained it best by identifying the inherent conflict between the mayor and the governor. Mayors have a desire to get more from Albany in order to solve city problems, while governors have limited resources and an entire state to look after (Benjamin 1988, 113).

Another example of the complexity of city-state ties is that, even if the governor and mayor are of the same party, a cordial relationship is not guaranteed. Mayor Koch and Governor Mario Cuomo, who ran against each other both at the city and state levels, were fierce political rivals, in addition to the above-mentioned constraints that influenced their relationship as governor and mayor. And although the relationship between Governor Cuomo and Mayor Dinkins was certainly more cordial than the Cuomo-Koch relationship, there was still a great deal of tension due to Dinkins's expectations about how the city would be treated in Albany and the reality that was in part due to the economic constraints facing the state during the Cuomo years. And while Governor Rockefeller recruited John Lindsay to be the Republican candidate for mayor in 1965, he later came to resent Lindsay's liberal policies and persona (Tobier and Espejo 1988).

Such tensions can occur despite the frequency with which city officials go to Albany to deal directly with state officials. In addition, most key state executive branch officials have offices in New York City, including the governor, the state comptroller, and the attorney general. As a result, contact between city and state officials and their staffs occur on a day-to-day basis.

Mayors go to Albany to lobby on behalf of the city, but they must be careful to choose their battles. As the symbolic representative of the city, the mayor's appearance in Albany is viewed as a sign that the issue in question is especially critical to the city. A mayor spending too much time in Albany risks diluting the importance of this symbolism. While mayoral visits to Albany are not routine in any way, many are tied to the state budgetary cycle. As a result, mayors are frequently seen in Albany in January around the time the governor's proposed budget is announced and again in May when the state legislature is completing its modifications and approval of the state budget before it goes back to the governor for his signature.

In February 2003, Mayor Bloomberg traveled to Albany to lobby for the city. The city was facing a three-billion-dollar deficit for fiscal year 2004 even after raising property taxes 18 percent in November 2002, and cutting the city's budget by over 2.5 billion dollars (Cooper 2003a). Several days before his visit to Albany, the governor had released details on the state's preliminary budget for fiscal year 2004. Not only did the governor's budget not include any new aid for the city, it cut state funding for the city in critical areas such as education and Medicaid. The mayor met with legislative leaders and spoke before a joint committee of the legislature. He noted that the governor's education cuts would force the elimination of the city's pre-kindergarten program. It would also cause the loss of approximately 1,900 teaching positions that would result in increased class sizes in early grades. He stated further that the governor's proposed Medicaid reform would cost, not save, money for the city. The mayor also lobbied for the reinstatement of the commuter tax as well as for tort reform. These items were not addressed in the governor's budget, but clearly would have an impact on the city's fiscal health (Bloomberg 2003). While pointing out the deleterious impact that the governor's budget would have on the city, however, the mayor refused to publicly criticize the governor and, as a result, Democrat Sheldon Silver, Speaker of the State Assembly (from Lower Manhattan), accused the mayor of being "insufficiently zealous as an advocate for the city" (Haberman 2003). Bloomberg responded, "I just don't know why everybody can't accept that people with different views still are trying to do what's right. . . . And you work collaboratively and try to solve the problem, rather than try to provide fodder for a column or a sound bite. . . . I know that is a unique approach to government. . . . I'm here to do a good job, not to entertain" (quoted in Cooper 2003b).

Not every mayoral visit to Albany is budget related. Mayor Giuliani lobbied in Albany with regard to the city rent control and the reorganization of the city's educational system. Mayor Bloomberg also traveled to Albany to lobby on behalf of education reform.

The mayor is not the only city official who lobbies on behalf of the city at the state level or attempts to convey the city's interest to state decision makers. The comptroller, as the city's chief financial officer, occasionally accompanies the mayor to Albany during the state's budget deliberations. As an independently elected city official, the comptroller's perspective on city fiscal matters can serve to corroborate the mayor's position or it may serve to modify or critique the position the mayor is pursuing in Albany. Both officials are well aware of the potential damage to the city's interests in Albany if their positions are contradictory and so, unlike governor-mayor tensions, mayors and comptrollers try hard to work in tandem. The city council also attempts to get its views articulated in Albany. This is sometimes done through resolutions that convey to the state legislature the position of the city council as an institution. More often, individual council members, especially the Speaker of the Council, will lobby the state government. In 1999, Council Speaker Vallone joined Mayor Giuliani in traveling to Albany to lobby against a repeal of the city's commuter tax. City council activity at the state level occurs more often when there is divided party control of the city government. In 2003, City Council Speaker Gifford Miller did not travel to Albany to lobby against the governor's budget, but used his "State of the City Address" to attack the governor and the impact that his budget would have on city schools. Taking a much more aggressive tone than did the mayor, Speaker Miller stated, "We're trying to turn our schools around. We cannot possibly absorb these cuts to public education and our children cannot be forced to languish in a second-rate school system. Remember this: it costs the state more to sacrifice a generation of students than it does to invest in them. Governor Pataki, please stop your assault on public education. If the governor was serious about addressing our real problems, he wouldn't resort to false solutions" (Miller 2003).

Conclusion

The legal power, and the residual political clout, that the state exercises over the city evolved over two centuries. While issues affecting the fiscal health of the city have dominated the recent relationship between the city and the state, it is the state's legal position via Dillon's Rule and home rule that structures the relationship. Regardless of the issue, the state retains, via the rule, the ultimate legal authority to respond in a way that serves its interests over the city's in a conflict. The state's relationship with the city is not a federal one. New York State is a unitary political system with all power emanating from the state. Vague home rule legislation leaves the city little legal ground on which to contest state actions but says nothing about the city's shifting political strength at the state level. The city may not be able to influence state actions by calling on its legal relationship with the state but it certainly can use its political influence to make a case on its behalf. The city's exercise of political influence is complex, shifting, and dependent upon a number of factors including partisanship at the state and city levels, state economic conditions, and the specific policy area in question.

The most significant impact of the state upon the governance of New York City concerns the funding and delivery of public goods and services. To a great extent, the array of public goods and services delivered by the city to its citizens has been mandated by the state and is controlled at the state level. In policy areas as diverse as education, the environment, and child welfare, the city's service delivery activities are, to a considerable extent, a response to state laws and regulations. Just as important as state policy and program mandates, the city has remained dependent upon state revenues, as well as state taxation and debt authority, to finance city service delivery activities. As noted in this chapter, the city's dependence on state funds and state revenue-raising authority can become contentious at times. Although it is less visible on a day-to-day basis, the state also has a significant impact on democratic accountability within the city's political system. By giving the city home rule powers, the state has ceded to the city the ability to structure its own procedures for the establishment and maintenance of representative government. At the same time, given the extent to which decisions affecting the city are made at the state level, democratic accountability via representative government is as important at the state level as it is at the city level, for the city's citizens and policymakers. The Public Authorities Board, a state agency, controlled the key decisions in both the Jets/Olympic Stadium and Nets Arena cases. Compared to its roles in the city's delivery of public goods and services and its influence on democratic accountability in the city's political system, the state's impact on civil harmony in the city is minimal. To the extent that civil harmony is a function of leadership, governors and other state officials have rarely been perceived as being a part of the city's political system, even when they are from the city. To the extent, however, that civil harmony is a function of perceptions of a just (i.e., fair) political system, those seeking justice in the city's political system have on occasion used the state constitution and the state courts to promote equity, as in the case of the Campaign for Fiscal Equity and the litigation for the homeless.

Clearly since the 1975 fiscal crisis, the city's need for increased revenue and/or the policy flexibility to alleviate spending obligations has been at the crux of any state-city tension. The state responses to city requests for assistance have varied. They have ranged from the creation of the Municipal Assistance Corporation and the EFCB, to the state's mandating that the city share in the cost of Medicaid and welfare. More recently, the state responses have included at first resistant and then apparent acquiescence to city demands for more educational assistance.

The state may want to avoid fiscal responsibility for the city's activities while exercising maximum legal control, but the state's legal and political relationship with the city dictates that the state spend a great deal on the city. While the perennial upstate concern with the city may be based primarily upon the city's fiscal pull on the state budget, the historical relationship includes partisan differences that still structure the city's relationship with the state government as well as social differences that remain as pronounced today as a century ago, even if the racial and ethnic groups have changed. State-city relations also are based on state dependence on the city as the economic engine of the state. Whether the state gets pulled into city affairs by city officials or interest groups, or whether the state involvement is self-initiated via the state constitution, laws, or budget, there is little that goes on in the city that is not influenced by the state.

4

The Federal Government
and the City

New York City's relationship with the federal government is very different from its relationship with New York State. As seen in the intergovernmental relationships surrounding the fiscal crisis, the federal government is not legally responsible for the actions of the city or its officials, while the state is. The federal response to the city during the fiscal crisis, similar to the response after the September 11 attacks, was not based upon any constitutional obligation. It was solely based on political calculations by officials at the federal level as well as lobbying in Washington by New York State and New York City officials. In addition, the relationship that the city has with the federal government today has evolved since the 1930s. Prior to that point, the relationship was minimal. Based primarily upon fiscal assistance (i.e., intergovernmental grants) coming from the federal level, the relationship peaked in the late 1970s, declined substantially during the 1980s, never recovering fully. Much of the evolving federal-city relationship centered around programs such as urban renewal, model cities, and the Community Development Block Grant. These programs represented the federal government's efforts to target financial assistance to urban areas. They do not, however, represent the entire impact that the federal government has had on urban areas. Federal programs with a broader scope such as the funding of the interstate highway system and the interest on home mortgage tax deduction were not directed specifically at urban areas, yet they had a significant impact on urban and metropolitan development, not all of it positive.

Beginning with the New Deal, but accelerating in the 1960s and 1970s, New York City, like most large cities and many local governments, developed a relationship with the federal government independent of its relationship with the state. During this period, the federal government made available to cities billions of dollars in aid covering many policy areas. Between 1970 and 1978 alone, federal grants to cities increased by over 700 percent (Fossett 1984). While some cities were reluctant to become entangled with the federal regulations accompanying the federal funds, and other cities selectively chose only a few federal programs to pursue, New York City aggressively sought federal funding across the broad array of available funds. The resulting relationship between New York City and the federal government was both cooperative and conflictual, depending upon the policy or program area.

City fiscal dependence on the federal level reached its peak during the late 1970s, in part due to the federal loan guarantees that helped the city out of its fiscal crisis, and in part due to the increased use of federal grants as mechanisms to assist local governments in selected program areas. Although the level of federal fiscal assistance to the city surpassed state assistance to the city for only a few years during the mid- to late 1970s, the rapid rise and fall of federal assistance and its overall volatility was a very significant factor in the city's fiscal health. Since the Reagan years, urban policy has not received the attention on the federal government's agenda that it received in the prior decades. The Clinton administration implemented some programs that were targeted toward cities, but these never approached the magnitude of the programmatic or fiscal commitment that the federal level exhibited toward the cities prior to Reagan. Aside from the aid the city has received as a result of the September 11 attacks, the Bush administration has not implemented any new urban initiatives.

In addition to federal fiscal assistance, the other major instrument of federal-urban relations is the mandate. Similar to state mandates, federal mandates are orders or regulations imposed on the city by the federal government that may or may not be accompanied by funding to implement the mandate. During the early 1980s, Mayor Koch became a national leader in local government criticism of federal mandates, some of the most expensive of which concerned federal environmental regulations (Koch 1980). Many of these mandates continue to affect the city. Throughout the late 1990s, the city faced the prospect of having to construct a filtration plant for its water system in response to U.S. Environmental Protection Agency regulations regarding water quality (Wakin 2001). In 1998, as the result of a federal court order, the city agreed to filter water from the Croton Reservoir in Westchester County, responsible for about 10 percent of the city's drinking water. Finally, in 2003, after contentious city council hearings, several years of litigation, deliberations by the state legislature, and intervention by the governor, the city decided to build the water filtration plant in Van Cortlandt Park in the Bronx. The cost of the plant was almost a billion dollars, with the federal government paying very little of the cost (Baker 2003). Without federal environmental mandates, the city would not have had to undertake this activity and it is doubtful that the city would have undertaken such activity on its own.

The Evolution of Federal Relations with Cities

New York City's relationship with the national government was in large part a result of malapportionment of the state legislature. Facing growing problems and unresponsive state political systems in the middle of the last century, New York City and other large cities focused their efforts on the federal government. An increasingly liberal national political system, dating back to FDR, responded to the needs of cities with a series of federally funded programs. Throughout the history of federal financial assistance to states and localities, the primary tool of intergovernmental fiscal transfer has been the categorical grant. Categorical grants give funds for narrowly defined purposes, allowing the grantor to dictate to the grantee how the money is going to be used. The receipt of categorical grants from the federal government, similar to the receipt of all federal aid, is voluntary. Local governments are always free not to apply for federal funding if they feel the strings attached to the assistance are too burdensome or if the goals of the grant go against local program priorities. Over time, however, the amount of federal aid available to cities and the variety of programs being funded became too much for most large cities to ignore. Although the categorical grants were accompanied by narrowly defined categories and tight spending restrictions, the variety of grants across policy and program areas gave city officials a large number of programs from which to choose. In many cases, the program areas being funded by federal categorical grants corresponded to the problems being experienced by large cities and the categories of funding for which city officials expressed a need.

Most categorical grant monies were distributed through an application process, with prospective grant recipients competing for a limited amount of funding. Federal bureaucrats in the agency administering the grant would assess the applications and make a determination about which applications would be funded. There were a few categorical grants, such as Aid to Families with Dependent Children (AFDC) (now Temporary Assistance to Needy Families, or TANF) and Medicaid that were distributed automatically to recipients according to a formula established by Congress, but most of these grants went to the states and not to cities. The application format for categorical grants created a process whereby cities wanting federal funds had to demonstrate that there was a need for the money and also that the city had the bureaucratic infrastructure to spend the money wisely once it was received. This skill became known as grantsmanship. Cities seeking to maximize federal intergovernmental fiscal assistance hired good grant writers. As the number of federal grants and availability of federal funds increased, successful grant writing became more important for cities. Some cities shied away from this competition. New York City did not.

As the number of categorical grants increased throughout the 1960s and early 1970s, mayors and other local officials complained to federal officials about the burdensome and repetitive application and reporting requirements that accompanied each grant. They also complained about the lack of flexibility in tailoring the use of categorical monies to local needs, due to the specific and detailed federal requirements regarding how the money was to be spent. Mayors in particular were concerned that since much of the categorical money went from a federal agency distributing the money to a local bureaucracy that had applied for the money, elected officials were being left out of the process.

To respond to these concerns, the federal government employed two additional intergovernmental fiscal devices during the 1970s: block grants and general revenue sharing. The two new grant types were both creations of President Nixon's New Federalism, an attempt to rationalize but not drastically alter intergovernmental relations in the early 1970s. Both types of grants gave the city a great deal more discretion than categorical grants over how federal funds could be used. In addition, both types of grants distributed monies through a congressionally established formula rather than through a competitive application process, thereby lessening the dependence on grant writers. General revenue sharing, initiated in 1973, gave recipients almost unlimited flexibility over the use of its funds.

Block grants occupied a middle ground between general revenue sharing and categorical grants. They gave recipients considerable flexibility within a programmatic area such as community development or public health but fell far short of the near unlimited programmatic discretion that accompanied revenue sharing. Block grants were established in one of two ways. Some block grants were established by collapsing existing categorical grants in a related area into one large block grant. This type of block grant formation gave cities the ability to fill in programmatic gaps that existed between related categorical grants, and gave them greater discretion over federal funds within a given policy area. A second group of block grants was established simply by legislating broad recipient discretion over federal funds in a new policy area that was not previously occupied by categorical grants. Although general revenue sharing and block grants received a great deal of attention during the 1970s and early 1980s, the dollar amount accounted for by these new grant types never equaled the dollar amount of categorical grant assistance.

Giving cities greater discretion over the use of federal funds created some controversy over how the money was being spent. Many, but clearly not all, federal categorical grants had a redistributive goal; that is, the federal grant money was targeted to low-income areas of the city or for programs benefiting predominantly low-income individuals. Paul Peterson et al. (1986) have argued that the array of active interests in local political systems inhibited local political officials from spending discretionary funds for redistributive purposes. Peterson notes that those interests supporting redistributive programs are generally weak at the local level compared to those interests supporting distributive or developmental programs. Distributive programs such as law enforcement tend to spread spending more evenly across the city while developmental spending focuses on economic development in those parts of the city where development is attractive. In addition, local officials are reluctant to embark upon broad redistributive programming for fear of what it will do to economic development in their localities, and ultimately to their reelection chances (Peterson, Rabe, and Wong 1986).

As a result, there was concern on the part of some federal officials and interest groups at the national level representing the interests of the poor that block grants and general revenue sharing would result in less spending on the poor. Locally elected officials, with discretionary power over these funds, would spend them in response to politically active constituents, and not the poor.

The limited research that has been conducted in this area suggests a somewhat more complicated local political system than what was initially described by Peterson et al. (1986). In some cases, advocates for the poor at the local level were successful in making a claim on the discretionary funds coming from the federal level. In particular, in those cities with a record of categorical grant experience, there were entrenched interests, including local bureaucrats who had been administering federal categorical monies and they pushed for continued redistributive spending despite increased local discretion over the funds (Kettl 1980; Peterson, Rabe, and Wong 1986).

Whatever controversy arose concerning increased local discretion over federal funds was almost immediately overshadowed by the cuts in federal aid to cities that occurred during the 1980s. The decline in federal intergovernmental assistance that began during the Carter administration and was stepped up during the Reagan administration became the dominant theme of federal-urban relations during the 1980s and 1990s. The level of federal aid to cities achieved during the seventies was never reestablished after the decline in federal funding that occurred during the 1980s.

New York City and the Federal Government, 1930–1964

In response to the economic hardships created by the Depression, the Roosevelt administration created a set of programs that connected cities to the federal government to a much greater degree than before.

One of the more lasting impacts of Roosevelt's New Deal on the city was in the area of housing. The Depression exacerbated the problems of an already deteriorating urban housing stock. The federal Public Works Administration (PWA), created by the 1933 National Industrial Recovery Act, awarded a small number of grants for housing (Plunz 1990). Under the PWA, low- and middle-income housing projects such as the Williamsburg Houses in Brooklyn and the Harlem River Houses in Manhattan were constructed. The housing component of the PWA gave way to one of the first federal-urban categorical grant programs through the Housing Act of 1937. The act, sponsored in part by New York Senator Robert Wagner, provided federal funding for the construction and administration of local public housing projects. The program also attempted to create a link between publicly funded housing and slum clearance. Ultimately, the program was responsible for the construction of high-rise, high-density public housing projects that in retrospect have received a great deal of criticism for their aesthetic failures as well as the fact that they served as incubators of the culture of poverty and dependence that have since plagued low-income areas of the city.

The Federal Housing Act of 1949 went well beyond its predecessor by promoting urban renewal through large-scale slum clearance and commercial as well as residential development of cities. According to Title I of the act, the federal government would give money to local urban renewal authorities for the purpose of condemning and clearing slum neighborhoods. While the hope was that for every deteriorating housing unit cleared, a new unit of low- or moderate-income housing would be built to replace it, this did not occur. Since the federal program gave local authorities discretion in replacing dilapidated slums with commercial or residential developments, many local authorities opted for commercial redevelopment. In addition, the law allowed for up to 30 percent of the cleared land to be used for private commercial purposes; and private developers brought in by local development authorities to develop recently cleared land under the program saw little economic advantage in building low- or moderate-income housing. As a result, many more housing units were destroyed than replaced (Smith and Klemanski 1990). Whatever vagaries existed in the 1949 Housing Act were clarified in the 1954 Housing Act. Local governments were given considerably greater freedom to engage in economic development projects with federal funds without having to build new housing (Flanagan 1997). New York City aggressively sought these categorical funds and was successful in receiving a significant percentage. Throughout the first fifteen years of the program, New York State accounted for almost a third of all national urban renewal construction under the 1949 Housing Act, and virtually all of this was in New York City (Anderson 1964).

The one project that best represents both the positive and negative aspects of urban renewal was the city's leveling of the San Juan Hill area of the Upper West Side and the building of Lincoln Center for the Performing Arts. In 1956, Robert Moses, head of Mayor Wagner's Committee on Slum Clearance, began to plan for the development of the Upper West Side. Since the 1930s, Moses had been involved in all aspects of public construction in the city, serving as Mayor Fiorella La Guardia's Parks Commissioner as well as occupying several positions at the state level. When the San Juan Hill planning began in the mid-1950s, Moses had already been instrumental in obtaining urban renewal funds for the clearing of land and construction of the New York Coliseum, situated on the southern border of San Juan Hill (present-day Columbus Circle). Moses's plan was to raze the eighteen square blocks of the neighborhood and replace it with a new cultural center for the city and a number of other educational and cultural institutions that had agreed to relocate in the urban renewal area. The area would also include luxury housing as well as some low- to moderate-income housing primarily for the elderly (Salwen 1989)

In the 1950s, San Juan Hill was a low-income neighborhood populated predominantly by Blacks and Puerto Ricans (Jackson 1995). To make way for urban renewal, residents were moved out and the tenement buildings in the neighborhood were demolished. In 1959, President Dwight Eisenhower presided over the groundbreaking for Lincoln Center for the Performing Arts; by 1966, the project was completed. While the project demonstrated what could be done to renew the cities with federal help, the project also demonstrated the costs of urban renewal. Low-income neighborhoods saw the necessity and possibility of organizing to resist the loss of their homes, and some federal officials were made aware of the need to include local residents in redevelopment plans. As a federal categorical grant, urban renewal monies were restricted to slum land purchase and clearance. The grant gave the city sufficient discretion to determine what land would be cleared and what would be done with it once it was cleared. The indigenous businesses and residents of the area were not included in the process (Frieden 1966).

By the mid-1960s many federal policymakers were well aware of the problems of the urban renewal program and the need for greater community involvement in redevelopment decisions. They were also becoming aware that in dealing with low-income communities, a "bricks and mortar" solution was insufficient. If individuals and communities were going to be brought out of poverty to take advantage of redevelopment, effective services would have to be targeted to individuals and possibly entire neighborhoods. As a result of the early urban renewal experience as well as the emerging civil rights movement, urban minority groups felt particularly committed to achieving greater involvement in decisions regarding their own communities and to developing the needed political power to have a positive impact.

Federal Relations with New York City, 1964–1980

In response to the rising public awareness of urban problems, the Johnson administration sought to implement a policy that would concentrate federal dollars in low-income urban and rural areas through a series of targeted categorical grants. In contrast to earlier urban renewal values, the Johnson administration's antipoverty program adopted a strategy of community empowerment through community control over social services delivery. The concept of community action and empowerment as an antipoverty strategy had its roots in two pilot projects in New York City, Mobilization for Youth and Harlem Youth Opportunities Unlimited (HARYOU), partially funded by the federal government. Operating out of the Lower East Side, Mobilization for Youth was a joint project of the Henry Street Settlement House, Columbia University's School of Social Work, the Ford Foundation, President Kennedy's Commission on Juvenile Delinquency, and the National Institute of Mental Health. The goal of the project was to develop strategies for preventing juvenile delinquency by improving the economic opportunities of those at risk. One of the strategies explored by Mobilization for Youth was the organization of the poor for political action and the "maximum feasible participation" of the poor in the administration of social service program delivery to the community (Clarke and Hopkins 1968; Jackson, 1995). The HARYOU program went one step further by arguing that the primary reason for the predicament of the poor was not a lack of services, but political powerlessness. For the HARYOU program, the purpose of community action was to obtain and use political power on behalf of the community (Clarke and Hopkins 1968). These ideas were embodied in the 1964 Federal Economic Opportunity Act (EOA), the legislative foundation for President Johnson's War on Poverty. The legislation created a cluster of categorical grants designed to create economic opportunities in part through greater community involvement and control of service delivery. Unlike the previous federal categorical grants targeted to urban areas, federal funds under the EOA would not be administered by government officials. They were supposed to be administered by community residents.

Among the categorical grants established by Johnson's War on Poverty were Project Head Start, the Job Corps, the Neighborhood Youth Corps, and Volunteers in Service to America (VISTA). In retrospect, the most controversial of the programs funded through the EOA was the Community Action Program. The program funded the creation of local community action agencies that would administer the War on Poverty monies at the community level. It was the goal of these local agencies to encourage the "maximum feasible participation" of the poor in those targeted communities. In part, poverty was being defined as a political condition as much as an economic one.

Community control of the programs created an initial tension between the federal government and the mayors of most large cities. Mayors wanted control over the War on Poverty monies but federal program planners opted for community control. Just as urban renewal and public housing monies had bypassed the states and gone directly to cities, War on Poverty monies were designed to bypass city governments. The authors of the War on Poverty viewed mayors as not acting in the interests of the poor, as witnessed by what many city officials had done with urban renewal monies, destroying many low-income communities and not including residents in decision making. Testifying before a congressional committee in 1964, however, Mayor Wagner argued that mayors "should have the power of approval over the make up of the (community action program) planning group, over the structure of the planning groups, over the plan" (Donovan 1967, 55).

Greenstone and Peterson (1973) report that the War on Poverty program in New York City became part of the conflict between Democratic Party regulars and reformers. Republican and Liberal Party Mayor Lindsay sought to encourage greater community involvement, in order to keep control of the program out of the hands of Democratic Party regulars entrenched via patronage in city social service agencies. In fact, the Lindsay administration increased the participation of the poor on the city's poverty policymaking body from 42 percent, the percentage under the previous Wagner administration, to 50 percent. Mayor Lindsay saw the community groups as far less threatening to his weak political base than the Democratic Party regulars and their allies in the city bureaucracy. Nevertheless, some have argued that the participation of the poor in the decision making and administration of these programs in most cities was symbolic at best (Greenstone and Peterson 1973).

The War on Poverty programs affected the city in several ways. The federal requirements for low-income community participation fostered the further development of Black and Puerto Rican leadership. Some have suggested that New York City, unlike many other large cities, already had an indigenous community leadership developing in impoverished neighborhoods prior to the War on Poverty. To some extent, the existence of organizations such as Mobilization for Youth and HARYOU prior to the War on Poverty served as incubators for low-income community leadership.

This increased power, however, created greater competition among local groups for control of local poverty organizations. Greenstone and Peterson (1973) reported that in East Harlem, Bedford-Stuyvesant, and the Lower West Side of Manhattan, the competition became fierce. More specifically, there was evidence that the conflict taking place in some low-income communities was between Black and Puerto Rican groups. In the Bronx, Puerto Rican groups accused the city's Council Against Poverty of acting in a discriminatory way toward Puerto Rican residents of the poverty communities. The groups claimed that when they complained about a lack of adequate representation on some community poverty boards, they were told to "campaign better"; but when Black groups complained of poor representation on the Hunts Point Community Corporation, the city Council Against Poverty overruled an election won by Puerto Ricans and ordered the corporation to appoint un-elected Blacks to its board of directors (Beck 1969; Clarke and Hopkins 1968; Greenstone and Peterson 1973; Kihss 1968).

Complaints from mayors about the conflict created by the War on Poverty and about problems stemming from the inexperience of low-income community groups in administering federal monies were influential in producing the Model Cities program. The Demonstration Cities and Metropolitan Development Act of 1966, otherwise known as Model Cities, was an attempt by the Johnson administration to promote comprehensive urban development as opposed to the narrow goal of the eradication of urban poverty, the focus of the War on Poverty. The principle goal of the Model Cities program was for the cities to utilize federal spending for a concentrated attack on the physical and social problems of blighted neighborhoods. The few federal strings attached to the program were designed to allow local governments to employ their own ingenuity in solving urban problems by coordinating their own resources along with the federal funding. In the short history of federal urban-oriented legislation, the Model Cities program was unique in that it provided funding for a wide variety of activities including slum clearance, crime and poverty reduction, housing improvements, job training, and the creation of job opportunities. Unlike prior federal grants to cities, the Model Cities program gave city officials broad, but not unlimited, discretion in how to spend federal funds. Model Cities was not a typical categorical grant. In granting broad program discretion to cities, the program was a forerunner to later block grants that gave cities increased discretion in how to spend federal monies. Unlike War on Poverty monies, Model Cities monies were meant to be controlled by city officials, and not by community representatives, although there was a community participation requirement in the legislation. And unlike urban renewal, Model Cities promoted urban development that included social programs such as health clinics, senior centers, and early childhood programs.

There were requirements to include community groups from the Model Cities neighborhoods in the planning of the programs. In arguing against community involvement in the Model Cities program, Bronx Borough President Herman Badillo claimed that antagonisms among groups in the Community Action Program would be exacerbated in the Model Cities program. Supporting a Model Cities program with more centralized control, Badillo critiqued the idea of decentralization, "It's a very bad procedure. . . . It will produce the same disaster as the poverty program. People will compete for jobs on an ethnic basis—Negro against Puerto Rican" (Roberts 1967b). Above Badillo's objections, Mayor Lindsay gave local communities a veto over the selection of the directors of the program in the Model Cities communities. Throughout the brief history of the Model Cities program in New York City, however, the mayor slowly but steadily increased the level of centralized control in an attempt to move the program above the feuding that took place at the community level (Washnis 1974).

New York City was the only city to receive funding for more than one Model City neighborhood, as Harlem, the South Bronx, and Central Brooklyn were designated to be included in the program. The city's application to the federal government for Model Cities funding stressed three areas of concentration: educational improvements; job training and day care; and housing repair and maintenance. Even concentrated in small areas of the city and on a limited number of projects, the funding was insufficient (Roberts 1967a).

Although the Nixon administration did not attempt to eliminate the Model Cities program, it was not entirely supportive of the program either. Throughout the Nixon years, the budgetary growth of Model Cites and other urban-oriented programs were constrained far below what Johnson administration officials had earlier estimated program budget targets to be for the program's successful implementation (Herbers 1969). In addition, the allocation of urban-oriented grant monies under Nixon was altered, spreading the monies out more broadly to small- and medium-sized cities that in many cases were experiencing urban problems of their own (Herbers 1970). While this reallocation of federal monies was viewed by some as a more equitable distribution, larger cities such as New York were the losers. The fact that most large cities were governed by Democratic administrations, whereas the administrations of small- and medium-sized cities were far more mixed, was lost on no one.

In early 1973, the Nixon administration took its transformation of Model Cities one step further, according to its principles of New Federalism. The Nixon administration proposed a block grant, which would allocate money to cities for community development. The funding for the block grant would come from eliminating several project categorical grants, including urban renewal and Model Cities, and collapsing their programmatic authority into the new broader grant (Herbers 1973). Big city mayors, including Mayor Lindsay, objected to the block grant proposal because it did not require cities to apply to the federal government for funding but instead distributed block grant funds via a formula. Mayor Lindsay and others were concerned that their cities' allocations of federal funding under the new block grant would be less than their cities had been receiving previously, when the funds were distributed in categorical grant form (Kovach 1973). The mayors were also concerned that the block grant regulations did not require cities to spend the money in low-income neighborhoods but instead gave local officials maximum discretion in spending the funds on community development anywhere in the city. Deliberations on the Community Development Block Grant (CDBG) took place throughout 1973 and 1974. The legislation creating the block grant was signed into law by President Ford shortly after he took office.

CDBG effectively eliminated seven categorical grants that had been all administered by the Department of Housing and Urban Development, and created one larger grant oriented toward community development. Central cities in standard metropolitan statistical areas (SMSA's) and other noncentral cities with populations over 50,000 as well as urban counties were eligible to receive CDBG funding. Recipients would no longer apply for each grant. Instead, they would submit one simplified application and the application process would no longer be competitive. Funding would be allocated according to a formula established by Congress. Recipients would have broad yet limited discretion in spending CDBG funds in all activities allowed under the seven collapsed categorical grants (U.S. Congressional Budget Office 1980). The one controversial regulation included in the program requirements was that the activities funded by the program be "planned to actively benefit low and moderate income families or blighted areas" (U.S. Advisory Commission on Intergovernmental Relations 1977). The Carter administration attempted to make this requirement more formal and rigid by establishing a percentage of CDBG funds that must be spent on low-income persons or neighborhoods, but Congress prevented those rules from being promulgated.

One issue raised by the CDBG was the funding formula established by Congress. The 1974 legislation created a three-variable formula that included: number of overcrowded housing units; population; and population living below the poverty line. Within the formula, the third variable, population living below the poverty line, had twice the weight of the two other variables. Studies done in the early years of CDBG discovered that according to the 1974 formula, cities in the Northeast and Midwest were getting less CDBG money because they were losing population, creating less overcrowded housing, relative to cities with growing populations in the South and West. As a result, in 1977 a new funding formula was added to respond to the needs of older, declining cities. The newer formula also had three variables: number of housing units built before 1940; population growth relative to that in all cities entitled to CDBG funds; and population living in poverty. The relative weights assigned to the variables in the 1977 formula were 50 percent, 20 percent, and 30 percent, respectively. The use of a variable reflecting the age of the housing stock was an attempt to simplistically measure the needs of aging urban areas. Cities were able to choose either the old (1974) or the new (1977) formula, under the assumption that they would choose the one that gave them the most funding (U.S. Congressional Budget Office 1980).

Another issue concerning cities was the dollar amount of the CDBG allocation relative to the amount each city had been receiving prior to the block grant's implementation when the monies were in categorical grant form. Since categorical grant monies were distributed primarily according to a competitive application process and CDBG funds were distributed according to a formula allocating funds to all eligible cities and urban counties, it was obvious that some cities would be gaining federal funds while others would be losing. Those cities that had made a concerted effort to apply for categorical grant funds in the seven grant areas being collapsed, prior to the creation of the CDBG, believed that they stood to lose a great deal of money, while those cities that had never made an attempt to get federal funds in these areas stood to receive a fiscal windfall. Once the proposed formula was published, New York City officials discovered that under CDBG, New York would get additional funding. Many declining cities, primarily those in the Northeast and Midwest, lost money in the transition (Savitch 1999). New York fared well in the transition, in part because the city's large population base relative to other cities counteracted both the declining population as well as the fact that the city had aggressively and successfully sought categorical grant funds.

In the early years of CDBG, the impact of the grant on city programs was minimal. New York had prior experience with most of the categorical grants that were collapsed into the block grant. As a result, the organization of political interests outside of government as well as the organization of bureaucratic interests inside government created a bias toward continuing the funding of those programs and projects previously funded by the collapsed categorical grants. The city's Model Cities and urban renewal experiences as well as the entrenched interests and professional staffs defending these programs shaped CDGB funding decisions (Van Horn 1979). Throughout the 1980s and the 1990s, however, the city used more of its CDBG funding for the rehabilitation and maintenance of its increasing stock of *in rem* housing. *In rem* housing, or property, is that which a government obtains due to tax foreclosure. In New York City in the mid-1970s, approximately 40,000 units of housing were being abandoned per year. Owners unable to make a profit off their buildings, primarily in low-income areas of the city, abandoned their properties in record numbers (Smith and Klemanski 1990). Since there was little or no market for these properties, the New York City government rapidly became the largest landlord in the city. With this role came the responsibility of rehabilitating and managing the buildings so as not to displace the tenants, which would have created an even greater housing problem.

Throughout the late 1970s and the 1980s, the budget demands for dealing with the *in rem* properties grew and CDBG block grant funds became a source of meeting these needs. In the mid-1990s, the national average for CDBG spending on housing was 32 percent. New York City's percentage for CDBG spending on housing was 69 percent. This disparity simply reflects the fact that New York City had the largest stock of *in rem* housing in the country (New York City Independent Budget Office 1998a).

Two years prior to the passage of the Community Development Block Grant, the federal government had established general revenue sharing through the State and Local Fiscal Assistance Act. Revenue sharing was similar to CDBG in that federal funding was allocated according to a congressionally determined formula. The program differed from CDBG in that all states and localities were eligible to receive funds and the recipient's discretion in spending the monies was virtually unlimited. The program also differed in that the amount of money being allocated in revenue sharing was considerable. Throughout the life of the program attempts were made by researchers to discover the fiscal and programmatic effects of revenue sharing on New York City and other recipient governments. In those jurisdictions where the revenue sharing funds were earmarked or dedicated to a specific purpose and in those jurisdictions where special hearings were held to determine how the money would be spent, researchers were somewhat successful in tracking the impact of these federal funds on state and local spending (Nathan and Adams 1977). In New York City, however, the money was placed into the city's general fund. As a result, it is difficult to assess what impact the money had on the city except to conclude that it accounted for approximately 3 percent of the city's nonschool budget during its years of existence (Gruson 1987). States were cut out of the program in the early 1980s and the entire program was eliminated in 1986.

The Carter administration served as a transition for federal policy toward the cities in two ways. First, it was during the Carter administration that federal aid as a percentage of city revenues reached its peak and began to decline. In combating simultaneous high unemployment and inflation that was increasingly being attributed in part to rising federal budget deficits, the Carter administration began to cut federal spending. In most cases, Congress was a willing partner in this effort. One program whose death had a significant impact on New York City's fiscal health was countercyclical revenue sharing. This was a formula grant initiated in the mid-1970s, which gave cities funds based on their unemployment rate relative to a national average. While the grant was extended during the early years of the Carter administration, President Carter's attempt to make the program permanent failed and the program was ended in 1978. New York City lost an annual grant of forty-five million dollars in the middle of its fiscal recovery due to the death of the program (Stanfield 1978). Two related programs, a local public works program designed to stimulate the construction industry in depressed communities and a public service employment program designed to provide public sector jobs to the long-term unemployed, were expanded during the Carter years. Unlike countercyclical revenue sharing, these programs were not eliminated in 1978, but the federal appropriation did begin to decline during those years. New York City used the public sector employment program to hire additional police officers, parks employees, and day care personnel. The programs were eventually eliminated by the Reagan administration (Fossett 1984). As a result of the actions of the Carter administration, when Ronald Reagan took office in 1981, New York and other large cities were already experiencing a decline in federal aid. Shortly after the November 1980 election, Mayor Koch stated his concerns about the federal aid cuts under the coming Reagan administration: "sure, I'm worried about federal budget cuts.... I worried about the Carter budget, too. You have to understand that while the Carter people were quite good to us in terms of grants for specific programs over the three years of my administration, they actually cut us back in budget support by over $500 million" (quoted in Morehouse 1980).

Second, during the Carter administration, Congress passed and the president signed into law the Urban Development Action Grant (UDAG). What was unique about the UDAG program was the intent of the program to take advantage of private investment opportunities or to stimulate private investment in deteriorating areas of cities. UDAG funds were targeted to cities that met minimum standards of economic and physical distress as determined by the U.S. Department of Housing and Urban Development (HUD) (Rich 1982).

HUD regulations required that funded projects be accompanied by a firm commitment of private resources. UDAG funds were to be used to leverage private dollars in distressed urban areas. This program was similar to urban renewal in its employment of private development. UDAG funds, however, were far more flexible in that they could be given directly to a private developer to assist in a wide range of development activities as long as the developer committed their own funds to the project as well (Webman 1981).

In New York City, UDAG funds had a role in two significant development projects in the 1980s. In the early 1980s, UDAG funds were joined with city and state monies to subsidize the Rouse Corporation's rebuilding and commercialization of South Street Seaport in Lower Manhattan. In the late 1980s, UDAG monies were significant in the building of the Metrotech Center, a commercial office complex built by the Forest City Ratner Corporation in downtown Brooklyn. Metrotech eventually became the home for companies including Brooklyn Union Gas, Bear Stearns, and a major operations center of Chase Manhattan Bank. The UDAG program underscored the necessity of private sector involvement in urban revitalization. The grant encouraged New York City and other distressed urban political systems to reach an accommodation with private developers, instead of relying on federal programming and funds to play a lead role.

Federal Relations with New York City, 1980–1992

When the Reagan administration took office in 1981, they inherited a federal government relationship with the cities that had been radically transformed over the two previous decades. The number of federal grant programs funding city activities had grown from fewer than fifty to over four hundred. Big city dependency on federal revenues had more than doubled, and in some cases, tripled. Through fiscal assistance and mandates, the federal government had become a major presence in most large urban political systems. President Reagan's urban policy was to a great extent an artifact of his administration's overall attempt to balance the budget and decrease taxes while at the same time bolstering U.S. defense spending. Many domestic programs were targeted for significant budget cuts throughout the Reagan years, and although Congress did not cooperate entirely with the Reagan budget proposals, growth in many federal urban-oriented programs was slowed, if not reversed, during these years. At the heart of the Reagan approach to cities was the belief that less government in the guise of lower taxes and fewer regulations would fuel private sector economic growth and prosperity. The Reagan approach promised urban policy makers regulatory relief and block grants, albeit with less money, which would allow them to respond to local problems with greater flexibility and less control from Washington. His intergovernmental program attempted to drastically reduce the federal role in helping cities. The Reagan administration viewed prior federal urban policies as not only ineffective but counterproductive. The Reagan domestic policy advisors believed that market forces and local preferences should be what drives urban policy, not the federal government (Randall 1986). While Reagan budget cuts gave cities significantly less money, Reagan block grants also reorganized intergovernmental funding primarily through the consolidation of categorical grants into block grants, in many cases giving states control over funds that had previously flowed directly from the federal level to cities. Thus, not only did cities receive less federal money, but they were also forced to compete for remaining federal funds in a new venue, the state capital.

The shifts in federal policy during the Reagan years negatively affected New York City in several ways. According to Alair Townsend, the city's budget director during the Reagan years, the city lost approximately 500 million dollars in federal aid annually from 1981 to 1985 (Liebschutz 1991). The actual dollar amount of federal aid increased from 1981 to 1985, although at a rate much slower than previously and clearly not enough to keep up with inflation or need. Between 1985 and 1988, the actual dollar amount of federal aid to New York City dropped, primarily due to the elimination of General Revenue Sharing (Liebschutz 1991). Table 3.1 in the previous chapter tracks the decline in federal aid as a percentage of all city revenue.

Another big loser in the Reagan budget reductions was the MTA. During the first term of the Regan administration, the MTA saw its federal subsidy decline by 70 percent, mostly in the operating subsidy it had been receiving. This placed a strain on the MTA and ultimately resulted in several fare increases during this period (Brooke 1985). For the Metropolitan Transit Authority, the operating subsidy was a considerable windfall, equaling 8 percent of the Metropolitan Transit Authority's budget in 1981 (Holsendolph 1981). In 1982, the actual dollar operating subsidy was frozen and subsequent years' operating subsidies were based on a percentage of the 1982 subsidy. The overall grant, which includes both capital and operating subsidies, declined throughout the 1980s.

The city was also affected by the decline in federal aid to the state, especially in those programs targeted to the poor. With a large proportion of the state's poverty any cut in federal programs for low-income citizens was felt disproportionately in the city. During the first four years of the Reagan administration, New York State saw a real dollar decline in the amount of federal money received for Aid to Families with Dependent Children. Related programs such as food stamps and Medicaid received federal aid only sufficient to maintain a level of service established in the early 1980s, but did not allow for an increase. In addition, the Reagan administration consolidated a number of categorical grants primarily targeted to low-income individuals into block grants in 1981, and these grants experienced budget cuts as high as 50 percent in Reagan's first term alone. All of these cuts were additionally burdensome since during the early eighties, the nation and the city were experiencing a severe recession and rising unemployment rates (Liebschutz and Lerner 1987).

The one area of federal-city relations where the Reagan administration appeared to offer help to New York City was regulatory relief. During the two prior decades, when federal aid to cities had grown significantly, federal mandates requiring local government action had also increased. Many mandates were not supported by federal funds and therefore required local government funding. The mandates covered a wide range of policy areas including bilingual education, handicapped access to transportation, solid waste disposal, and civil rights. In many instances, the mandates required local governments to carry out activities in which they had no prior experience, creating a significant fiscal burden. By having to divert its own resources to implement the federal mandate, the city was forced to transfer funds from its own locally determined priorities to those established by Congress or the federal bureaucracy.

Although Mayor Koch, while a congressman, had been involved in the creation of many mandates, as mayor, he adopted a very different perspective toward this method by which federal priorities were imposed on local governments. Koch demanded that the federal government become sensitive to the fiscal burden being placed on cities by the proliferation of unfunded mandates. Specifically, he recommended that the imposition of mandates be deferred until a fiscal impact report was conducted so that all levels of government would recognize the cost of the mandate to the local government prior to implementation. More important, Koch argued for waiver provisions that would give local governments some flexibility in meeting the mandate's objective (Koch 1980).

As an example, Koch argued that the regulations created by the Department of Transportation in response to Section 504 of the 1974 Rehabilitation Services Act, which required the city to provide access to public transportation for disabled persons, did not give the city the flexibility to achieve the goal within its fiscal capacity. Not only was the federal government mandating that disabled individuals be given access to public transportation, but it was also mandating how the city should go about doing it. Koch noted that the federal Department of Transportation requirements mandated that over the next thirty years, over 50 percent of the subway stations should be made wheelchair accessible in order to achieve this mandate. He cited, however, a Congressional Budget Office study that concluded it would be less expensive for the city to pay for a taxi ride or paratransit service, door to door, for all disabled individuals than it would be to retrofit the subway system to accommodate wheelchair-bound individuals. Moreover, Koch argued that in addition to being ignorant of its cost, the federal government frequently mandated local government activity without knowing whether technology was available to fulfill the mandate (Koch 1980).

The Reagan administration made regulatory relief a key element in its "New Federalism" initiatives. The reduction of federal mandates was an integral part of the Reagan strategy. By strengthening White House oversight of executive branch agency rule-making and by relaxing enforcement of existing regulations, the Reagan administration realized some moderate successes in relieving the burden of mandates on local governments. Koch saw the Reagan administration position on regulatory relief as producing significant gains for the city. "My position has been if the mandates are imposed by the federal government, the federal government should pay for them. . . . President-elect Reagan agreed. He said he believed that if the federal government mandated a locality to do something, it should pay for it. He said he would lift the mandates if the federal government doesn't pay for them" (quoted in Morehouse 1980). Many of the disabled access to public transportation regulations Koch had cited were deleted and replaced by a vague requirement that local transportation operators make "special efforts" to assist the disabled (Nathan and Doolittle 1983).

Despite the weakening or elimination of some regulations, the Reagan administration, on occasion, was accused of replacing old mandates with new ones. In late 1983, the federal Department of Transportation issued rules compelling states to allow trucks up to 80,000 pounds in double-trailer combinations, and more than 65 feet long and 102 inches wide to use the interstate highway system. These rules were more liberal than existing New York State or New York City rules regarding commercial trucks. New York City had a law banning double trailers from all of its roads. The sanction for not complying with these new federal rules was the possible withholding of federal highway funds. New York City and New York State officials were concerned about the impact of these larger trucks on the city's crumbling roads as well as their impact on traffic safety (Holsendolph 1983). While neighboring Connecticut sued the federal government over the new regulations, New York State entered into negotiations with the federal Department of Transportation and was able to exempt many of the roads in New York City from this regulation (Madden 1984).

The Clinton Years

Despite ending twelve years of Republican control of the White House, the Clinton administration did not significantly reverse the decline in federal aid to cities begun by Presidents Carter and Reagan. Clinton's lack of an urban orientation was due to his neoliberal, New Democratic, political values that focused more on balancing the budget and promoting national economic growth than it did on responding to the needs of one of the traditional Democratic Party constituencies, the cities. During the first six years of the Clinton administration, three pieces of legislation were passed by Congress and signed by the president that had an impact on cities: the Empowerment Zone program, the crime bill, and welfare reform.

New York Congressman Charles Rangel was one of the prime sponsors of the Empowerment Zone legislation. As part of the 1993 Omnibus Budget and Reconciliation Act, the federal Empowerment Zone and Enterprise Communities Act was a distant relative of the urban enterprise zone program that had received a great deal of attention during the Reagan administration but had never been seriously considered by Congress at that time. Similar to the Empire Development Zone program implemented by New York State (chapter three), the enterprise zone concept was based on an assumption that private sector location and expansion decisions could be affected by offering generous tax incentives that would promote movement or expansion of businesses into economically depressed areas of the city. There was little or no direct subsidy or "up-front" capital involved in the program. The federal empowerment zone legislation included wage and tax credits as well as tax-exempt bond financing. The 1993 federal legislation created a ten-year pilot project for a limited number of cities. As a result, competition for urban empowerment zone status was intense. Cities wanting empowerment zone status had to document the high probability that jobs for low-income residents of the empowerment zone communities would be generated by the program (Riposa 1996).

Six cities, including New York, were granted Empowerment Zone status. New York City's empowerment zone application included a commitment by both the city and state to match the one hundred million dollars in federal funds over the ten-year life of the program. According to the city's proposal, funds would be spent on job and workforce development, children, and housing (United Stated Department of Housing and Urban Development 1998). A major part of the city's proposal was the funding of a Harlem International Trade Center that would serve as headquarters for the trade offices of developing countries. Critics were quick to note that most countries preferred their trade missions closer to Midtown Manhattan (Moss 1995). The federal government also committed itself to provide 250 million dollars in tax incentives to businesses located within the zone. New York City's empowerment zone, the Upper Manhattan Empowerment Zone (UMEZ), includes parts of Harlem and Washington Heights in Manhattan, and a small section of the South Bronx. The UMEZ began with a $300 million development fund and $250 million in tax incentives to distribute over ten years, ending in 2009 (*New York Times* 2001b). UMEZ also takes advantage of city and state "as of right" economic development tax incentives such as those offered through the Commercial Expansion Program (New York City Department of Finance).

The empowerment zone financed a number of projects including a job training and counseling center run by a Harlem church in conjunction with local banks (Bumiller 1997). It has supported a number of cultural activities in Harlem including the restoration of the Apollo Theater and the historical preservation of a number of churches (UMEZ 2001). In 1998, the empowerment zone was instrumental in getting a nationally known producer to open an 8,600-square-foot video duplication factory in Harlem. By locating in the zone, the company, Broadway Video, qualified for an $878,000 low interest loan as well as a $3,000 tax credit for each of its employees who live within the zone. The company projected that, at its peak, it would employ twenty residents of the zone (Lueck 1998). As of mid-1998, the empowerment zone was responsible for creating over 1,300 jobs. In 1998, the Upper Manhattan Empowerment Zone was also instrumental in the financing and construction of Harlem U.S.A., a 275,000-square-foot shopping complex that included Magic Johnson Movie Theaters, the Disney Store, and Old Navy (New York State Governor's Office 1998).

It is difficult to assess how successful the empowerment zone concept has been to the development of Harlem. Given the health of the national and local economies in the mid- to late 1990s, development in Harlem, particularly along 125th Street, was beginning to take off at the same time that the Upper Manhattan Empowerment Zone got its start. In addition, the UMEZ has been criticized for supporting national over local, more indigenous businesses (Pristin 2001; Shipp, 2006). It also has been accused of ignoring small businesses. By 2001, the Business Resource and Investment Service Center, started by UMEZ to assist small businesses, had only given out three million dollars in loans while incurring approximately five million dollars in administrative costs (Pristin 2001).

In 1994, Congress approved and the president signed a series of bills, collectively labeled the "Taking Back Our Streets Act"—the shorthand name for the legislation became the Crime Bill. This bill combined legislation that produced stiffer penalties for certain federal crimes, a ban on the sale and possession of nineteen types of assault weapons, federal funding for the construction of state prisons, and the hiring of additional police officers, as well as funding for a variety of programs focused on community-based crime prevention strategies (O'Neil and Sheehan 1995). While there was a great deal of skepticism nationally about the long-term impact of the legislation, New York City officials were extremely satisfied with the legislation's impact. Commenting on the legislation,

Mayor Giuliani noted that "no one thing in this bill turns around the problem of crime. . . . But it helps us in every single area in which we have been doing things" (Treaster 1994). The component of the legislation viewed most important to New York City officials was the allocation of federal funds for the hiring of additional police. The Giuliani administration, through then Brooklyn Congressman Charles Schumer, was able to negotiate some flexibility into the legislation that allowed New York City to use some of the federal funds to hire civilians to work in the New York City Police Department. The lower paid civilian workers were used to replace uniformed personnel working at desks, and this resulted in more police on the street (Treaster 1994). As of 1998, the federal funds were responsible for an additional five thousand New York City police on the streets. The one problem with the federal funding component was that the federal share of the cost declined each year. After six years, the city would have to bear the entire burden of financing the additional police (Johnston 1994). New York City also received funding for a variety of crime prevention programs, such as after school, weekend, and summer programs for children, school programs to help troubled youths, anti-gang training programs, and drug treatment (Lewis 1994).

Possibly the single most significant change in policy promulgated during the Clinton administration was the 1996 Personal Responsibility and Work Opportunity Reconciliation Act (PRWORA). This piece of legislation, otherwise known as welfare reform, changed the structure of income maintenance assistance that the federal government had maintained for the previous five decades under Aid to Families with Dependent Children (AFDC). AFDC had operated as an open-ended matching grant; that is, the federal government was obligated to fund the states' welfare programs for federally designated categories of families regardless of the number of families and amount of money spent at the state level. For New York State, the federal share was approximately half the cost of the assistance. The 1996 legislation replaced this open-ended obligation on the part of the federal government with a capped block grant, Temporary Assistance for Needy Families (TANF). This replacement meant that there would be a finite limit to the funding support of state welfare programs by the federal government, as opposed to the open-ended obligation that existed under AFDC. The second major change under welfare reform was a shift in the receipt of assistance by eligible families. Under AFDC, the income maintenance assistance received by eligible families was an entitlement as long as they remained eligible. There was no limitation on the number of years a family could receive assistance. Under PRWORA, families would be subject to a five-year lifetime limit. Finally, under the new law, all able-bodied recipients would be required to work after receiving two years of assistance. Under AFDC, the federal government had made work experience and/or training an option, but they had never mandated it for all eligible recipients (Criscitello 1997).

New York City's interest in welfare reform was based on several conditions. First, since the inception of federal income maintenance programs during the

New Deal, New York City has had a large number of families living in poverty and eligible for federal welfare assistance. City officials were concerned with any change in federal law that might have changed the eligibility status of large numbers of its families. In particular, they feared that families eliminated from federal welfare roles would end up enrolled in programs in which the city would pay a larger share or the entire share, consequently raising the city's cost for these families. Legal aliens were the group hit the hardest by the PRWORA. According to the new program, most classes of legal aliens were no longer eligible for Supplemental Security Income, a federally funded income maintenance program for the disabled. They were also no longer eligible for food stamps. In addition, immigrants entering the country after August 1996, would not be eligible to receive any form of federal public assistance for five years (New York City Independent Budget Office 1998b). Second, since counties in New York State were required to pay half the cost of the state's share of federal income maintenance, any change in federal welfare laws had a significant impact on New York City's budget. In 1996, the year before the new welfare law was to take effect, New York City spent $1.8 billion on welfare (Criscitello 1997). Since the new federal welfare law gave states considerable discretion in how they would implement the new welfare provisions, New York City was a keenly interested participant in the gubernatorial and legislative deliberations that took place in Albany during the first half of 1997.

A third significant condition of welfare reform was the federally mandated work requirements, known as workfare, requiring most welfare recipients to work or participate in job training. New York State gave its local governments the responsibility for structuring this part of the welfare reform program. For several years prior to the passage of welfare reform, New York City had been experimenting with a workfare program, the Work Experience Program (WEP). What distinguished the WEP program from other welfare-to-work programs was the emphasis on work experience and the lack of emphasis on vocational training or schooling. Program participants spent approximately twenty hours a week working for a city agency or contractor. A smaller amount of time was spent either looking for a job in the private sector outside of the WEP program or receiving some job training skills. The Giuliani administration claimed the program was responsible for a dramatic decrease in the welfare rolls, from a high of 1.1 million persons to fewer than 800,000 in late 1997, prior to the implementation of federal welfare reform (Swarns 1997). Critics argued, however, that for the most part, WEP had failed to move former welfare recipients into real jobs. Although WEP participants cleaned parks and swept streets, only a tiny percentage picked up job skills and obtained a permanent private sector job. Of the 125,000 individuals who went through the WEP program during its first three years, less than 10 percent reported finding a permanent job. Two thirds of the participants left the program and gave up their welfare benefits (Firestone 1997a). Critics also claimed that although negotiations between Giuliani and public employee unions had produced an agreement that city employees would not be replaced by WEP workers, this had not stopped the Giuliani administration from reducing its workforce through attrition or buyouts and then giving workfare workers jobs for which no city employees were available (Firestone 1997b). Under the new federal welfare reform law, half the adults receiving federal assistance would have to be participating in a workfare program by 2002. Once given the option by the state, New York City officials simply interpreted this mandate by expanding the city's WEP program.

In implementing the new federal welfare program, some decisions by New York City officials brought them into conflict with the federal government. One provision of the federal welfare legislation mandated that local employees turn in illegal immigrants who sought public services such as police protection, hospital care, or public education. In October 1996, shortly after the passage of the federal welfare reform law, the Giuliani administration filed suit against the federal government regarding this provision. If this clause was implemented, it would serve to overturn a 1985 mayoral executive order mandating that illegal aliens receive city services and forbidding local employees from turning in illegal immigrants (Firestone 1995). In speaking out against such a clause, Mayor Giuliani argued that illegal immigrants would be denied due process of law because they would be afraid to call the police if they were in trouble, for fear of exposing themselves as illegal immigrants and being turned in by city officials. The mayor also expressed the fear that if the federal provision was implemented, illegal immigrants would stop sending their children to school or seeking treatment for contagious diseases in public hospitals (New York City Mayor's Office 1996; *New York Times* 1996). The mayor argued that the federal provision also violated the Tenth Amendment of the Constitution, since it usurped the city's police power (Firestone 1996).

September 11: Federal Disaster Relief

George W. Bush did not include any urban initiatives in his 2000 campaign for president. The events of September 11, 2001, changed his administration's national agenda, placing increased emphasis on foreign policy and domestic security. The events also altered the agendas of state and local governments, forcing them to become more cognizant of security issues. In the wake of the terrorist attacks, the Bush administration made available to New York City over twenty billion dollars in federal aid for the cleanup and rebuilding of Lower Manhattan. In addition, the federal government began distributing aid to governments to deal with increased security responsibilities. Much of this was done in an environment of intense lobbying by the city and considerable controversy over the amount and type of funding.

The Federal Disaster Relief program that the Bush administration and Congress developed for New York City was a response to the attacks and the attacks' immediate impact on the city. Of the over twenty-one billion dollars of disaster relief appropriated for New York City, the largest piece of the funding was administered through the Federal Emergency Management Administration (FEMA). FEMA funding responded to claims related to the cleanup and recovery effort. This included "overtime and personnel expenses, and replacement costs of lost equipment such as fire and police vehicles" (New York City Comptroller's Office 2002, 46). In addition to the promised aid, the federal government also relaxed regulations in order to ease the city's reconstruction and recovery efforts. FEMA usually required local governments to provide a 25 percent match to its aid for rebuilding public facilities. Less than two weeks after the attacks, FEMA announced that New York was being relieved of this requirement (Barstow 2001). Another portion of the funds administered through FEMA supported the construction of a major transportation hub in lower Manhattan (NYC Comptroller's Office 2002, 46). Lower Manhattan had long been a commuting nightmare, and the destruction of the World Trade Center offered infrastructure planners a chance to improve a chaotic transit system. At the center of the transportation hub concept was the integration of the PATH trains that connect New Jersey and Lower Manhattan with the city's subway system. Some transportation planners had larger visions of bringing the Long Island Rail Road as well as the commuter trains from Westchester (Metro-North) to the new downtown hub as well. The Bush administration modified the FEMA funding regulations to allow the city to build the transportation hub (Perez-Pena 2002).

A second piece of the Federal Disaster Relief package funded the creation of the "Liberty Zone" in Lower Manhattan. This created tax incentives and subsidies to promote economic growth and the retention of business in the area. Many of the tax benefits would accrue over a ten-year period, with most of the benefits targeted for the first five years, through 2007. The program included accelerated depreciation of equipment and capital improvements, and authority for the state and the city to issue eight billion dollars of tax exempt bonds to finance new offices, housing, and public utility improvements. The Liberty Zone program also included a Work Opportunity Tax Credit for businesses with two hundred or fewer employees. This gives a $2,400 tax credit per employee for two years to any business that moves into the area. The Liberty Zone program is primarily a tax expenditure program, not a grant program. The federal government is not giving grants to businesses directly (New York City Comptroller's Office 2002, 47–48). Less than a year after the program was created, it was criticized by city officials because much of the aid was dependent on the development in Lower Manhattan. There was little demand for new offices in Lower Manhattan and very few businesses were expanding (Wyatt et al. 2002). In fact, through mid-2003, Liberty Zone funding had been used more for residential development than commercial development (New York City Independent Budget Office 2003). In late 2002, less than half a billion of the 5.5 billion dollars allocated to the Liberty Zone program had been utilized (Wyatt et al. 2002). There was concern among city officials that the city would not be able to use all of the bonding authority prior to the December 31, 2004, expiration date (New York City Independent Budget Office 2003).

A third piece of the Federal Disaster Relief program included funding that is administered through the Lower Manhattan Development Corporation (LMDC) and the Empire State Development Corporation (ESDC). The largest portion of this funding went to those agencies through the Community Development Block Grant (CDBG). The LMDC used this money to fund commercial and residential rebuilding activities in Lower Manhattan. In addition, the LMDC received federal funding to provide job training to employees displaced by the September 11 attacks. The distribution and use of the CDBG monies was unique. Usually, the federal government requires state governments to pass on CDBG monies to local governments. In this case, the federal government was allowing New York State to spend the money directly in Lower Manhattan through the LMDC and the ESDC. Also, CDBG monies usually must be spent on programs that predominantly benefit low- and moderate-income individuals. Using the CDGB funds, the LMDC was given the discretion to negotiate job retention and creation agreements with large corporations in lower Manhattan (Pear 2002). The only stipulation was that the firms agree to stay in Lower Manhattan for seven years (New York State Comptroller's Office 2002, 48–49). Some of the employers that received federally funded grants from the LMDC had never considered leaving Lower Manhattan. Many of them had long-term leases. City and state officials believed, however, that it was important to secure long term commitments to Lower Manhattan from a critical mass of major employers before approaching those employers who were less sure about their future in the area. Critics of the grants argued that more funds should have gone to job training and toward directly addressing the needs of the low-wage workers who lost their jobs as a result of the attacks (Bagli 2002). The LMDC, however, found that there was little demand for employment training. As a result, they moved to reallocate those funds to business recovery activities (New York City Independent Budget Office 2003). Federal funding also allowed LMDC to offer residential grants to people committed to living downtown for at least two years. Depending upon one's proximity to the World Trade Center, the grant offered to subsidize the monthly rent, mortgage, or maintenance payments up to twelve thousand dollars over two years. These grants were also criticized because of the number of high-income individuals and families living in Lower Manhattan who would benefit (Wyatt 2002). The Federal Internal Revenue Service exempted Lower Manhattan residents from paying income taxes on much of the federal aid received (Fried 2002). Finally, some of the CDBG funds were joined with FEMA funding for transportation activities (New York City Independent Budget Office 2003).

As part of the disaster assistance package, Governor Pataki wanted the federal government to reimburse the state and city for lost tax revenues, but he was criticized by members of Congress for making this request. Critics noted that the federal government had not bailed out local governments for lost taxes after earthquakes or hurricanes (Hernandez 2001a). While FEMA did reimburse the city for overtime and equipment costs directly related to the attacks and their aftermath, the federal government did not reimburse the city for lost revenue (Cooper 2002).

In the aftermath of the September 11 attacks, counterterrorism and terrorism preparedness became a major area of concern in the city's relationship with the federal government. Late in 2002, NYPD Commissioner Raymond Kelly went to Washington to lobby federal officials for additional aid for the city's Police Department. Kelly argued that since September 11, the NYPD had redeployed a thousand officers to deal with counterterrorism and that the federal government needed to recognize this and reimburse the city accordingly (Rashbaum 2002). Earlier in the year, the U.S. Conference of Mayors had lobbied Homeland Security Director Tom Ridge for similar aid (Brinkley 2002).

At a meeting of mayors in Washington in late October 2001, Mayor Giuliani joined other mayors in asking the Bush administration for additional federal aid to cover the cost of additional policing and security responsibilities in the post–September 11 environment. Specifically, the mayors were asking for funding to set up command centers as well as the provision of additional training and the purchase of protective equipment (Becker 2001a). In the mayors' meeting with Ridge, no additional aid was promised (Becker 2001b). Later, when the Bush administration and Congress initiated the funding of local antiterror activities, Mayor Michael Bloomberg and other city officials expressed frustration with the amount the city was receiving, particularly in comparison to other states and cities perceived to be less likely terror targets. Testifying at a city council hearing in 2004, the city's Commissioner of the Office of Emergency Management noted that while Wyoming received $38 per capita in anti-terror aid, New York City received $5 per capita according to the funding formula established by Congress (McIntire 2004). Mayor Bloomberg added that "this is pork barrel politics at its worst" (Wyatt 2004). After Congress rejected an amendment that would have given high-risk cities additional anti-terrorism aid, Mayor Bloomberg complained: "everybody can always say, 'Well, we have security issues.' . . . You know, one guy said to me that 'Yeah, the corn and soybean crops are our food supply and therefore this country needs a food supply, we've got to protect it.' You know, I've never seen a terrorist with a map of a cornfield in his pocket. Come on. Let's get serious to what this is about, why this money should be going to places like New York City" (quoted in Hernandez 2004b).

The city was receiving more anti-terror aid than any other city, according to federal officials, but the amount appeared to be declining over time (Hu 2004; Lizza 2004). The Urban Areas Security Initiative, the one federal program that distributed money based on a site's probability of being a terror target, allocated aid to seven states in 2003 with New York City receiving a quarter of its funding. By 2004, over eighty sites have been added to the list of possible terror targets and New York City received less than 7 percent of the funds (Lizza 2004).

In addition to anti-terrorism aid, the city also sought to establish better ties with federal intelligence agencies regarding terrorist threats. At the meeting of mayors in October 2001, some mayors expressed concern that the FBI was not sharing terrorism intelligence information with local police departments (Becker 2001a). At a Congressional hearing on security that had been scheduled before September 11 and held at City Hall, Mayor Giuliani asked for federal legislation that would increase information-sharing between federal and local law enforcement agencies. Mayor Giuliani expressed some anger that the city was not immediately informed of the October 2001, anthrax threat even though part of it occurred within the city. Giuliani stated that there had been cooperation in this area in the past, citing how several federal agencies helped the city refine its Office of Emergency Management when it was established in 1996 (Steinhauer and Chen 2001). Police Commissioner Bernard Kerik testified that local police officials should have security clearances to receive sensitive information. "Anything that would affect the safety and security of the people of the city I need to know, and I need to know it now. . . . I can't wait until it goes through a committee and it goes through a number of jurisdictions and people, and somebody determines 'maybe we should tell them'" (quoted in Steinhauer and Chen 2001).

In early November 2001, Senators Charles Schumer and Hillary Clinton introduced legislation that, if passed, would permit federal officials to share information obtained from "grand juries, wiretaps, foreign intelligence operations, and confidential banking and educational records" with local law enforcement officials (Clymer 2001). No such legislation was approved by Congress. In March 2002, Homeland Security Director Ridge informed Governor Pataki and Mayor Bloomberg that they would be told of all "credible threats against New York in the future" (*New York Times* 2002).

New York City Lobbying at the Federal Level

The growth in federal government relations with urban areas, especially in fiscal assistance, has necessitated an urban presence in Washington, D.C. New York City, similar to many other large cities, has attempted to influence federal policy toward cities in several ways. First, as in the case of the fiscal crisis of the 1970s and the city's efforts to obtain aid in the aftermath of September 11, the mayor has lobbied both the Congress and the White House as the representative of the city. During the fiscal crisis, in several instances the mayor was joined by the governor. Less than two weeks after his election and six weeks prior to his inauguration, Michael Bloomberg went to Washington to meet with members of the Bush administration, Congressional leaders, as well as members of the city's congressional delegation (Steinhauer 2001a). As the mayor-elect lobbied for increased aid to the city, one of his aides stated, "he has to walk a fine line. . . . He is a new member of the Republican Party, so he can't attack the White House right now. . . . But at the end of the day, you're either for New York or you're not. And I think he gets that" (quoted in Steinhauer 2001a).

A month later, as the city was seeking additional federal aid, Bloomberg contacted former U.S. Senator Alphonse D'Amato, seeking to use the senator's Republican Party contacts to influence congressional leaders (Steinhauer 2001b). As chief executive of the country's largest city and a national political figure in his own right, the mayor can communicate directly with federal officials and be assured of gaining a level of access.

As national political figures, mayors of New York City have used their "bully pulpit" to communicate with the federal government through the media. For example, Mayor John Lindsay openly castigated the federal government for not expediting New York City's Model Cities application (Roberts 1967c). Mayor Koch's article in *The Public Interest* criticized the federal government's use of mandates (Koch 1980). Shortly after the election of Bill Clinton, Mayor David Dinkins wrote President-elect Clinton a letter and released a copy of it to the news media. The Dinkins's letter, based on the assumption that the first Democratic president in twelve years would be a friend of the cities and New York City in particular, laid out the mayor's urban policy agenda (McKinley 1992). Not only do mayors communicate directly with Congress and the White House, they also communicate with relevant members of the federal executive branch who are involved in the administration and implementation of programs relevant to the city. In 1971, when HUD officials accused the city of not spending Model Cities funds fast enough, Mayor Lindsay wrote to the Assistant Secretary at HUD who administered the Model Cities program and defended the city's record. Mayor Lindsay also released the letter to the news media (Shipler 1971).

Since 1970, the mayor has been assisted in his lobbying efforts at the federal level by the New York City Federal Affairs Office in Washington, D.C. This office is part of the Office of the Mayor, which monitors federal government activity in all three branches and lobbies the federal legislative and executive branches on those issues where the mayor's presence is not needed (Lizza 2004).

The second mechanism through which the city attempts to influence the federal government is the city's congressional delegation. In 1998, there were fourteen members of the House of Representatives whose legislative districts fell wholly or partly within the boundaries of New York City. The city used to have more than fourteen representatives, but since the 1970 census the city has gradually lost representatives due to the stabilization of its own population combined with population growth in other parts of the state and other regions of the country. Of the fourteen representatives from New York City in 1998, all but one was a Democrat. The fact that many of the New York City congressional seats are safely Democratic means that in periods when the Democrats control the House of Representatives, legislators from New York City enjoy considerable seniority and play major roles on some of Congress's most important committees. Representative Charles Rangel, Democrat from Manhattan, was instrumental in the creation and passage of the Federal Empowerment Zone program during the early years of the Clinton administration.

When the Republicans controlled the House of Representatives from 1994 to 2006, and the Senate for much of the same period, the Democratic representatives from New York City were unable to influence federal policy as much as before. The defeat of Senator Alphonse D'Amato in 1998, combined with the retirement of several upstate Republican congressmen who had considerable seniority, also affected the city's influence in Washington (Hernandez 2004a).

In the aftermath of September 11, the city's congressional delegation was extremely active in getting the federal government to assist the city. Senators Schumer and Clinton lobbied the White House and sponsored legislation. The city's members of the House of Representatives, especially Jerrold Nadler, who represents Lower Manhattan, were also fighting for the city. Senators Schumer and Clinton were reluctant to attack the Bush administration for not giving the city enough assistance and for not immediately handing over the promised money. Members of the delegation from the House of Representatives, however, favored placing more pressure on the Congressional leadership and the Bush administration to deliver the aid already promised. One House aide stated, "you've got happy talk from the senators. . . . On the House side, we're much more realistic that if we don't get this money now, it will become a tougher sell later. If we keep being forced to come back for small amounts of money every time we need it, we'll eventually be told no by the Republican leadership. . . . We don't have the benefit of working in a Democratic body that tends to be friendly to New York" (quoted in Hernandez 2001b).

The third way that the city has attempted to influence federal policy is through interest groups or associations that represent cities at the national level. Two groups, the National League of Cities (NLC) and the United States Conference of Mayors (USCM), provide cities with a collective voice at the federal level. Since the National League of Cities is dominated by small- and medium-sized cities, larger cities such as New York have found more of a voice in the USCM (Farkas 1971). In 1986, Mayor Koch addressed the National League of Cities meeting in an attempt to get small- and medium-sized cities to assist larger cities in getting the federal government to do more in anti-drug efforts (Purnick 1986).

Mayors of New York City have also been involved in less formal attempts by big city mayors to lobby the federal level. In the early 1970s, Mayor Lindsay became part of a group, labeled the Big Ten, which was comprised of mayors of the largest cities in the United States. The group used their prestige to lobby Congress for increased federal aid to cities by testifying before congressional committees and meeting informally with members of Congress (Madden 1970). In 2006, Mayor Bloomberg was instrumental in creating a coalition of big city mayors in an attempt to decrease the level of illegal gun trafficking across the country. The Federal Bureau of Alcohol, Tobacco, and Firearms agreed to join the mayors in this effort (Baker 2006).

The Impact of Federal Grants on New York City

Throughout its relationship with the federal government, New York City has aggressively sought federal funds. Some federal grant programs funded activities in which the city was already engaged. When the city could substitute federal funds for city funds, local monies were freed up to be used to pursue other items on the city's agenda. In a small number of instances such as public housing, the city was a prime mover in getting the federal government to establish a grant in a program area in which the city was already active. With very few exceptions, between the New Deal and the Carter administration, both New York City and the federal government were governed by a liberal, progressive leadership. City officials and federal officials agreed on what problems urban areas faced as well as the possible programmatic solutions. More important, during this period, both city and federal officials shared a similar ethic about the role of government, and in particular the federal government, in solving society's problems. As a result, federal priorities for urban areas reflected in the array of grants made available to cities, and mandates imposed on cities were very similar to those areas of policy being pursued by New York City government. When the federal government offered the city funding through a grant, the city sought the funding enthusiastically not only because it needed the money but also because the programs being funded by the federal government were programs the city was already implementing or programs that it would implement if it had the fiscal resources. While federal regulatory strings or mandates attached to grants might have stopped some cities from applying for them, those regulations rarely stopped New York City.

New York City's successful pursuit of federal grants increased the amount of federal funds coming into the city. As the growth of federal grant monies being received by the city increased at a rate higher than that of city revenues, the city became more dependent on federal funds. It also became more vulnerable to budget disruptions at the federal level, as was experienced during the Reagan years.

James Fossett (1984) studied the comparative dependence of large cities on federal funds using data from 1978, one of the years in which federal funds to New York City surpassed state funds and clearly one of the peak years for the city's receipt of federal funds overall (Fossett 1984). Fossett's study offers two additional perspectives on New York City's dependence on federal funds. First, Fossett examined different definitions of dependence. While measures of federal revenue as a percentage of local revenue offer some insight into the extent of dependence of local governments on the federal government, they offer an incomplete view. In order to attain a more comprehensive perspective of big city dependence on the federal government, Fossett (1984) examined the percentage of federal monies used for basic services, as well as federal grant monies spent on basic services as a percentage of total spending on basic services by the city. According to Fossett, regardless of whatever else cities do, all cities must provide the basic services of police and fire protection, garbage collection, and maintain city streets and infrastructure. By using these additional measures, Fossett suggested that local governments that use federal grant monies for basic services are more dependent on the federal government than those who do not. Given the volatility of federal aid, those local governments who can deliver basic services without depending upon federal revenues are in better fiscal health than those who need the federal funds. In the case of New York for 1978, Fossett (1984) found that New York used over 50 percent of its federal aid for the delivery of basic services and that federal funds made up approximately 23 percent of the city's basic services budget.

The second perspective Fossett offered is a comparative one. New York City's fiscal dependence on the federal government was also considerable relative to other large cities. Fossett's data shows that of the ten cities studied for 1978, only Rochester surpassed New York City in the percentage of federal aid used to finance the delivery of basic services. Several large Midwestern cities, however, including Detroit, Cleveland, and St. Louis, came close to New York City's level of dependence (55.3 percent). Using his alternative measure of dependence, federal spending as a percentage of total city spending for basic services, New York City's level of dependence (22.7 percent) was slightly lower than Detroit, Cleveland, and St. Louis but it was still among the highest of the ten cities examined. Fossett's study concluded that New York City was one of a group of cities that was unable to insulate the financing and delivery of basic services from federal assistance, and that therefore created a level of dependence on the federal level greater than most cities.

Conclusion

New York City's relationship with the federal government is considerably different than its relationship with New York State. There is no direct constitutional linkage between the city and the federal government, and as a result the federal government is in no way legally responsible for financing or monitoring the complete range of services that New York City is delivering to its residents. During the middle of the twentieth century, however, the federal government established a strong fiscal relationship with cities. At its peak, federal government revenues accounted for almost a quarter of the money being spent by New York City across a broad range of policy and program areas. In part, this fiscal relationship was reflective of the power of urban interests at the federal level as well as the fiscal resources of the federal government.

Even after federal aid to cities declined during the Reagan and Bush Sr. administrations, the number of policy and program areas in which the federal government had an impact on the cities did not decline proportionately. A 1998 document published by the Mayor's Office listed over one hundred areas of federal policy where New York City officials believed they had an interest (Mastro 1998). The fiscal depth of federal involvement in New York City programs may have declined, but the breadth of involvement is still present. In 1997, federal revenues to New York City made up only 12 percent of the city's budget, but this figure did not include welfare, Medicaid, food stamps, or any of the direct payments made by the federal government to individuals or institutions other than the city government. Nor did it include federal environmental mandates or civil rights regulations that the city must follow. Thus, the importance of the federal government to the city goes well beyond direct intergovernmental transfers. Aside from the decline in federal aid, possibly the most significant change in federal aid over time was its decreasing redistributive orientation. Many of the categorical grants promulgated in the 1960s and 1970s were targeted toward low-income areas and citizens. But in the ensuing years, grants either did not include strong mandates that the funds be spent on the poor, or gave state and local officials discretion over where and how the money should be spent.

With the possible exception of the years immediately following the September 11 attacks, it is doubtful that federal assistance to New York City will ever approach the level it achieved in 1978. Nevertheless, the federal government continues to give the city billions of dollars in direct assistance and billions more indirectly. In addition, in the absence of growing financial aid, the federal government continues to mandate city behavior across a wide array of policy areas.

The federal impact on the governance of the city, while significant, does not equal the impact of the state. Moreover, one should not mistake the federal response to the city in the wake of the terrorist attacks as having a major impact on the governance of the city. While the federal funding was welcomed and needed, it was for the most part a one-time response to a disaster. In addition to the federal funds to help rebuild Lower Manhattan, the city now receives federal anti-terror aid that it did not receive before the attacks, but the aid is minimal, and according to city officials it is far less than what is needed. Since the 1970s, federal aid to the city, as a percentage of total city spending, has declined, and so has federal influence on city governance. At its peak in the late 1970s, federal aid to the city greatly affected the city's ability to delivery basic public goods and services. In addition, some federal grants, such as urban renewal, provided the city with significant capital funding to pursue large-scale economic development projects. This is much less the case now.

Although federal influence on city governance has declined, it is still significant in a number of areas. There are areas of service delivery such as welfare and social services where federal funding and regulations continue to play a critical role in city policy. And in many areas where the federal government provides minimal funding, such as the environment, federal mandates influence both what the city does as well as how it does it. Just as important, though, the federal government influences the governance of the city through the maintenance of democratic accountability and justice in the city's political system. Throughout the 1960s and 1970s, many federal grant programs and mandates pushed the city to include communities and citizens in decisions regarding economic development and the delivery of social services, thereby opening up the local public policymaking process to citizens and groups who had heretofore been excluded. And although some of these requirements were watered down in the 1970s, the legacy of community involvement remained. On its own, the city's political system might have achieved similar procedural reforms eventually but the federal government certainly served as a catalyst in this area.

As will be discussed in the next chapter, federal mandates guarantee the city's residents a level of fair representation through redistricting and U.S. Department of Justice review of city election procedures. These mandates and procedures also promote civil harmony by allowing minorities and disadvantaged groups access to processes that they previously lacked as well as an alternative venue at the federal level to seek redress if they feel they have been unfairly treated at the city or state levels. Federal procedures and the ability of all groups to appeal to the federal level lend legitimacy to the city's political system.

5

Racial and Ethnic Diversity

Throughout New York City's history, racial and ethnic groups have looked to advance themselves up the economic and political ladders. For reasons of discrimination, choices made by the group's members, or circumstances connected to the economy and the political system when they arrived in the city, advancement up those ladders has not occurred at the same rate for each group. Groups assess their own socioeconomic and political status against the success or failure of other groups. Social relations among groups in the city are based in part on a group's relative position in the economic and political system. Where they live, where they work, and their ability to influence political outcomes all serve as indicators of this status.

The role of the political system in the city's social relations is complex and subtle. Groups want to be treated fairly and justly by the political system. This fairness certainly includes all of the constitutional rights of participation in the political process. Beyond the issues of procedural fairness, however, justice means being treated equally by the political system in a relative sense. If one group is being subjected to incidents of police brutality more than another group, then the victimized group may not perceive the political system as fair. If one group is receiving the benefits of a public program more than another group, then the group being shortchanged may also not view the political system as fair. In addition, if a group perceives that other groups are improving their economic or political status because of assistance from the political system, then the political system also will not be perceived as being fair. With few exceptions, procedural democracy and due process for all citizens have been achieved. What issues remain concern the specific treatment of groups by the city's political system and how that treatment affects relative group advancement up the economic and political ladders.

In August 1991, Blacks and Hasidic Jews faced off against one another in Crown Heights, Brooklyn, in what was quite possibly one of the low points of interethnic/racial relations in the city's recent history. The rioting that occurred was touched off when a Hasidic driver ran over a Black child, resulting in the boy's death and the subsequent stabbing death of a Hasidic Jew in the same neighborhood. The Blacks and Hasidim rioted against each other as well as against the New York City police, who were sent in to quell the disturbance. One of the perplexing aspects of the Crown Heights conflict was that both groups perceived that they were being treated unfairly by the political system. At various points during the conflict, each group perceived that the other group was receiving preferential treatment. In 1996, several years after the rioting, some Crown Heights Hasidic security patrol members were arrested by the New York Police Department (NYPD). The Hasidim complained of being treated "worse than criminals" by the police (Gonzalez 1996). A local black resident responded to the complaints by the Hasidim: "We've been crying out police brutality for years and nobody ever listens. . . . It's nothing new. It happens to everybody except them. Things are equaling out" (Gonzalez 1996).

One of the more controversial issues in discussions of race and ethnicity in New York City is whether the politics of race and the politics of ethnicity are similar. In their first edition of *Beyond the Melting Pot*, Nathan Glazer and Daniel Moynihan (1970) argued that Blacks in New York City were merely the latest group in a long line of new immigrant groups who started out at the bottom and would slowly work their way up the socioeconomic and political ladder, as other immigrant groups had done. Throughout the city's history, each new ethnic/racial immigrant group arriving in the city was treated with disdain by those groups that had arrived before. Most of the newly arrived groups sought to achieve political power as a means of raising themselves up from the bottom and delivering benefits to group members. Furthermore, their potential rise to power in the city's political system was viewed by more established groups as dangerous to the stability of the system. By 1970, however, the authors' second edition admitted that Blacks were not following the same pattern of assimilation and upward mobility as other immigrant groups had. They argued that race had "exploded to swallow up all other distinctions" (Glazer and Moynihan 1970). Blacks had not overcome poverty as fast as other groups had; and due to nonparticipation in politics, at least partially related to poverty, they had not been mobilized into the political system as fast as other groups. Glazer and Moynihan noted that when they published the first edition of their work in 1963, their beliefs about Black entry in New York City politics assumed that assimilation was possible; but by 1970, their discussion of Black involvement in city politics was centered more on concepts of separatism (Glazer and Moynihan 1970). At the same time, though, the authors noted that the primary ethnic patterns in city politics had not changed. Ethnic identity was still the primary grouping by which New Yorkers defined themselves, more so than class or occupation. But they also argued that religion had declined as a focus of ethnic identification. Congressman Charles Rangel (D–New York) agreed with the perspective of race and ethnicity discussed in the second edition of *Beyond the Melting Pot*. Rangel shared Moynihan's perspective on the political system's treatment of the early waves of immigrants but he disagreed with Moynihan on the issue of Black political ascendance. According to Rangel, when Blacks were ready to assume their position in the city's political system, "they threw away the old rule book because of who was up next" (Roberts 1993). Rangel saw Blacks, unlike earlier ethnic groups, being denied their rightful place in the city's political system even though they had waited their turn. Rangel saw the politics of race as more visible and indelible than ethnic politics.

Interviewed in the early 1990s, Moynihan seemed to retreat to his view of race and ethnicity in 1963. Looking back, he noted that "ethnicity was the organizing unit of New York politics" and that "race has acquired the pattern of an ethnic group interest" (Roberts 1993). According to Moynihan's perspective, the reaction on the part of some Whites to the rise of Black political power in the city during the later half of the twentieth century was no different than the Anglo-Saxon response to the rise of Irish political power in the mid-nineteenth century.

How Diverse Is New York City?

New York City's label as a majority-minority city, where Whites are in the minority and no single group makes up a majority of the city's population, does not do justice to the level of diversity in the city. As the city's percentage of White residents declined during the latter half of the twentieth century, it was not replaced by a single ethnic or racial group. Just as important, the White residents of New York City are far from a homogeneous group. Grouping them together for purposes of political analysis is just as faulty as grouping together all other non-White residents of the city.

Table 5.1 examines New York City's racial composition for 1980, 1990, and 2000, including the degree of change over the twenty years. In 1980, white non-Hispanics made up a majority of the population, but this decreased to 43 percent by 1990 and 35 percent by 2000. As the table shows, this decline occurred while the city's overall population was growing. Two White non-Hispanic subgroups, those with Irish ancestry and those with Italian ancestry, both declined over the twenty-year period. Asian groups experienced the greatest rate of growth over the twenty years. In 2000, they comprised approximately 10 percent of the city's population. The rate of growth for Asians in the city, however, was far greater during the 1980s than during the 1990s. In addition, among Asian subgroups the rate of growth over the twenty-year period differed significantly. The rate of population growth for Koreans has declined over the two decades. Population growth rates for Chinese and Indians have also declined over the twenty years, but the rates are still quite high. Although those of Hispanic origin grew steadily over both decades, there is a considerable difference among subgroups as well. While Puerto Ricans grew slightly during the 1980s, they declined both as a percentage and in real numbers during the 1990s. Non–Puerto Rican Hispanics increased at a significant rate during the 1990s. Of that group, Dominicans are the most numerous even though their growth rate declined over the two decades. The composition of Blacks in the New York City population held steady over the twenty-year period but West Indians, who were not even measured in 1980, made up more than 20 percent of the city's Black population in 1990 and 25 percent in 2000.

The racial and ethnic diversity of New York City's population was and continues to be affected by several factors including birthrates, death rates, out-migration, and in-migration. Each factor affects each group in different ways. The growth in the Hispanic population in the city is primarily due to birthrates but also is significantly affected by immigration. In contrast, white non-Hispanics have low birthrates and are leaving the city and dying faster than they are being replaced. While Black New Yorkers have a moderately high birth rate, they have a very low in-migration rate and a moderately high out-migration rate. Asians have the highest immigration rate of all the groups, but they have a low birthrate (Firestone 1995).

Although birthrates, death rates, and out-migration have certainly affected the city's racial and ethnic mix, immigration has had the largest impact on the city's population composition throughout its history. New York has been the port of entry for many of the nation's immigrants. As a result, much of its population at any single time has been foreign born. In 1990, 28.4 percent of the population was foreign born. By 1999, one third of the city's population was foreign born and half the population was either foreign born or the U.S.-born offspring of immigrants (Kraly and Miyares 2001, 33; New York City Department of City Planning 1999, 27). Although this figure is not as high as it was in the nineteenth or early twentieth centuries, when the composition of foreign-born residents in the city's population topped 40 percent, the percentage of foreign-born in the city in 1999 was higher than it had been in fifty years (Kantrowitz 1995; Kraly and Miyares 2001, 33).

The waves of immigration experienced by the city in the nineteenth and early twentieth centuries were predominantly white European. Although the early immigration waves gave New York City an ethnically diverse population compared to other American cities at that time, these waves were not as ethnically and racially diverse as the waves of immigration in the later half of the twentieth century. New York City has experienced immigration by over a hundred different nationalities since 1965, when immigration laws were liberalized (Sachs 1999).

During the 1990s, the city experienced immigration that averaged close to 200,000 people per year (Forman 2002). Western Europe, the region where the majority of immigrants came from in the nineteenth and early twentieth centuries, accounted for only 12 percent of the immigration during the 1970s; by the 1990s, Western European immigration accounted for less than 5 percent of the total. The Caribbean and Eastern Asia (including China) accounted for over half the immigration during all three decades. Non-Hispanic immigration from the

TABLE 5.1

New York City Population by Race Origin, 1980–2000

	1980 Population	%	1990 Population	%	% Change	2000 Population	%	% Change
Total population	7,071,639	100	7,322,564	100	3.5	8,008,276	100	9.4
White non-Hispanic	3,703,203	52.4	3,163,125	43.2	−14.6	2,801,267	35.0	−11.4
Italian ancestry	1,005,304	14.2	838,780	11.5	−16.6	692,739	8.7	−17.4
Irish ancestry	647,733	9.2	535,846	7.3	−17.3	421,646	5.3	−21.3
Black non-Hispanic	1,694,505	24.0	1,847,049	25.2	9.0	1,962,154	24.5	6.2
West Indian			391,744	5.3		549,664	6.9	40.3
Hispanic origin	1,406,389	19.9	1,783,511	24.4	26.8	2,160,554	27.0	21.1
Puerto Rican	852,833	12.1	896,763	12.2	5.3	789,172	9.8	−12.0
Other	553,556	7.8	886,748	12.1	60.2			
Dominican	125,380	1.8	332,713	4.5	165.4	406,806	5.0	22.3
Asian and Pacific Islander	239, 338	3.4	489,851	6.7	104.7	783,058	9.8	59.9
Non-Hispanic								
Chinese	124,372	1.8	238,919	3.3	92.1	361,531	4.5	51.3
Asian Indian	46,708	0.7	94,590	1.3	102.5	170,899	2.1	80.7
Korean	22,073	0.3	69,718	1.0	215.9	86,473	1.1	24.0
Filipino	25,391	0.4	43,229	0.6	70.3	54,993	0.7	27.2
American Indian non-Hispanic	9,907	0.1	17,871	0.2	80.4	17,321	0.2	−3.1
Other non-Hispanic	18,297	0.3	21,157	0.3	15.6	58,775	0.7	177.8

Sources: Data from City of New York Department of City Planning, *Demographic Profiles*, 1992, 2002.

Caribbean accounted for more immigrants in the 1970s and 1980s but Hispanic immigration moved ahead in the 1990s (New York City Department of City Planning 1996).

In part, the shift in immigration patterns can be explained by conditions in the countries and regions of origin. Many immigrants come to the United States to escape poverty, seeking economic security and a higher standard of living that could not be obtained in their country of origin. Other immigrants come to escape political repression or persecution. Restrictive emigration policies may affect the flow of immigrants, as was the case in the Dominican Republic and Haiti, due to repressive political regimes. At the same time, conditions in the United States and New York City explain some of the immigration shifts as well. As discussed in chapter two, beginning in the 1970s and continuing throughout the 1980s and 1990s, New York experienced growth in low-paid, low-skilled service sector jobs. And while job growth in the city was not greater than the national average, immigrants were assisted by a significant number of Whites leaving the city's labor force and by shifts in the structure of the city's economy (Wright and Ellis 2001, 89). The restaurant and personal services industries became major employers of immigrants. In addition, the apparel industry was also a major employer of immigrants. In some cases, New York City could have been attractive to immigrants because unlike other large cities where immigrants locate (e.g., Los Angeles) many of the industries that attracted immigrant labor were unionized or protected in some way by legislation. For instance, most, but clearly not all, of the Chinese garment workers in New York City are members of the International Ladies' Garment Workers Union (Waldinger 1995).

United States immigration laws also account for a great deal of the change in immigration patterns. In 1965, Congress passed the Immigration and Nationality Act. The legislation abolished the immigration quotas dating back to the 1920s that favored European immigrants and replaced those quotas with immigration regulations that emphasized family reunification, occupation skills needed in the United States, and political refugees. By emphasizing family reunification, the 1965 immigration laws favored immigrants from Latin America and Asia. Europeans who had lost their familial link with the United States found it more difficult to immigrate. Immigrants from the former Soviet Union are the only major immigrant group in the city who have used political refugee status. The law and its amendments in 1976 and 1978 resulted in major increases in non-European immigration. New immigration legislation in 1990 established three tracks for immigrant status: family; employment; and diversity. While the new law maintained the principle of family reunification, it placed greater emphasis on occupational skills by increasing the number of visas granted to several groups of immigrants including professionals, those with advanced degrees, skilled workers, unskilled workers, and those willing to invest at least $500,000 in businesses that would employ a minimum number of persons. The 1990 law also introduced regulations that would create greater diversity among immigrants.

The diversity visa program was developed for those wishing to immigrate who had no relatives in the United States. The increase in immigration from Bangladesh as well as Africa has been through the use of the diversity visas (New York City Department of City Planning 1999, 23).

New York is attractive to immigrants not only because of the economic opportunity that the city provides, especially when compared to the countries of origin, but also because the city has a tradition of accepting immigrants. In New York, as in most gateway cities, ethnic communities survive long after the initial waves of immigrants arrive (Salins 1997). This means that in some cases, new immigrants will find preexisting social networks where they can get assistance with housing and employment from family members or fellow countrymen. In addition, upon immigrating, they might find a community that is not completely alien from their country of origin. Some have suggested that immigration movements can become "self perpetuating," as established social networks in the country of destination lower the costs and reduce the risks of immigration (Foner 2001, 4).

Peter Salins (1997) has noted that as the population of ethnic enclaves grows, either through increased immigration or birth, the community's geographic shape takes on one of three patterns. Some groups simply move into adjacent neighborhoods, displacing other ethnic groups. In Washington Heights and the South Bronx, for example, the expanding Dominican community displaced Puerto Ricans, who several decades earlier had displaced Jews. In a second and third pattern of diffusion, some immigrants establish new communities in outer boroughs or the suburbs. The Chinese community centered in Manhattan established a second large community in Flushing, Queens, to handle its growth. Suburban ethnic enclaves are usually not as densely settled, and are usually settled by second- or third-generation descendants of immigrants.

Although Salins (1997) suggests that ethnic community expansion occurs usually without substantial interethnic conflict, there are examples of tension. In a 1996 *New York Times* interview, city council member Julia Harrison (D-Queens) expressed open hostility toward the influx of Asian residents into Flushing. "They were more like colonizers than immigrants. They sure as hell had a lot of money and they knew how to buy property and jack up rents of retail shops and drive people out" (Dugger 1996). Other longtime Flushing residents expressed similar resentment of the way in which Asian immigrants had taken over the commerce of Flushing. In Bensonhurst, Brooklyn, longtime Italian residents spoke similarly of the influx of Russian immigrants into their neighborhood. The president of a local community council stated that "no one indoctrinated the Russians before they got here. . . . They don't understand the American ways and consequently they are rubbing people the wrong way" (Pierre-Pierre 1993). Another longtime resident of Bensonhurst expressed resentment of the number of Russian immigrants on welfare. "They come here and get it like that. . . . They all have food stamps. That's my money and I resent it" (Pierre-Pierre 1993). In the 1980s, there was tension

between Blacks and Koreans in Bedford-Stuyvesant over increased Korean ownership of stores in the Brooklyn community. Black residents resented their relative
inability to start up businesses due to a lack of capital, while many Koreans were
able to get needed capital from their relatives and their community.

Some have noted that ethnic/racial enclaves develop for very different reasons. For some groups it is a matter of preference. Immigrants seek the advantage
and comfort of living among people who are similar. The community social networks are valued. For other groups, the development of enclaves may be as much
a matter of discrimination in the housing market as preference. Individual members of a group may not be able to find affordable housing in a nonhostile environment outside the enclave (Scott 2001). One individual's enclave may be
another's ghetto.

Immigrants to the United States may also find New York City attractive relative to other cities because of its expansive governmental and nonprofit social
service networks. The city's municipal hospital system and network of health
clinics as well as a broad array of community-based social services, many of them
oriented toward immigrants, complements the familial or friendship networks
of the enclave (Foner 2001, 8).

What may also make the city attractive to ethnic and racial group participation is its degree of political decentralization, the resulting opportunities for
political participation. This participation is enhanced by the fact that for the past
several decades no single racial or ethnic group has been able to amass sufficient
resources to control the city's political system on its own. As a result, New York
City's political system can offer benefits to many groups. Roger Waldinger (1995)
suggests that the system offers "many prizes" simply because of the number of
elected and appointed official positions that must be filled, including city council seats, state assembly seats, community board, and community school board
positions (when they existed). These multiple positions not only create additional means of access into the political system, but they also provide a means by
which groups can be recognized and rewarded for successful participation in
electoral efforts (Foner 1987).

Groups compare their success in the political system against the success of
other groups and assess their degree of progress and if they are being treated
fairly. Three factors make up the assessment of progress or fair treatment: representation; recognition; and equal treatment by the city's service delivery bureaucracy. Of the three factors, recognition may be the most symbolic form of
political system response to a group's existence. Simply stated, does the political
system or its officials recognize the existence of the group? Recognition usually
does not result in any substantive benefits, but for some groups it may be a sufficient response. For groups who may be too small or too new to the city to compete successfully in the political system, symbolic recognition may be the best
they can do. For new groups in particular, symbolic recognition may serve as
their orientation and initiation into political participation.

Unlike recognition, representation brings with it a greater possibility for substantive benefits from the political system, although representation does not guarantee these benefits. The concept of group representation also contains a constitutional component as the courts continue to address the meaning of equal protection as it relates to electoral outcomes and the drawing and redrawing of legislative boundary lines. The city's political system has a large number of elected and appointed positions, making representation at some level a realistic goal for many groups. Simply having a member occupying a position makes representation a symbolic benefit. If, however, ethnic or racial group representatives can use their appointed or elected position to gain benefits for members of their group, then representation brings with it substantive benefits. Finally, equal service delivery treatment deals with whether the city is responding to the specific demands of the group as they have been articulated, and how the group perceives it is being treated by the various service delivery agencies that make up the city government. Does one group perceive that other groups are being treated better? Do groups believe that they are getting the same quality of city services that all other citizens are getting?

Representation

In examining the issue of minority group participation in New York City politics, three types of representation can be identified. Formal representation addresses the processes and procedures by which a political system chooses it representatives, primarily in a legislative capacity. Do minority group members, by virtue of the established legal procedures, have a fair opportunity to attain positions of authority in the political system? Descriptive representation addresses the issue of whether the ethnic and racial composition of those in government is equivalent to the ethnic and racial composition of the general population. This includes not only those in elected office but also those in appointed positions. And interest representation addresses whether the policies and programs produced by the political system are responsive to the demands and needs of the array of ethnic and racial groups in society (Pecorella 1994, 131). Interest representation is similar to the concept of service delivery equity. As noted above, formal representation does not guarantee descriptive representation, and neither formal nor descriptive representation guarantees interest representation. Moreover, interest representation can be achieved without the presence of formal or descriptive representation. The chances, however, of a racial or ethnic group getting what it wants out of the political system are probably increased if formal and descriptive representation has been achieved. And of course, any racial or ethnic group's success in the political system will, in part, be a function of its presence, or size, relative to other racial and ethnic groups in the city's population.

One way groups seek to advance the interests of their members is through formal representation in the governmental process. The most direct mechanism of succeeding in formal representation is getting group members elected to office. At its most effective, having elected representatives assists groups in achieving policy goals in the political system. At its least effective, representation provides political symbolism that a group has arrived in the political system and has sufficient voting strength to advance group members to high levels of decision making. An additional means of gaining significant representation in the political system has been through obtaining executive branch appointments. City commissioners and high-level members of the city's executive branch are as visible as members of the city council and may have just as much ability to influence policy as legislators.

The population changes that occurred in the city throughout the 1970s and 1980s had a significant impact on the racial and ethnic mix of the city. To what extent are these changes reflected in the city council's racial and ethnic composition and in the composition of the higher-level positions in the city's executive branch? Tables 5.2 and 5.3 display the racial/ethnic composition of the city council and a sample of the city's executive branch leadership since 1974 at four-year intervals respectively. The four-year intervals represent the years immediately following citywide elections, so they should reflect any changes due to the elections or changes in appointments due to new mayoral administrations. Table 5.2 indicates that since 1974, White representation on the city council declined while Hispanic and Black representation increased. Descriptive representation has not been achieved, but minorities have made significant improvements in their presence on the city council over time. The explanation for these changes, however, goes well beyond simple increases or decreases in the city's population mix of these groups. Since 1974, the city council has gone through two structural changes in its legislative district design, plus the imposition of term limits. Both changes in the number of districts, in 1982 and 1990, resulted from changes in the city charter in response to suits filed against the city by groups seeking enhanced minority representation. The 1982 change, abolishing at-large seats on the council, produced a slight increase in the percentage of minority representation on the council. The 1990 change, however, had a much greater impact on minority representation.

In 1981, in response to a suit filed by the New York Civil Liberties Union, the U.S. District Court ruled that the city charter provision allowing for two at-large council members per borough violated the one-person, one-vote constitutional principle, since the boroughs varied widely in size (Benjamin and Mauro 1989). In both 1974 and 1978, all city council members occupying at-large positions were White. The abolition of these positions prior to the 1981 city council elections resulted in a small decline in the percentage of Whites in the city council and a small increase in the percentage of Black members, although the increase in seats occupied by Blacks was minimal. The shifting percentages in 1982 are more a result of declining seats for Whites as a result of the elimination of at-large seats than any real increase by minorities.

TABLE 5.2

Racial/Ethnic Composition of the New York City Council, 1974–2002, in Percentages (Frequencies)

	1974	1978	1982	1986–90	1992	1994	1998	2002
White	83.7	79.0	74.2	74.2	58.8	54.9	52.9	51.0
	(36)	(34)	(26)	(26)	(30)	(28)	(27)	(26)
Black	9.3	11.6	17.1	17.1	23.5	24.4	25.4	27.4
	(4)	(5)	(6)	(6)	(12)	(13)	(13)	(14)
Hispanic	6.9	9.3	8.5	8.5	17.6	19.6	21.5	19.6
	(3)	(4)	(3)	(3)	(9)	(10)	(11)	(10)
Asian	0	0	0	0	0	0	0	2.0 (1)

Source: Data obtained from New York City Council Website and New York City Municipal Archives Library.

TABLE 5.3

Racial/Ethnic Composition of Selected New York City Executive Branch/Appointed Positions, 1974–2002, in Percentages (Frequencies)

	1974	1978	1982	1986	1990	1994	1998	2002
White	75.0	75.7	78.7	75.0	51.5	60.0	64.5	62.5
	(22)	(25)	(26)	(24)	(17)	(20)	(20)	(15)
Black	20.6	15.1	12.1	18.7	24.2	12.1	19.3	20.8
	(6)	(5)	(4)	(6)	(8)	(4)	(6)	(5)
Hispanic	3.4	9.0	9.0	6.0	24.2	27.2	16.1 x	16.6
	(1)	(3)	(3)	(2)	(8)	(9)	(9)	(4)

Sources: Data obtained from New York City Website and New York City Municipal Archives Library.

Notes: Positions included in sample: New York City Commissioners of Buildings, City Planning, Consumer Affairs, Corrections, Cultural Affairs, Environmental Protection, Finance, Fire, Health, Housing Preservation Development, Human Resources, Mental Health Alcoholism and Drug Abuse, Parks, Police, Transportation, Taxi and Limousine, Housing Authority, Human Rights Commission, Corporation Counsel, Chancellor of the Public School System, Members of the Board of Education, Deputy Mayors.

For 2002, Board of Education members are not included since the board was abolished. In addition, Department of Health and the Department of Mental Health, Alcoholism and Drug Abuse were merged.

In 1989, the number of city council seats was expanded from thirty-five to fifty-one as the result of the city charter changes that abolished the Board of Estimate (chapter nine). The increase in the number of city council districts resulted in smaller districts. Combined with the increase in minority population over the previous two decades, this enabled the creation of more minority-dominated districts. The 1991 council elections produced a significant shift in the racial/ethnic composition of the city council. Table 5.2 shows that this shift toward greater minority representation increased slightly in both 1994 and 1998. By 1998, minorities had practically achieved parity with Whites on the council. More importantly, the percentage of Black and Hispanic representatives on the city council was approaching those two groups' percentages within the city's population. It is doubtful that the minority composition of the city council would have been close to what was achieved in 1991, 1993, and 1997 without the restructuring of the districts. While population shifts might have accounted for incremental change over a long period of time, increases in Hispanic population in various parts of the city would have been counteracted by the incumbent status of many non-Hispanic city council members representing increasingly Hispanic districts. The creation of new districts allowed for incumbents to keep their seats while creating new districts that reflected population changes.

Although as table 5.2 shows, the 1989 charter reform resulted in increased minority representation on the City Council, this created tension between Hispanic and Black groups over redistricting in areas where a minority council member had the potential of winning one of the new seats. Hispanic groups in the city were so critical of the initial districting plan for the city council after the charter revision that in 1991, the U.S. Justice Department was needed to referee a redrawing of the City Council district boundaries. The Justice Department agreed with Hispanic groups that the previous district lines favored Black candidates over Hispanic ones (Roberts 1991).

The 2001 city council election was the first to incorporate two-term limits, approved by the city voters in 1993. Thirty-six out of fifty-one incumbents were forced out of office due to term limits. Since some of the incumbents were Whites representing minority areas, the 2001 council elections was a chance for minority groups to pick up more seats in the council. As table 5.2 displays, the minority gains due to term limits were minimal, although the election did move minorities one vote away from controlling a majority of votes on the council, assuming minority council members would vote as a block. The 2001 elections also produced the first Asian member of the council.

Table 5.3 reflects changes in the composition of the city's executive branch leadership over time. These changes, however, occurred for very different reasons, since the positions displayed in table 5.3 are all appointed, not elected. All the positions examined in table 5.3 are appointed by the mayor except for five of the seven members of the City's Board of Education. The five borough presidents controlled these positions. The seven Board of Education positions are not included in the 2002 cells of the table because the board was abolished by the state legislature and the governor earlier in that year. In addition, the number of deputy mayors varies by mayoral administration, with some mayors appointing as many as seven and others as few as three. According to the data displayed in table 5.3, White representation in the appointed positions in the city's executive branch has declined while Hispanic representation has increased. Black representation has fluctuated over the twenty-eight-year period but has remained relatively stable. Similar to representation on the city council, descriptive representation has not been achieved but minority groups have increased their presence in the key appointed positions in the city administration.

The peak for minority representation in the executive branch occurred during the Dinkins administration. The percentage of Black officials increased slightly and the percentage of Hispanic officials increased significantly. Interestingly, the election of Rudolph Giuliani in 1993 resulted in no decrease in Hispanic representation in the executive branch, but a marked decrease in Black representation. Mayor Giuliani's courting of the Hispanic vote might serve as an explanation for this. It was uncharacteristic of Mayor Giuliani to mention the ethnic membership of his appointees. When his support among Hispanic New Yorkers began to drop during his first term, however, there were occasions when he made a point of noting the Hispanic origin of some of his appointees (Hicks 1995). In 1998, after Mayor Giuliani's reelection, the percentage of Hispanic officials in the Giuliani administration declined, but it did not drop back to the low levels of representation that occurred during the Koch administration. Black representation in the Giuliani administration did increase during his second administration. It appears as if elected officials have recognized the significant increase in the Hispanic population of the city and that this recognition is now being reflected in executive branch appointments. Table 5.3 shows no representation of Asian New Yorkers in the executive branch over the twenty-four-year period. Mayor Giuliani appointed an Asian American as Commissioner of the Department of Employment and Mayor Bloomberg appointed Asians to head the Health and Hospitals Corporation and the city Department of Employment, but these positions are not included in the sample examined in table 5.3.

Since the 1960s, there has been a great deal of legal and political controversy over the formal representation of minority groups in legislative bodies at the federal, state, and local levels. The controversies have their roots in the 1965 Voting Rights Act and the Supreme Court cases of the early 1960s concerning the reapportionent of legislative districts. These cases established that the Fourteenth Amendment's goal of equal protection would be served if the principal of one person—one vote was maintained. This meant that within a political system, legislative districts had to contain approximately the same number of residents so as not to advantage one group of citizens over another in having a greater weight in the election of their representatives and the resulting legislative decisions made by these representatives. It also meant that legislative district lines would have to be reviewed after every census and adjusted for population shifts to assure that the one person–one vote principle was upheld and maintained over time.

Given the impetus provided by the civil rights movement, the court's rulings, combined with the 1965 Voting Rights Act, meant that the impact of redistricting on groups suffering past discrimination became a major focus of attention. In particular, civil rights advocates, the courts, and the U.S. Justice Department were concerned with legislative district redrawing where minority groups were gerrymandered out of a representative. Gerrymandering is the practice, dating back to the early years of the American political system, in which legislative district boundaries take on strange shapes in order to enhance the electoral chances of a group or a particular legislator. Throughout the last four decades of the twentieth century, the U.S. Justice Department blocked state legislative redistricting plans if the plans were not deemed free of any racially discriminatory purpose. Section 2 of the Voting Rights Act bars any electoral law or procedure that results in minority voters having "less opportunity than other members of the electorate to participate in the political process and to elect representatives of their choice" (Greenhouse 1996). Section 2 applies to all states and their localities. Section 5 of the Voting Rights Act applies to selected states and portions of states with a history of discrimination. According to Section 5 of the federal Voting Rights Act, jurisdictions, due to a record of discrimination against minority voters or poor minority voter participation, have to obtain approval, termed pre-clearance, from the Justice Department before making any change in their election laws or procedures. Although most of the states subject to the "pre-clearance" requirement were southern, the Justice Department's list also included Manhattan, the Bronx, and Brooklyn (Pear 1991a).

The demographic changes that New York City experienced during the mid- to late twentieth century heightened the sensitivities of groups seeking formal representation and made it an issue in city politics on several occasions. Justice Department intervention in Brooklyn in the late 1960s resulted in legislative redistricting, which was responsible for the election of the first Black woman, Shirley Chisolm, to Congress. Brooklyn had a large concentration of Black voters that prior to the Voting Rights Act had been divided among several congressional districts (Sleeper 1992). During the 1980s, the Justice Department mandated that states take affirmative steps to insure that minority groups were clustered in districts to enhance their chances of electing a representative from their group.

Also as a result of the 1990 census, New York State legislators redrew the state's Twelfth Congressional District lines, creating a strangely shaped district including parts of Queens, Brooklyn, and the Lower East Side of Manhattan. This district enhanced the chances of a Hispanic being elected to Congress. At various points, the Twelfth Congressional District is connected only by parks and the Brooklyn-Queens Expressway. When it was created, the district was 58 percent Hispanic and about 19 percent Asian. Whites made up 14 percent of the district and Blacks 9 percent. In 1992, the district elected Nydia Velazquez, a Puerto Rican woman, to Congress. In 1995, however, the Supreme Court ruled unconstitutional a redistricting plan in Georgia in which race played a dominant factor (Hicks 1997a). Subsequent decisions regarding state redistricting plans around the country reiterated the court's antipathy with the use of race as a dominant factor. In most cases, the rulings had the effect of invalidating those districts, drawn after the 1990 census, in which district boundary lines were shaped, however strange, to give minority voters more electoral influence.

In February 1997, a federal district court declared the Twelfth Congressional District unconstitutional because "race and ethnicity were the dominant factors used to draw it" (Levy 1997). In its ruling, the court noted that "the number of Hispanic residents had been so important in drawing the district that a sophisticated computer program was used to find people with Hispanic surnames on voter registration lists" (Levy 1997). During the summer of 1997, the New York State legislature redrew the boundaries of the Twelfth Congressional District with surprisingly little controversy. The redistricting affected the boundaries of five other adjacent congressional districts. Under the change, the percentage of Hispanic residents in the district dropped from 58 percent to 48 percent. Many assumed that Congresswoman Velazquez would win reelection in the November 1998 elections not only because the percentage of Hispanic residents was still quite high, but also because she would be running as an incumbent (Hernandez 1997). She was easily reelected.

Section 5 of the Civil Rights Act became an issue in education and school reform policy during both the Giuliani and Bloomberg administrations. During the Giuliani administration, Schools' Chancellor Rudy Crew attempted on several occasions to discipline corrupt and/or malfeasant elected community school boards and their superintendents. In one case, the Justice Department initially blocked Chancellor Crew's suspension of an entire community school board and its appointment of a superintendent. In its ruling, the Justice Department argued "that the Chancellor's actions essentially denied the district's voters, who are pre-dominantly Black and Hispanic, the ability to choose the members of their school board" (Barry 1996). Chancellor Crew asked the Justice Department to reconsider, but he also submitted a revised plan for the district giving parents "a greater say in the appointment of trustees for the district" (Holloway 1996). The Justice Department reversed its earlier position and allowed Chancellor Crew to take over the district, barring the elected officials from the school district offices (Holloway 1996). In 1997, Mayor Giuliani and Chancellor Crew were successful in getting the state to approve legislation giving the chancellor the power to appoint all community school district superintendents. Although the chancellor had to choose from lists submitted by the community school boards, he was given the power to reject all nominees "until he receives a candidate he feels is qualified" (Steinberg 1997). This too had to be approved by the U.S. Department of Justice because of Section 5 of the Voting Rights Act. They approved the changes, noting that the law "did not have a discriminatory purpose or effect" (Steinberg 1997).

In 2002, Mayor Bloomberg was successful in getting the state to give him complete control over the city's school system, abolishing the Board of Education and entirely overhauling governance of the system. With the abolition of the Board of Education, the mayor was given the power to appoint the city schools chancellor. Going one step further than the reforms achieved by Chancellor Crew and Mayor Giuliani, under the Bloomberg reforms, the state gave the School's Chancellor sole responsibility to appoint the superintendents of the city's school districts, no longer taking names from lists submitted by community boards (Goodnough 2002). The Justice Department approved abolition of the city's Board of Education as well as the further modification of the community school boards' powers, stating that it was "not a change affecting voting" (Goodnough 2002). Finally, late in 2003, the U.S. Justice Department approved the abolition of the community school boards entirely and their replacement by parent councils. The new councils would not be selected via a direct vote, as had the community school boards (Bode 2004).

Recognition

Many ethnic groups in New York City lack the political clout to get one of their members elected to the city council or to be appointed to high-level executive branch positions by the mayor. For example, despite the fact that Asians are one of the fastest-growing groups in the city, they still comprise less than 10 percent of the city's population. Even though they are concentrated in parts of the city, they have only been able to get one of their members elected to the city council. Groups who lack representation at the highest levels of city politics, however, still seek to be recognized by the city's political system. In turn, city officials are well aware of emerging groups in the city's ethnic and racial milieu, as well as those ethnic groups whose population in the city is significant but not sufficient to elect their own representatives or warrant executive branch appointments. For those groups, the city's political system has created many ways they can be recognized without giving them formal or descriptive representation within the decision making structures of the system. Recognition placates those groups too small to be represented at the higher levels of the political system and serves as part of the socialization process whereby emerging group leaders and members are introduced to the political system, its officials, and procedures. Over time, the city's means of group recognition has become so institutionalized that all groups, even those with substantial representation in the higher levels of the city's political system, seek recognition.

Recognition is primarily symbolic. Given the degree of institutionalization that ethnic and racial group recognition has taken on in the city, however, issues of equity do arise, just as they do regarding more concrete issues of service delivery. Recognition includes appearances by city officials at ethnic parades, proclamations by city officials regarding ethnic events or holidays, street namings, statue unveilings, and the suspension of parking rules on ethnic or religious holidays. In August 1997, Mayor Giuliani welcomed representatives of the Pakistani community to City Hall, where he recognized the fiftieth anniversary of Pakistan's independence. He declared August 24 to be Pakistan Day to coincide with the Pakistan Independence Day Parade in Manhattan (New York City Mayor's Office 1997a). The next month, Mayor Giuliani hosted a reception at Gracie Mansion where he proclaimed German American Friendship Week in honor of the fortieth anniversary of the Steuben Day Parade. Joining the mayor on the occasion were New York Fire Department Commissioner Thomas Von Essen and Commissioner of the Department of Aging, Herbert Stupp, both of German ancestry (New York City Mayor's Office 1997b). A month later, the mayor joined with the Consul General of India and the president of the Association of Indians in America at South Street Seaport in the celebration of Deepavali, the Indian Festival of Lights, in honor of the fiftieth anniversary of India's independence (New York City Mayor's Office 1997c). Other ethnic events that the mayor participated in during 1997 and 1998 included the proclamation of the Hellenic Letters and Arts Day together with Greek Orthodox Archbishop Spyridon, a proclamation recognizing Puerto Rican Week in conjunction with the Puerto Rican Day Parade, a similar proclamation for Bronx Dominican Parade Week, and the hosting of a reception to celebrate the completion of the reading of the Talmud (New York City Mayor's Office 1997d, 1997e, 1998a, 1998b). During 1997, the mayor participated in no fewer than fifty events where racial or ethnic groups were recognized by the city. Among the events in which the mayor took part, seventeen different racial and ethnic groups were recognized. The mayor is not the only city official who presides at ethnic events and occasions. The comptroller, the public advocate, and members of the city council also take part in ethnic/racial group recognition events on as regular a basis as the mayor. Frequently, city council meetings begin with the recognition of an ethnic group representative or representatives, visiting the council chamber.

While certain types of group recognition may create problems in other sectors of the political system, these conflicts represent the political system's attempt to deal with the cultural diversity of the city. Many groups have sought the suspension of alternate side of the street parking regulations on religious and ethnic holidays. These parking rules allow the Sanitation Department to clean the streets by clearing one side of the street of parked cars at least two days a week. In 1992, two Muslim holidays were added to the list of days on which parking rules were suspended. This brought the total number of suspension days to thirty. In 1998, representatives of the Chinese community requested that the city suspend the parking rules on the Chinese New Year. The Sanitation Department expressed concern about the steadily increasing number of suspended streetcleaning days and the negative impact that further suspensions would have on the cleanliness of the city's streets. Members of the city council argued that to deny the request would be an insult to the Asian community and that other groups who happened to arrive in the city prior to this point had their holidays recognized by parking rules suspensions (Allen 1998).

Group recognition also became controversial in 1997 when the city's Chinese community protested the Giuliani administration's enforcement of a citywide fireworks ban. There had been a citywide ban on all fireworks for many years. Up until 1997, however, mayors had not enforced the ban in Chinatown during the New Year celebrations out of recognition for the Chinese community. Citing the fact that lighting firecrackers during the Lunar New Year celebrations had been a practice in the city for over a hundred years, representatives from the Chinese community sought to have enforcement of the ban curtailed during the New Year celebrations, or at least have the mayor allow a controlled display of firecrackers during the holiday (Lii 1998).

Muslims sued the city school system for the display of the Muslim star and crescent alongside symbols of other religious holidays such as Christmas and Hanukkah. The suit was settled prior to being litigated when the school board concluded that the star and crescent were cultural and not religious symbols. At first, city school officials had argued that the Muslim star and crescent were not secular or cultural symbols like the Christmas tree or the menorah, but that they were religious symbols and thus could not be displayed in public schools. A spokesperson for the plaintiffs, the National Council on Islamic Affairs and the American-Arab Relations Committee, claimed that the symbols were used to counter the cross Christians had used during the Crusades. In the agreement reached between school officials and the Muslim groups, the Board of Education also agreed to encourage city school districts to allow students who are fasting during the month of Ramadan to be seated separately from other students at lunch if they request it. In addition, they agreed that the Muslim holiday that ends Ramadan, Eid Al-Fitr, would be added to the list of days when Muslim students could be legally absent from school (Fried 1997).

Service Delivery Equality

In seeking recognition from the city's political system, some ethnic or racial groups have implicitly made the claim that their group simply wants to be treated as other groups are being treated. The Muslim claim against the public school system was based in part on the fact that other symbols from other religious groups were already being displayed. Similarly, the claim for the suspension of alternate side of the street parking rules by some groups is based on the fact that the city already suspends the parking rules on other holidays, some of them religiously or ethnically based. Claims to be treated equally by the city's political system go well beyond the symbolism of school religious displays and parking rules. The city's service delivery bureaucracy delivers tangible benefits to all citizens. If a group perceives that it is receiving less than other groups, then this is a cause for concern and possibly political action. The Campaign for Fiscal Equity suit, discussed in chapter two, is an example of the city claiming inequities in school funding. The primary plaintiffs in the suit were minority parents.

Race Relations and the NYPD

Clearly the most visible example of minority groups in the city claiming unequal treatment by the city's service delivery bureaucracy is in their relationship with the NYPD. It was the claim of unequal treatment by the police, in part, that was at the root of the tension in Crown Heights; although at times during the Crown Heights conflict, both Blacks and Hasidics were alleging unequal treatment. The most serious instance of unequal treatment of minorities by the police is brutality. In 1996, Amnesty International, a human rights organization known for publicizing cases of human rights violations and torture primarily in nondemocratic countries, issued a report on the practices of the NYPD. The report concluded that "police brutality and unjustifiable force" is a "widespread problem" throughout the NYPD and that the vast majority of abuses occur in Black, Hispanic, and Asian neighborhoods (Krauss 1996). The federal government has also been involved in investigating a number of cases of police brutality against minorities in the city. Some of the federal investigations have involved individual cases of abuse where civil rights violations were alleged, while other investigations have examined broader patterns of abusive behavior by the NYPD (Weiser 1998). In many cases, the federal investigations have come as the result of requests from community group leaders. In 1997, after a grand jury decided that there was insufficient evidence to indict a police officer in the shooting death of a Hispanic youth in Washington Heights, the Reverend Al Sharpton personally delivered a letter to U.S. Attorney General Janet Reno from the youth's family requesting a federal investigation of possible civil rights violations in the teenager's death (Van Gelder 1997).

Police brutality is only one claim that many minorities in New York City make against the police. The claim is part of a much broader view on the part of some minorities that they are treated with constant suspicion and disrespect by the NYPD. Mayors and police commissioners have always acknowledged that the problem of brutality and insensitive behavior toward minorities exists, but they have differed significantly in how much attention they give the problem and how sensitive they appear to be to the corresponding demands of the minority communities and the police. In at least one case, an officer who was found innocent of criminal charges in using an illegal choke hold that led to the death of a Hispanic man was fired by the police commissioner following an administrative hearing (Kocieniewski 1997). Nevertheless, minority groups and their leaders have been uniformly unsatisfied with the political system's handling of this problem. A 1997 New York Times poll found that 82 percent of Blacks and 71 percent of Hispanics felt that the police did not treat White and Black New Yorkers with equal fairness. The fear of abuse resulted in a variety of responses from the minority community. Minority parents reported training their children, especially their sons, to deal with police encounters, believing that such encounters were inevitable. The president of the NYPD Latino Officers Association told a *New York Times* reporter that as a result of the racial inequity he had seen in law enforcement, he had begun to counsel young people on how to deal with the police. A public defender service in Harlem reported offering a course for young minorities on how to deal with police encounters (Lee 1997).

Critics of the NYPD's service delivery record in minority communities have suggested that a link exists between descriptive representation and interest representation. That is, they have argued that the NYPD's problems in minority communities are in part due to the fact that minorities are underrepresented on the police force. In 1999, Whites made up 67.4 percent of the NYPD while comprising 43.4 percent of the city's population. In addition, Whites comprise 94 percent of all captains and 92 percent of all inspectors in the department (Wilgoren and Cooper 1999). These statistics placed the city's police department among the most racially imbalanced of all big city police departments. In the late 1990s, the city had a better record of attracting Hispanics to the force than Blacks. Although the Giuliani administration made some attempts to recruit more diverse police cadet classes, the administration was accused of not paying as much attention to diversity in the NYPD as had prior administrations (Wilgoren and Cooper 1999). Comparing the minority recruitment and advancement efforts made by the Giuliani administration with former mayoral administrations, a Dinkins administration official stated that the Dinkins and Koch administrations "constantly looked at numbers and looked at assignments: Where did we have blacks assigned? Are they in positions where they could move up? How many blacks are being put into the detective list? How many blacks are sent to the F.B.I. academy. . . . I'm not sure anybody is doing that now to make sure there is an equal playing field" (quoted in Wilgoren and Cooper 1999). The head of the organization that represents Black police officers claimed that there was an "unwritten rule" that kept Blacks out of the more prestigious divisions of the NYPD (Wilgoren and Cooper 1999). Critics also noted that during the Giuliani administration, some prominent minority members of the NYPD left. Minority members of the department also complained that they were disciplined more frequently than Whites in the department (Wilgoren and Cooper 1999).

In its defense, the NYPD stated that it conducted recruitment campaigns at churches, job fairs at city colleges, and even distributed leaflets at subway stations. These efforts did not significantly increase diversity in the NYPD. Some have suggested that the reason for the failed recruitment attempts is the self-perpetuating problem that minorities lack a connection to police work. They know no one on the police force while many White police prospects have family members and friends on the force (Youngblood 1999). In addition, in selecting cadets and those for promotion, the NYPD has used a competitive examination.

During the Giuliani administration, Police Commissioner Howard Safir stated that he was "going to select the most talented people" regardless of race or residency (Wilgoren and Cooper 1999). A spokesperson for the NYPD added that, "We try to encourage diversity as much as possible. . . . It's an open competitive examination—everyone can see it's fair. Whether everybody takes advantage of it is something else" (quoted in Wilgoren and Cooper 1999). Minorities successfully challenged the examinations used by the NYPD to hire and promote in the mid-1980s, but NYPD minority recruitment and promotions did not change significantly as a result (Wilgoren and Cooper 1999).

In the late 1990s, NYPD relations with the city's minority communities deteriorated further following two events, the beating and torture of Abner Louima and the shooting of Amadou Diallo. Early in the morning of August 13, 1997, police broke up a fight outside a Haitian club in the Flatbush section of Brooklyn. After a brief scuffle, several arrests were made, including Abner Louima. Mr. Louima later told police investigators that at the Seventieth Precinct station, he was beaten, subjected to racial slurs, and had the broken wooden handle of a toilet plunger shoved into his rectum and then into his mouth. Both Mayor Giuliani and Police Commissioner Howard Safir visited Louima in the hospital and then met with leaders of the Haitian community to assure them that action would be taken to apprehend and prosecute all police who were responsible for the beating (Barry 1997).

In 1997, New York City had approximately 300,000 Haitian Americans. They lived primarily in the Queens neighborhoods of Jamaica and Cambria Heights and Crown Heights in Brooklyn. Prior to the Louima incident, the Haitian community had been relatively inactive in New York City politics. As a community, they were focused far more on events in Haiti than events in New York or the United States in general (Pierre-Pierre 1997a).

The beating of Abner Louima served to change the focus of the New York Haitian community away from Haiti and more toward the city, and it also served to politically mobilize them. On August 29, 1997, a march to protest police brutality sponsored by the Haitian American Alliance drew over ten thousand people. Approximately a year later, the Haitian American Alliance had moved beyond the Louima beating and was beginning to pursue other issues. Some Haitian leaders complained about the lack of a business development corporation to assist Haitian merchants with loans or business assistance. Others were concerned about the housing problems faced by Haitian immigrants. The alliance and other Haitian groups had designated a New York State Assembly district in Brooklyn as the first test of Haitian electoral power. In that district, they identified over twenty thousand French-sounding names and planned an intensive campaign to mobilize and register Haitian voters in support of a Haitian candidate for the State Assembly seat (Pierre-Pierre 1998).

Less than two years after the Louima incident, on February 4, 1999, Amadou Diallo, a Black West African male, was shot to death by four members of the

NYPD's Street Crimes Unit. The Street Crimes Unit was a plainclothes division that focused on illegal guns and had a reputation for being aggressive. It also had a reputation for being underrepresented by minorities. While the NYPD was approximately 30 percent Black or Hispanic, the Street Crimes unit was estimated to be less than 10 percent minority (Koceiniewski 1999). As a result of the shooting, the U.S. Civil Rights Commission also decided to conduct a broader investigation into the practices of the NYPD in minority neighborhoods (Holmes 1999). In addition, the State Attorney General announced an investigation into the stop-and-frisk practices of the NYPD (Cooper 1999). The attorney general's study, published in December 1999, found that "Blacks and Hispanics are much more likely than whites to be stopped and searched by New York City police officers, even when the numbers are adjusted to reflect higher crime rates in some neighborhoods where members of minority groups live" (Flynn 1999b). Police officials argued that the variance in stop-and-frisk rates among various racial and ethnic groups was due to the fact that most of the police activity takes place in high crime areas. The attorney general's study refuted the NYPD's defense by comparing how often members of a racial/ethnic group were stopped compared to how often those stops resulted in arrests (Flynn 1999b).

In March 1999 the National Congress for Puerto Rican Rights filed a class action lawsuit in federal court on behalf of people who had been subjected to stop-and-frisk by the Street Crimes Unit. Alleging that the Street Crimes Unit had engaged in racial profiling when stopping over thirty-five thousand individuals on whom no further action was taken, the suit sought to disband the unit (Weiser 1999). In 1998, the Street Crimes Unit stopped and frisked 27,061 people, but only 4,647 were arrested (Cooper 1999). In a *New York Times*/CBS public opinion poll in mid-March 1999, less than a quarter of those New Yorkers asked believed that the police treated Whites and minorities equally. Almost 90 percent of Blacks questioned thought that the police engaged in acts of brutality against Blacks (Barry and Connelly 1999). Despite these poll results, by December 1999, 75 percent of Blacks and 83 percent of Hispanics sampled agreed with the statement, "I respect the New York City Police Department and its officers" (Flynn 1999c). The Diallo incident caused many to ask whether it was possible to achieve drastic reductions in crime through aggressive policing without violating the rights of those who live in crime-ridden neighborhoods (Herbert 1999).

To protest the Diallo shooting and the perceived lack of sensitivity to the issue on the part of the mayor and the NYPD, the leadership of the minority community in New York City, led by Reverand Al Sharpton, engaged in protests and acts of civil disobedience outside of the police headquarters in Manhattan. Those arrested included former Mayor David Dinkins, Borough President Ruth Messinger, and the head of the NAACP (Barry 1999).

By late March, NYPD Commissioner Safir had decided to reorganize the Street Crimes Unit, adding more minorities and having the unit wear uniforms so they would be more recognizable in minority communities (McFadden 1999).

Several months later, Safir decided to break up the Street Crimes Unit into eight separate units and have them report to regional commanders (Blair 1999).

Environmental Racism

Environmental racism involves the placement of facilities, public or private, which produce toxic or hazardous air or water quality, into communities that are heavily populated by minorities, particularly low-income minorities who lack the political power to oppose the facility or the economic ability to relocate (Berger and Chapel 1998; Weisskopf 1992). Environmental racism is premised on the hypothesis that environmentally hazardous sites are not equitably distributed across the city and therefore constitute an insidious form of service delivery inequity (Bowen et al 1995, 641). It is as much an issue of class as it is race or ethnicity, but in urban areas, race and class are frequently linked (Weisskopf 1992). Whether the location of hazardous facilities in low-income minority areas has been a matter of public policy or merely a function of diffuse, but systemic, values regarding race and class, is the subject of debate among those who study the concept (Bowen et al 1995, 658; Maher 1998, 360). Environmental racism has an impact not only on the health of the individuals living nearby, but also on the economic development prospects for those affected communities. Labeling these areas "environmental sacrifice zones," one researcher noted that the placement of hazardous sites create "obstacles to normal development" (Maher 1998, 360).

Environmental racism is as much an artifact of urban economic development as it is racial and ethnic politics. Pollution and the production of waste are two of the negative byproducts of economic development. Clearly, some types of economic development produce more pollution and waste than others, but there are very few types of economic development that do not create some type of negative impact on the environment. In densely populated urban areas, the management of pollution and waste creates financial and logistical challenges for planners and politicians. Moving residential and commercial waste far away from population centers for disposal becomes expensive. Finding a place for waste disposal close to population centers reduces transportation costs, but may expose populations to the disposal's harmful effects. Given the high cost involved in the transportation of waste or waste disposal it is not surprising that a disproportionate number of facilities that produce harmful environmental effects are placed in communities where those who have the least political power reside.

In 2006, the city council debated Mayor Bloomberg's citywide solid waste management plan that would ostensibly make each borough responsible for housing its residential solid waste prior to its being trucked or shipped out of the city. One of the most controversial aspects of this plan was the placement of a waste transfer station on the East River in Manhattan, adjacent to some very affluent White neighborhoods on the Upper East Side. Councilpersons representing the Upper East Side of Manhattan vigorously opposed the measure on health and aesthetic grounds. Brooklyn Councilperson Charles Barron responded to these protests. "I find it interesting how now people are concerned about waste transfer stations in densely populated areas. . . . Where have you been for all these years when we had 19 in Brooklyn, 15 in the Bronx and none in Manhattan? Where were all you people of conscience? . . . We've been concerned about environmental racism for decades. You have to share the burden. It is disingenuous now when you raise the issues because it is coming to your neighborhood but as long as it was in our communities, it was alright" (New York City Council Committee on Sanitation and Solid Waste Management 2006).

Environmental racism has been closely associated with the incidence of asthma among the city's minority children. In addition, asthma rates were highest in those areas of the city that were the most underserved by the health and medical community and where higher percentages of those who lacked health insurance lived. In the late 1990s, asthma was the leading cause of hospitalization among the city's children. It was responsible for approximately three hundred deaths in the city per year, an approximately 50 percent increase since 1980 (Calderone 1998; Egbert and Calderone 1998). Within individual boroughs, especially the Bronx and Manhattan, there was significant divergence among neighborhood child asthma hospitalization rates. In Manhattan, East Harlem had an asthma hospitalization rate of almost thirty children per one thousand. The rate for the Upper East Side, a more wealthy neighborhood, was four per one thousand. In the Bronx, the child asthma hospitalization rate was twenty-three per one thousand for the Hunts Point/Mott Haven community, but seven per one thousand for the more affluent Riverdale (New York City Department of Health 1999, 6).

In the ensuing debate over the causes of asthma, community groups from low-income minority areas focused on environmental racism. Citing diesel fuel–powered busses and the continued use of coal-burning furnaces in many of the city's public schools, environmental groups and their researchers argued that air pollution was a significant part of the problem as well (Kassel and Kennedy 1996). An environmental group in the Bronx cited the large number of diesel exhaust vehicles that drive through low-income communities, such as Hunts Point where an estimated sixty thousand trucks passed through in a month (Calderone et al. 1998; Stolberg 1999). In 2000, when the MTA proposed using new diesel-powered buses in the city, the proposal was opposed by environmental groups as well as public health experts. They argued that a number of medical studies had "established a direct link between diesel emissions and respiratory ailments" (Lueck 2000). Another factor that environmental and community groups cited as a possible cause for increased asthma in parts of the city was the placement of waste transfer stations. In the late 1990s, there were approximately seventy-five waste transfer stations in the city, and most of them were located in low-income minority-populated areas. The Greenpoint and Williamsburg sections of Brooklyn had twenty-four waste transfer stations alone (Stewart 2000). In a small section of East Harlem, there were four waste transfer stations and four bus depots, in addition to the automobile exhaust created by the Triborough Bridge traffic (Wakin 2001).

In 1998, the city adopted a comprehensive approach to treat asthma in the city's high incidence areas. The Department of Health implemented a multifaceted program, the Asthma Initiative. One of the principal strategies of the initiative was to foster partnerships with community groups, health providers, and schools, many of whom were already dealing with childhood asthma (New York City Department of Health 2001). In 2001, the Department of Health reported that hospitalization rates for children with asthma had fallen. In 1997, the hospitalization rate had been ten per one thousand. In 2000, the rate was down to 6.4. The report noted that children with asthma in some low-income areas of the city were still ten times more likely to end up in the hospital than asthmatic children in wealthier neighborhoods of the city. Officials credited the hospitalization rate decline to efforts by the city and others to educate parents and children about managing the illness as well as providing them with the needed medications and medical devices in some instances (Flanders 2001). Despite the decline in asthma hospitalization rates, asthma remained the "leading cause of hospitalization among children" in the city (New York City Department of Health 2002).

Racial and Ethnic Interest Groups

Groups representing ethnic and racial minorities have been part of the city's political fabric since the nineteenth century. Benevolent associations, fraternal organizations, and immigrant aid societies have played a socialization as well as a mobilization role in the lives of the city's minorities for almost two centuries. In the twentieth century these groups were joined by organizations fighting discrimination and seeking to assert legal rights of minority groups. More recently, municipal unions as well as other occupational groups representing a heavily minority constituency and groups representing the poor have also represented minority concerns.

Legal Rights Groups

The Puerto Rican Legal Defense and Education Fund (PRLDEF) was founded in the early 1970s in New York City. Although the group's activities go well beyond the borders of the city, the principal founders of the group were all New Yorkers and some of the group's major victories have had a significant impact on New York City politics in the areas of legal rights and service delivery equity. In addition, the group's activities have benefited many minorities other than Puerto Rican New Yorkers. The group's first lawsuit, *Aspira v. New York City Board of Education*, addressed the needs of non–English speaking students in the New York City public schools. The consent decree resulting from the case mandated that the city Board of Education "provide transition bilingual education services to all Puerto

Rican and other Spanish speaking youngsters in the system needing it" (Rappaport 2002, Preface). The decision was central to New York City's establishment of a bilingual education program throughout the school system.

PRLDEF has also been involved in voting rights issues. In 1981, the group went to the U.S. Supreme Court and succeeded in postponing the city's Democratic Party primary due to allegations that the city had violated the 1965 Voting Rights Act. PRLDEF alleged that the city's redrawing of city council district lines after the 1980 census discriminated against Puerto Rican and other Hispanic voters by denying them equal representation. The council district lines were redrawn in response to the complaint (Puerto Rican Legal Defense Education Fund Website, Voting Rights Reauthorization 2006). In 1991, PRLDEF went back to court and used the Justice Department's Voting Rights Act pre-clearance provision to halt the city's redrawing of city council district boundary lines. On this occasion, PRLDEF alleged that some of the districts created favored Black candidates rather than Hispanic candidates and resulted in potential imbalance in Black and Hispanic representation in the city council relative to Black and Hispanic composition in the city's population. As a result of the group's activities, the Justice Department informed the City Districting Commission that it could not approve the city's redistricting plan for the council because it "consistently disfavored" Hispanic voters (Pear 1991b). The Districting Commission was forced to redraw its original plan in order to give Hispanic voters greater strength in two districts (Lee 1991).

Formed at about the same time as the PRLDEF, Asian Americans For Equality (AAFE) focus much of their activity around Chinatown in lower Manhattan. While its early activities dealt with discrimination against Chinese workers and employment rights, much of its activity today deals with housing and immigrant services (Asian Americans For Equality Website, AAFE History, 1st Decade 2006). The organization not only deals with tenants' rights, but it has also become a provider of affordable housing in the Chinatown community. As a result it has an economic development focus in addition to its original goal of protecting the rights of Asian Americans.

AAFE has used federal legislation and programs to further its goals. In building affordable and senior housing in Chinatown, AAFE is a recipient of Community Development Block Grant funds through the city (Asian Americans for Equality Website, Congressional Testimony 2005). AAFE has also used the federal Community Reinvestment Act to increase bank-lending activities in Chinatown (Asian Americans for Equality Website, AAFE History, 2nd Decade 2006). In the aftermath of the September 11, 2001, terrorist attacks, AAFE became more involved in rebuilding the Chinatown economy, damaged due to the neighborhood's proximity to Ground Zero (Asian Americans for Equality Website, AAFE History, 3rd Decade 2006). Similar to the PRLDEF, AAFE has also been involved in city council redistricting battles, but it was not successful in sending an Asian to the council from Chinatown (Lin 1998, 143).

Municipal Unions

Over the last three decades, minority groups have taken control of several of the city's major municipal unions as their membership in these unions has increased. As the composition of the city workforce changed, including more minorities and women, the composition of municipal unions changed as well. Municipal union leadership in the city became outspoken supporters of civil rights and programs for the poor. As minorities obtained leadership positions in these unions, some of them took on broader leadership roles within the city's political system.

Probably no labor official reflects this type of union leadership more than Dennis Rivera. During the late 1980s and throughout the 1990s, Rivera earned a reputation as a militant labor leader. His union, Local 1199, representing over one hundred thousand health care workers, was one of the few city unions to strike during that period. Yet during the same period, Rivera appeared willing to work with politicians from both parties to advance the cause of his membership. During the mid-1990s, the Pataki administration requested a waiver from the Clinton administration to move New York State's 3.5 million Medicaid recipients to managed care plans. Rivera used his contacts in the Clinton administration to block the granting of the waiver. He feared that the plan would result in many of his members losing their hospital jobs due to the reduced business from Medicaid. Given that the Pataki plan was projected to save the federal government hundreds of millions of dollars in Medicaid expenditures by moving Medicaid recipients into managed care plans, Rivera proposed that the federal government provide New York State with some of the savings in order to cushion the impact on the state's hospitals and their workers. He was able to broker a meeting between Governor Pataki and Vice President Al Gore in 1996 to discuss his proposal, and he was able to get both to agree to his plan. Kenneth Raske, executive director of the Greater New York Hospital Association, a group that is usually across the bargaining table from Rivera's union, praised Rivera's participation and leadership in the deal. Of Rivera's participation, Raske noted, "If it wasn't for Dennis's persistence, this thing would have never happened" (Greenhouse 1997). In 1998, Rivera's union merged with the Service Employees International (SEIU), giving Rivera leadership of the largest union in New York State, the National Health and Human Service Employees Union.

Although initially linked to the Democratic Party, under Rivera's leadership SEIU became far more bipartisan. Rivera did not endorse the Democratic candidate for mayor in 1997, Ruth Messinger. Negotiating a 5.4 percent pay increase for his union's home health care workers with the Giuliani administration in 1997, Rivera endorsed the mayor in his run for a second term. Citing his continued commitment to liberal principles at the time, Rivera defended his endorsement by noting, "it would be fair to say that we felt it did not make the most sense to alienate a mayor who was going to win" (Bumiller 1998). In 2002, Rivera endorsed a number of Republican candidates at the state level, including Governor Pataki and State Senate Majority Leader Joseph Bruno, due to their support for health issues being pursued by his union (Greenhouse 2002a).

The Transport Workers' Union (TWU) is another of the city's labor organizations that over the last few decades has been comprised of a large minority membership. Roger Toussaint, born in Trinidad, joined the MTA as a subway cleaner in 1983, working his way up through the union ranks. In the late 1990s, he became leader of a militant union caucus that took the position that the incumbent leadership was not aggressive enough in its negotiations with the MTA management. In 2000, Toussaint became president of the union (Greenhouse 2002b). The TWU has had a history of labor union militancy, having gone out on strike in the late 1960s under the leadership of Mike Quill, who was jailed during that strike. In late December 2005, Toussaint led his union in a strike against the MTA in response to management's demand for pension concessions. Toussaint and the TWU faced fines and jail due to New York State's Taylor Law, which makes public employee strikes illegal. Facing the wrath of both Governor Pataki and Mayor Bloomberg, Toussaint portrayed the strike as a "civil rights campaign" to rally the union membership, invoking both Martin Luther King, Jr. and Rosa Parks (Greenhouse 2005).

Groups Representing the Interests of the Poor

A majority of New York City's low-income citizens are minorities. As a result, groups whose focus is poverty and low-income communities also respond to the needs of many of the city's minority citizens. One such group is the Association of Community Organizations for Reform Now (Association of Community Organizations for Reform Now 1999). ACORN is a national organization with local affiliates in many urban areas. Its goal is to promote and mobilize political action by residents of low-income communities. In the Atlantic Yards Nets Arena case, ACORN played a major role in brokering the community benefits agreement (Brick 2005).

In 1997, ACORN issued a report entitled "Secret Apartheid." In the report, it documented a study that used volunteers who, posing as parents, attempted to get information from school officials about "gifted and talented school programs." The study found that "Black and Latino parents were permitted to speak with an educator less than half as often as White parents." White parents received tours of schools more than twice as often as minority parents. And White parents received preferential treatment throughout their interaction with school officials compared to minority parents. The ACORN study concluded that access to information about gifted and talented programs in the city's public schools was dependent upon the race of the individual seeking the information. The report also found that in heavily minority-populated middle schools, courses required for the city's elite high schools were frequently not offered, effectively barring many minority students from those schools (ACORN 1997). In a response to the study, Chancellor Rudolph Crew acknowledged the imbalance, but also accused ACORN of ignoring his efforts to publicize gifted and talented programs so that everyone had access to the information (Sengupta 1998).

Despite these successes ACORN's attempts to promote political action by the poor in New York reflects the difficulty of this strategy. After the passage of welfare reform, ACORN was at the forefront of the attempt to unionize the city's workfare workers in the late 1990s. They collected signatures from 17,000 workfare participants, over one-half of the total, demanding union recognition from the city (Firestone 1998). When they organized a march on City Hall, only four hundred Work Experience Program (WEP) workers participated (Finder 1998). The attempt fizzled.

Within New York City's political system, there are numerous advocacy groups comprised of middle- and upper-income citizens who represent or claim to represent the interests of low-income citizens. Advocacy groups speak out on behalf of the poor and represent them at various stages of the policymaking process. They attempt to get the political system to respond to the demands of the poor by publicizing system inaction or wrongdoing, lobbying political officials, and litigating where there is legal basis for redress. In 1995, Children's Rights Incorporated, a national advocacy organization comprised of attorneys, filed a suit against New York City's Child Welfare Administration (CWA), the city agency that oversees the disposition of abused and neglected children. Alleging that the CWA was a mismanaged and ineffective city agency, Children's Rights Incorporated was seeking through litigation to have a court-appointed receiver take over the agency. The group had filed similar suits in other parts of the country, and had been successful, for example, in getting the federal courts to take over the District of Columbia's child welfare agency earlier in the decade. The New York City suit was a class action filed on behalf of eleven children, all minorities, who were the subjects of cases being overseen by the CWA. One of the children had been returned to her biological mother, a drug abuser, after which she had spent six months locked in a closet. The Children's Rights Inc. suit alleged that after CWA had returned the girl to her mother, they had ignored reports of abuse (Bernstein 1995). In early 1999, Children's Rights Inc. and the city's Administration for Children's Services (ACS) (the name was changed when the agency was reorganized in 1997) settled their lawsuit. Since the lawsuit had been initiated in 1995, Mayor Giuliani had reorganized the agency, given it new leadership, and reduced the case load of the child welfare workers overseeing individual cases. Children's Rights Inc. agreed to withdraw their call for a court takeover of the agency. ACS agreed to be guided for two years by a panel of experts who would offer advice. The independent panel was given access to all ACS records and Children's Rights Inc. retained the right to seek a court takeover of the agency if after two years the independent panel deemed that the ACS had not acted in good faith (Swarns 1998). When the two-year period was completed, the groups withdrew the suit, announcing that the city's child welfare system had made progress in addressing its problems.

Some interest groups not only advocate for the city's poor and minority citizens but they also deliver services to low-income New Yorkers. The services being delivered are either partly or entirely funded by the political system. In the delivery of social services to the poor, New York City contracts with a very large network of not-for-profit groups. The city's reliance on not-for-profit social service delivery agencies dates back to the nineteenth century when numerous ethnic, religious, and other charitable societies were formed to deal with the needs among immigrants and the poor. Some of the largest social service delivery organizations in the city are associated with mainstream religious denominations. Catholic Charities and the Jewish Board for Family and Children's Services are both broad networks of service agencies that include family service centers, health care facilities for the elderly, nursing homes, child welfare agencies, day care centers, hospitals, homeless shelters, mental health centers, visiting nurse services, maternity services for unwed mothers, and various youth organizations. Most service delivery groups engage in advocacy as well as service delivery activities since, in many cases, the two activities are so closely related. Service delivery groups claim to speak for their low-income clientele, and the fact that their clientele lack the resources and the skills to represent themselves in the political system means that the voice of the service deliverers is frequently the only voice for the poor heard by the political system.

There are a large number and a wide array of groups advocating on behalf of minority New Yorkers. It is difficult to gauge the extent to which the activities of these groups provide racial and ethnic minorities with adequate representation within the city's political system. Minorities, and especially low-income minorities, frequently lack the resources to organize and approach the political system on their own in any sustained and effective manner. Their reliance on others to speak on their behalf remains a weakness in their representation.

Assessing Racial/Ethnic Group Political Power

A group's success in gaining representation, recognition, and service delivery equity from the political system is in part a function of the political power they have amassed. Racial/ethnic group political power is usually a function of several components. First and most important, the group must have sufficient strength at the polls in order to use the electoral process to reward public officials who provide the group with benefits, punish those officials who ignore group demands, and if possible elect group members to office. While there is a relationship between electoral strength and population, it may not be direct. A group with a certain percentage of the city's population is not always assured of a similar percentage of votes within the city's electoral system. In 1990, Hispanics made up approximately one quarter of the city's population; however, in the 1989 and 1993 elections, they comprised less than 15 percent of the electorate. By 1997, they comprised a little more than 20 percent of the electorate, but this was still less than their corresponding percentage of the city's population that by the late 1990s was approaching 30 percent. Asians also have voted in smaller percentages than their composition of the city population would suggest.

Blacks in New York display a very different pattern of political activity. Similar to Hispanics, Blacks comprise approximately one quarter of the population; however, in the 1989 and 1993 elections, Blacks made up approximately 28 percent of the vote. The fact that this figure declined to 21 percent in 1997 suggests that the candidacy of David Dinkins might have influenced Black turnout at the polls in 1989 and 1993. Low voter turnout among minorities partly explains how White voters continue to dominate New York City electoral outcomes even though they comprise less than 40 percent of the population. During the 1980s, the percentage of white non-Hispanics in the city declined below 50 percent. In the 1989, 1993, and 1997 mayoral elections, however, White voters still made up a majority of the electorate although the 1997 percentage was only 53 percent (New York Times 1997a; Associated Press 1997). In part, White voters remain the largest block because minority groups have low voter turnout rates with the exception of Black voters during the David Dinkins candidacy.

There are several explanations as to why voter turnout rates for some racial/ethnic groups may be lower than population composition percentages. For some groups who have experienced recent increases in immigration, new immigrants may not have become citizens and are therefore ineligible to vote. For some immigrant groups, New York City is not viewed as their permanent or long-term home. Some immigrants plan on returning to their place of origin after having accumulated some wealth in the United States. A scholar on Asian American immigrants suggested that low voter turnout rates are in part due to a strong emphasis on work over other activities as well as an aversion to politics resulting from living in authoritarian political systems. As in the case of many Haitian New Yorkers, prior to the Abner Louima incident, the political orientation of many immigrant groups is focused more on the politics of their homeland than that of the United States. As a result, they tend not to become citizens, or delay their citizenship, and therefore cannot register to vote. It took the Abner Louima incident to sufficiently politicize the Haitian population and reorient its focus toward New York.

Another reason why the voter turnout rates of some racial/ethnic groups are low is demographic. For some groups, immigration practices and birthrates have produced large numbers of group members below the age of eighteen, the age at which voter registration is possible (Dao 1999).

A second factor that affects a racial/ethnic group's political power is the degree of group cohesion or unity. A common group identity that stems from common experiences or ancestry serves to create and strengthen group cohesion. It may also serve to politically mobilize a group if its past experiences are tied into political events. Racial or ethnic groups that have a history of political activity and unified political behavior, such as block voting, have a greater tendency to attract the attention of candidates running for office. At the same time, however, racial and ethnic groups who continuously vote as a block for one party may be ignored by candidates from the other party who believe that it is not a good investment of campaign time and resources to pursue the group's vote. Black voters in the city have been one of the most unified groups, especially in recent city elections. The Dinkins candidacy mobilized Black voters more than any previous election and polarized their vote. In 1989, candidate Dinkins was assisted by the presidential candidacy of Jesse Jackson in 1984 and 1988, which politically mobilized the African American community in New York City. African Americans in the city very much see themselves as sharing a common experience of racism in America, which serves to focus their political behavior more so than other racial or ethnic groups. Black West Indians, on the other hand, do not share the African American experience even though they are part of the same broad racial group. As a result, although West Indians joined with Afro-Americans in middle decades of the twentieth century, they have recently become more independent in their political behavior as their population in the city has increased (Kasinitz 1992).

Unlike African Americans in the city, Hispanic New Yorkers do not share a common experience or ancestry, although they do share a common language. The two major Hispanic groups in the city, Puerto Ricans and Dominicans, see themselves as two distinct groups. Dominican immigration occurred at least a decade after the major waves of Puerto Rican immigration had subsided. The two groups have their own organizations, and city public officials have quickly learned to address the identities of each group. Hispanics are still grouped together for purposes of vote analysis and it is difficult at times to assess differences in political behavior between Dominicans and Puerto Ricans. Hispanics as a group, however, have not voted in as concentrated a block as Black voters have.

Particularly for smaller ethnic/racial groups, settlement patterns may play a major role in the group's political activity or recognition. As discussed earlier in this chapter, the existence of a racial or ethnic enclave within a neighborhood gives a group a sense of place in the city. Enclaves play a critical social and economic role for new arrivals by offering immigrants familial or old country links, socialization experiences, and possibly employment opportunities. The enclave also offers the group a means of political communication and mobilization. For group leaders seeking to build a political constituency or politicians looking for a critical mass, the enclave represents a political opportunity. At the same time that the enclave may offer a point of ethnic identity and mobilization conducive to increased political awareness and participation, the enclave can also delay a group's entry into the city's political arena. The enclave as a community may keep the immigrant's focus on the politics of their country of origin rather than on city politics. The enclave community may also reinforce political attitudes and practices from the country of origin rather than encouraging assimilation into the city's political system. All of this could result in fewer voter registrations and less political participation.

Given that no racial or ethnic group can win citywide elections on their own, coalition-building among racial and ethnic groups has been a necessity. According to McNickle's (2001) analysis of mayoral elections, there were three different principal racial/ethnic coalitions responsible for electing the mayor throughout the twentieth century. From the early part of the century through the early 1960s, a Democratic coalition led by Irish Catholics and supported by Jewish immigrants and a minority of Italians were successful in electing the mayor in eleven out of sixteen elections. The candidate of this coalition was an Irish Catholic in fifteen of the sixteen campaigns. This coalition promoted a liberal progressive social agenda. From the early 1960s through the mid-1980s, the dominant coalition was led by Jewish politicians. They ran a Jewish candidate for mayor in five out of six elections and were successful in four. This coalition relied on Democratic borough party organizations cooperating with each other. In addition, the relative conservatism of the coalition appealed to less liberal outerborough Irish and Italians. While McNickle argues that the third coalition was made up of Blacks, Latinos, and White liberals, this group was only successful in electing a mayor in 1989, while failing in 1993, 1997, 2001, and 2005. In fact, the coalition responsible for electing the Republican mayors recently is very similar to the earlier coalition of Jews and more conservative Irish and Italians. What distinguishes this coalition from the earlier one is the obvious lack of Democratic Party backing (McNickle 2001). As McNickle (2001) points out, Republican mayoral candidates have won when the minority/liberal coalition is unstable. Liberal-leaning ethnic and racial groups in New York City have a long history of cooperation in the civil rights and labor movements as well as in the development and delivery of social services. Coalition formation, however, for the purpose of electing a minority candidate as mayor has been elusive, with the exception of David Dinkins. As a result, Dinkins has been the only member of a minority to serve as mayor, and he only served for one term. As previously discussed, Blacks and Hispanics have had considerable success in getting members elected to the city council, and this success has been replicated at the state legislative level and in New York City's representation in the U.S. House of Representatives. At the mayoral level, however, Black and Hispanic leaders have rarely been able to coalesce around a single candidate (White 2000).

John Mollenkopf (1997) notes that although the city's Black-Hispanic coalition has failed to elect a mayor other than Dinkins, New York City as compared to other cities still produces policies that are responsive to the demands and needs of minority groups. And even though the Koch and Giuliani administrations were not heavily supported by minority voters, they still included a significant number of minorities among the mayoral appointees. These conditions serve to weaken minority group cohesion and make the formation of minority group coalitions less urgent than in other cities where mayoral appointments and public policies may not be as solicitous of minority interests unless a minority or minority-supported mayor is in office.

A third factor contributing to ethnic/racial group power is leadership. Ethnic/racial group leaders represent the group in the larger political system and define the group's identity and demands for the larger political system. Ethnic/racial group leadership is more significant for less affluent groups, who are not as economically powerful or politically active. Less affluent groups look to their leaders to deliver public policy benefits as well as symbolic recognition within the political system. Lacking political efficacy, they look to leaders to succeed in the political system where the group as a whole has not been successful. At the community level, group leaders can use the issues of fairness and justice to mobilize support, build organizations, and maintain their positions of leadership. Leaders not only offer individual group members heightened identification with others in similar positions, but they also offer those individuals the opportunity to advance the group through collective action.

Leaders benefit through building supportive constituencies that hopefully can be mobilized at future times for personal or group advancement. Union leaders, including Denis Rivera and Roger Toussaint, have an organizational constituency behind them. Other minority group leaders have to build their own constituencies. The appearance of the Reverend Al Sharpton in Crown Heights in 1991 after the automobile accident death of a Black child and the stabbing death of a Hasidic Jew was just such an event. As in the case of Sharpton, group leaders can be perceived as exploiting community issues to enhance their own leadership position or visibility, or leaders can make a genuine contribution to resolution of intergroup conflict, the solution of group problems, and the advancement of group status.

To be effective, group leaders must be able to maneuver through the world of mainstream politics but also relate to group constituents. The fact that no racial/ethnic group comprises a majority of the population in the city means that in order to succeed in the political system, group leaders must engage in coalition behavior. In his study of Caribbean New Yorkers, Philip Kasinitz (1992) noted the dual roles of the ethnic entrepreneur. They must be seen as strong advocates in order to maintain credibility within their community, but they cannot be seen as so militant that they inhibit a working relationship with the political establishment (Kasinitz 1992).

Probably no politician reflects this dilemma of group leadership better than Reverend Al Sharpton. He is a political maverick who has sought to lead New York City's Black community. Sharpton had his roots in the church, a major source of African American community and political leadership. The African American church survived slavery and throughout twentieth-century urban America it was one of the more stable institutions in the Black community (Lowery 1990).

Sharpton did not work his way up through the Democratic Party organization in the city. His background was more as a community activist than as a political regular. During the early 1970s, he worked for Jesse Jackson's Operation

Breadbasket, which organized boycotts and demonstrations against businesses that refused to employ Blacks (Robinson 1995). Sharpton came to prominence during the 1980s, when he established himself as a citywide Black leader following bias attacks in the Howard Beach section of Queens and the Bensonhurst section of Brooklyn. Following the Howard Beach incident—in which a Black youth was killed by an automobile after being chased onto a highway by White youths—Sharpton was successful in pressing the governor for the appointment of a special prosecutor. In the early 1990s, Sharpton became involved in the Crown Heights conflict between the Black and Hasidic communities where he was accused of promoting Black anti-Semitism. In addition, Sharpton had been criticized by Black moderates and White liberals throughout the late 1980s and early 1990s for failing to denounce the anti-Semitic and anti-White rhetoric of Reverend Louis Farrakhan of the Nation of Islam. Sharpton never established mainstream credentials. He became a spokesperson for that segment of the Black community that felt neglected by mainstream Black officials. Sharpton used that support to try to break into the mainstream. His success was due in part to his ability to use the media, and also the fact that the frequently divided Black and minority political mainstream produced few leaders other than David Dinkins (Gottlieb and Baquet 1991). In 1992, Sharpton became a candidate for the Democratic nomination for U.S. Senate. During the race, Sharpton moderated his rhetoric and, unlike his three White opponents, who engaged in bitter personal attacks on each other, he addressed the issues and ran a credible campaign. He received 15 percent of the total vote and 70 percent of the Black vote, finishing ahead of one of the White candidates. Two years later, Sharpton ran against incumbent Senator Daniel Patrick Moynihan in the Democratic primary and received 26 percent of the vote statewide (Hicks 1997b).

During the Dinkins administration, Black political leadership was united, deferring to Mayor Dinkins to set the Black community's political agenda, even if some disagreed with the substance of the agenda (Horowitz 1994). Elected officials, party leaders, or those appointed to high-level positions within the city government often become the de facto leaders of their ethnic group. Dinkins assumed this position when he was Manhattan borough president and strengthened it when in 1988 he was instrumental in helping garner Jesse Jackson's plurality of votes in the city's Democratic presidential primary. After Dinkins' defeat, there was fear among Black leaders that Black political support would splinter, giving the Black community little voice in the Democratic mayoral race. In addition, there was hope that other groups might rally around a Black mayoral candidate as they had around Dinkins, giving the Black community another chance at occupying City Hall.

Sharpton's 1996 announcement that he was running for mayor was not well received among mainstream Black leaders. They believed that while Sharpton had a core constituency of staunch supporters, he would have difficulty gaining support beyond that constituency given his past polarizing statements and behavior. Some minority and Democratic party leaders feared that if Sharpton lost in the primary he would not back the winner in the general election (Hicks 1996). Moreover, despite his respectable showings in the two Senate races, Sharpton was still seen by many as a radical politician. In a 1997 *New York Times* poll, 36 percent of Black respondents had an unfavorable view of Sharpton while only 24 percent had a favorable view. Among Whites, the unfavorable rating rose to 73 percent (Hicks 1997b).

In 1997, Reverend Sharpton ran in the Democratic primary for mayor against Manhattan Borough President Ruth Messinger. He ran an issue-oriented campaign in which he tried to escape some of the more controversial aspects of his past. He supported reforms that would have required the police to reside in the city as a means to make the NYPD more diverse. He also supported strengthening the city's Civilian Complaint Review Board in their attempt to curb the excessive use of force by some members of the NYPD. At one point during the campaign, he was asked whether he was trying to get White voter support. His response was, "Sure. But I'm not going to compromise or sell my soul to get them!" (Hicks 1997b). He agreed to support Messinger should she win the Democratic nomination for mayor, and she agreed to support him. Sharpton received 32 percent of the vote in the September 1997 primary, losing to Messinger, who received just over 40 percent. Sharpton's critics explained his performance by arguing that with a low voter turnout, Sharpton had done nothing more than hold on to approximately the same number of core voters that had supported him in his Senate races. The critics also claimed that Messinger had been a weak candidate and that Sharpton had benefited from a high turnout of Black voters due to close races for Manhattan Borough President and several city council seats involving Black candidates (*New York Times* 1997b). Despite the negative analysis of Sharpton's electoral performance in the mayoral primary, it appeared to be another example of Sharpton moderating his image in order to challenge the mainstream leadership of the Black community. Shortly after the primary, Sharpton was approached by former Mayor David Dinkins and was urged to run for Congress against Edolphus Towns, an incumbent Black congressman from Brooklyn who had supported Giuliani for mayor (Bruni 1997). Sharpton declined the invitation.

After the shooting of Amadou Diallo in 1999, Sharpton was at the center of the protests in front of the NYPD headquarters, playing a major organizational role as well as assisting the Diallo family (Nagourney 1999). Commenting on his leadership, former Democratic Congressman Floyd Flake stated, "He just stepped in and began the process of trying to move the agenda, as he does in all these cases. I like to tell people this is his career. When you look at this situation in relation to Los Angeles and Rodney King, regardless of what anybody says about him, his presence and his finding a way to give people a means to vent probably saved this city from having the same kind of rioting. . . . I don't know if anybody else could have done that" (quoted in Nagourney 1999).

Although he did not run for mayor in 2001, Reverend Sharpton played a significant role in the campaign. Less than two weeks before the scheduled primary, Sharpton endorsed Bronx Borough President Fernando Ferrer in the Democratic primary. Ferrer was the only minority among the four candidates (Filkins and Nagourney 2001). The Sharpton endorsement gave Ferrer the strong but not unanimous endorsement of the city's Black leadership. Congressman Charles Rangel and Manhattan Borough President C. Virginia Fields had also endorsed Ferrer, but former Mayor David Dinkins endorsed Mark Green (Filkins and Nagourney 2001). Green and Ferrer received enough votes in the September 25 primary to appear in a runoff election two weeks later. During the campaign for the runoff election, Sharpton's endorsement of Ferrer became a campaign issue. In a debate, Ferrer denied that, if elected, Sharpton would be selecting his police commissioner. Ferrer needed additional White votes to win a runoff against Green. A close link with Sharpton would frustrate this effort. Green's advisors were attempting to link Sharpton and Ferrer in order to galvanize moderate White voters while attempting to avoid criticizing Sharpton for fear of alienating minority supporters (Nagourney 2001). Although Green won the runoff election, he did not escape accusations that some of his supporters and staff had used Sharpton's endorsement of Ferrer as a weapon in the final days of the campaign.

Unlike Sharpton's hostile relationship with Mayor Giuliani, his relationship with Mayor Bloomberg has been cordial. Mayor Giuliani refused to meet with Sharpton throughout his two terms as mayor, whereas Bloomberg met with Sharpton before his inauguration and attended Sharpton's annual celebration of Martin Luther King's Birthday and promised to attend every year he was mayor (Cooper 2003).

Conclusion

Race and ethnicity has been a recurring theme throughout American political history. For New York City politics, however, race and ethnicity has been more than a recurring theme. It has been one of the driving forces. What makes race and ethnicity a more intense and constant factor in the city's political system than in the national political system? First, the city's political tradition and culture are anchored in ethnic and racial politics. New York City's social history is defined by the arrival of wave after wave of immigrant groups. Immigration accounts for approximately five times more of the population growth in the city than in the country. In 2000, over half the families in Brooklyn, the city's largest borough, had parents who were foreign born. With few exceptions, group after group assimilated and worked its way up the socioeconomic ladder. In part, immigrant groups defined their success through access to the political system as a societal rite of passage. Successful participation in the political system became a symbol of group success but it also provided substantive benefits. Second, the city's continued status as a gateway city means that newly arriving groups can still find the same type of enclave settlements that their ancestors found or that other immigrant groups found well over a century ago. While ethnic/racial group enclaves assist the assimilation process by translating and interpreting the new political and social culture for the immigrant, the same factors may serve to frustrate assimilation by fostering an inward, isolated perspective on the larger political system and the other groups in it. Political mobilization may occur under either perspective but it is likely that isolated and inward-looking groups will be more oriented toward politics in their homeland than in New York City. Third, as has been stated throughout this chapter, the city's extreme diversity is complemented by the fact that no group comprises a majority of the population or has sufficient resources to control the political system on its own, as was the case in the distant past. Although they make up less than a majority of the population, non-Hispanic Whites still make up a majority of the electorate. This slim and declining majority, however, does not assure this group of electoral success. They are too diverse as a group and rarely vote as a bloc. Non-Hispanic Whites are by no means unified in their political views or behavior. As a result, on those public issues where race and ethnicity are critical factors, groups must coalesce if they want to advance their position.

For the above mentioned reasons, racial and ethnic relations continue to play a critical role in the governance of the city. With regard to the political system's goal of establishing and maintaining democratic accountability, the elections and the institutions of representative government have been both assisted and disrupted by the presence of racial and ethnic groupings in the city's political system. At times during the city's recent political history, the shifting patterns of racial and ethnic diversity have forced the city to reform its institutions of democratic governance. Within this changing institutional framework of governance, the leadership of racial and ethnic groups is often significant in how groups interact with the political system as well as the quality of the group's representation. The leadership of racial and ethnic groups also plays a critical role in the political system's maintenance of civil harmony. As in the cases of Crown Heights, police brutality, or environmental racism, group members look to leaders for an assessment of whether the political system's actions are fair and just. Leaders socialize members as to whether the political system is friendly or hostile and, by their own behavior, leaders educate members on how to respond.

In their book *Beyond the Melting Pot*, Glazer and Moynihan (1970) argued that the politics of race and ethnicity in New York City was nearly synonymous with class politics. Racial/ethnic politics in New York City has frequently served as a shorthand for the politics of class; however, the two factors are far from identical in how they influence the city's political system. For groups with low socioeconomic status, ethnic/racial mobilization and organization has served as a means of overcoming a lack of resources. In these cases, ethnic/racial group identity becomes an additional political resource. As the group or group members become more affluent, they find less of a need to rely on ethnic/racial group mobilization as a way to advance their demands on the political system.

While racial/ethnic politics and class politics overlap, there are also areas where they work at cross-purposes. On some occasions, the politics of race and ethnicity inhibit class politics. The groups in the Crown Heights conflict had similar socioeconomic status, yet rather than cooperate to advance their common needs in the political system, they chose to battle over turf. Similarly, during the War on Poverty, the negotiations over building the Pathmark supermarket in East Harlem, and in discussions within the Democratic Party regarding mayoral candidates, the opposing Black and Hispanic groups occupied similar socioeconomic positions. The politics of race and ethnicity preempts class politics in New York City. In some cases it may serve as surrogate for class politics, but in others it stifles coalition-building that would advance the interests of lower socioeconomic status groups. Moreover, ethnic entrepreneurs use group identity as a means to advance their own interests in the political arena. Their success in mobilizing their group behind them frequently comes at the expense of cooperation across groups.

Once described as a melting pot in reference to the evolution of individual racial and ethnic cultures, New York City is now more often described as a tossed salad, or to use former Mayor David Dinkins's term, a beautiful mosaic. It is difficult to assess the degree to which the melting pot was ever achieved in New York City. Clearly, some immigrant groups assimilated and acculturated rapidly. Second and third generations moved up the economic ladder and moved out of the ethnic enclave into more heterogeneous communities that were distinguished more by the similarities of socioeconomic status than by ethnic/racial group membership. Societal institutions including schools, churches, and the media served as engines of socialization, assisting these groups to adapt to the dominant culture. Other groups, however, were slower to assimilate. They had less success moving up the economic ladder and out of the enclave. While this inability might be attributed to ethnic/racial group decisions to develop an inward perspective, in as many if not more cases, the inability to assimilate was due to discrimination on the part of those groups who had already arrived. Simply stated, the failures of the melting pot are due to the fact that some racial/ethnic groups were not allowed into the pot until long after they arrived. As the economic and political advancement of some groups was blocked, ethnic and racial enclaves became ghettos. Even when these groups were allowed entry, the process was slow and begrudging. Following the 1997 Abner Louima police brutality incident, many Haitians, while acknowledging the achievement of middle-class status, noted that they found themselves often judged by the "triple status as immigrants, blacks and non-English speakers" (Pierre-Pierre 1997b).

The civil rights and minority empowerment movements of the 1950s, 1960s, and 1970s, along with the critique of American middle-class values that took place during the 1960s, encouraged ethnic and racial groups to reassess their rush to assimilate and acculturate. Once an ideal, the dream of the melting pot became a thing to be avoided. Groups who were once encouraged to shed their roots now were being encouraged to celebrate them. It is unclear what impact the death of the melting pot had on New York City. As a gateway city for immigrants, New York had always experienced a level of racial/ethnic diversity and identity seen in few other cities. This was supported by the city's political culture, which had traditionally sought to politically mobilize ethnic and racial groups, thereby supporting a level of ethnic identity and isolation. Some would question whether the melting pot myth was ever accepted in New York City's political culture during the period of time when it was receiving support throughout the national political culture.

6

Political Parties in
New York City Governance

Political parties structure the electoral process, the most important aspect of achieving democratic accountability in the governance of the city. Just as significant, however, the evolution of interparty as well as intraparty politics in New York City explains some of the shifts in attitudes of the political system toward issues of race and ethnicity. To a lesser extent, inter- and intraparty politics explains the city's economic development imperative as well as the city's relationship with the state and federal governments. Party politics are usually most visible just before and during election campaigns. Primary and general election campaigns become the battlegrounds where the values, or ideologies, that control the direction of the political systems are debated. What role will the political system play in the promotion of economic development? To what extent will the demands of minority groups get a positive or negative response? What role for other levels of government will the city seek? As the stewards of electoral politics, political parties have a role in the continuous debates that seek to answer these questions. Party competition or the lack of party competition may affect the quality of these debates.

New York City: A One-Party Town?

With the exception of the mayoralty, the Democratic Party has dominated electoral politics in New York City for the last several decades. Registered Democrats outnumber registered Republicans by a factor of more than four to one. For the past several decades the Democrats have occupied most of the elected positions in the city's political system. How did the party come to enjoy this advantage? In many parts of the city, the Democratic Party has had a superior organization that reaches down to the neighborhood level. In some cases this organization dates back to the nineteenth century. As a result Democrats have been and continue to be capable of responding to wave after wave of new immigrants. Throughout the twentieth century, city Democrats naturally aligned themselves with the national Democratic Party. Through President Roosevelt's New Deal, President Truman's Fair Deal, Democratic Party leadership in the civil rights movement, and President Johnson's Great Society, city Democrats took credit for and advantage of the national party's response to the demand of urban areas and particularly of urban minorities. Finally, the Democratic Party has benefited from the collapse of third parties situated to the ideological left of the Democrats at the same time that the national Republican Party was moving further to the right.

Despite its dominance the Democratic Party is far from unified. It is organized on the borough/county level, not citywide. There is no party hierarchy that spans the city. As a result, citywide party decisions, other than the party primary election, are a function of informal bargaining and compromise, not an accepted set of rules or procedures.

In some but not all of the boroughs, the party organization has been or is being challenged by reformers, or insurgents, who are seeking to wrest control from the party hierarchy, or machine. This intraparty conflict between the reformers and regulars has been waged over the last six decades. The power of the Democratic Party machine was based on a rigid organizational hierarchy highly dependent on the dispensation of patronage (e.g., jobs) to those at the bottom in return for support of those at the top. At the top of the hierarchy was the county Democratic Party leader. In part, the success of the Democratic machine in New York City was due to the continuous wave of immigrants who needed the patronage the machine had to offer. Immigrants were willing to trade political support (votes) for jobs and a modicum of social services dispensed through the Democratic Party organization. Reformers resent the closed decision-making process by which the party organization makes public decisions. In the past they opposed the material patronage base upon which the party sought and obtained support from the mass electorate. And when necessary they sought to expose the corrupt, or at the very least unethical, ways in which the party conducted the business of government that was profitable to the Democratic Party organization leaders personally and helped to keep the party in power. Reformers favored open membership of political clubs, control of leadership by the club members, complete and open disclosure of club finances, and a free and open flow of ideas and debates on current issues (Costikyan 1966, 35).

The strength of the Democratic Party political machine is its hierarchical organization at the county level, with most, if not all, significant decision-making power flowing down from the county Democratic Party leader. In the 1950s, the base of this organization was the local Democratic club. Each assembly district had at least one club that served as the headquarters of party activity in that area. Each assembly district also had one vote in the election of the county leader. Thus, whoever had control of the party organization in the assembly district also had the ability to participate in the election of the county party leaders. Assembly districts were made up of smaller electoral districts. Every assembly district had two leaders, a man and a woman, and every electoral district or precinct had a captain who reported to the district leaders. At the end of World War II, clubs were controlled by Democratic regulars. They were viewed as closed groups. Prospective members were closely scrutinized and went through a lengthy probation period before being accepted (Costikyan 1966, 23–24)

After World War II, however, returning veterans such as Ed Koch were not satisfied to remain passive until they were invited to participate in the political system via the Democratic clubs. The war had piqued their interest in politics and they resented the fact that many clubs were controlled by nonveterans (Costikyan 1966, 24). The reformers, initially labeled insurgents, began to form their own clubs and compete with indigenous "regular" party clubs for control of the assembly district organizations. Most of the early conflicts between reformers and regulars took place within the New York County (Manhattan) Democratic Party organization, otherwise known as Tammany Hall. Note that although the Democratic Party county organizations were well-run hierarchical machines, the Democratic Party at the city level was made up of five independent county/ borough organizations.

The borough organization base of the party as well as the reformer-regular split has at times been exacerbated by ethnic and racial differences, making city-wide party unity that much more difficult to achieve. In addition, at times in the city's recent history, reformers/insurgents have also adopted policy positions further to the left of the party regulars on such issues as race and economic development.

The reform movement's success in democratizing Democratic Party politics together with the increased role of the media in political campaigns significantly compromised but did not eliminate the power of Democratic county leaders. Writing on the eve of the 2001 city elections, one commentator listed the following powers of the county party leaders: endorsement by a county organization can mean help from loyalists who go into the streets and door to door to gather signatures on nominating petitions; party leaders also provide lawyers to make sure those petitions comply with all the technical rules that can trip up unsuspecting candidates; those same party lawyers also help kick unblessed challengers off the ballot in cases that are argued before judges who owe their seats to the very party organizations whose lawyers are appearing before them; picking judges remains the one power that party leaders retain virtually unchecked control over; with term limits clearing all three citywide officials and thirty-five members of the fifty-one-member city council out of office (in 2001), the party leaders can lend credibility to first-time candidates who may be veterans of party wars but little known to the public at large; and party leaders, by the weight of their endorsements, can clear the field of wannabe elected officials, who figure "stepping aside in the short run stands them in good stead for future possibilities" (Liff 2001).

In the 2001 city elections, there were several examples of candidates dropping out of the race after not receiving the endorsement of their Democratic county leader, particularly in races for borough president. At the same time, however, county leaders must build coalitions among their district leaders, which requires compromise. As the election campaign progresses, the significance of the county leader declines as endorsements by "unions and prominent pastors" become more important. These local leaders can also provide campaign workers and telephone banks to support a candidate's efforts (Liff 2001).

Republicans

The Republican Party competes in New York City with some significant disadvantages. The party is small and in parts of the city the party has little or no organization. Only on Staten Island do the Republicans have an organizational base that comes close to the Democratic Party organizations in the other four boroughs. In addition, the party has suffered from ideological differences. The more moderate wing of the party centered in Manhattan has frequently disagreed with the more conservative wing centered in the outer boroughs.

Between the 1965 election of John Lindsay and the candidacy of Rudolph Giuliani in 1989, the Republican Party had no success in electing a mayor, with the exception of Ed Koch in 1981. In the three elections between 1965 and 1981, the Republicans placed third in two of the mayoral election and in the other they placed a very distant second. Lacking any serious citywide presence, the Republican Party nominees for mayor were usually state legislative officials who had a local base, but had little citywide visibility. Unlike the Democrats, who had strong party organizations in all five boroughs, the lack of strong hierarchical borough-based organizations made it difficult for the Republicans to build an electoral base, let alone compete with the Democrats. In 1969 and 1973, their candidate was John Marchi, a state senator from Staten Island. In 1977, their candidate was State Senator Roy Goodman from Manhattan's Upper East Side. Neither Goodman nor Marchi had served in any citywide office. In those three mayoral elections leading up to 1981, the Republican candidates had received 22.8, 16.1, and 4.1 percent of the vote, respectively. And some of these votes were received on the Conservative Party line. In 1981, Ed Koch ran for mayor on both the Democratic and Republican ticket. In 1985, when Koch ran for reelection but only on the Democratic line, the Republican candidate was Diane McGrath, a virtual unknown. Similar to the Republican failures of 1969, 1973, and 1977, McGrath came in third, with less than 9 percent of the vote (Brecher and Horton 1993, 102).

Recently, however, Republican Party weaknesses reflected in their inability to win most elected positions in the city have translated into an advantage at the mayoral level when competing with the Democrats. Divided by borough-based organizations and a large number of potential candidates now exacerbated by term limits for all city elected offices, the Democratic Party has found it difficult to coalesce around a single candidate for mayor. The Republican Party, given its lack of hierarchy and few potential candidates, has been able to seek out candidates who can run a credible campaign and draw votes away from the

Democratic nominee. As a result of their lack of organization, the Republicans are not tied to candidates who arise from a decentralized, and sometimes protracted, process. Of course both Rudolph Giuliani and Michael Bloomberg were considerably more moderate than most Republicans. This made them more acceptable to many Democratic voters.

Third Parties

In the recent past, third parties have frequently joined the two-party competition in the city. The significance and decline of third party politics in New York City is best illustrated by examining the rise and fall of the Liberal Party.

The Liberal Party was born in the mid-1940s by a splinter group of American Labor Party (ALP) members who disagreed with the radical left-wing stances of the ALP in the final days of World War II. David Dubinsky of the International Ladies' Garment Workers Union and Alex Rose of the Hatters Union, founders of the Liberal Party, were concerned about communist influences within the Labor Party. Throughout the remainder of the 1940s and into the 1950s, the Liberal Party supported liberal, as opposed to socialist and communist, positions on domestic and foreign policy issues. Although the party occasionally ran their own candidates for office, more often they endorsed liberal Republicans or Democrats (Ludington 1995). They supplied the vote margin that was the difference in Robert Wagner's mayoral victories and the margin that gave New York State to John Kennedy in 1960 (Pleven 1998). To a great extent, the birth of the Liberal Party in New York State marked the beginning of the end of socialist and communist influences into mainstream New York City politics that had been present since the 1920s. It also ended any hopes of a united labor front in New York City politics. The American Labor Party, which received over 10 percent of the vote in citywide elections throughout the 1940s, was disbanded in the mid-1950s, at the height of the Cold War (Freeman 2000, 55–62; Isserman 1995).

John Lindsay's reelection in 1969 illustrates the role of third party politics in New York City. After defeating incumbent Mayor Lindsay in the Republican primary, State Senator John Marchi received only 23 percent of the vote in the general election. Moderate-conservative Democratic Party regular Mario Procacino received 35 percent of the vote while Lindsay received 42 percent. Liberal and reform Democrats had nowhere to go except to Lindsay on the Liberal Party line. Given Procacino's questionable views on race, many minorities who might have normally supported the Democratic candidate, be it regular or reformer, also shifted to Lindsay on the Liberal line (Brecher and Horton 1993, 86–91). In addition, Mayor Lindsay had been supportive of minority community control advocates in their conflict over school control with the United Federation of Teachers (UFT) in the Ocean Hill–Brownsville section of Brooklyn several years prior. During that conflict the UFT received support from Democratic Party regulars.

New York State election law encourages third party involvement by allowing smaller third parties to cross-endorse candidates. That is, parties may "nominate candidates already endorsed by other parties" (Spitzer 1994). In New York City, the ability of a third party to cross-endorse led to candidates running on "fusion tickets" where they would incorporate multiple endorsements into their campaign (Spitzer 1994). Cross-endorsing also allowed third parties to appeal to voters who were afraid of wasting their vote. Voters could vote on a third party line, if they so chose, and demonstrate their independence from the two major parties, but still vote for a candidate who had a chance of winning. With both the Lindsay and Giuliani candidacies on the Liberal Party line, the Liberal Party offered Democrats a way to vote for these men without having to vote on the Republican Party line. Assuming Democrats and members of the Liberal Party voted on the Liberal Party line and Republicans voted for Lindsay and Giuliani on the Republican line, it became easy to calculate the extent to which the Liberal Party or any third party in a fusion campaign contributed to the winner's total vote. The Liberal Party vote played a crucial role in Giuliani's two successful elections and obviously played a major role in Lindsay's 1969 victory.

There have been very few elections in the city where a third party candidate played the role of spoiler, taking votes away from the nearest major party candidate to deprive them of a victory. The Lindsay election in 1969 stands out as a very unique case as he ran only on the Liberal Party line (Spitzer 1994). While third parties can cross-endorse anyone, even individuals who are not members of their party, only members of the third party can challenge the leadership-endorsed candidate in a primary. In response to this legal predicament, a *New York Times* editorial responded, "Parties that endorse non-members should not be able to keep other non-members out of their primaries. Parties that endorse non-members should also not be rewarded with an automatic position on state ballots, while other third parties that field their own candidates have to go through the difficult process of collecting signatures. Election laws should be directed at encouraging competition, not rewarding tiny political cliques that regard their line on the election ballot as so much real estate, to be rented out to the highest bidder" (*New York Times* 1997a).

What do third parties seek in exchange for their support of major party candidates? The Liberal Party, probably the most successful of the third parties, sought and received patronage for its support of Rudolph Giuliani. Two sons of Liberal Party leader Ray Harding, as well as other Liberal Party officials, received important positions in the Giuliani administration (Chou 2000).

A second possible quid pro quo that third parties seek in cross-endorsing major party candidates is the candidate's support for some aspect of the party's ideology (Spitzer 1994). At the same time, however, it is doubtful that major party candidates will compromise their backing by the major party by acceding to the ideological demands of third parties. As a result, some third parties have become more flexible regarding their original ideology in the course of cross-endorsing candidates. This creates a dilemma for third parties, since their long-term success is due partly to their ability to stake out a position on the ideological spectrum that allows them to maintain a group, however small, of core supporters and to attract some voters from the major parties during an election. The decline of the Liberal Party may be due to its failure to maintain its ideological position on the left side of the spectrum. Once a haven for very liberal reform Democrats who would not support the Democratic Party regulars, the Liberal Party lost its liberal cache after endorsing Rudolph Giuliani in three successive elections.

In the 2001 mayoral election, the two most liberal Democratic candidates, Bronx Borough President Fernando Ferrer and Public Advocate Mark Green, did not even seek the Liberal Party nomination. The two moderate Democrats, City Council Speaker Peter Vallone and Comptroller Alan Hevesi, sought the Liberal Party nomination along with the two Republican candidates, Michael Bloomberg and former Congressman (and Democrat) Herman Badillo. Former Democratic mayor David Dinkins claimed that he would not support any Democrat who sought the endorsement of the Liberal Party (Nagourney 2001). Alan Hevesi, the recipient of the Liberal Party endorsement in the 2001 mayoral campaign, believed that the endorsement was important in his appeal to centrist "middle of the road Democrats who voted for Giuliani in recent elections" (Lentz 2001). Beginning in the 1990s, the popular joke about the Liberal Party was that it was neither liberal nor a party. It was no longer perceived as "pursuing a left of center agenda" and it no longer held primaries or conventions, having become the vehicle of one individual, Ray Harding (Kolbert 1998).

In the late 1990s, the Liberal Party was challenged by a new third party, The Working Families Party, established by several left-leaning unions (Cardwell 2001). Formed in 1998, the new statewide party was formed by a group of labor unions and community groups, seeking to bring together a coalition of poor and working-class voters around a platform promoting social justice (Chou 2000). The leaders of the party stated that they were not breaking away from the Democratic Party, rather they were concerned about "its recent drift toward a more conservative agenda" (Goodnough 1998). Similar to the Liberal Party, the Working Families Party has adopted a strategy of cross-endorsing candidates rather than running its own in order to maintain ballot access. While expressing the new party's loyalty to the Democratic Party, one official stated, "we felt it would be useful to have a force to keep the Democrats honest" (McCarthy 1998). In the 2001 mayoral election, the party endorsed Mark Green. The party also took a very active role in the 2001 city council elections. The Working Families Party endorsed twenty-nine candidates, fifteen of whom were elected. Immediately after the election, the party brought the successful candidates together with party staff and union leaders in an attempt to construct an agenda for the city council (Cardwell 2002).

Party Politics and the Politics of Race

As the city's minority population grew over the last five decades, minority leadership sought to control more of the city's elected positions with the ultimate prize being the mayoralty. With few exceptions the Democratic Party became the vehicle through which minority leaders worked to achieve this goal.

The election of Ed Koch and race relations during his three terms as mayor serve as the basis of the politics of race and ethnicity within the Democratic Party today. The 1977 Democratic Party primary for mayor was a mix of reform-regular and racial-ethnic political competition. In the wake of the fiscal crisis and with the city still under considerable fiscal/budgetary pressures, there were five strong candidates seeking the nomination including the incumbent, Abraham Beame. There were reformers (Koch, Mario Cuomo) and regulars (Beame, Percy Sutton, Badillo). No one received more than 25 percent of the vote in the September primary, forcing a runoff between the two top vote-getters, Koch and Cuomo. Mario Cuomo received the endorsement of the Liberal Party, so he would be on the November ballot regardless of the results of the runoff. Since they were both reform-minded Democrats, they were forced to decide whether to seek the support of the regular party organizations of the outer boroughs and/or to seek alliances with candidates Badillo and Sutton in order to obtain the support of Hispanic and/or Black voters, respectively. Koch met with the Democratic county leaders of the Bronx (Stanley Friedman), Queens (Donald Manes), and Brooklyn (Meade Espositio), and received the endorsement of all three county organizations (Koch 1985, 17–18). Koch also received the endorsement of Badillo and Percy Sutton's Harlem Democratic Party organization after a meeting with Harlem Congressman Charles Rangel. Koch won the primary runoff with 55 percent of the vote. The endorsements clearly paid off. Koch received a majority of the vote in the assembly districts (ADs) carried by Beame, Sutton, and Badillo in the primary. Cuomo did best in the White ethnic Catholic areas of the city (Mollenkopf 1992, 105). In the general election, Koch faced Cuomo on the Liberal Party line and State Senator Roy Goodman on the Republican Party line. Koch won with 50 percent of the vote (Brecher and Horton, 1993, 95). From the assembly districts carried by Koch in both the runoff and the general election, it appeared as though Koch won by bringing together New York City's liberal coalition comprised of minorities and reform Democrats (Mollenkopf 1992, 105–108).

Some argue that Koch's turbulent relations with minorities during his three terms as mayor was foreseen in the years before. In the early 1970s, the Lindsay administration unveiled plans to construct federally funded scattered site public housing in New York. The idea behind scattered site housing was that rather than concentrate low-income housing solely in poverty-stricken areas of the city, smaller projects would be spread throughout the entire city, including in middle-class neighborhoods. One of the areas designated for a housing project by the Lindsay administration was the middle-class Jewish neighborhood of Forest Hills, Queens. Some residents of the neighborhood, fearing the influx of low-income minorities, organized to stop the project. Even though Forest Hills was nowhere near Ed Koch's own district, but possibly anticipating a later run for mayor, Koch decided to join the fight on the side of the Forest Hills residents. Koch attended a rally in Forest Hills in which he encouraged the residents to carry on their fight with the Lindsay administration. According to Koch, "I wanted them to know they were not racists because they opposed the project" (quoted in Browne, Collins, and Goodwin 1985, 110). Koch argued further, "I firmly believed that we should not destroy our middle class communities, black or white, for any reason. They were all precious. You would find the same resistance on this issue in a black middle class area as you would in a white middle class area. People work all their lives to get out of poverty and the problems that go with it. I didn't think there was anything wrong, or contradictory about my position. It was common sense, but it really pissed off the reformers and the liberals who had been my political base until that moment" (Koch 1992, 116).

Some liberals in the city reacted harshly toward Koch's actions, and Koch himself later recognized the significance of his actions in terms of his own political career, both positive and negative (Koch 1992, 117). In another instance, during the 1977 mayoral campaign, Koch had been asked by leaders of the Black community to cease using the term "poverty pimp" in his criticism of the corruption and ineffectiveness of the community-based administration of War on Poverty programs in the city. The term specifically referred to those minority leaders who were using federal antipoverty funds to build small patronage empires in low-income communities in the Bronx. In some cases these federally funded poverty organizations were closely tied to local political clubs in minority neighborhoods (Browne, Collins and Goodwin 1985, 154–155; Koch 1984, 83).

Mayor Koch's relations with the Black community suffered a series of setbacks throughout his twelve years in office. Partly in response to the fiscal crisis and partly in response to federal regulations to curb rising health care costs, the Koch administration targeted several municipal hospitals for closing early in his administration. One was Sydenham Hospital in Harlem. Not only was Sydenham located in the middle of Harlem, but it had symbolic significance for the minority community as well. Established in 1925, for years it had been one of the few hospitals that accepted Black physicians as residents or specialists. The hospital's closing was marked by demonstrations and a sit-in that went on for several days (Koch 1984, 206–222). The fact that in the middle of these very sensitive policy decisions, an article was published by Ken Auletta in which Koch accused the Black community of being anti-Semitic, only exacerbated Koch's relationship with the minority community and with liberal New York (Koch 1984, 152).

Crime was another policy area where Koch, in his ambivalent pronouncements more than through his policies, distanced himself from the minority and liberal wing of the Democratic Party. From the outset of his campaign for mayor in 1977, Koch was an outspoken proponent of the death penalty, not a liberal position. And his pronouncements on crime and the treatment of criminals was much closer to the conservative law-and-order perspective than the typical liberal perspective that sought to treat the social and economic roots of criminal behavior. Throughout his twelve years there were a number of racially motivated crimes that, as mayor, Edward Koch could have made clear his views on race and crime. In the aftermath of each incident, however, Koch's attempts to speak for the city lacked the clarity to be perceived as attempts to engage in racial healing (Koch 1985, 227). Toward the end of Koch's twelve-year tenure, a Black youth, Yusef Hawkins, was killed in a racially motivated attack in Bensonhurst, Brooklyn. Koch's attempt to dissuade Reverend Al Sharpton from marching through Bensonhurst in protest was not well received by the minority community (Koch 1992, 231–232). No one was accusing Koch of causing these incidents, but there was considerable criticism of the mayor for not using his bully pulpit sufficiently to engage in citywide racial healing.

Mayor Koch's attitudes on race at times took on an ideological perspective. True to a neoconservative perspective on equal opportunity, Mayor Koch was an opponent of affirmative action. While Koch believed that no group should suffer discrimination, his definition of equality of opportunity disagreed with the concept of preference for groups who had suffered previous discrimination (Koch 1984, 152). This more limited concept of equality of opportunity was a core difference between neoconservatives and liberals. Koch's public pronouncements on this issue, along with his perspective on welfare and the policies of his administration with regard to the cutting of services, made him an adversary of minority groups in the city, and of the Black community in particular.

By 1981 Mayor Koch lost much of the minority support that had backed him in 1977, and the outerborough White ethnics who supported Mario Cuomo in 1977 were now backing Mayor Koch. For someone who had participated in the civil rights movement and whose Congressional voting ratings placed him in the mainstream of American liberalism, Koch was appealing to a very different constituency than who elected him in 1977. In 1981, Koch ran for reelection as mayor occupying both the Democratic and Republican Party lines. While this shift and the controversial positions he took as mayor did not appear to hurt Koch's reelection in 1981 and 1985, the cumulative effect of Koch's battles with the Black community were clearly part of his downfall in 1989.

Koch's victories in 1981 and 1985 were, in part, due to his strength as a candidate and performance as a mayor in the post–fiscal crisis environment. His victories were also due to the failure of White liberals and minorities to coalesce around a candidate. Blacks and Hispanic Democratic leaders failed to find a consensus candidate in 1981 and 1985. In 1989 they finally coalesced around Manhattan Borough President David Dinkins, who defeated Koch in a close primary and then defeated Rudolph Giuliani in a close general election. Mayor Dinkins served only one term. His administration suffered from a national as well as local recession. In addition, his administration was accused of poorly handling two separate incidents of racial turmoil in the city; one between Blacks and Hasidic Jews in Crown Heights and another between Blacks and Korean storeowners in the Bedford-Stuyvesant section of Brooklyn.

The Democratic Party coalition that elected David Dinkins has been unsuccessful in electing a mayor since 1989. In 1997 and 2001, a White liberal headed their ticket after defeating a minority in the Democratic primary. In 2005, the Democratic Party nominee was a Hispanic. Only the 2001 election was close. In both 1997 and 2005, the Democratic candidate faced very popular, well-funded Republican incumbents. Michael Bloomberg's run for reelection was not handicapped by any racially polarizing events. And in 2001, Democratic unity was marred by charges of race-baiting against Mark Green's campaign when Al Sharpton endorsed Fernando Ferrer. While Ferrer endorsed Green against Michael Bloomberg in the general election, it was clear that the Bronx County Democratic Party organization was not enthusiastic about the Green candidacy in the wake of his campaign's behavior during the primary.

With regard to Rudolph Giuliani's position on race, one might assume that as a high-ranking member of the Reagan administration Justice Department, he shared Edward Koch's views on the issue of affirmative action; however, Mayor Giuliani was far less outspoken on the issue of race than was Mayor Koch. According to Wayne Barrett, senior editor of the *Village Voice*, Rudolph Giuliani waffled on the issue of affirmative action prior to his becoming mayor. Once he became mayor, however, Giuliani discarded the previous administration's charter-mandated Affirmative Employment Plan and took almost his entire first term to replace it with a watered-down version. Moreover, according to Barrett, once he became mayor, Giuliani "pretended, as he accommodated himself to many mainstream Republican ideas, that an aversion to racially conscious hiring was a matter of ideology to him" (Barrett 2000, 225). In addition, Mayor Giuliani's views on welfare policy, his success in reforming welfare and cutting the welfare rolls in New York City placed him in a similar adversarial position with the minority community. His disagreements with the leadership of the Black community over his handling of several shootings by the New York City Police Department in minority neighborhoods, discussed in chapter five, exacerbated this relationship.

After his first election, Mayor Koch made no effort to include the Black community in the coalition for whose votes he campaigned. He assumed the Black leadership was seeking someone to run against him and that the Black voters would be mobilized to vote against him. Running against a Black incumbent twice, Rudolph Giuliani similarly assumed that seeking the support of the Black community would have little payoff at the polls. Their respective relationships with the Black community may simply be a matter of coalition-building and constituency politics. But whatever caused Mayors Giuliani and Koch to not have the support of the Black community at the polls, in retrospect, they did not need it, and as a result they made little effort to reach out to the Black community once in office. At the same time, however, the apparent neoconservatism of these two mayors cannot be dismissed as a coincidence and should be part of a broader explanation of city politics over the last several decades.

Party Politics and the Economic Development Imperative

The recent history of city politics suggests that there has been convergence in party attitudes toward the necessity of promoting economic development. Two events played a critical role in this convergence. First, the fiscal crisis of the mid-1970s forced city governing elites to think creatively about maintaining a positive fiscal flow. Second, beginning in the late 1970s, the slow but steady decline in federal aid to the city also encouraged governing elites to seek new revenue streams. Throughout the middle of the twentieth century, federal aid had funded, or at the very least subsidized, some of the city's largest economic development projects including Lincoln Center via urban renewal, the city's acquisition and maintenance of *in rem* housing via the Community Development Block Grant, and the building of Metrotech and South Street Seaport via the Urban Development Action Grant. The impact of the fiscal crisis and the decline in federal aid was exacerbated nationally by a "tax revolt" in the late 1970s and early 1980s. Either through referenda or legislative action, popular pressure to lower taxes inhibited elected officials' abilities to raise revenue by way of tax increases across the country.

Prior to the fiscal crisis, a liberal, mostly Democratic regime governed economic development decisions. Liberal economic development programs have both a developmental and redistributive component. They seek to contribute to the city's overall tax base yet also advance the city's low-income citizens. The liberal Democratic economic development agenda was also directed primarily by governing elites, not the private sector. These elected officials maintained control over economic development through public funding via tax revenues and intergovernmental assistance. The fiscal crisis of the mid-1970s was a major factor in the city turning away from these liberal roots. This change in orientation occurred simultaneously with the rise of neoconservatism and the increased attention given to the failures of the Great Society liberal social programs. Neoconservatives prefer a more market-driven, private sector approach to economic development. Unlike liberalism's approach toward economic development, neoconservatives view a more limited role for government, including tax reductions and targeted tax incentives.

Amid sagging federal intergovernmental assistance and national economic decline, the Koch administration responded to the city's sagging revenue base by promoting economic growth through tax incentives, cutting services, and increasing taxes only when necessary. The service cuts, such as the controversial closing of Sydenham Hospital in Harlem, and the corporate tax incentives were opposed by many in the New York City liberal establishment who supported Mayor Koch's initial election in 1977. Given these policy initiatives, it is not surprising that the Koch administration was seeking a new electoral base during its first term (Mollenkopf 1992).

The Koch administration made a concerted effort to keep taxes low, particularly in regards to businesses and corporations. The Koch administration sought to promote economic development in hopes that stable tax rates could produce more revenue in a growing economy. Together with a growing array of tax incentives for business, the mayor hoped to keep city businesses from moving out and to attract new businesses into the city. This aspect of Koch's tax policy is compatible with neoconservatism. Another related explanation, however, offered by John Mollenkopf (1992), is that between Koch's elections in 1977 and 1981, the core constituencies the administration courted had shifted. Corresponding with changes in the city's economy, the Koch administration sought the support of the rising real estate, financial, and corporate services sectors. According to Mollenkopf:

> The rising economic constituencies had a clear, if latent or partially expressed, agenda for city politics. The city's corporate leaders wanted city government to reduce its tax burden on the private economy, shrink its functions and employment base, reduce seemingly unchecked claims for social services, and increase services relevant to the private sector and the middle class. Real estate developers and their investment bankers and corporate lawyers wanted city government to promote private investment more aggressively through a capital program that would restore economically relevant infrastructure and through regulatory and tax incentives that would foster specific projects. (Mollenkopf 1992, 63–64)

Using political scientists Wallace Sayre and Herbert Kaufman's concepts, Brecher and Horton (1993, 77) suggest that Koch's core constituencies between 1977 and 1981 shifted from those demanding services from the city to those providing revenue to the city. The policy changes that occurred due to Koch's relationship with the financial services and real estate sectors, and the fact that these policy changes were part of a broader shift by Koch away from service demanders and toward money providers, is certainly compatible with a shift from a liberal to a neoconservative ideology.

Although the Giuliani administration inherited a city fiscal system only somewhat healthier than that inherited by Koch, the Giuliani administration quickly became the beneficiary of a period of national economic growth unequaled in recent history. In addition, by the time Mayor Giuliani took office, neoconservative approaches to economic growth and fiscal health were far more acceptable in New York City and the nation than they were in 1977. As the city's fiscal health was restored under the Giuliani administration, the mayor continued along neoconservative lines by reducing taxes, and shrinking the size of city government as a means to promote continued economic growth, partly with tax incentives.

The one area that clearly distinguishes the Koch and Giuliani administrations is taxation. This may be the result of their differing partisan roots. The Giuliani administration was able to decrease several different taxing instruments during its two terms. Mayor Giuliani believed that tax decreases would spur investment and economic growth (Giuliani 1999a). Of course, the Giuliani administration was able to take advantage of one of the longest periods of sustained economic growth in the nation's and the city's recent histories. During this period, the city realized increased tax revenues and returns on its investments while lowering taxes. For example, the Giuliani administration reduced the hotel occupancy tax but was able to realize increased revenue from the tax because of the increase in tourism in New York City (Giuliani 1999a).

Peripherally related to economic development, a second area of distinction between the tone of the Koch and Giuliani administrations was their perspective on welfare. Koch had attacked welfare programs in the city, but his attack was targeted primarily at the administration of War on Poverty categorical grant programs, not at the federal government's income maintenance program for low-income families, Aid to Families with Dependent Children (AFDC). In fact, in his 1984 State of the City Address, Mayor Koch said, "New York has always been a haven for the poor—our harbor beckoned them, our residents embraced them, our government and social agencies fed and clothed them. We have and will continue to maintain this tradition" (*New York Times* 1984). Moreover, in those years when the fiscal constraints on city revenues and spending were not as burdensome, the Koch administration made efforts to restore some of the social programs that had been cut since the fiscal crisis of the 1970s, as well as respond to growing social problems. Probably the most notable Koch administration policy in this effort was a set of programs designed to increase housing availability for low- and moderate-income New Yorkers.

In contrast to Koch, Giuliani's critique of the welfare state was far more severe. With regard to the social programs of the Great Society, Giuliani stated, "I believe that the welfare programs of the sixties and seventies, although well intentioned, were a terrible social mistake that created serious personal problems for people, for families ..." (Giuliani 1999b). At the core of Rudolph Giuliani's perspective on welfare was the belief that the jointly funded federal-state-local income maintenance program should not be an entitlement. He believed that the receipt of welfare should be temporary at best (Giuliani 1999d). Whereas liberals defined a progressive society by how it treated those in need, Rudolph Giuliani and the neoconservatives suggested that a society was progressive when "an increasing number of people are able to take care of themselves" (Giuliani 1999d). Mayor Giuliani believed that many social programs created dependency and asked nothing in return from welfare recipients, many of whom were capable of work. In accordance with neoconservative views of the growth of the state, Giuliani criticized the social welfare bureaucracy in New York City for seeking to increase the welfare rolls, making more people dependent (Giuliani 1999d). In the early 1990s, when Giuliani became mayor, approximately 1.1 million people out of a total population of 7.3 million were on welfare.

The Giuliani administration was at the forefront of the workfare movement, implementing some welfare for work requirements prior to the 1996 national welfare reform legislation that mandated workfare or job training for most welfare recipients. In the later days of the Giuliani administration, welfare offices were converted into "job centers," and welfare workers were encouraged to become employment agents for their clientele. In a related policy area, homelessness, Mayor Giuliani also disagreed with liberal perspectives. Contrary to the views of homeless advocates, the Giuliani administration adopted a policy that no one had the right to sleep on the streets, a right that homeless advocates had defended successfully in the courts. And although the Giuliani administration adhered to the state mandate that all individuals had a right to shelter, his administration added the additional requirement that all able-bodied homeless persons would have to work in exchange for shelter (Giuliani 1999c).

The one exception to the recent neoconservative mayoral succession was the four years of Mayor David Dinkins. The Dinkins administration attempted to return the city to the liberalism of the pre-Koch years. Yet Mayor Dinkins may only have been successful in returning New York City to a more liberal orientation in his rhetoric, goals, and the electoral coalition that he gathered to support his candidacy. The Dinkins term was constrained by depressed economic growth, both nationally and locally. The lack of additional city revenue and the fact that Mayor Dinkins had to address budget deficits for his four years in office prohibited his administration from successfully pursuing a more liberal policy agenda. In fact, Dinkins angered many of his supporters by pursuing an economic development agenda fueled by corporate tax incentives during the later years of his administration. Most significant, the Dinkins administration only lasted four years.

The final years of the Dinkins administration overlapped with the first years of the Clinton presidency. As discussed in chapter four, Mayor Dinkins expected that the first Democratic president in twelve years would adopt a city-friendly agenda with an infusion of federal aid. President Clinton's neoliberal policies, however, focused more on economic growth than on intergovernmental aid transfers. Programs such as Urban Empowerment Zones comprised mostly of tax incentives and little direct assistance reflected this shift in Democratic Party thinking.

Party Politics and Intergovernmental Relations

The two-party system spans all three levels of government. Given the dominance of the Democratic Party in New York City, there are differing expectations by governing elites in the city when Democratic or Republican administrations control the state and/or federal levels. The city's recent run of Republican mayors has produced some expectations regarding the city's relationship with Republican administrations in Washington as well as in Albany. As noted in chapter three, partisanship is an influential factor in the city's relationship with the state. These partisan differences at the state level are at times exacerbated by upstate-downstate differences. The Republicans dominate upstate politics and their interests are most well-represented in the State Senate, while the Democratic Party–dominated city interests are most influential in the State Assembly. Partisanship is also perceived to be an important factor at the federal level. Since Democrats dominate the city's federal congressional delegation there is an expectation that city interests will get a positive response when the Democrats control Congress. Moreover, since New York State normally gives its electoral votes to the Democratic nominee for president, and since New York City is the Democratic Party stronghold in the state, there is the expectation that the city's interests will be better served if there is a Democratic president.

Expectations that having elected officials of the same party at the state and city level will be beneficial for the city have not always been met. While Democratic governors and Democratic state legislators all claim allegiance to the same core set of values as the elected Democrats in the city, having a Democrat in the statehouse and a Democratic-controlled assembly has not always produced the optimal results for the city's interests. Democratic governors, although heavily dependent upon Democratic voters in the city, have to look to other parts of the state to complete their winning electoral coalition. Democratic support from New York City is not sufficient to elect a governor. Similarly, the expectation that a Republican governor is going to ignore city interests is equally erroneous. Governors, regardless of party affiliation, cannot totally ignore the city. There may not be enough city voters to elect a governor, but there are clearly too many city voters for a gubernatorial candidate to forget. Even within the assembly, one cannot always assume that a Democratic majority will respond to the interests of city officials. Differences between upstate and city Democrats, differences between reform and regular Democrats, and occasionally differences of race and ethnicity have inhibited the unity and resulting effectiveness of the Democratic Party in Albany. A common constituency may be a much stronger bond than partisan ties. Upon Rudolph Giuliani's election as mayor, one Democratic State Assemblyperson noted that, "the concern members have is for their constituents. They will be happy to get whatever additional state support they can, even if it makes Rudy look good" (Dao 1993).

In 2002, Republican Mayor Bloomberg endorsed and actively campaigned for Republican Governor Pataki. He was one of the principal financial backers of the governor's campaign. During the gubernatorial campaign, when city deficits for the current and coming fiscal years were looming, the mayor did not discuss the need for tax increases or state assistance until after the governor's reelection (Sargent 2003). As of early 2003, Governor Pataki had provided New York City with little assistance in dealing with its deficit and budget problems. Granted, the state was facing a much larger deficit than the city for fiscal year 2004. At the same time, however, much of what the city was seeking from the state was not direct fiscal assistance, but the authority to raise the money via taxation (e.g., the commuter tax). In his preliminary budget message and subsequent discussions, the only aid the governor was willing to offer the city was approximately one billion dollars in one-year ("one shots") fiscal assistance, as opposed to continuing assistance from some of the state's public authorities (Cooper 2003a). In addition, while the state gave the city $275 million in additional revenue in fiscal year 2003, an election year, to fund pay increases for teachers, the governor's preliminary budget for fiscal year 2004 proposed a $450 million dollar decrease in city aid (Cooper 2003b). As noted in chapter three, Mayor Bloomberg refused to openly criticize the governor.

Just as a common party affiliation between the governor and mayor has not guaranteed cordial relations, having a mayor from one party and a governor from another has not necessarily created tension from the outset. In 1940, Republican Mayor Fiorella La Guardia endorsed incumbent Democratic Governor Herbert Lehman over Republican challenger Thomas Dewey. Democratic Mayor Robert Wagner and Republican Governor Nelson Rockefeller got along so well that Wagner reported better relations with Governor Rockefeller than with Democratic Governor Averill Harriman (Benjamin 1988, 113–114).

In the 1994 gubernatorial election, Mayor Giuliani crossed party lines and endorsed Democratic incumbent Mario Cuomo in his race against Republican challenger George Pataki. There were several reasons for Giuliani's move. First, George Pataki was a supporter, if not the hand-picked candidate, of Republican Senator Alphonse D'Amato. Relations between D'Amato and Giuliani had been cordial early in their political careers and D'Amato had even supported Giuliani's appointment as U.S. Attorney. The relationship declined, however, when D'Amato attempted to intervene in an organized crime investigation being conducted by Giuliani's office (Purdum 1994). Second, there were similarities between Giuliani and Cuomo that might have brought them together. Both were perceived as mavericks within their respective parties who had not depended on machine support for their elections. Third, both Cuomo and Giuliani shared a political base. Giuliani, according to his advisors, concluded that city voters would neither be courted by George Pataki nor would they be helped by his election. Pataki's political base was upstate (Purdum 1994). Giuliani believed that Cuomo had done all he could as governor to help the city, even during a recession. Pataki's promised tax cut, on the other hand, did not portend well for state aid to the city. Therefore, both from a prospective as well as retrospective vantage point, Mayor Giuliani assessed that he had nothing to lose from endorsing Governor Cuomo.

Mayor Giuliani made no budget trip to Albany in January 1995, possibly figuring his endorsement of Governor Cuomo in the 1994 gubernatorial election would gain him little from the new Pataki administration (Sack 1995). In retrospect, even though Pataki won the election, the mayor and the city did not appear to suffer unduly as a result. Shortly after his election, Governor Pataki was instrumental in settling a dispute between the city and some upstate communities over the city's watershed. In 1996, Governor Pataki vetoed a piece of legislation that would have required the city to automatically promote sergeants or lieutenants in the New York Police Department who had served at least eighteen months as supervisors in some of the police department's bureaus. The Patrolman's Benevolent Association (PBA), the union that represents the police in New York City, had successfully navigated the legislation through the Democratically controlled assembly and the Republican-controlled senate. The Giuliani administration opposed the legislation, claiming that it would compromise the city's ability to manage its workforce, and the governor cooperated by vetoing it (*New York Times* 1996). In 1997, the governor obliged the mayor again by vetoing another piece of legislation that would have complicated the city's ability to manage the police department. This bill, also supported by the city PBA, would have eliminated the police commissioner's power to dismiss police officers and given it to an outside arbitrator (*New York Times* 1997b). In early 1998, shortly after endorsing the governor's reelection bid, Mayor Giuliani publicly recognized the governor's valuable support in vetoing those pieces of legislation that retained the Giuliani administration's ability to manage the police department. At the same press conference, Giuliani reiterated his support for the governor, noting how supportive he had been of New York City (Giuliani 1998).

Expectations on the part of the mayor for help from his party at the federal level have produced disappointment on occasion as well. As previously discussed, Mayor Dinkins expressed disappointment that the city did not receive more assistance from Democratic President Clinton and a Democratic-controlled Congress. And in 2006, Mayor Bloomberg was openly critical of the Bush administration and the Republican-controlled Congress when they cut the city's homeland security assistance by 40 percent.

There is also a link in intergovernmental legislative relations. Members of the city council, members of the state legislature, and members of Congress from the city not only share a common constituency, they frequently have their political roots in the same local party organizations. In addition it is not uncommon to find members of Congress and members of the state legislature who formerly served in the city council. This gives them an affinity for city issues and further strengthens the intergovernmental partisan connection. In 2006, five members of the New York State Senate and three members of New York City's congressional delegation were former members of the city council. The implementation of term limits in New York City's political system has put some strain on the intergovernmental linkage. The fact that the fifty-one members of the city council can only serve two four-year terms means that those with political ambitions must seek higher office. Given the limited number of higher offices, New York City's political system is producing a greater number of politicians seeking higher office after they have served their two terms in the city. In 2006, there was at least on New York State Senate race and one Congressional race in which members, or former members, of the city council were running against each other.

Conclusion

Similar to most other democratic political systems, political parties in New York City play a significant role in the governance of the city. As the institution that structures elections, parties are closely linked to the maintenance of the system's democratic accountability; but the absence of competition between the two parties in most city elections decreases their impact. In many city elections the lack of two-party competition is replaced by competitive Democratic intraparty races. The issues in these races, however, usually fail to address major issues such as race, economic development, or the role of the state and federal governments in the city's political system. Term limits have exacerbated this problem by depriving the voters of more elections where candidates run on their record as incumbents.

If New York City had a more competitive two- or multiparty system, it is possible that party politics would be a stronger factor in explaining the impact of race and ethnicity on the governance of the city. It is also possible that party politics would be more of a vehicle for how these forces affect the governance of the city. At present, the most intense party competition takes place inside the Democratic Party. The current divisions in the party are primarily based on inter-borough conflicts, or insurgents versus party regulars. Since minorities have been successful in the last two decades in achieving control of some of the borough-based party organizations and have become party regulars, the insurgent-regular split does not fall clearly along racial or ethnic lines. When it comes to electing the mayor, race and ethnicity stills play a significant role in Democratic intraparty politics, with borough-based party organizations occasionally acting as surrogates for ethnic or racial groups.

Interparty competition would be less helpful in explaining the workings or the impact of the economic development imperative on city governance because, at the national and state levels, there has been convergence among the two parties with regard to economic development strategies. The Democrats are no longer proposing that urban development be pursued through large infusions of federal money. Like their Republican opponents, they have opted for a far more private sector directed strategy, with the manipulation of land use regulations and tax incentives as the primary governmental tactics. There is little or no discernible difference on this issue across the various factions of the city's Democratic Party with the possible exception of those very liberal Democrats who do not want the political system to subsidize private development in any way. Even when there was greater party competition in the city, during the days of fusion candidates such as Mayors La Guardia and Lindsay, the liberal wing of the Republican Party was not that different than the Democrats on the issue of public sector involvement in the pursuit of economic development.

The mayoralties of Rudolph Giuliani and Michael Bloomberg have further muddled the city's politics of intergovernmental relations as it relates to partisanship at the state and federal levels. As Republican mayors, both know that they owe their election and reelection to a Democratic party base. In his 2005 reelection, Michael Bloomberg received more Democratic votes than his Democratic challenger. Mayors Giuliani and Bloomberg are both perceived as mavericks within their party, with Bloomberg's Republican credentials questioned due to his only recently changing parties. Both candidates have taken moderate, if not liberal, positions on issues where the vast majority of Republicans have adopted a more conservative stance. These issues include abortion, gun control, gay rights, and immigration. As a result, both politicians have openly opposed positions take by the governor and the president; and Mayor Giuliani went so far as to endorse a Democrat for governor. As stewards of the city, Mayors Giuliani and Bloomberg appeared willing to forsake party loyalty if the politics of their party at the state and federal levels was not perceived to be working in the city's interest.

7

The Charter, the Mayor, and the Other Guys

The City Charter

Chapter three discussed the control that the state can exercise over New York City. It discussed the concept of home rule whereby states give local governments limited authority to govern themselves. Home rule includes, in most cases, the power of the local entity to "frame, adopt and amend charters for their government and to exercise powers of local self government, subject to the constitution and general laws of the state" (Adrian and Fine 1991, 86). Charters are not constitutions. They are similar to constitutions in that they normally determine the basic structures of the government and significant processes. Similar to constitutions, charters lay out how the institutions of government function as well as the roles and responsibilities of each government official. Charters may also describe basic governmental procedures, such as how a municipal budget gets approved or how decisions are made about land use (Goodwin 1982). They do not, however, structure the rights of citizens inside the political system, as most constitutions do. This power is reserved to states and their constitutions.

New York State did not give New York City the power to define and modify its own charter until 1924 (Benjamin 1995, 208). From 1924 to 1989, New York City had a modified strong mayor–council structure of government as described in its charter. Since 1989, the New York City governmental structure has had a strong-mayor model without the modification. This model of municipal governance has several key characteristics. First, the administrative function of government is controlled by a mayor elected by the citizens of the political system. The mayor, as chief executive, is responsible for the implementation of policy. In this capacity, the mayor has the ability to appoint the heads of all administrative agencies as well as prepare the government's budget. Second, the mayor and an elected legislative body, the city council, share the law-making function. The city council in its legislative capacity is responsible for the passage of laws, but the mayor has veto power. The city council also has the power to adopt the budget once it is prepared and presented by the mayor. In what way is this a strong-mayor system?

"The mayor's legal position allows for both powerful political and administrative leadership. Not only does the mayor have the veto power and the right to recommend legislative policy to the council ... but complete control over administration also allows for constant oversight of the needs of the city as a whole and furnishes a vantage point from which to recommend policy" (Adrian and Fine 1991, 195). The strong-mayor model makes the mayor the focal point of city government. The mayor is the spokesperson for the political system and is accorded the media attention and scrutiny that accompany this role (Adrian and Fine 1991, 195).

What made the structure of city government a modified strong-mayor model prior to 1989 was the existence of the Board of Estimate. Although the structure of this body has changed over time, its establishment in 1873 was supposed to inject greater fiscal responsibility into the exercise of government (Hammack 1998). The board was given significant control over the city's fiscal decision making. In 1873, the Board was composed of the mayor, comptroller, President of the Board of Alderman, and the head of the Department of Taxes and Assessment. In 1924, the composition of the Board of Estimate included the mayor, the comptroller of the city, the President of the Board of Alderman (later the President of the City Council), and the five borough presidents (Benjamin 1995). This composition remained until the board was abolished in 1990.

No event in recent New York City political history better illustrates the impact that race and intergovernmental relations have on city public decision-making than the 1989 charter revision. In 1981, the New York Civil Liberties Union filed a suit in the Federal District Court in Brooklyn claiming that the Board of Estimate's voting system was unconstitutional because it violated the one-person-one-vote principle. Each of the five borough presidents on the board had one vote. The other three members of the board—the mayor, the city comptroller, and the president of the city council—each had two votes. The borough president vote apportionment gave the fewer than 400,000 residents of Staten Island as much clout on the board as the more than two million residents of Brooklyn. Minorities and all citizens in the boroughs other than Staten Island were being denied equal protection because of the board's voting system. If the Board of Estimate had little or no substantive power, it is possible that few would have noticed or cared about the malapportionment of votes. This was not the case. According to the city charter, the Board of Estimate had "exclusive power on behalf of the City to grant franchises or rights or make contracts providing for or involving the occupation or use of any of the streets of the city, whether on, under or over the surface thereof, for railroads, pipes or other conduits or ways or otherwise for transportation of gas, electric, steam, light, heat or power" (Kivelson 1990, 35). The board also had authority over the disposition of city land and final authority on most land use issues. Moreover, it shared budgetary approval authority with the city council. Next to the mayor, the Board of Estimate was the second most powerful governing institution in the city's political system. New York City had initially defended the existence of the Board of Estimate and its voting system by arguing that it was not a legislative body and was therefore not subject to the one-person–one-vote principle. None of the individuals on the board had been elected as legislative officials except for the president of the city council, who could vote in the council in the case of a tie by the regular members. The court's response was that the principle of one person-one-vote applied to all elected officials. The court also noted that given the functions assigned to the Board of Estimate by the charter, it was difficult to argue that the board was not acting in a legislative capacity. The case alleging the unconstitutionality of the Board of Estimate, *Board of Estimate v. Morris*, was ruled on by the U.S. Supreme Court in March 1989. Affirming the decision of the Court of Appeals, the Supreme Court ruled that the voting structure of the board was "inconsistent with the Equal Protection Clause of the Fourteenth Amendment" (Mauro and Benjamin, 1989, 53–55). A federal court responding to a suit filed in the interest of the city's minority citizens had mandated that the structure of city governance be changed.

In responding to the ruling in *Board of Estimate v. Morris*, the Charter Revision Commission appointed by Mayor Koch had to deal with a number of significant issues regarding the future of governance in New York City. First, the commission had to decide whether the Board of Estimate should be retained. The ruling in *Board of Estimate v. Morris* had not mandated the elimination of the Board of Estimate, but only its voting system. Some within the city's political system, and in particular some of the borough presidents from the larger boroughs, proposed that the Board of Estimate be retained with a different voting system that weighted the votes of the borough presidents based on population (Purdum 1989b). The commission ultimately decided to eliminate the board. While weighted voting system was considered, there were fears that it would violate the Federal Voting Rights Act due to the fact that at-large elections, such as the borough presidents, suppress the chances of minorities being elected. A second issue the commission had to grapple with was how to reallocate the powers that had previously belonged to the Board of Estimate. As previously noted, the board's powers were considerable. The two likely recipients of board powers were the mayor and the city council. The commission sought to strike a balance of power between these two institutions. They did not want to give the mayor too much power for fear of his running roughshod over the other institutions of city governance. Yet at the same time, the commission did not want to give the city council too much power for fear of promoting gridlock, via the council's ability to frustrate the mayor's agenda.

A third issue facing the commission was how to enhance the participation of minorities in the city's governing structures through charter revision. The litigation that resulted in the court mandate for charter revision was initiated by those claiming that the city's governing structures had been biased against minority representation and participation. Interestingly, at the time of the board's elimination, it had two minority members, David Dinkins, the Borough President of Manhattan, and Fernando Ferrer, the Borough President of the Bronx. Despite the court ruling in the *Morris* decision, Dinkins believed the Board of Estimate could effectively represent minority interests (Purdum 1989a). Much of the commission's discussion of this issue focused on expanding the size of the city council so that more minority legislators could be elected. A fourth and related issue was procedural. Once the commission had constructed a set of proposals for charter revision, the proposals had to be approved not only by the voters of New York City, but also by the U.S. Justice Department. The federal Voting Rights Act mandated that any modification of legislative or election procedures in New York City would have to be scrutinized by the Justice Department to certify that they were not discriminatory.

The final recommendations of the 1989 Charter Revision Commission included:

- the elimination of the Board of Estimate;
- a city council expanded in size from thirty-five to fifty-one members (with no at-large members);
- the city council has power over the municipal budget, proposed by the mayor, and authority over zoning, land use, and franchises;
- a new City Planning Commission has the power to recommend zoning changes, make decision on the use of city owned land, and grant special land use permits (zoning variances);
- the mayor will appoint seven of the thirteen members of the City Planning Commission, with the city council president (now Public Advocate) and the five borough presidents each appointing one member;
- borough presidents will have the power to propose capital improvements equal to 5 percent of the city's capital budget;
- the city council president, now Public Advocate, will serve as a municipal watchdog or ombudsman, responding to complaints by citizens and making sure that executive branch agencies supply the public with information as requested;
- a new Independent Budget Office will be established to evaluate the mayor's budget proposals and revenue estimates;
- the mayor, through the executive branch, has the power to approve contracts, subject to guidelines set by a board appointed by the mayor and the comptroller. (Benjamin 1995, 207; Finder 1989c; Purdum 1989c)

On November 7, 1989, New York City voters went to the polls and approved the proposed charter revisions by a margin of 55 to 45 percent (Finder 1989d). On the same day, city voters narrowly voted for David Dinkins over Rudolph Giuliani in the mayoral election. The U.S. Justice Department approved the charter revisions approximately five weeks later, noting that each of the major changes in the structure of New York City's government would not reduce the voting power of minorities (Finder 1989e). Although the minority community in New York City was split over the charter revisions, most saw the changes as positive, particularly the expanded city council that would allow for greater minority representation. Neighborhood advocates however were hopeful that the expanded city council would represent the local constituencies in making land use decisions (Lueck 1989). Clearly the biggest losers in the charter revision were the borough presidents and the president of the city council, now called the public advocate. They had lost much of their power within city government when they lost their votes on the Board of Estimate, and the new charter changes had not come close to making up for this loss. The office of the city comptroller also lost its votes on the Board of Estimate, but it did retain its ability to perform financial and performance audits on city agencies.

After the 1989 city charter revision, the only other significant charter reform was the 1993 adoption of term limits for all city elected offices (chapter eight). Mayor Giuliani attempted charter reform several times during his two terms as mayor. On one occasion, he successfully used a minor revision of the charter to keep off the ballot a city council–sponsored referendum on city funding of a proposed new Yankee Stadium on Manhattan's Far West Side. On other occasions, he attempted either to abolish the position of public advocate, or at least limit the public advocate's ability to succeed the mayor in office, should the mayor have to resign. On many of these attempts, Mayor Giuliani was criticized for making the charter revision process an overly partisan activity (Goodnough 1999; Schwarz 1998). During his first term as mayor, Michael Bloomberg attempt to institute nonpartisan elections for all city elected offices through the charter revision process. This attempt failed.

The Mayor

On September 11, 2001, upon hearing that a plane had crashed into the World Trade Center, Mayor Rudolph Giuliani and his aides headed for the scene of the disaster; that was his custom as mayor. He was at the scene when the second plane hit. The New York City Office of Emergency Management center located in 7 World Trade Center was evacuated since it was too close to the site. In the early hours after the collapse of the World Trade Center towers, the mayor and his staff attempted, amid the chaos of Lower Manhattan, to set up a new emergency command center in the vicinity. The mayor established three goals: "First, I had to communicate with the public, to do whatever I could to calm people down and contribute to an orderly and safe evacuation (of lower Manhattan). Second, I wanted to prepare for the injured. . . . The third track I was considering was, 'What will happen next?'" (Giuliani 2002, 16–17).

The mayor spoke to the governor and the White House, and by late afternoon, a make-shift command center had been set up at New York City's Police

Academy (Giuliani 2002). In the days and hours that followed the attack, Mayor Giuliani was the most visible public figure. In the words of one reporter, "he seems to realize that New Yorkers need a symbol of stability, need to know someone is in control when everything is out of control" (Purnick 2001). What enabled the mayor to so successfully lead New York in the weeks following the attack on the World Trade Center? And what was it about the mayor's leadership that resulted in the response it received by New Yorkers and those all over the country?

What made the mayor so visible in the days following the attack was the fact that he was performing multiple roles. As chief executive, he directed and monitored the cleanup of the site as well as looking after the continued safety and security of the city. As chief spokesperson for the city, he led the city and the nation in mourning for those lives lost and in comforting the victims' families (Steinhauer 2001a). After reports that some New Yorkers of Arab descent had been harassed, the mayor admonished those who engaged in acts of hatred (Purnick 2001). As the city's biggest advocate, the mayor urged New Yorkers, amid the mourning and fear, to try and be more optimistic and to try and return to normal (*New York Times* 2001; Steinhauer 2001c). Throughout all of this, the mayor maintained daily meetings with his staff to address the orderly running of the city, held daily press conferences to communicate with the public through the media about progress being made at the site, and met with state, federal, and foreign dignitaries who wanted to assist the city or simply pay their respects. Even some of his harshest critics had high praise for the mayor. "A Giuliani the city had never seen before surfaced at just the right time. He had the requisite air of command, but also the sensitivity and even gentleness that was so necessary for such a tragic and frightening sequence of events. There was, if such a thing is possible, a kind of awkward grace that he exhibited that was perfect for the moment" (Herbert 2001a).

In part, what made Mayor Giuliani so effective in the days following the attack was not only the multiple roles that he was playing, but also the fact that the public recognized that the mayor had played many of these roles prior to the crisis; maybe not all at once, and maybe not in as intense and crisis-ridden a situation as September 11, 2001. Moreover, he brought the same personal style to these roles that he had previously. As one reporter noted, "Mr. Giuliani's flaws are some of the same qualities that make him so attractive in a crisis: confidence, authority, intransigence" (Tierncy 2001). He brought the same confidence, resolve, and administrative style to September 11 and its aftermath as he had to his desire to dismantle the Board of Education or his monitoring of city art exhibits (Steinhauer 2001b). In the weeks following September 11, Mayor Giuliani was involved in popularly supported attempts to suspend term limits so he could run for a third term, or at the very least extend his term several months to ease the transition to a new mayor. Both attempts failed and to an extent brought back some of the criticism that had been leveled at the mayor prior to

September 11 (Herbert 2001b). Nevertheless, because of his actions on September 11 and in the days and weeks following, Mayor Giuliani left office a considerably more popular mayor than he had been prior to September 11.

Mayoral Roles

As the Constitution of the United States lays out the formal and official roles for the president, the New York City Charter lays out the formal and official roles for the mayor. Similar to the president, however, the mayor of New York City has over time acquired additional, more informal roles not specifically discussed in the charter that enhance the mayor's power and authority. The combination and conjunction of the various roles of the mayor, both formal and informal, give his office considerably more power than any other office in the city's political system.

The city charter establishes two formal roles for the mayor. These roles result from the charter's establishment of a strong-mayor form of municipal government. One primary aspect of this governmental structure is that the mayor is popularly elected, as opposed to being selected from among the members of the city council or from among a number of city commissioners. The fact that the mayor is popularly elected makes him the de facto head of the city's political system. The city charter does not discuss a chief of state or a ceremonial head of state, but in New York City's strong-mayor structure, the mayor fulfills that role. The mayor is the spokesperson for the city at a wide variety of events. Mayors or their surrogates represent the city when the city needs representation. Many of Mayor Giuliani's activities in the aftermath of September 11, such as funerals or briefings to foreign dignitaries, were fulfilling this role. Less than a month after September 11, Mayor Giuliani was invited to speak before the General Assembly of the United Nations. He did so as the city's chief of state. Several days later, the mayor rejected a ten million dollar gift to the city from a Saudi prince who had previously criticized U.S. policy in the Middle East (Steinhauer 2001c). Here again, the mayor was acting as the city's chief of state.

A second role given to the mayor by the city charter, and another requisite part of the strong-mayor governmental structure, is chief executive. The mayor directs the executive branch of the city government. The mayor is the chief administrative officer of the city. He directs and monitors the entire city bureaucracy and is responsible for the implementation and execution of city laws and programs (chapter nine). There are a number of significant powers that accompany this role. The mayor has the power to appoint and remove the heads of all city executive branch agencies. Unlike the President of the United States, who needs approval of the U.S. Senate for cabinet appointments, the mayor does not need city council approval for most of his executive branch appointments. To control the activities of the entire executive branch, the mayor needs the support of a large staff. For this purpose the charter creates an Office of Operations to assist the mayor in his duties as chief executive. The mayor also has the ability to appoint deputy mayors who assist in directing the activities of the executive branch. Unless the city council disapproves within ninety days, the mayor has the ability to reorganize the executive branch, transferring functions from one agency to another or effectively eliminating and/or establishing new agencies (New York City Charter, Chapter 1 2004). Under Mayor Giuliani, when the Child Welfare Administration, an agency in the Department of Human Resources, was experiencing difficulty monitoring child abuse activities, the mayor removed the Child Welfare Administration from the Human Resources Department. He gave the agency a new name (the Administration for Children's Services) and appointed a new commissioner in an attempt to restructure and improve the agency's performance.

As chief executive, the mayor has the responsibility to propose a budget for the executive branch for each fiscal year. The budget, however, must be approved by the city council. The mayor can use his budgetary authority to punish poor-performing agencies, reward effective ones, or simply change the policy direction of city government by giving some programs or agencies more money and others less. In 1989, the new charter gave the mayor an additional power, the approval of contracts, which further enhances his power as chief executive (New York City Charter, Chapter 1 2004).

One area in which the chief of state role and the chief executive role complement each other is when the mayor lobbies on behalf of the city at other levels of government. Even before his inauguration, Mayor Bloomberg visited Washington for the purpose of lobbying the Bush administration for additional federal aid in the wake of the events of September 11 (Steinhauer 2001b). As chief executive, the mayor can speak for how the city spends the revenue it receives. He has a staff who can gather and analyze information on the impact that additional or less revenue will have on the operations of the city. And as chief of state, the mayor is a citywide elected official who can claim to speak for (i.e., represent) the entire city. No other official combines these two roles.

In addition to the official roles given to the mayor by the charter, there are unofficial, or less formal, roles played by the mayor that enhance the power of the office. One such role is chief legislator (Pohlman 1993, 235). As the functions of government have become more diverse and more complex, the mayor, in his responsibility as chief executive, controls a large bureaucracy that is increasing in size, diversity, and expertise. These bureaucrats not only implement policy and administer the law, but they also have the ability to report back to the mayor through appointed agency heads or through mayoral staff about problems occurring throughout the city. While the mayor does not have a monopoly of information about problems occurring in the city, he certainly has better access to information regarding emerging problems through the bureaucracy or his staff than any other actor in the political system. As a result there is an expectation among those in the political system, including those in the city council, that the mayor will help set the city's legislative agenda. The city charter facilitates this role in a number of ways. It requires the mayor to communicate to the council at least once a year on the state of the city (New York City Charter, Chapter 1 2004). This provides the mayor with an excellent venue to set his priorities for the coming year. The budgetary process is another activity through which the mayor can influence legislation. The mayor's power to veto legislation, as stated in the charter, is another way in which the mayor can influence legislation. Of course, the council can always override a mayoral veto with a two-thirds majority vote.

Another unofficial role for the mayor is opinion leader (Pohlman 1993, 239). As spokesperson for the city, citizens look to the mayor to respond to problems or public concerns. In his position, the mayor can pick and choose which public concerns to address and which to ignore. Given the mayor's visibility and resources, however, he does not have to wait until an issue arises before it is addressed. Throughout their terms in office, both Mayors Giuliani and Bloomberg held press conferences four or five times a week. In addition, they both had their own radio shows that aired approximately once a week. This gave them the ability to address the public on any topic of their choosing. According to Mayor Giuliani, "one of the great advantages of being New York City mayor was that I could communicate directly. Because it was such a visible job, I didn't have to be a slave to press coverage. A leader who cannot access the airwaves or draw people to a meeting risks having the media shape the public's impression of him. Someone with as high a profile as the mayor of a big city can create his own impressions, and can ensure that the press becomes just another element that factors into decisions" (quoted in Giuliani 2002, 188).

The literature on the presidency speaks of a "bully pulpit" that presidents can command to take on any issue or problem because of his status, visibility, and the media attention he receives. Within New York City's political system, and possibly beyond, the mayor is in a similar position. The mayor has the ability to define problems as being worthy of public/mayoral attention merely by informing the citizens of the city that the problem, in his or her view, exists. Throughout his two terms, Mayor Giuliani used his bully pulpit frequently to criticize New York City's Board of Education and the educational bureaucracy, in the hopes that his criticism would be a catalyst for reform and reorganization of public education in the city. In 1999 and again in 2001, Mayor Giuliani brought to public attention art exhibits at the Brooklyn Museum of Art that he found offensive. In 1999, the mayor followed up his public indignation with an unsuccessful attempt to cut public funding from the Brooklyn Museum of Art (Barstow 2000). The 2001 incident resulted in the mayor forming a decency panel to review art exhibits in publicly financed museums (Bumiller 2001). The mayor's role as opinion leader gives him a great deal of influence on the maintenance of civil harmony, as evidenced by both Mayor Koch's and Mayor Giuliani's statements following incidents involving racial bias.

Political scientist Marcus Polhlman suggests that an additional unofficial role for the mayor might be as leader of his/her political party (Pohlman 1993, 240).

While this might be a role that the mayors of some large cities play, it does not appear to be accurate in the case of New York City. As discussed in chapter six, the Democratic Party in New York City is decentralized to the borough/county level. The mayor may be a product of one county's Democratic Party organization, as was the case with Abe Beam (Brooklyn) and David Dinkins (Manhattan), but their election as mayor in no way makes them the leader of the other county organizations. And although Edward Koch was from Manhattan, the maverick style he exhibited throughout his political career suggested that he may not have even been a product of, let alone a leader in, Democratic Party politics in the city. Democratic Party county organizations, or those organizations below the county level, support candidates for mayor and expect benefits in return. They are not looking for, nor would they in most cases accept, party leadership from a mayor, especially one from a different county organization. At best, Democratic mayors are brokers between organizations. The Republican mayors of the city illustrate even better than the Democrats the inability of the mayor to play a party leadership role. John Lindsay, who was active in the city's Republican Party prior to becoming mayor, lost the Republican primary as an incumbent and ended up winning a second term running on the Liberal Party line. Even while Lindsay was an active and loyal Republican, his leadership was being challenged by the more conservative wing of the party and by Governor Rockefeller. Rudolph Giuliani, a former appointee in the Reagan administration, had little or no experience in New York City Republican Party activities prior to his first run for mayor. Even during his administration, his relationship with the New York City Republican Party was minimal. And Michael Bloomberg was a Democrat up to approximately one year before being elected mayor on the Republican Party line. Recently, in order to win the mayoralty, the Republican Party has had to look beyond its own organization to someone who could attract a sufficient number of non-Republican voters to win an election. This individual will be the mayor, but he/she will not be a leader within the party.

Mayoral Behavior as a Function of Economic Development Needs, Race and Ethnicity, and Intergovernmental Relations

It is the primary thesis of this book that the city's political system and the public policy decisions it produces are constrained and/or significantly influenced by the need to engage in economic development activities, racial and ethnic diversity, and the influence of the state and federal levels of government on the city. As the most important single actor in the governance of the city, the mayor is affected by these forces more than any other official. In addition, the tensions created by the simultaneous influence of the forces should be most discernible through the behavior of the mayor.

Remove the external forces that influence mayoral decision making and one will find that most mayors are driven by several rather simplistic goals. First, once in office, they want to be reelected. For the last fifty years, there has not been an individual who served as mayor of New York City who did not seek a second term in office and occasionally a third or fourth. In addition to reelection, some mayors have sought other elected offices including president, governor, and senator, after serving as mayor, although recently none have been successful in obtaining these other offices. A second goal of most mayors is to maintain a level of popularity among the citizenry. A mayor's level of popularity is usually obtained through one of several polls that include questions regarding the mayor's performance or more simple questions gauging popularity. Mayor Koch used to ask people, "How'm I doing?" There is a strong relationship between a mayor's popularity and being reelected, but popularity or performance in office is measured far more frequently than elections occur. Third, and much less immediate, mayors want to be remembered as effective and decent leaders long after they have left office. They want to leave a legacy that will be remembered as positive and valuable for the city. This may include a specific policy or program agenda.

ECONOMIC DEVELOPMENT. How much credit can a mayor take for economic development that occurs in the city and for the city's overall fiscal health? National economic conditions significantly influence how successful a mayor can be in promoting economic development, but these conditions do not leave the mayor helpless. Mayors can take advantage of healthy national economies by enacting policies that further enhance growth and development, or they can enact policies that inhibit local growth despite national economic health. Of course, it is always difficult to factor out national economic conditions from local policy in assessing how much credit or blame the mayor should take for the city's economic development track record.

In the opinion of many, given the set of economic circumstances that was presented to the Giuliani administration in the mid-1990s, Mayor Giuliani was able to enact a set of complementary policies and programs that enhanced the city's ability to take advantage of national economic growth. These programs included tax decreases that promoted tourism and decreased taxes on businesses, targeted tax breaks to corporations, as well as law enforcement policies that decreased the city's crime rate much faster than the national average and consequently made the city a more attractive place to visit and to conduct business activity (Bagli 2001). The result was economic development and job growth in the city. A good example of the confluence of national economic health and mayoral policies combining to produce economic development is tourism during the Giuliani administration. According to Mayor Giuliani, "In the year before the hotel occupancy tax was cut, the city received $127 million in hotel tax revenue. This year [1997] the City is projected to receive $172 million in tax revenue, clearly showing how a reduction of this tax has been good for the city as well as good for business. Between 1994 and 1996, we gained almost 21,000 jobs in the tourism and restaurant industries" (Giuliani 1997).

Mayor Giuliani took credit for the increase in tourism in New York City, as he should. In the speech cited above, he neglected to mention that his law enforcement policies also played a significant role in attracting tourists to the city, given the reduced rates of crimes. Neither, however, did he mention the role that national economic growth had played in the city's own economic health and the growth of tourism nation-wide. In contrast to the Giuliani administration, Mayor Dinkins presided over one of the city's weakest economies. Prior to Dinkins's term, from 1980 through 1988, the city experienced an average annual revenue growth of 9.8 percent. In fiscal year 1989, his first year in office, the rate of growth was 2 percent (Purdum 1990a).

The mayor has significant influence over zoning and land use, and the overall shape of the budget including capital spending, taxation, and which business will receive targeted subsidies. Given that the mayor's performance in office will be measured in part by the economic health of the city, the mayor must act to promote economic development. Regardless of whether the actions taken produce positive results, he is expected to take affirmative steps to promote economic development. The appearance of inaction may be worse than action taken that produces few results. As long as the mayor is doing something to promote economic development, he may be able to justify poor results by citing other forces beyond his control that influence the city's economic health.

When Mayor Dinkins took office, there were very low expectations on the part of the business community as to what his administration would do to promote economic development. Some perceived the attitude of the Dinkins administration to be anti-business and anti-development (Lipper 1989). Initially, the Dinkins administration did little to assuage these concerns. An interview with Mayor Dinkins' Deputy Mayor for Economic Development, Sally Hernandez-Pinero, prior to the mayor's inauguration, made clear that the city could no longer afford the kind of targeted tax incentives that the Koch administration employed (Berkowitz 1989). When Hernandez-Pinero resigned midway through Mayor Dinkins' first term, the mayor appointed Barry Sullivan, a career banker and retired chairman of the First Chicago Corporation. Many took this as a sign that the Dinkins administration was seeking greater cooperation with the corporate community (New York Times 1992). The Dinkins administration employed tax incentives, personal attempts by the mayor to entice businesses to move to New York from other cities, and even the appointment of an individual from the financial community as deputy mayor in order to instill more confidence in the city government on the part of developers and investors. Despite these attempts, the city continued to lose jobs and experience budget crises. Yet the attempts by the Dinkins administration to create economic growth allowed it to deflect some of the failure on other forces: the sluggish national and regional economy as well as insufficient intergovernmental assistance.

There are several ways in which economic development and the desire of political systems to promote it influences mayoral decision making. First, the city's economic performance has become a major political issue with which mayors must contend. The primary way that this performance is gauged is through job creation and job loss, particularly private sector jobs. Although mayors throughout the history of the city have used economic development as a way to measure their success, this has normally been accomplished by pointing to specific projects for which they could take credit: a bridge, a subway, better roads. Up until the 1960s, most in the political system assumed that new jobs would be created as the city expanded and the population increased. When manufacturing jobs began to leave the city and it began to experience a decline in total employment, job creation became a significant political issue. Recently, mayors have taken credit for job growth that occurs during their administration whether they were responsible for it or not. Their opponents, in turn, have attempted to blame them for any job loss. Public sector job creation, on the other hand, has not been viewed as an integral part of economic development in the city. Some have viewed increased public sector employment as an inhibitor or deterrent to private sector economic development since funds being spent on more or better-paid public bureaucrats cannot be spent on economic development activities or tax decreases. In fact, some recent mayors have publicized and taken pride in their decreasing the size of the public sector.

Another measure of the economic health of the city is done through the bond rating agencies. Bond ratings are not as clear an indication to the public of the economic health of the city. Yet those in the city government and the investment industry believe that bond ratings have more to do with the performance of the mayor and his administration than the number of jobs the city losses or gains in a year. Corporations such as Standard and Poor and Moody produce assessments of the city's ability to manage debt. The ratings of these corporations significantly affect the city's ability to borrow money to finance capital spending.

Cities with lower rated bonds frequently must offer investors higher interest rates on their debt. New York City bonds had a below investment grade rating from 1975 to 1981. When the rating was raised, the Koch administration claimed responsibility for this sign of the city's fiscal health (Haberman 1981). Some economists took issue with Mayor Koch's claim by arguing that the national economy had begun to turn around the year before Koch took office and that high rates of inflation had given the city unexpected additional revenue through its sales and income taxes. In 1995, when Standard and Poor lowered the city's ration from an A− to a BBB+, Mayor Giuliani publicly criticized Standard and Poor for not recognizing that his administration had decreased the municipal workforce and decreased the city's budget. The mayor also argued that the rating downgrade was not fair because Standard and Poor had not downgraded the city's bond rating while Mayor Dinkins was in office (Gasparino and Perez-Rivas 1995). In 2003, Standard and Poor gave city bonds an A rating, and raised "the city's bond rating outlook to stable from negative" (Saul 2003). In response to this, a Bloomberg administration official stated that the administration was grateful that Standard and Poor had "recognized the extraordinary efforts the mayor had made guiding the city through its fiscal crisis" (quoted in Saul 2003).

As discussed in chapter two, one of the most visible mayoral activities in pursuit of economic development is the targeted tax incentive. As previously noted, this economic development tool is employed primarily to keep corporations from leaving the city. The Giuliani targeted tax incentive program was not much different from the Koch and Dinkins programs, although Mayor Giuliani promulgated more tax incentive deals than either of the two previous mayors. The Giuliani administration claimed that its tax incentive packages cost the city less and that the deals were connected to job growth, not job retention (Bagli 1997). This concept of linking additional tax incentives to job growth began during the Dinkins administration (Deutsch 1993). In another high visibility act, Mayor Dinkins traveled to Atlanta and Europe to woo businesses to move to New York, just as Mayor Koch had gone to Chicago for the same purpose (Dugas 1992; Marinaccio 1990). As noted in an earlier chapter, the Bloomberg administration has not used the targeted firm-specific tax incentive as much as the Giuliani administration.

The mayor has no control over global, national, or even regional economic forces. Nor does the mayor have any influence over the national government's response to shifting economic trends or forces, short of lobbying the federal level for desired policy changes. On these issues, the mayor is merely one of hundreds or thousands of officials and groups seeking to influence the direction of U.S. economic and fiscal policy. Given their insignificance in this process, most mayors rarely make a concerted effort to influence federal policy in this area.

One very unique way that the national and global economies affect the city and the economic development decisions of the mayor is through the city's relationship with Wall Street and the investments industries. In 1987, the securities industries accounted for 12.8 percent of the city's private sector revenue. By the late 1990s, this figure had increased to almost 18 percent (Johnson 1997). And while the securities industries only comprise about 5 percent of the city's labor force, there are many other workers in the city, "accountants, office cleaners, lawyers, printers, caterers, limousine drivers, computer technicians, and temporary workers," all of whom depend on the health of Wall Street (Eaton 1998). As a result of the importance of the securities industries to the city as a source of employment and tax revenue, when the stock market is strong, the city and metropolitan area benefit more than other parts of the country. When the market is weak and declining, the city is more adversely affected. In October 1987, the stock market collapsed, dropping 20 percent of its value in a single day. The layoffs in the investments industries plus the reduced salaries and end of year bonuses forced the Koch administration to significantly lower its tax revenue expectations for the current fiscal year (Lueck 1987). Mayor Koch responded immediately by ordering a ninety-day freeze on city hiring in order to restrain city government growth in the face of decreased revenue projections (Purnick 1987). For much of the Giuliani administration, the opposite phenomenon occurred. At the beginning of the bull market of the mid-1990s, the Giuliani administration underestimated the tax revenues emanating from Wall Street's performance. It could not foresee Wall Street's contribution to the city's personal income tax or corporate business tax revenues (Levy 1996b). Throughout the late 1990s, the Giuliani administration established a practice of underestimating Wall Street performance so as not to overestimate city tax revenues. In 2000, as the market began to level off and decline, city revenue from Wall Street declined (Eaton 2001).

RACIAL AND ETHNIC DIVERSITY. As the leader of the political system, the mayor is influenced by the political significance attached to race and ethnicity. In addition, the mayor has an important impact on racial and ethnic relationships in the city through the multiple roles that the office includes.

Mayoral elections provide one of the most significant means by which race and ethnicity influence mayoral decision making. In New York City mayoral elections, candidates seek to build a coalition of voters sufficient to win the election. To a great extent, the blocks of voters that make up the coalition are defined by their race and/or ethnicity. Mayoral candidates construct a strategy to put together a winning coalition by focusing on issues that appeal to specific groups, by campaigning with and being endorsed by racial and ethnic group leaders, and by focusing their campaign on certain neighborhoods and parts of the city. Candidates seek to mobilize blocks of favorable voters who will show up at the polls. The racial and ethnic identity of the candidate may also be a crucial element in constructing a winning coalition. In 1977, Ed Koch became mayor by putting together a broad coalition of Democratic regulars, minorities, and White liberals. In the Democratic primary runoff and the general election, the only ethnic group of New Yorkers he did not carry was White Catholics (Arian et al. 1991, 25–27). He received the endorsement of former congressman and mayoral candidate Herman Badillo, which helped him with Hispanic voters. Badillo later became a deputy mayor under Koch. He also received the support of a majority of New York's Black leadership as a result of a meeting with Congressman Charles Rangel. In the meeting, he agreed to appoint minorities to his administration and to stop using racially charged language such as "poverty pimp" to describe some of the leadership of the War on Poverty program in the city, which was primarily minority run (Arian et al. 1991, 24). The 1977 winning coalition that was based in part on Koch's liberal record yet conservative mayoral campaign only lasted one term. By 1981, he did not receive the endorsement of any of the minority leaders from the Black and Hispanic communities he had received four years earlier. His spending policies on social programs, service cuts, and his courting of the city's financial community to the exclusion of minority groups damaged his relationships with minorities in the city. At the same time, the groups who did not support him in 1977, outerborough White ethnics and particularly White Catholics, supported him in 1981 (Mollenkopf 1994, 4–10). They saw him as a moderate to conservative mayor seeking to put the city back on sound financial footing. According to political scientist John Mollenkopf, the latter Koch coalition "centered among white, ethnic, middle class voters, augmented by support from the more conservative, property owning elements of the black population and from the poor but more conservative Latino population" (Mollenkopf 1994, 4).

The tenor of the Koch administration was conservative enough that he received the Republican nomination for mayor in 1981. And although he did not receive the GOP nomination for mayor in 1985, the Republican Party could not find a competitive candidate to run against Mayor Koch. Both in 1981 and 1985, White liberals and minorities sought to unseat him in the Democratic primary but could not coalesce around a candidate.

In 1989, Manhattan Borough President David Dinkins beat Mayor Koch in the Democratic primary for mayor, defeating him by over eight percentage points. Corruption in the Koch administration that was uncovered during his third term and a recession were factors in voters seeking a change. The principal reasons, however, for the Koch loss were racial. First, the Jesse Jackson presidential candidacy in 1988 had mobilized minority voters in higher numbers than they ever had. In the 1988 Democratic Party primary, Jesse Jackson carried New York City with a plurality of the vote, defeating Governor Michael Dukakis and Senator Al Gore (Arian et al. 1991, 50). During the primary, Mayor Koch endorsed Al Gore, who came in third out of three; but more importantly, he was openly critical of Jesse Jackson for making some apparent anti-Semitic comments, for accepting the endorsement of Black radical Louis Farrahkhan, and for supporting Palestine Liberation Organization leader Yasir Arafat (Arian et al. 1991, 44; Mollenkopf 1994, 172–173). The extent to which Mayor Koch criticized Jackson angered New York's minority community. Second, several weeks before the Democratic primary, a black youth, Yusef Hawkins, was surrounded, shot and killed by a group of Whites in Bensonhurst, Brooklyn. The incident itself and Mayor Koch's handling of it served to underscore the degree of racial tension in the city and the level of dissatisfaction with the mayor's handling of racial issues (Mollenkopf 1994, 178).

In the 1989 general election, David Dinkins beat Rudolph Giuliani in a very close race. Dinkins had less than a 50,000-vote margin out of 1.8 million votes cast (Arian et al. 1991, 94). He received 97 percent of the Black vote and 71 percent of the Hispanic vote but only 31 percent of the White vote (Guttenplan 1989). In their analysis of the 1989 mayoral election, Arian et al. (1991) concluded that race played a major role in his narrow margin of victory. While few voters said that they voted for Giuliani because Dinkins was Black, Arian et al. encountered an attitude among 39 percent of the electorate that they labeled "racial anxiety—mistrust of what the other fellow will do" (Arian et al. 1991, 113). In addition, Arian et al. (1991) identified a number of "racially correlated agenda items," policy issues on which Blacks and Hispanics differed from Whites. These issues included homelessness, housing, education, crime, and corruption (Arian et al. 1991, 112–113). They also concluded that Rudolph Giuliani's defeat in 1989 was in part due to the fact that the Giuliani campaign had viewed Black and Hispanic voters similarly when in fact Hispanic voters are a far more politically diverse group. In 1989, Hispanics were twice as likely than Blacks to vote for a Republican candidate (Arian et al. 1991, 117). The Giuliani campaign did not make this mistake in 1993. Moreover, although David Dinkins received 65 percent of the Hispanic vote in the 1989 election, midway through his term, his popularity among Hispanic voters began to fall. Mayor Dinkins himself noted that there was a perception that he had not done enough for the Hispanic community, even though he disputed the accuracy of the perception. In 1992, approximately a year before the mayoral election, Mayor Dinkins began meeting with the Hispanic members of the city council on a regular basis. He also supported the creation of a second congressional district where there would be a high probability of electing a Hispanic. Rudolph Giuliani also supported this measure (Finder 1992).

In 1993, Giuliani beat incumbent Dinkins by a similarly narrow margin that Dinkins received in defeating Giuliani in 1989. One significant factor in the Dinkins defeat was his two most supportive constituencies, Black and Hispanic voters, not showing up at the polls as strongly as they had in 1989. There was no Black presidential candidacy the year before that would serve to politically mobilize the minority communities as there had been in 1989. Moreover, those who supported the Dinkins candidacy in 1989 had hopes that the new mayor would heal the city's racial wounds. When this did not happen, some disappointed former Dinkins supporters did not show up at the polls in 1993, and many who did voted for the challenger (Mollenkopf 1994, 213–217). Similarly to Arian et al's. (1991) discussion of "race correlated agenda items," those voters who saw crime and the quality of life as the most important issues were more likely to defect from Dinkins to Giuliani than were other voters (Mollenkopf 1994, 218). These are issues that concern White and middle-class voters more than minority and poor voters.

John Mollenkopf suggests that the coalition of voters who supported Rudolph Giuliani in 1993 was similar to the coalition that supported Mayor Koch throughout the 1980s (Mollenkopf 1994, 219). Giuliani's focus on crime and his tough demeanor made him popular among middle-class homeowners and outer-borough White ethnic voters. Due to Mayor Giuliani's successes in bringing crime down plus building a strong economy, minorities and White liberals were unable to unseat Mayor Giuliani in 1997. Although Ruth Messinger, Mayor Giuliani's Democratic challenger, was a weak opponent, it is doubtful that a much stronger Democratic candidate could have won. Given Giuliani's popularity in the city, potentially stronger candidates, such as Bronx Borough President Fernando Ferrer, decided not to enter the race. In 2001, with Mayor Giuliani leaving office due to term limits, the Democrats appeared to be unable to coalesce around a single candidate. The Democratic primary runoff between Public Advocate Mark Green and Bronx Borough President Ferrer was particularly divisive along racial and ethnic lines, so much so that Michael Bloomberg, a well-funded political neophyte, was able to win running as a Republican.

Of course, in the wake of the events of September 11, the voters of New York were looking for a mayor who could play a leading role in rebuilding the city. And Bloomberg, with Mayor Giuliani's endorsement, had an advantage given his non-partisan business background. Yet similar to the problems that Democratic liberals had in the 1980s attempting to unseat Mayor Koch in primary elections, infighting in the Democratic Party between the Green and Ferrer camps was as much to blame for Green's loss as any other factor.

During mayoral campaigns, racial and ethnic groups develop a set of expectations about what the candidate will do (for them) if he/she is victorious. These expectations include areas of public policy that the mayor will emphasize once in office as well as mayoral appointments. Any promises or commitments made by the candidate during the campaign obviously influence these expectations. And while the vast majority of voters lose interest in tracking the mayor's accomplishments after the election, racial and ethnic group leaders will closely watch the chief executive. Through the actions and pronouncements of their leaders, racial and ethnic constituencies that are disappointed by a mayor's performance will seek to publicly remind him of his previous commitments. Groups that are consistently disappointed by the mayor they supported will seek to unseat him in the next election. When Mayor Dinkins took office, there was an expectation by his liberal supporters that a Dinkins administration would focus on social issues much more than the Koch administration had. Mayor Dinkins took office, however, in the middle of a recession with projected budget deficits, rising crime, and a drug epidemic (Finder 1993c). One liberal union leader commented that "the challenge for Mayor Dinkins was to maintain his coalition at the same time he made overtures to the financial community" (Preston 1991b). But another liberal interest group leader charged, "he sure is changing his political base" (Preston 1991b). A Black leader suggested that the mayor had to do something "demonstrable . . . to show he's not just cutting everything to satisfy the Wall Street people" (Roberts 1991). Mayor Dinkins was able to balance the budget and to stem the rising crime rate, but this did not please many of his supporters (Finder 1993c). In an interview, Dinkins himself admitted, "Given that I care so much about children and those that are disabled and homeless . . . it has been very frustrating, not to have the ability to do all the things that I wish. . . . We have had to cut some of these areas. It is painful for me to cut back on libraries, art and cultural programs, to say nothing about health and hospitals and the Board of Education" (Preston 1991b).

That Mayor Dinkins was not able to significantly move the city's political system in a new direction speaks to the influence that external factors have on mayoral decision making. In Dinkins's case, the economic development imperative created by the city's fiscal plight combined with the lack of assistance from the federal and state levels handicapped his ability to respond to his core constituency. Studies of other cities have suggested that other minority mayors have experienced the same constraints (Pelissero et al. 2000).

The election of David Dinkins was significant for two reasons. He was New York City's first minority mayor. Just as important, however, he was also the first mayor elected as a liberal since John Lindsay's second term in 1969, with the possible exception of Ed Koch's election in 1977. There have been no liberal mayors elected since. Liberal New York is a multiracial/ethnic coalition of Whites, Blacks, and Hispanics. None of these groups can elect a mayor on their own, and in the early to mid-1980s, they were not even able to win a Democratic primary, albeit against an incumbent. In 1981, 1985, 1997, and 2001, this coalition experienced difficulty coalescing around a single candidate.

The expectations that voters established for Rudolph Giuliani were considerably different than those established for David Dinkins. And while there was little in Giuliani's background, except for a position in the Reagan Justice Department, that suggested that he would be antagonistic toward minority interests, the fact that he ran against and defeated Mayor Dinkins created an instant animosity between him and the minority community. Upon taking office, Mayor Giuliani ended the practice of having mayoral liaisons to the various ethnic and minority communities (Barry 1999). Not only did Mayor Giuliani do little to reach out to the minority community in the early days of his administration, he took several actions that antagonized them. He cancelled a program that set aside city contracts for minorities and women. In addition, "he stopped advertising for [city] jobs and contracts in Black and Latino newspapers" (Cottman 1995).

To outerborough White ethnics and middle-class homeowners, however, Rudolph Giuliani was a godsend. He was one of them, and he pursued many of the issues on their agenda. He refused to meet with the Reverend Al Sharpton. He brought the crime rate down by hiring more police and employing more effective police practices as well as stepping up enforcement on quality-of-life crimes. He lowered the welfare participation rates and required many of those remaining on welfare to work, even prior to the federal welfare reform law. The Giuliani administration made a point of claiming that reduced crime and welfare rates were as beneficial to the minority communities as they were to anyone else in the city, but few minority leaders agreed (Bumiller 2000; Traub 2001). The response of most minority leaders was that reduced crime rates came, in part, at the expense of the civil liberties of minorities living in high-crime areas and that lower welfare rates did not always mean better lives for individuals being taken off of welfare. Mayor Giuliani did remark cynically at one point in his first term that welfare and Medicaid cuts might result in some recipients leaving the city and that that would be beneficial (Conason 1995).

Another way that race and ethnicity affect the decision making of the mayor concerns the mayor's response to issues and events that take on racial and/or ethnic significance. These issues or events range from specific incidents of crime to proposals to eliminate alternative side of the street parking on religious or ethnic holidays. The mayor's roles as chief executive and chief of state give him the ability to play a significant role in mediating ethnic or racial conflict, maintaining or enhancing civil harmony. In 1989, Mayor Dinkins based his campaign for mayor on the promise that he would decrease the level of racial and ethnic division. He used the phrase "gorgeous mosaic" to describe the city's diversity in a way that would decrease divisiveness (Blumenthal 1990). In several responses to racially charged incidents that occurred during his term in office, Dinkins failed to deliver on his promise to be a healer of racial and ethnic tension. Shortly after he took office in 1990, Blacks in Flatbush, Brooklyn, were boycotting a Korean-owned grocery store because the owner allegedly assaulted a Haitian women shopping in the store. Ultimately, a jury acquitted the storeowner but the boycott turned racist and very anti-Korean. A judge ordered the protesters to remain fifty feet from the store, but Mayor Dinkins as chief executive did not enforce the order. The editorial boards of several newspapers in the city urged Mayor Dinkins to go to the store and buy something in order to symbolically end the boycott. The mayor, acting as chief of state, did not act promptly and only showed up at the store eight months after the boycott began (Tomasky 1993). In the Crown Heights riots of 1991 Mayor Dinkins again failed to act promptly or take any action to mediate or resolve tensions, this time between the Hasidic and Black communities. While some suggested that Mayor Dinkins's failure to act promptly in both instances was a function of his leadership style, others have suggested that he did not take action in these two cases because he did not want to "alienate his base" (Purdum 1993; Tomasky 1993). Both supporters and critics, however, did praise him for keeping the city peaceful after the verdict acquitting the police officers involved in the beating of Rodney King in Los Angeles (Calderone 1992).

While Mayor Giuliani was able to take a great deal of credit for the decline in the city's crime rate, the aggressive police tactics that were employed occasionally resulted in incidents of the police using excessive force. Many viewed Mayor Giuliani's behavior in the wake of these events as exacerbating racial tension in the city, not quelling it. In 1997, however, Mayor Giuliani received very high praise for his statements and actions after the assault on Abner Louima in a police station bathroom by members of the NYPD. Commenting on the mayor's reaction to the Louima attack, Black Congressman Floyd Flake of Brooklyn stated, "I would say that the level of racial tension is the lowest now that it's been in the twenty-one years that I've lived in the city" (Siegal 1999).

Early in his second term, Mayor Bloomberg dealt with a shooting and death of an unarmed African American individual in Queens by plainclothes police. The level of outrage and protest coming from the minority community was far less than had been the case for similar events during the Giuliani administration. Unlike in the Giuliani years, civil harmony was maintained in the aftermath of the Queens shooting in 2006. This can be attributed not only to the swift and measured response by Mayor Bloomberg following the shooting, but also to the fact that the Bloomberg administration had, since its inception, established effective lines of communication with the minority community, something the Giuliani administration had failed to do.

INTERGOVERNMENTAL RELATIONS. The impact that the state and federal levels of government have on mayoral decision making is primarily fiscal. Mayors and the city's political system look to the other levels of government as a major source of revenue. As discussed earlier, mayors make occasional trips to Washington and more frequent trips to Albany to lobby state and federal officials for continued and increased assistance.

David Dinkins provides an illustration of a mayor being constrained by intergovernmental issues. Mayor Dinkins was unable to obtain significant financial assistance at either the federal or state levels. The Bush administration in the early 1990s was decreasing aid to cities, and in the early 1990s, the state's fiscal position was as weak as the city's (McKinley 1991b). Only a few days after his election and almost two months before his inauguration, Dinkins traveled to Washington to lobby the New York City Congressional delegation and other members of Congress for increased federal aid to the city. During his term in office, Mayor Dinkins took an active role in the U.S. Conference of Mayors and other organizations in order to place additional pressure on the federal level to support urban issues (Walsh 1990). In 1990, when the Bush administration proposed a federal tax on securities transactions, Mayor Dinkins joined the financial community lobbying against the tax, noting that it "would have a crippling effect on an already fragile local economy" (Dutt 1990). And in early 1991, when President Bush published his proposed budget for the next fiscal year, Mayor Dinkins and members of New York City's Congressional delegation noted that if the budget was implemented, it would cost New York one hundred million dollars (King 1991).

The same year, Mayor Dinkins requested additional state aid from Governor Cuomo to help the city balance its budget. Earlier in the year the mayor had negotiated wage increases for some of the city's public employee unions. Governor Cuomo's response to Mayor Dinkins's request for aid signaled the governor's displeasure with the wage increase and intimated that wage rollbacks or givebacks would be necessary before the state gave the city any additional aid. The governor stated, "How do I explain to this state and its workers that instead of taking wealth and finding a way to share it with them, I in effect shared it with a city that used wealth it didn't have—otherwise they wouldn't be asking you for money—to give to its employees?" (Sack 1991).

Shortly after the election of Bill Clinton in 1992, the Dinkins administration began to construct a budget for the fiscal year beginning in July 1993, based on an assumption that there would be a significant increase in federal aid. The mayor hoped that with the additional aid, the city could maintain the current level of service delivery and possibly expand a little (Powell and Moreno 1992). In an attempt to make the assumption a reality, Mayor Dinkins and other mayors from large cities lobbied Vernon Jordan, the chair of President-elect Clinton's transition team (Sirica 1992). Yet as early as December 1992, the state Financial Control Board and the city's other fiscal monitors warned the mayor not to balance the budget for the next fiscal year with federal and state aid that had not yet materialized (Liff 1992). In March 1993, Mayor Dinkins met with Senator Moynihan and was warned that President Clinton's first budget may contain many cuts in federal programs being implemented by the city (Liff 1993). By April 1993, Dinkins began hinting that if intergovernmental aid from the state and federal levels was not forthcoming, the city might have to cut services to balance its budget (Finder 1993a). Given that it was an election year, Mayor Dinkins did not want to cut services, and thought that a Democratic governor and a Democratic president would help him out (Finder 1993b). In lieu of state aid, Mayor Dinkins also hoped that Governor Cuomo might relieve the city of some of the more burdensome state mandates that could save the city hundreds of millions of dollars (McKinley 1993). By May 1993, it was apparent to the Dinkins administration that the assumed intergovernmental fiscal assistance was not going to arrive. They began to revise their budget by factoring in five hundred million dollars of cuts including day care programs, outreach programs for the homeless, and park and playground maintenance (Mouat 1993). In late May, Dinkins and other city officials made several trips to Albany in search of additional aid, but were unsuccessful (Finder 1993d). When the mayor released the final budget in June, it not only included the above-mentioned cuts but also the expectation that the city's workforce would have to be reduced. He and his advisors placed much of the blame on the Republicans in the New York State Senate and Congress (Finder 1993e).

Similar to the actions of David Dinkins, Michael Bloomberg was in Washington before his inauguration lobbying for federal aid, particularly in light of the financial impact of September 11 on the city. He made other trips to Washington early in his administration and even attended a Republican Policy Conference retreat, attempting to become more familiar with national Republican leaders. He appointed a former aide to Senator Moynihan to advise him on dealing with the federal government and to reorganize the city's lobbying office in Washington (Steinhauer 2002). According to Joseph Lhota, a deputy mayor in the Giuliani administration, Mayor Giuliani's lobbyists had concentrated more on dealing with the Justice Department than on pursuing fiscal assistance (Steinhauer 2002). Due to the strong economy during much of the Giuliani administration, there was less of a need for the city to pursue federal assistance.

As discussed in chapter three, New York State also influences mayoral fiscal and budget decision making by controlling how the city raises revenue. In September 1990, responding to a rising crime rate and several highly publicized incidents of crime over the summer, Mayor Dinkins proposed hiring an additional six thousand police officers. Governor Cuomo pledged his support for the program including the issuance of new taxes to support new hires, as did other state leaders (Flynn 1990; Flynn and Smith 1990). By early October, Mayor Dinkins had constructed a proposal for hiring the new officers. According to the proposal, approximately half of the cost would have been financed through a payroll tax "levied on all workers drawing paychecks in New York City, and their employers, including commuters." The Dinkins administration clarified that poorer New Yorkers would pay the tax but would receive refunds. According to the Dinkins proposal, the remainder of the cost of the police would be paid for through higher property taxes. The city council, not wanting to raise property taxes, proposed paying for the remainder of the program through a twenty-five cent surcharge on state lottery tickets (Purdum 1990b). The city can raise property taxes on its own without state approval but the payroll tax and the surcharge on lottery tickets required approval by the state legislature and the governor, and it was an election year at the state level. Once Mayor Dinkins released his plan for financing the additional police, the reaction at the state level turned from supportive to negative. Speaker of the State Assembly Mel Miller suggested that the tax on commuters and surtax on lottery tickets "would go over like a dead weight" (Goldman 1990). Republicans in the State Senate expressed anger at the plan, noting that Mayor Dinkins had just given the city's teachers a 5.5 percent pay increase and now he was asking the state to raise taxes to finance his police plan. Governor Cuomo asked Mayor Dinkins to present some alternatives to his proposed financing plan (Kolbert 1990). Mayor Dinkins stated that if state officials did not favor his financing plan, they should tell him what taxing mechanisms they prefer. Responding to the mayor, a spokesperson for Republican State Senate Majority Leader Ralph Marino stated, "We don't think it works that way at all. . . . It is incumbent on whatever chief executive is coming up with a plan to come up with a way to carry it through. . . . We have previously said the payroll tax is not acceptable because it affects commuters and because it might not be a good thing for business in the city in this economic climate" (Purdum 1990c).

In mid-November, a *New York Times* editorial criticized Mayor Dinkins for not preparing state legislators prior to the publication of his plan, and it also criticized the mayor for appearing to lose interest in the plan as well (*New York Times* 1990). In December, the mayor, compromising with the city council, came up with a scaled down plan that hired fewer police. The plan no longer relied on a tax on commuters but called for increased property taxes, an extension of the city income tax surcharge that was supposed to expire in 1993, and the creation of a new city lottery game (Purdum 1990d). The mayor and council opted for a lottery game that would be sold only in the city instead of a surcharge on existing state lottery tickets. This was in response to state concerns that the surcharge would have depressed sales of lottery tickets, decreasing total lottery revenue (Purdum 1990d). The income tax surcharge and the new lottery game required state approval. The state finally approved the program in February 1991, partly because the incidence of the program would fall primarily on city residents.

Since the fiscal crisis of the 1970s, mayors have also had their budgets and fiscal policies reviewed by the State Financial Control Board, which was created specifically to oversee financial and budget decisions made by New York City officials. Knowledge that the Financial Control Board will review and must approve the city's fiscal plan has served as a constraint on mayoral fiscal decision making. In April 1991, Mayor Dinkins created plans to furlough thousands of city workers on a staggered basis through the end of the fiscal year in response to Governor Cuomo's hints that it might be necessary for the Financial Control Board to take over the city's budget in order to balance it (Preston 1991a). Later that same year, Mayor Dinkins put together a budget for the next fiscal year that included one billion dollars in aid from the Municipal Assistance Corporation, the state agency that issues bonds for the city. The chair of the Municipal Assistance Corporation, Felix Rohatyn, would not make the money available until the Financial Control Board approved the city's long-term (four year) financial plan (Purdum 1991). In the next two months, the Financial Control Board sent the mayor's four-year fiscal plan back to him twice for revisions before it was finally approved in early 1992. Once it was sent back to the mayor because the staff of the Financial Control Board disagreed with the mayor's fiscal advisors on how fast the country would come out of a recession (McKinley 1991a). The second time it was sent back because the Financial Control Board and the Municipal Assistance Corporation wanted the mayor to cut more city spending (Moreno 1992). During this period, a former executive director of the Financial Control Board suggested that the mayor should be using the planning requirements of the board as a mechanism to impose his own plan on New York City's political system, rather than view the board in an adversarial fashion (Berger 1991).

In 1994, after Mayor Giuliani and the city council had agreed on a budget for the 1994–1995 fiscal year, the mayor ordered the executive branch to identify an additional $450 million of budget cuts, partly in response to a Financial Control Board critique of Mayor Giuliani's budget (Mitchell 1994a). The critique suggested, among other things, that the Giuliani administration had overestimated federal assistance the city was to receive, that Mayor Giuliani's long-term financial plan did not sufficiently account for the impact of his proposed tax cuts on city revenue, and that the administration was not adequately auditing its contracts with service providers (Newsday 1994).

Mayors also are constrained by federal and state mandates and regulations in a variety of policy areas. In 1997, the U.S. Environmental Protection Agency (EPA) informed the city that it was going to fine the city for "failing to commit to a firm plan to build a filtration plant" for its drinking water coming out of the Croton watershed reservoirs, the city's water supply east of the Hudson River (Revkin 1997). According to the EPA, the city had been in violation of the Federal Safe Drinking Water Act since 1993, because the water from the Croton reservoir system had not been filtered (Rohde 1998). In 1992, the city had agreed to build a filtration plant, but in 1995, Mayor Giuliani had stopped the process because the city was unable to find a location to build the plant (Martin 1998a). The Giuliani administration had questioned the need for building a filtration plant that would cost the city over six hundred million dollars. The mayor was seeking to delay the EPA deadline for the construction of the plant as well as delay the political conflict on where the filtration plant would be located (Revkin 1997). By delaying the construction, Giuliani was also hoping he could reach an agreement with the EPA that would allow the city to avoid building a filtration plant altogether by controlling development in and around the Croton watershed. Van Cortlandt Park in the Bronx was identified as the most likely location for the plant (Martin 1998b). In early 2001, however, a New York State court blocked the city's attempt to locate the filtration plant in Van Cortlandt Park in response to a suit by those living near the park. The ruling was based on a New York State law that requires legislative approval before park land is used for any other purpose (Perez-Pena 2001). In response to the state court ruling, the EPA did not change its position and New York City began amassing federally imposed fines of over $400,000 for its failure to meet federal drinking water standards (Baker and Steinhauer 2003). An EPA spokesperson stated that the city must continue with planning to build the filtration plant or face millions of dollars in fines (Waldman 2001). The federal government was pressuring the city to build a water filtration plant, but the city had nowhere to build it. Finally, in 2003, the state gave the city permission to build the filtration plant in Van Cortlandt Park (Baker and Steinhauer 2003).

As discussed in chapter three, at times mayors must lobby at the state and federal levels to achieve their policy goals. In order to take control of New York City's school system, Mayor Bloomberg had to go to the state level to obtain this control. He was forced to lobby both houses of the state legislature to pursue the specific type of school system reform that he wanted. Although the state legislative bodies gave him most of what he wanted, there were some areas where he was forced to compromise. To obtain the support of Sheldon Silver, Speaker of the State Assembly, the mayor had to agree not to decrease that part of the city budget devoted to classroom spending unless total city revenue decreased (Goodnough 2002). As part of the reform, the mayor wanted New York City's thirty-two locally elected school boards to be abolished and replaced with parent councils (Steinhauer 2002). The New York State Senate refused to do this. The final state legislation called for the abolition of the community school boards only after a task force devised a replacement for them and hearings were held in each borough (Goodnough 2002). In 2003, Mayor Bloomberg announced that the thirty-two community school district boards would be abolished and replaced with thirty-two district parent councils elected by the officers of the parent associations of the schools in their respective districts, with each board having two appointees by the borough president. There would also be a citywide high school parent council and a council for special education (Gootman 2004a). In arriving at the abolition of the District School Boards and their replacement with parent councils, Mayor Bloomberg and School Chancellor Joel Klein were forced to compromise with members of the New York State Senate. The compromise forced the city to retain some of the district structure despite the abolition of the elected school boards (Herszenhorn 2003a). In addition, as in all cases where the city modifies election procedures, the U.S. Justice Department had to approve the reform (Gootman 2004a).

Conclusion

Mayors play a dominant role in the governance of the city. The mayor's combination of roles and accompanying political power gives him/her the ability to take part in every major political decision made by the political system. As the most visible elected official, the mayor is accountable to the electorate. Given his/her visibility, the mayor may be the only elected official in the city who runs for reelection on their record where there is a good chance that much of the public is knowledgeable about the substance of their record.

As the political system's chief executive, the mayor plays a leading role in decisions regarding the delivery of public goods and services. As in the case of school system reform, the mayor combines the role of chief of state along with chief executive. This enables the mayor to not only set the agenda regarding which public goods and services need modification, but also to lead the political system in attaining the desired modifications. Through the responsibility to create a budget for the city government, the mayor influences the mix of public goods and services being delivered, dominating discussions as to how the city's budget will stay in balance, either through tax increases, service cuts, or appeals to other levels of government for funding. Once the budget has been approved, the mayor continues to dominate service delivery issues through his ability to influence the direction of the city bureaucracy.

Mayors also play a leading role in the establishment and maintenance of civil harmony. With the combination of roles they occupy, mayors have a "bully pulpit" similar to presidents. The citizenry, through the media, look to the mayor for leadership in times of conflict. Mayors must decide not only if they are going to respond to conflict, but how. David Dinkins was elected mayor in part because the public perceived Ed Koch to have failed to guide the city through some racially tense events in the 1980s. Dinkins ran for office as a healer and someone who could raise the level of civil harmony in a racially and ethnically diverse city. Dinkins's failure to rapidly address the Brooklyn boycott of the Korean grocery store and his mishandling of the Crown Heights riots severely damaged his status as a healer, and did little to raise the level of civil harmony in the city as promised. Dinkins's successor, Rudolph Giuliani, was not elected as a healer. Giuliani's combative style frequently lowered the level of civil harmony. His aggressive attacks on the school system and some of its chancellors polarized educational politics in the city and inhibited his ability to achieve any substantive reform of the school system while in office. Giuliani's response to incidences of police brutality at times contributed to the racial polarization of the city, although in at least one case, he was praised by Black leaders for his fair and level-headed public pronouncements, immediately after the shooting of Abner Louima.

The Other Citywide and Borough-wide Elected Officials

In 1989, once the decision was made by the Charter Revision Commission to elim-inate the Board of Estimate, one issue that arose was what to do with those city officials who in the past had gotten most of their power from their seat on the board. Although the City Charter gives these officials responsibilities beyond the votes that they had on the Board of Estimate, it was their membership on the board that gave them significant influence in the city's political system. Each of the borough presidents had a single vote, while the comptroller, president of the city council, and the mayor each had two votes. Realizing how diminished the political role of the city council president and the borough presidents would be, the 1989 Charter Revision Commission seriously considered eliminating the city council president's position and also gave some thought to abolishing the bor-ough presidents (Lane 1998; Schwarz 1998). Intense lobbying by Andrew Stein, the city council president, in 1989, to save his position was successful and the charter revision commission appeared reluctant to take on the meaning of borough identity, so the borough presidents' positions were retained as well (*New York Times* 1989). Eighteen years later, these positions and the individuals who occupy them are still struggling to identify a function for themselves within the city's political system. Due to its fiscal and accounting responsibilities, the comptroller has not experienced the same struggle as the other positions. Nevertheless, the loss of visibility the comptroller suffered when the Board of Estimate was abolished forced the comptroller, as a politician, to attempt to make the role more visible.

With the onset of term limits, these offices may fulfill a new role within the political system. They may provide former council members or other politicians with a way to remain in the political system and the public eye, gaining eight additional years of visibility in another elected position before running for mayor or some other office at the state or federal levels. In 2001, three of the candidates for mayor were the term-limited comptroller, public advocate, and a borough president. With regard to the city council in the 2001 city elections, two term-limited members of the council became borough presidents. Several others ran and lost. Two term-limited members of the council made unsuccessful bids for public advocate, one was unsuccessful in running for comptroller, and one was unsuccessful in running for mayor. In 2005, large numbers of term-limited city council members ran for borough president as well as public advocate.

The Public Advocate (formerly President of the City Council)

The 1989 charter revision eliminated the city council president's office and cre-ated the office of public advocate. Aside from its two votes on the Board of Estimate, the office of city council president never had any substantive responsi-bilities. The primary responsibility of the president was to preside over council meetings, but this minimal responsibility was taken away in a charter revision referendum in 2002. The public advocate is first in line to replace the mayor if the city's chief executive cannot fulfill his or her term of office.

Frederick A. O. Schwarz, the chairman of the 1989 Charter Revision Commission, explained that, "With a strong mayor, which the City Charter creates, it was particularly important to have a number of checks and balances to that mayoral power. And we thought the Public Advocate was and would be an important element of the checks on that power" (Herbert 1998).

In its endorsement of Mark Green for the position in 1993, the editorial board of *Newsday* suggested that if Mr. Green was so concerned with efficiency in government, he should consider abolishing the position for which he was running (*Newsday* 1993). In 1993, when the title of the position was changed to public advocate, it came with a salary of $105,000, a staff of approximately seventy, and a budget of almost four million dollars (Dwyer 1993). This was cut by a million dollars by the city council for fiscal year 1994 (Hicks 1993b). Mark Green, who won the election for public advocate in 1993 and again in 1997, was able to define the position primarily because of his experience as Mayor Dinkins's Commissioner of Consumer Affairs, his early experience working with Ralph Nader, and his very liberal ideology (Hicks 1993a). Green initially defined his role as an ombudsman for citizens and a government abuse watchdog (Carroll 1994). Calling the public advocate the city's second-highest elected position, he described himself as a "quality of life cop patrolling the bureaucracy beat, no matter whose toes we may have to step on" (Hicks 1994). As public advocate, Green and his staff shed light on managed care abuses, nursing home issues, homeless shelter food purchases, toxic chemicals used by dry cleaners, and the city's administration of foster care. He was one of the first government officials to look into the impact of pharmaceutical prices on the elderly (Lueck 2000).

Although Green performed the role of consumer advocate and government watchdog, within a year of taking office, he also became the in-house critic of the Giuliani administration. The issue that Green and the Giuliani administration fought over most frequently was the police. Green constantly sought information that would enable him to monitor how police misconduct cases were being handled by the police department. The Giuliani administration made multiple efforts to block his access to this information. On more than one occasion, the public advocate and the mayor ended up in state court litigating over the mayor's ability to withhold this information. The public advocate won most of the cases (*New York Times* 1998). For its part, the Giuliani administration early on did little to establish an amicable relationship with the public advocate. In Green's first year, Mayor Giuliani proposed cutting the public advocate's budget by 23 percent (Perez-Rivas 1994). The cut was eventually decreased to 11 percent (Herbert 1998). In the late 1990s, Giuliani-appointed charter revision commissions undertook several attempts to abolish the public advocate's position through a charter revision referendum. Short of abolishing the position, Mayor Giuliani sought to minimize its role in succeeding the mayor if the chief executive could no longer serve, something the Bloomberg administration was able to do in 2002.

Green's successor, Betsy Gotbaum, was also a former commissioner under David Dinkins. Gotbaum lacked the consumer advocacy experience as well as the aggressive political style of Mark Green. As a result, almost a year into her tenure as public advocate, she was struggling to redefine the role and some were again questioning the necessity for the position (Cardwell 2002). Assuming the office of public advocate is not abolished, it will continue to evolve, partly based on Mark Green's initial attempt to define the position and in part as a function of whoever occupies the role.

The Comptroller

Similar to the public advocate and the borough presidents, the office of the Comptroller of the City of New York lost most of its political clout when the Board of Estimate was abolished. Unlike the other offices, however, the city charter gives the comptroller a substantive role in the governance of the city. The comptroller is the city's chief fiscal officer. The office has the responsibility and power to perform both fiscal and performance audits on any aspect of city government. Not only is the office responsible for assessing whether the city's money is being spent in appropriate ways, but it is also responsible for assessing the extent to which program goals are being met. As one of the city's fiscal monitors, the comptroller reviews the mayor's revenue estimates, the executive budget, and is expected to issue reports on the state of the city's economy. The comptroller also monitors and reviews all city contracts and has the power to temporarily suspend the awarding of any contacts if he/she believes it to be corrupt. The comptroller participates in the awarding of city franchises and appoints two of the five members who serve on the city's contracts policy board. In addition, the comptroller manages the city's money, including billions of dollars in pension funds for city employees (Finder 1989c; New York City Charter 2004, Chapter 5, Section 93 2004). In order to carry out his functions, the comptroller has a staff of over seven hundred, compared to the public advocate's staff of less than a hundred (Levy 1996a). Also significant, the comptroller is a member of the State Financial Control Board.

In 1997, Alan Hevesi used his role as manager of the city's pension funds to influence Swiss banks to expedite their establishment of a fund for Holocaust survivors. He did this in response to reports by the federal government that the banks had frustrated efforts by Holocaust survivors to recover money placed in Swiss banks by their families in the 1930s (Sanger 1997).

Since the 1989 charter revision, comptrollers have had much less conflict with the mayor's office than has the public advocate. This is probably due to the fiscal conservatism of both Mayors Giuliani and Bloomberg. In 1994, when the mayor and the city council went to court over differences in how much and what should be cut from the city's budget, Comptroller Hevesi angered both sides by implementing both sets of proposed cuts until the dispute was settled (Mitchell 1994b). Late in Mayor Giuliani's second term, Comptroller Hevesi's critiques of the mayor's budgets grew more negative. This was in part due to the fact that as the Wall Street boom began to subside, the comptroller became more concerned with the fact that the mayor was using stock market–created surpluses to balance the city's budget. In addition to using these one-time revenue sources to balance the budget, the mayor was implementing tax decreases that threatened the stability of future budgets when Wall Street would not be as strong (Lipton 2000a).

The most contentious issue over which Mayor Giuliani and Comptroller Hevesi disagreed concerned the comptroller's charter-granted ability to hold up city contracts. In March 2000, the comptroller refused to approve a city contract with a Virginia-based company, Maximus, as part of the city's welfare-to-work program. The company was being hired to run job training and employment programs for the city's welfare recipients. Comptroller Hevesi alleged that in awarding the contract, the Giuliani administration had not engaged in the required competitive bidding process. In December, after the Appellate Division of the State Supreme Court ruled in the mayor's favor, Hevesi decided not to pursue the issue further. The court ruled that after the mayor rejected the comptroller's objections, the comptroller had no choice but to approve the contract. Hevesi maintained that the contract with Maximus should not be approved but added that "because the charter provision regarding the mayor's discretion was poorly drafted, we were not certain of winning on appeal" (Lipton 2000b).

William Thompson, former President of the New York City School Board, was elected to the comptroller's position in 2001. As the city's chief fiscal analyst, Comptroller Thompson played a role in the city's recovery after September 11, 2001. His reports, "One Year Later: The Fiscal Impact of 9/11 on New York City" and "911: Three Years Later-Securing the Federal Pledge" established benchmark calculations on the impact of the World Trade Center attacks on the city's budget and the city's economy, as well as the role that federal aid has played in the recovery (New York City Comptroller's Office 2002a; 2004). Thompson also examined the increase in commercial insurance premiums in the city after September 11, 2001, as well as their impact on business health (New York City Comptroller's Office 2002b). Among the numerous audits that the comptroller performed in his first year were:

- the implementation of the Police Department's Domestic Violence Tracking System;
- the financial and operating practices of the Columbus/Amsterdam Business Improvement District;
- monitoring of senior citizen center conditions by the Department of Aging;
- funds raised by the New York City Department of Parks and Recreation and maintained in custodial and restricted accounts by the City Parks Foundation;

- New York Yankee rental credits for the third quarter of 2001; and
- effectiveness of the Department of Environment Protection's Help Center Hotline (New York City Comptroller's Office 2002c).

Similar to his predecessor Alan Hevesi, the one area of disagreement between Comptroller Thompson and the Bloomberg administration has been contracts. In 2003, the city signed a contract with the Snapple beverage company giving it "exclusive rights to sell beverages in city schools and other municipal properties" as well as the right to market itself as the city's official beverage (Herszenhorn 2003b; Peterson 2004). Comptroller Thompson questioned whether the Bloomberg administration had followed city regulations regarding competitive bidding practices and suggested that the entire contract needed the approval of the city Franchise and Concession Review Committee. Thompson also expressed the concern that a potential conflict of interest existed because Octagon, the marketing firm that served as a consultant to the city on the contract, was also under contract to Cadbury Schweppes, the parent company of Snapple (Gootman 2004b; Heszenhorn 2003b). The Bloomberg administration argued that there was no conflict of interest and that they had followed appropriate procedures in striking the deal with Snapple. In 2004, after further investigation and audit of the contract process, the comptroller sued the Bloomberg administration, seeking to void the contract with Snapple. According to Thompson, "Snapple was selected through a tainted process with a predetermined outcome" (Gootman 2004b). The comptroller argued that some of the companies competing with Snapple for the bid had not been given complete information. The comptroller also charged that Snapple "was the only company given an opportunity to improve its offer after final bids had been submitted (Gootman 2004b). In July 2004, a state court upheld the city's contract with Snapple but ruled the city Franchise and Concession Review Committee should have reviewed the entire contract, especially the part of the contract giving Snapple the right to market itself as the city's official beverage (Peterson 2004).

The Borough Presidents

During the 1989 charter revision discussion, one of the ideas to strengthen the role of the borough presidents, given the elimination of the Board of Estimate, was to give them a vote on the city council, in effect acting as at-large members. The idea was rejected. Aside from questioning the need for borough presidents, some on the commission went so far as to question the need for boroughs (Finder 1989a). Past and present borough presidents testified before the commission that, despite the increasing diversity of the city, borough identities were real. One borough president expressed fear that if the borough presidents disappeared, the outer boroughs would become colonies of Manhattan (Finder 1989a). Thus, the charter revision commission did not eliminate the borough presidents.

Within the larger political system, borough presidents do play a minimal representation role, but without the Board of Estimate, they have no venue other than the media or informal meetings with city officials, through which they can play this role. Borough presidents participate in the budgetary process, but their role is consultative at best. They and their offices also perform a minimal ombudsman function for the citizens and businesses of their borough who encounter difficulty dealing with the city's vast bureaucracy (Serant 1999). The public advocate and members of the city council also perform these functions. In the area of land use and zoning, borough presidents have the power to appoint one member of the City Planning Commission, and they also chair the Borough Board, which is part of ULURP. Borough presidents chair the board but they have only one vote. And the board's decision is not determinative. Prior to reform of the school system, borough presidents also had the power to appoint one member each to the seven member school board, but the state legislature eliminated the city's school board as part of the 2002 reform.

Would the boroughs be any less represented in the city's political system if the borough presidents' offices were eliminated? At present, council members collectively represent their boroughs as well, if not better, than the borough presidents. They share the borough identity, to the extent that it still exists, and they are certainly in a better position to represent as well as deliver public goods and services.

8

The City Council

Term Limits

In 1993, Ronald Lauder, millionaire and cosmetics heir, initiated a campaign to place a charter amendment before the voters in November calling for term limits for all city elected officials. In 1989, Lauder had unsuccessfully run for mayor, losing to Rudolph Giuliani in the Republican primary even though he spent approximately fourteen million dollars, four times more than Giuliani (Roberts 1993a). In his campaign for term limits, Lauder was seeking to limit all elected city officials (mayor, comptroller, public advocate, borough presidents, and city council members) to two four-year terms. In a letter to the *New York Times* in September 1993, Lauder argued that term limits would address the advantages of incumbency and would "return citizen legislators to office, remove much of the incentive for incumbents to manipulate the rules to insure lifetime incumbency, provide a safeguard to eliminate the multiple abuses that can come with unlimited tenure in office, bring fresh views and opinions to political office, and provide a wider choice of candidates" (Lauder 1993).

The supporters of term limits focused on the advantages of incumbency. In recent city council elections, incumbents had won over 90 percent of the time and some members had been on the city council since the 1970s. Some believed that term limits would "reinvigorate the political grassroots" and involve more citizens in government (Roberts 1993b). Other interest groups, however, believed that the turnover of so many city council members would cripple the effectiveness of the city's legislative body (Roberts 1993b).

Opponents argued that if citizens wanted elected officials out of office, they could always vote them out by choosing another candidate. Term limits would deprive the voters of electing an effective legislator to a third term. Opponents were also concerned about who would serve on a term-limited city council. Although term limit supporters claimed that one of the benefits of term limits is that it would get rid of career politicians, opponents wondered who would be motivated or aspire to become a candidate if they could only spend eight years in office. Would only the wealthy or those who could afford to interrupt their careers temporarily decide to run (Barry 2001)? And some opponents of term limits extolled the virtue, if not the necessity, of career politicians. Most important, the opponents of term limits believed that a term-limited city council would give the mayor much more power within the political system. The mayor has a large staff and the entire executive branch supporting him. The city council has staff but it does not compare to the mayor's. A non-term-limited city council can counter the power of the mayor with its experience and institutional memory. Frederick A. O. Schwarz, the chairperson of the 1989 Charter Revision Commission, expressed concern that term limits would destroy the balance of power between the executive and legislative branches that his commission's charter revisions had created (Roberts 1993b). Speaker of the City Council, Peter Vallone, the leading opponent of term limits, echoed Schwarz's opinion. "You can make a good argument for term limits on a mayor, a governor, a president, but in a legislature individuals only become powerful as they gain seniority. . . . All of a sudden, in one fell swoop, they're saying a Council member is as powerful as a chief executive from the moment you're elected and that is absurd. . . . You're facing a chief executive who's the head of everything and has 300,000 people working for him" (quoted in Roberts 1993b). Vallone was concerned that a term-limited city council that was full of inexperienced legislators would become too dependent on legislative staff and even upon the mayor (Liff 1993). Other opponents argued that term limits would strengthen lobbyists and interest groups (*Newsday* 1993).

The council and term limit opponents tried to block Lauder's attempt to get term limits on the November ballot, so supporters were forced to go to court. The court had to decide whether the voters of New York City could amend the city charter to include term limits under the state's home rule provision. Since the city appealed the decision of the state courts at every level, it was not until October 19, two weeks before the November election, that the state's highest court, the Court of Appeals, ordered the City Clerk to let the voters decide on term limits (Roberts 1993b). Good government groups had urged Speaker of the City Council Vallone to propose an alternative to the Lauder proposal, or at the very least hold hearings on the issue of term limits to better educate the media and the public. Speaker Vallone and the opponents of term limits believed that they could stop Lauder in court (Collins 1993). In the two weeks between the favorable court ruling and the election, Lauder used his wealth to blanket the airwaves with pro–term limits advertisements. One ad depicted politicians sitting around a legislative chamber with one fat member chomping on a cigar, several council members asleep, and one "cutting a paper chain of dollar signs" (Lueck 1993). In November 1993 the voters of the city amended the charter, approving the terms limits law with 60 percent voting in favor (Bunch 1993). Under the new law, anyone in a city elected position in 1993 could serve until January 2002. They would be unable to run in the 2001 city elections for the same position (Bunch and Mangaliman 1993). Subsequent attempts by the city council to amend or abolish term limits failed.

The November 2001 city council elections produced thirty-eight new legislators out of fifty-one total members. Given the number of open seats in the council, the Democratic primary in September 2001, had been a free-for-all. In some districts there were as many as four or five candidates running. The winners in eighteen of the districts won with less than 40 percent of the vote, and in only six council districts was there no Democratic primary. Did Ronald Lauder and the pro–term limits forces get the citizen legislature they fought for? Of the thirty-eight new members of the city council in January 2002, below is a brief summary of some of their political backgrounds:

- seven of the new members of the council were former council staff members, most of them serving as chiefs of staff for the council member they replaced;
- four members served on other legislative staffs either at the state or federal level;
- four members had served in elective office before, all of them in the two legislative bodies in Albany;
- four members were the children of outgoing council members, each of them having been elected to replace their parents;
- three members were the children of elected legislators at the state or federal levels;
- one member was a former mayoral appointee to a city agency; and
- one member managed a statewide campaign for the U.S. Senate (Hicks 2001c: New York City Council 2002a).

Twenty-four of the thirty-eight new members took office with considerable political experience. Many of them were as much career politicians as the council members they replaced. Those who supported term limits could not be satisfied with the results of the first term limits elections. At the same time, the opponents of term limits cannot bemoan the absence of legislative experience or institutional memory, although the voters' right to choose has still been abridged.

1989 Charter Changes

The 1989 charter revision increased the size of the city council from thirty-five to fifty-one members. More important, though, the 1989 charter revision abolished the Board of Estimate, dividing the board's power between the mayor and the council. Prior to the 1989 charter revision, the city council had little or no role in land use and zoning decisions. The new charter gave the council a major role in this policy area. In addition, while it existed, the Board of Estimate played the leading legislative role in reviewing the mayor's budget. The city council's role in the budgetary process was minor compared to the board's. With the board's departure, the city council assumed the major legislative role in the revision and passage of the mayor's budget. With the abolition of the Board of Estimate, mayor-council relations became the new focus of institutional conflict in the city government.

Prior to the board's abolition, the city council was viewed as a junior partner in the city's political system. Until 1974, members of the city council were not even required to show up at City Hall and vote. They could simply give the leadership their proxy and they would get paid (Finder 1988; Vallone 2002a). In the 1960s, Henry Stern, then member of the city council but later Commissioner of Parks and Recreation under Mayors Koch and Giuliani, suggested that the city council was "less than a rubber stamp, because a rubber stamp at least leaves an impression" (quoted in Hicks 2001a). Speaking of the place of the city council within the city's governing structures, Councilman Edward Sadowsky, a twenty-four-year member of the council and chair of the council's Finance Committee during the early 1980s, stated, "There is really one elected official in the city, and that's the Mayor. . . . We have divided the traditional legislative power between the City Council and the Board of Estimate, and that makes it very difficult to take legislative initiatives" (quoted in Purnick 1985).

In their 1990 book, Jewell Bellush and Dick Netzer devoted an entire chapter to the mayor and an entire chapter to the bureaucracy, but placed the city council and the Board of Estimate in a chapter entitled, "The Other Elected Officials" (Bellush and Netzer 1990). In this chapter, author David Eichenthal spent considerably more time discussing the Board of Estimate than the city council. After a very brief discussion, Eichenthal concluded that "despite . . . efforts to enhance its power, the council has never emerged as a potent legislative body" (Eichenthal 1990, 89). Moreover, Eichenthal noted that the city council's legislative power was further constrained by the state legislature's ability to intervene in local affairs using its own law-making powers (Eichenthal 1990, 90). State policymakers have control over policymaking in education, labor relations, rent regulation, and much of the transportation arena (Eichenthal 1990, 92).

City Council Roles

The 1989 charter revision had a significant impact not only on who performed the primary roles of a legislature—representation and lawmaking—but also on how these functions were performed. Legislatures are lawmaking bodies. There is an expectation that legislators as a group will seek to address the significant problems of society through the formulation and passage of laws. According to the City Charter, Chapter 2, Section 28, "The council in addition to all enumerated powers shall have power to adopt local laws which it deems appropriate, which are not inconsistent with the provisions of this charter or with the constitution or laws of the United States or this state, for the good rule and government of the city; for the order, preservation of the public health, comfort, peace and prosperity of the city and its inhabitants; and to effectuate the purposes and provisions of this charter or of the other laws relating to the city" (New York City Charter 2004).

While it is the responsibility of the legislature as an institution to formulate and pass laws for the good of the city, it is also the responsibility of each individual legislator to represent the citizens/constituents from the legislator's home district. Legislators are expected to look out for local interests and to represent the opinions and perspectives of those in their home district who elect them. This frequently results in a conflict between the representation and lawmaking functions of the legislature (Barbour and Wright 2001, 244). Those who study the U.S. Congress speak of its "dual nature" in referring to the "unresolved dichotomy" between the legislature's lawmaking and representation functions (Davidson and Oleszek 2002, 2–5). Citizens expect legislators to look after the local interest, but what is good for the district may not be what is good for the entire political system. In their representative capacity, legislators are supposed to defend parochial interests and points of view; but the lawmaking function of the legislature requires that, at some point, legislators set aside their parochial concerns and compromise for the good of the city. If legislators as lawmakers refuse to bend from representing their districts, then the potential for law responding to societal problems is compromised. At the same time, too much compromise for the sake of enacting legislation in the interest of all results in poor representation.

In light of the conflict between lawmaking and representation, the existence of the Board of Estimate and the city council, prior to the board's abolition, was a creative institutional method for addressing the lawmaking and representation functions. The board had a number of strengths as a lawmaking body. It had only eight members, resulting in extremely low decision-making costs. In addition, given the apportionment of votes on the board, each of the three citywide elected officials having two votes and the five borough presidents each having only one vote, those board members with a citywide perspective could outvote those members with a more parochial, borough-wide, perspective. Representation was present on the board, but not to the extent where it would inhibit lawmaking in the interest of the entire city. Moreover, given the board's structural emphasis on lawmaking, the former thirty-five-member city council could use what power it had for parochial representative purposes, and it frequently did. What made the Board of Estimate such an attractive lawmaking institution was partly responsible for it being such a poor representative body.

Much of the lawmaking power of the board was transferred to the city council. At the same time, the size of the city council was increased from thirty-five to fifty-one members to enhance its ability to represent minority groups in the city. This created quite a challenge for the members of the city council and for the council as an institution. They were being asked to become the primary lawmaking body in the city's political system, something they had never been before. Simultaneously, the council's representational function was being emphasized through the addition of more members. Given the city's increasing ethnic and racial diversity, more city council members increased the probability that the representatives would more closely resemble their constituents (Muzzio and Tompkins 1989, 84). In their article on finding the optimum size for the city council, Muzzio and Tompkins cite the 1988 Charter Revision Commission's "core values" in assessing the size of a legislative body: "representativeness; responsiveness; public participation and confidence in government; limiting the concentration of governmental power; attracting quality people to public service; accountability; increasing the ability of officials to make difficult and wise decisions for the public good; and enhanced efficiency and effectiveness" (Muzzio and Tompkins 1989, 90). The authors claim that increasing the size of the council enhances the representation, public participation, and accountability values. With regard to responsiveness, Muzzio and Tompkins (1989) state that while larger legislative bodies make legislators more responsive to their constituents, similar to the accountability value, they may exacerbate the legislator's lawmaking function. The authors suggest two ways of dealing with this dilemma. First, relieve some of the legislator's representational duties through community boards or ombudsmen, who could respond to constituent needs. The second possible solution would be to structure the council with staff and leadership positions that would enhance the lawmaking function (Muzzio and Tompkins 1989, 91). This second solution is linked to another core value, limiting the concentration of governmental power. Larger legislative bodies need hierarchy and organization. Increasing the size of the city council would require centralizing some of the procedural as well as housekeeping functions in leadership positions in order to keep the council functioning. Finally, Muzzio and Tompkins state that to the extent that increasing the size of the council results in more specialization on the part of council members as well as more staff and greater expertise, it would also increase the ability of the council to make better decisions (Muzzio and Tompkins 1989, 93).

Although it is difficult to compare the lawmaking function of the fifty-one-member city council with the old Board of Estimate, one example might illustrate the lawmaking-representation dilemma that these two bodies depict. In 1996, Mayor Giuliani proposed a plan to allow megastores to locate in New York City as of right. The Giuliani administration saw megastores bringing jobs to the city as well as keeping city residents from going out to the suburbs to do their shopping. The plan would have required the city council to amend the city's zoning laws to create areas where megastores could locate without going through ULURP, a potentially long and expensive process. The council rejected the mayor's plan, arguing that it did not give the neighborhoods where the megastores might locate sufficient control over their "quality of life" (Holloway 1997a). The council's decision represented a victory for representation. Most council members did not want megastores locating in their districts, or did not want to be held responsible for megastores locating in their districts. At the very least, they wanted to control the location process to the extent that they were not willing to amend the zoning code to allow megastores to locate in their districts as of right even if the land was pre-designated as being appropriate for this use. In place of the Giuliani megastore plan, the council proposed and implemented a plan where community boards in each of the council districts would be asked to identify areas where megastores could locate. Several months later, however, only five of over fifty community boards responded to Speaker Vallone's directive by the set deadline, and the council plan fizzled (Holloway 1997b). What would the Board of Estimate have done with Mayor Giuliani's megastore plan? Was the city council's rejection of the plan an example of good representation, bad lawmaking, or both? In the absence of any plan on the part of the city to house megastores, these stores continued to locate in the city, but going through ULRUP first (Pristin 1999).

Aside from the passage of local laws, the city council's lawmaking function includes three key aspects. First, the council has jurisdiction over the passage of the city's expense and capital budgets. Related to this, when the mayor wants to modify the budget during the fiscal year, if the modification varies from the original authorization by more than 5 percent or fifty thousand dollars, council approval is needed (Kivelson 1991, 36). The budgetary process will be discussed in greater detail later in this chapter. Second, the city council has jurisdiction over the property tax rates. The council can levy other taxes, but only if the state legislature gives its permission. This is done after the council passes a home rule message asking the state to enable the city to levy or raise the tax (Kivelson 1991, 35). Third, the council has jurisdiction over most land use decisions. Land use decisions coming out of the City Planning Commission related to zoning, as well as most decisions regarding the use of city-owned residential property, must be approved by the council. Other land use decisions such as special zoning permits and nonresidential city-owned property go to the council if the relevant borough president or community board has disapproved of the project or if the council votes to consider it (Kivelson 1991, 37).

The representation function that council members perform involves more than including the district's perspective in the discussions and debates over the formulation and passage of prospective legislation. Representation also involves performing a considerable amount of constituency service or casework for the residents of the legislator's district. Every council member maintains an office in his or her district. This helps the councilperson maintain a presence and it makes the council member accessible to constituents. To a great extent, casework or constituency service involves acting as a liaison or ombudsman between the constituents and the agencies that make up the executive branch. New York City's bureaucracy is so vast that citizens may not know where they need to go in the executive branch to get what they want. For example, a local group wants a parade permit. Do they go to the police, the Department of Transportation, or the Department of Parks and Recreation? A homeowner wants to renovate his single family home and rent out the basement as an income-producing apartment. Does he go to the Department of City Planning, the Department of Housing and Buildings, the local Community Board, or all three? The city council member and his or her staff can obtain that information. On other occasions, the citizen will know where to go but will not be successful in getting what they want from the relevant agency. At that point, they may ask the city council member to intercede on their behalf. Residents are upset about a bar on their block that is noisy at very late hours, and the several visits by the police over the past months have not been effective. A senior citizen may be unhappy with the delivery of Meals on Wheels administered by a local nonprofit group but contracted through the city's Department of Aging. Calls to the nonprofit group and the Department of Aging have not produced satisfactory service. A member of the city council may be able to get the results the citizen could not get.

Not all constituents are equal. Council members interact with community activists, leaders of community organizations, and participants on community boards much more frequently than with other citizens. The relationship that the councilperson establishes with these groups is reciprocal. Council members spend a great deal of their time responding to the needs of these individuals, including using some of their discretionary budget to fund community projects. In exchange, these groups become the councilperson's eyes and ears in the district (Eristoff 2001, 4).

In addition to lawmaking and representation, a third significant function of the city council is its oversight of the executive branch agencies and the complementary function of investigation. The city charter distinguishes the oversight function from the investigation function, but they are very much related (New York City Charter Revision Commission 2004, Chapter 2, Section, 29). From the charter's perspective, oversight implies a routine and periodic examination of the activities of an agency or agencies in the executive branch by the council or its relevant committee. This is usually conducted through a public hearing in the council chambers where agency heads (e.g., commissioners) come to testify about the actions of their agencies. Other interested parties may be invited to testify or may ask to be included. The budgetary process and the publication of the Mayor's Management Report (MMR) provide the council with the opportunity for a regular, annual review of agency activities. Beyond these reviews, the council does not usually conduct systematic hearings on the activities of the executive branch agencies (chapter nine), but rather holds oversight hearings on various aspects of the agencies as the need arises. The city charter also gives the council the power to "investigate any matters within its jurisdiction relating to the property, affairs, or government of this city or of any county within the city, or to any other powers of the council, or to the effectuation of the purposes or provisions of this charter or any laws relating to the city or to any county within the city" (New York City Charter Revision Commission 2004, Chapter 2, Section 29). This very broad and open-ended mandate allows the council to investigate and hold a hearing on practically any matter it wants. Since much of the council's oversight activities are not routine or periodic, they are practically indistinguishable from council investigations. The Council's Committee on Education has periodically held oversight hearings on the city school system's ability to hire, train, and retain qualified teachers. They have done this, in part, because for well over a decade, there has been a shortage of qualified teachers in the city's schools. In another example, in response to several assaults on young women at city-run pools in the late 1990s, the Council Committee on Parks and Recreation held a hearing on safety at public pools and beaches. After an electrical power failure in Queens in the summer of 2006, a city council committee held an investigative oversight hearing on the performance of Consolidated Edison, the local power company.

Finally, the city charter gives the council the power of "advice and consent" over a small number of mayoral appointees including members of the Art Commission, the Board of Health, the Board of Standards and Appeals, the City Planning Commission, the Landmarks Preservation Commission, the Tax Commission, the Taxi and Limousine Commission, and the public members of the Environmental Control Board (New York City Charter Revision Commission 2004, Chapter 2, Section 31). This gives the council the power to approve or reject mayoral nominations within thirty days after the nomination is made. If the council fails to act within that time, the nomination is considered to be confirmed (New York City Charter Revision Commission 2004, Chapter 2, Section 31).

City Council Organization and Leadership

The city charter allows the council to elect a speaker or majority leader from among its members and to establish its own rules and procedures for internal operations and governance (New York City Charter Revision Commission 2004, Chapter 2, Sections 44 and 45). Since the Democrats hold the vast majority of seats in the council, the council's Democratic Party caucus, comprised of all Democratic council members, controls all major positions within the council. Although the Speaker's responsibilities are not discussed in any detail in the charter, he or she has a considerable amount of power, especially when compared to the other members. He or she is the operational and symbolic leader of the council, and is responsible for hiring its staff and has the power to appoint the chairs and members of council committees, but these decisions are ratified by the entire council (Kivelson 1991, 35). The speaker also has a discretionary fund of several million dollars that he or she distributes to council members for chairing committees or for doing good works in their home districts (Hicks 1995d).

Similar to most large legislative bodies, the city council does most of its substantive work in committees, with each member of the council serving on at least three committees. Committee work allows the council to address a wide variety of issues simultaneously by dividing up jurisdiction over those areas of public policy and city government the council deems important. Members seek positions on those committees that will allow them to get benefits for their districts, advocate for significant issues and programs, or exploit their expertise in a specific policy or program area. Committees hold hearings on proposed legislation and hold oversight and investigative hearings on those areas of public policy and the agencies of the executive branch that fall under their jurisdiction. These hearings may involve testimony from representatives of the mayor, officials from executive branch agencies, interest groups, and the general public. Proposed legislation receiving a favorable vote at the committee level will then go to the entire council for a vote. Over time, the number of committees and committee jurisdiction may change to reflect the council's new areas of interest or changing emphasis. Prior to the 1989 charter revision, the council had no committees that dealt with land use issues, since land use policy and zoning was under the control of the Board of Estimate. After the charter revision, the council added a Committee on Land Use, the second most important committee, as well as a Subcommittee on Landmarks, Public Siting and Maritime Uses, a Subcommittee on Planning, Dispositions and Concessions, and a Subcommittee on Zoning and Franchises. A Committee on Aging was added in the mid-1980s and a Committee on Mental Health, Mental Retardation, Alcoholism and Drug Abuse was added in the 1990s (Boorstin 1986; New York City Department of Citywide Administrative Services 1985, 23; 1996, 35–36). In the aftermath of the attacks on the World Trade Center in September 2001, the council taking office in January 2002, added a Select Committee on Lower Manhattan Development (New York City Council 2002b). The most important committee is the Finance Committee. It coordinates the council's review, modification, and approval of the mayor's budget and has jurisdiction over all taxation issues.

Prior to term limits, council chairs who maintained their positions over a number of terms generally became experts in the policy areas over which their committee had jurisdiction. One of the significant disadvantages of term limits for the council is the loss of this expertise as committee chairs are now replaced at least once every eight years.

Speakers customarily give the most important committee chairs to members of the council who supported their candidacy. Aside from the status and power of being a committee chair, there are also financial implications. Each of the committee chair positions comes with an annual salary stipend ranging from one thousand to fourteen thousand dollars depending on the importance assigned to the committee by the speaker. These stipends are called payments in lieu of expenses, affectionately nicknamed "lulus" (Hicks 1995d). The speaker's stipend in 1986 was thirty thousand dollars, and was raised to thirty-five thousand dollars by 1995 (Barbanel 1986a; Hicks 1995d). When he became speaker, Gifford Miller lowered the stipend (Gotham Gazette 2002). A councilmember's salary in 1986 was forty-seven thousand dollars a year (Barbanel 1986b). In 1995, a councilperson's salary was fifty-five thousand dollars. This was raised to seventy thousand in 1996 (Hicks 1995d). It is currently ninety thousand dollars a year.

During his years as speaker, Peter Vallone (1986–2001) took a number of steps to enhance the position's power and to increase the visibility and power of the city council as well. During his first year in office, he increased the size of the council's staff by more than 50 percent (Daley 1986). By the mid-1990s, the council's staff had quadrupled under Vallone's leadership (Hicks 1995d). Part of the staff increase was the establishment of the council's first investigative unit. In addition, under Vallone, the council hired a lobbyist to represent it in Albany, independent of the mayor's lobbyists (Daley 1986). Several years later, the council hired a lobbyist in Washington as well (Finder 1988). Despite the increase in the size of the council staff, the Mayor's Office of Management and Budget has ten times as many people as the Council's Finance Division; and the mayor's Law Department has over a thousand people working, while the council's legal staff is fewer than forty (Hicks 1995d).

Although the operations of the council under Speaker Vallone were far more open and equitable than they were under previous speakers, he still wielded a great deal of discretionary power and used it to move the council under his direction. Although Speaker Vallone claimed that he did not coerce members to vote his way, there were a few members who lost their committee chair positions because they did not vote according to his wishes (Jacobs 1996). Moreover, Speaker Vallone distributed a discretionary fund to members of the council for community projects in their home districts. In 1995, the average grant given by the speaker was eighty thousand dollars; some council members, out of favor with the speaker, received as little as fifty thousand (Hicks 1995d). One council member noted that she was pressured to vote for the 1996 fiscal year budget even though she thought that the cuts in education and social services were too high. She reported being told that her district "would suffer" if she did not vote for the budget (Hicks 1995d). The budget appeared to be the single most important issue over which Speaker Vallone demanded the loyalty of council members (Liff 1994). In addition to his discretionary fund that assisted council members with district projects, Speaker Vallone also had a political action committee that he used to help fund the campaigns of council allies (Jacobs 1996). Even most of Vallone's critics recognized that he succeeded in elevating the status of the council as an institution within the city's political system, beyond the impact of the abolition of the Board of Estimate. And some went even further by arguing that in order for Vallone to make the council an effective counter to the mayor, he had to centralize power under the speaker's position (Cardwell 2001).

Peter Vallone's retirement due to term limits, the election of Michael Bloomberg as a Republican mayor, and the impact of term limits on the city council created some challenges for the council as an institution. With term limits plus retirements, thirty-eight of the fifty-one council members taking office in January 2002 were new. Due to Speaker Vallone's retirement, one of the first responsibilities of the new council would be to elect a leader. Other than the knowledge that the speaker would be selected by a majority of the council, the selection process was unclear. Vallone's selection as speaker in the mid-1980s had been structured primarily by county Democratic leaders. Sixteen years later, though, the strength of the county Democratic leaders was less certain since some of the new members of the council were not tied to the county party organizations. The party organizations in the boroughs had been unable to manage replacing the massive number of term-limited council retirements. As a result, in the September 2001 Democratic Party primary, a number of city council candidates endorsed by the county party organization lost to more independent candidates (Hicks 2001b).

Twenty-one of the new and more independent council candidates began meeting before the November election. Calling themselves the Fresh Democracy Council, they initiated discussions regarding the operations of the city council. Their primary focus was on decentralizing power within the legislative body, taking authority away from the speaker by inhibiting his ability to reward and punish members. The Fresh Democracy Council was proposing that the operating budgets of council members be equivalent and that the speaker provide the council with an itemized list of council expenditures in order to make the speaker more accountable (Cardwell 2002a). Also, under Speaker Vallone, Committee chairs had been unable to hire their own staffs. All the hiring was done centrally by Speaker Vallone. The Fresh Democracy Council was seeking to give some of the speaker's power to committee chairs (Hicks 2001b; Ruiz 2001). They also wanted a rule that "bills considered favorably by committees come to the full council for a vote" within six weeks of their proposal (Cardwell 2002a). Despite this activity to decentralize the power of the speaker, some expressed the view that if the power of the speaker were weakened, the power and status of the city council as a whole would diminish.

The council speaker selection race began shortly after the November 2001 election with as many as eight council members, some of them new, seeking the position. The process was more open than had been the case in 1986, with candidates engaging in public debates and significant lobbying by labor unions seeking to influence the choice of a speaker (Hicks 2001d). A spokesperson for the Central Labor Council stated, "The labor movement put unprecedented emphasis on City Council elections in 2001 in order to accomplish two things. . . . The first goal was to elect pro-labor council members, and the second goal was to elect a pro-labor speaker" (quoted in Hicks 2001d).

Gifford Miller, a councilman from Manhattan's Upper East Side, ultimately won because Thomas Manton, leader of the Queens Democratic Party, and Roberto Ramirez of the Bronx Democratic Party, met privately and decided to give their organizations' support to Miller (Cooper 2002). Thus, Miller's ascendancy to the speaker's position was not entirely different from Vallone's. There were also other reasons that explain Miller's success. He supported the Fresh Democracy Council's platform of procedural changes (Ruiz 2002). He also had his own political action committee that he used to support new candidates in their first run for the council, and he personally campaigned for many of them (Cooper 2002). The relationships that Miller established while supporting candidates in the outer boroughs helped deflate any criticism that he was too Manhattan-oriented (Hicks 2002). Moreover, he received the support of several large labor unions including Dennis Rivera's Service Employees International Union (1199) (Cardwell 2002b).

After his election as speaker, Gifford Miller had the task of filling the council committee leadership positions. The Queens and Bronx Democratic Party organizations and their leaders played a significant role in committee assignments. As a repayment to the Queens Democratic Party organization for their support of his candidacy, Miller appointed two Queens council members, David Weprin and Melinda Katz, to the chairs of the finance and land use committees respectively (Cardwell 2002c). Councilman Bill Perkins, who dropped out of the speaker's race and gave his support to Miller, was appointed chair of the Government Operations Committee. Councilman Joel Rivera, part of the Bronx Democratic Party organization, was appointed the Majority Leader of the Council, the position with the second highest stipend (Citizens Union 2002a). Due to the city's fiscal problems, Miller cut the stipends (lulus) going to many of the chairs of the committees. He even cut his own Speaker's stipend, giving himself approximately ten thousand dollars less than Speaker Vallone had given himself in his last year (Cardwell 2002d).

Although the Fresh Democracy Council played only a small role in the selection of the speaker, Gifford Miller did support most of their reforms. In January 2002, the council approved a number of reforms that significantly weakened the power of the speaker and made him more accountable to the members of the council. To prevent the speaker from using his power to punish or reward members, council rules require the speaker to equitably allocate discretionary funds for district projects. The speaker's powers to control legislation were also weakened. The sponsor of a piece of legislation can call for his or her bill's consideration by the entire council if it has not appeared on the council's stated meeting agenda forty-five days after it receives approval from its respective committee (Chester 2002). This means that the Speaker can no longer hold up legislation with which he or she disagrees. Some of the most significant rule changes voted in by the new council involve council staff. Under Speaker Vallone, council members complained that the central staff was better paid than the council member's staff in the district offices. The new rules required a more equitable, but not completely equal, allocation of resources. Another rule regarding staff required that the central staff provide its legislative drafting (bill writing) talents on a more equitable basis. Finally, in response to the complaint by committee chairs that the speaker hires all committee staff, a new rule allows each committee chair to hire their own senior staff person. While this appears more democratic, some have expressed the concern that some chairs might use this new power to respond to patronage needs and not hire the best staff person for that committee. Although Speaker Vallone did all the hiring, he received high marks for the quality of his staff (Chester 2002).

Under Peter Vallone's leadership and the old rules, the speaker had numerous tools to bring the council together, even if the use of those tools was not perceived as democratic. The rules changes promulgated by the council under Gifford Miller weakened the Speaker but did not leave him powerless. In November 2002, the city council faced a difficult vote on increasing property taxes in response to the city's budget shortfalls. Only three Democratic council members opposed the vote to raise the property tax by 18.5 percent. In February 2003, Council Speaker Miller moved to sanction the three council members by taking away a committee chair from each of them. Speaker Miller needed the support of the council to punish the three members. Only four Democrats opposed his move. While many saw the move as a mild rebuke, Speaker Miller made the point that he would not tolerate dissent on critical votes (Steinhauer 2003).

Gifford Miller was term-limited out of the council in 2005. Councilwoman Christine Quinn of Manhattan replaced him as speaker, with the support, as in Miller's case, of the major borough/county Democratic Party organizations: Queens; the Bronx; and Brooklyn. Councilwoman Quinn was viewed as an ally of Miller on the council and, like Miller, had been a vocal opponent of the Olympic/Jets Stadium, which would have been build in her district (Hu 2006a). Similar to Miller and Vallone, Speaker Quinn awarded council committee chair assignments to council members from those party organizations that supported her candidacy (Hu 2006b).

The Budgetary Process

The city's annual budget describes how the resources of the political system are to be allocated and who is going to pay for them. In most democratic political systems, budgets are constructed on an annual basis as part of a process that involves the legislative and executive branches. For urban and most local political systems, budgets establish the parameters within which services will be delivered as well as how these services will be financed. As a result, the annual budgetary process at times can become very visible and highly conflictual, especially if the budget under discussion deviates significantly from the previous year's budget, or if the political system is experiencing fiscal stress.

Much of the city's budgetary process is mandated by the city charter. The new fiscal year begins on July 1. The budgetary process formally begins in January with the mayor's publication of his preliminary budget for the coming fiscal year.

Prior to January, the mayor and his or her staff collect information on projected revenues and needed expenses for the next fiscal year, and in conjunction with the agencies of the executive branch they construct a preliminary budget that reflects how the mayor wants to use the city's resources within the limits of available revenues and spending needs. The city council then examines the budget, holds public hearings that attempt to examine the service delivery and program impact of the mayor's proposed budget, and produces its own set of recommendations by late March. Frequently during these hearings, interest groups representing those who deliver or receive city services lobby the city council in an attempt to restore any cuts in their programs, or to increase their program's budget. The mayor then submits an executive budget to the council by late April, based on updated estimates and any revisions in preliminary budget. The council holds public hearings again, and enters into a period of negotiations with the Mayor's Office of Management and Budget to work out any differences between the proposed executive budget and the council's own spending and revenue priorities. At this point in the process, the need for tax increases or the possibility of tax decreases is also addressed. After the council votes and approves the budget, in early June, the mayor has several days in which he or she can veto any increase or addition the council has made to the budget. The mayor may not veto decreases the council has made to his executive budget. The council can override a mayoral veto with a two-thirds vote.

There are three pieces to the city's budget. The expense budget includes the city's annual operating expenses. The capital budget includes spending on facility construction and improvements such as buildings, roads, or very expensive equipment. The revenue budget lists the resources the city is using to pay for the expense and capital budgets. It includes taxes, fees, intergovernmental fiscal assistance, and debt. According to state law, the city's budget must be balanced; that is, all expenditures must be accounted for by equivalent revenue (New York City Council 2002c). During the budgetary process, state, city, and private fiscal monitors issue reports and statements assessing the accuracy of the city's revenue projections for the coming fiscal year and issue their opinions as to whether the proposed budget is balanced (expenditures versus revenues). At the state level, these monitors include the Financial Control Board and the state comptroller. At the city level, the monitors include the Independent Budget Office and the city comptroller. And in the private sector, the bond rating corporations also publish their opinion of the city's budget.

The New York City budget process has traditionally provided an illustration of the city council in its representation role. The mayor submits a budget, including reduced expenditures, to the council, and the council proceeds to restore some of the cuts in response to constituent and group demands. The mayor's budget represents a citywide perspective, although one that is biased toward the mayor's own ideology and policy choices. The mayor has a much larger budget staff than the council, and therefore has the superior ability to construct a budget based on accurate projections of city revenue as well as accurate predictions of the impact of budget cuts or enhancements. The council's perspective on the budget is more parochial, as its efforts are usually supported by interest and advocacy groups who descend on the council seeking the restoration of cuts, or enhancements. Many of these groups are equipped with the information to educate council members on the impact that cuts will have on his or her district. In discussing the budgetary process, Mayor Giuliani admitted that his budget staff purposefully subjected programs to budget cuts in anticipation that some, if not all, of the cuts would be restored by the council. "This is the game we play every year, if you have not figured it out yet. . . . We take things out of the budget, we put them back. . . . In order to make sure the budget does not grow by 7 percent, 8 percent, 10, 12 percent, that is what you do. . . . Every year you have to be willing, if you are the mayor to have a good sense of humor and have the New York Times and the Post and the Daily News and everybody else write that you are cutting pacemakers for people and you are putting old people in the zoo or something. I mean it is ridiculous, it is ridiculous" (quoted in Lipton 2001). The mayor, members of the city council, and interest group representatives have all criticized the budgetary process and the roles each party play, but there has been no major movement to reform the process.

Although the budgetary process gives a political system the opportunity to periodically review its priorities, some areas of city public policy go unaddressed by the budget. The budgetary process has traditionally not provided a mechanism through which a political system can review tax expenditures, that is, the use of tax forgiveness as a means to subsidize actions valued by the political system. This includes most of the tax incentives discussed in chapter two. Simply stated, the budget does not consider uncollected revenue as a cost. While budgets could include tax expenditures as expenses, or as foregone revenue, most public budgets do not do this. This does not mean the council cannot or does not review these programs. The council has held hearings on economic development tax expenditures in the past but it does not routinely consider them as part of the budgetary process.

In the years following the 1989 charter revision, there was tension between the mayor and the city council over the budget due to both institutions jockeying for position under a new process and rules. During the Dinkins administration and in the early Giuliani years, this tension was exacerbated by a poor economy forcing the city to make significant budget cuts, raise taxes, or both. In 1991, the council and Mayor Dinkins compromised with the council, agreeing to raise property taxes more than it had initially wanted in exchange for the mayor restoring some cuts in services (Purdum 1991b).

In 1994–95, the Mayor Giuliani and the council went to court over control of the budgetary process. At issue was a mid–fiscal year budget modification needed to balance the budget. When negotiations between the mayor and council broke down, the council attempted to pass a budget modification over the mayor's veto, but the mayor claimed the charter did not give the council that authority. The mayor, as chief executive, refused to certify the council's budget modification and ordered city agencies to implement his own budget cuts. Comptroller Alan Hevesi, the city official who distributes the city's money, decided that he would implement both branches' budget cuts. Comptroller Hevesi explained that this was being done in part because, not knowing who was going to prevail, implementing both sets of cuts was the fiscally prudent move (Mitchell 1994a). In early December, the mayor and Speaker Vallone attempted to negotiate their differences one more time, but were unable to reach an agreement (Myers 1994a). An editorial in the *New York Times*, chided the city council: "This confrontation is over political muscle, not fiscal details. The revised city charter gave the council substantially more power than before. Up to this point, the council has not exploited that power aggressively. Now its Democratic majority is embarrassed by its failure to press for more changes in the new Republican's mayor's original budget when it could have done so last June. Members are also angry that he now proposed to cancel some of the few changes they made. June was the time to fight. Not now" (*New York Times* 1994).

On December 8, 1994, the city council filed suit in the New York State Supreme Court to stop the mayor from implementing his budget cuts (Myers 1994b). On December 22, the judge in the case issued her ruling, throwing out both the council's and the mayor's proposed budget modifications. The mayor's modifications were thrown out because they had not been approved by the council, and the council's modifications were thrown out because the mayor had withdrawn his budget modification before the council's initial vote, giving it nothing to consider and no reason to come up with its own plan. Nevertheless, the ruling left the government without a budget modification. As a result, with the budget out of balance, the mayor was able to use his impoundment power with little or no council input (Mitchell 1994b).

Even surplus budgets can create conflict. In the fiscal year 2001 budget cycle, the mayor and council fought over which taxes would be rolled back and who would benefit. At issue was a reduction of an income tax surcharge that had been initiated during the Dinkins administration. In this case the council got most of what it wanted. Those taxpayers earning seventy thousand dollars a year or less would get a 12 percent reduction, with more affluent New Yorkers getting less of a reduction. Those taxpayers earning over a million dollars a year would receive less than a 1 percent reduction. This tax cut required state approval (Lipton 2000).

City council speakers frequently view a vote on the budget as a "key institutional vote" (Hicks 1994). In 1994, there was evidence that Speaker Vallone used his resources, committee chairs, discretionary funds, and perks to reward supporters and punish dissidents in order to build a majority coalition (Hicks 1994). Councilman Lloyd Henry from Brooklyn stated, "I was being lobbied from all sides. . . . The unions wanted a no vote and the Speaker's staff, of course, wanted me to go along with them. . . . As a junior member of the Council who was just elected last year, I wanted to be able to bring something back home to my district. . . . By voting no, I risked losing everything my first time at bat" (quoted in Hicks 1994). The speaker promised Councilman Henry fifty-two thousand dollars for a senior center and a youth center plus additional money for a Caribbean cultural center at Medgar Evers College in his district (Hicks 1994). Facing a similar dilemma, Councilwoman Una Clarke from Crown Heights, Brooklyn, reached a similar decision. "It was a tremendously difficult decision for me. . . . But for the residents of my district, a no vote would have been an irresponsible act on my part" (quoted in Hicks 1994).

Councilwoman Virginia Fields of Manhattan reached a different conclusion. "In the final analysis, I just couldn't vote for a budget that had such a severe impact on health care, on education and on social service in my district" (quoted in Hicks 1994). Councilwoman Fields was well aware that her vote would cost her thousands of dollars in discretionary funds distributed by Speaker Vallone and possibly a chair of a subcommittee (Hicks 1994). Regarding the fact that many minority council members voted for the budget in response to the speaker's lobbying and largesse, Fields stated, "If they take it, they take it. . . . It will be their loss. I'm constantly surprised by how important these positions are to some people in the council. But it really is a question of integrity. The Speaker asked me to vote for it. But I just can't vote for something I oppose" (quoted in Hicks 1994).

The Legislative Process

The city council is at the center of the process through which proposed legislation becomes law. The legislature is the political system's legitimizing body in the production of law and public policy. Yet similar to any other political system's legislative process, legislators in New York City are only one of the many actors participating in the production of law and public policy. The legislative process is initiated in one of several ways. The mayor can initiate it by finding legislators to introduce and sponsor the legislation for him/her. Interest groups can lobby members of the city council and have them introduce legislation on their behalf. And of course, legislators can introduce legislation on their own. Contrary to the rules of some legislative bodies, legislation introduced into the New York City Council can only address one subject. Non-germane amendments are not allowed (Kivelson 1991, 36).

After legislation has been introduced, the speaker assigns it to a relevant committee or committees that hold public hearings. At that point interest groups, citizens, and any other interested individuals can come and testify either in favor of or opposed to the legislation. The committee then modifies the legislation if they believe modification is necessary. This precedes a vote by the committee on the legislation. If the vote is positive, the legislation is then scheduled by the speaker for a vote by the full council.

In the New York City Council, most substantive debate and discussion of the legislation takes place in committee. There is rarely debate or discussion of the legislation by the entire council, although each council member is entitled to explain their vote. If there is still significant disagreement over the legislation after it leaves committee, the speaker can direct further modifications in the legislation prior to it coming to a vote by the full council. Speaker Vallone had the power to schedule full council votes, delaying a vote indefinitely if necessary. One of the rules changes after the 2001 council elections eliminated the power of the speaker to delay indefinitely committee-approved legislation from coming to the full council for a vote. Once the full council considers and passes the bill, it goes to the mayor for signing. If the mayor "takes no action" after thirty days of receiving it from the council, the legislation becomes law. If the mayor vetoes the legislation, it is returned to the council, which then has thirty days to override the veto by a two-thirds majority (Kivelson 1991, 36).

The legislative process often illustrates the tension between the legislator's roles as lawmaker and representative. On occasion, the council deals with legislation that, if passed, would benefit the entire city but at the same time might have a negative impact on a neighborhood or borough. Legislators in their representative role defend their constituencies and oppose the legislation. Legislators in their lawmaking role either seek to compromise to move the legislation forward or sacrifice the parochial interest of their constituents for the greater good of the city. In 2006, the council debated and passed Mayor Bloomberg's Solid Waste Management Plan. In the spirit of environmental justice, the plan attempted to allocate the burden of waste transfer stations across all five boroughs. Although the plan passed overwhelmingly, several members of the council from Manhattan opposed the plan, since their districts were slated to be the site of new waste transfer stations.

Since the 1989 charter revision and the increase in the number of seats on the city council, the council has been virtually veto-proof. There have been fifty-one seats on the city council since 1991. Since that time, the greatest number of seats the Republicans have occupied on the council is seven. Under Speakers Vallone, Miller, and Quinn, most votes on legislation taken by the full council passed with a veto-proof (i.e., more than two-thirds) majority (Citizens Union 1997; Citizens Union 1998; Citizens Union 1999; Citizens Union 2000a; Gotham Gazette-City Government-City Laws). In many cases the Republican minority voted on the losing side of the issue. During Speaker Vallone's tenure, there were also a number of votes, including a controversial piece of legislation on lead paint regulations, in which the most liberal Democrats on the council found themselves voting on the losing side.

The recent voting record on the council suggests that the Democratic Party has a leadership that knows how to use its majority. The small number of negative votes that each piece of legislation received reflects the speaker's ability to use resources wisely, build consensus, as well as avoid divisive issues. Due in part to Speaker Vallone's moderate position on most policy issues, Mayor Giuliani vetoed council legislation only about a dozen times during his eight years as mayor, and a majority of those were overridden. Under Speaker Miller, Mayor Bloomberg vetoed council legislation three dozen times, all of which were overridden (Gotham Gazette–City Government–City Laws).

There were occasions in which the council's overriding a mayoral veto resulted in the mayor initiating litigation to check the council. In late 1994, the council voted to create an independent agency to monitor police corruption. The mayor did not like the legislation because of the selection process of the five members of the monitoring panel; the mayor only appointed two, the council appointed two, and the chair and fifth member of the panel was selected jointly by the council and the mayor. The mayor vetoed the legislation and the council overrode it (Hicks 1995). The mayor then filed suit against the council in state court, arguing that the council's action infringed on his powers as chief executive (Hicks 1995b). In June 1995, a State Supreme Court judge ruled that the council had gone beyond its authority and that the creation of the independent commission to monitor the police would "curtail the Mayor's executive prerogatives" (quoted in Hicks 1995c). The mayor and the council went through a similar battle over an independent police review board in 1998 that also ended up in court (Onishi 1998).

The City Council and Economic Development

The city council as an institution, and individual council members, are not constrained or influenced by economic development issues or concerns similar to the mayor. The council is not held responsible for the city's poor economic performance and there are few expectations on the part of the electorate that the council will act to promote economic development. In most areas of economic development, the council has been far more adept at playing its representative role than its lawmaking role. Due to each council member's desire to protect the interests of his or her district, the council rarely, if ever, initiates economic development programs. It is the executive branch with its superior resources and citywide focus that initiates these types of proposals while the council's role is more reactive.

When the Board of Estimate was abolished, the council took on much of the board's land use policy functions. The 1989 charter revision established a land use approval process in which the council and the mayor share responsibility. Prior to that point, the council played little or no role in land use policy and zoning. Due to the impact that land use modifications and policy could have on individual districts, the council took its new responsibility very seriously. The committee structure of the council was reorganized with multiple subcommittees feeding into the council's new committee on land use. The previously discussed megastore zoning proposal by the Giuliani administration as well as the

Willamsburg-Greenpoint rezoning (chapter two) illustrate the way that the council can either thwart economic development attempts by the mayor or force him or her to accommodate the council's representative role before a policy is approved. Although the council's approval is needed for the establishment of a business improvement district (BID), this approval process is little more than an exercise in logrolling and distributive politics. The council will usually defer to the indigenous council member in deciding if the proposed BID should be created. There is usually no reason for its not being approved other than significant opposition in the community. The local community gets an organization that will improve the economic development profile of the neighborhood. The fact that BID creation is rarely controversial and allows members of the council to simultaneously play both a representative and lawmaking role explains the council's positive, albeit limited, role in their creation.

The council in its legislative capacity is involved in the creation of many of the as-of-right tax incentives. One of the more conspicuous aspects of the city's economic development tax incentive policy is the fact that more lucrative "as of right" benefits are offered to developers and businesses for activities in the outer boroughs and north of Ninety-sixth Street in Manhattan, than to developers active in the central business district and south of Ninety-sixth Street. This is one way that council members from outside the central business district attempt to redress the perceived Manhattan-centered imbalance in the city's economic development policies. The council plays little or no role in the firm-specific incentives negotiated by the mayor individually with corporations threatening to leave or thinking about moving to the city. The council has held hearings on the use of firm-specific tax incentives as an economic development policy tool. At these hearings, those testifying have criticized the use of incentives by the mayor and requested greater involvement by the council in this policy (New York City Council Committee Economic Development 2002). The council has not, however, attempted to abridge the power of the mayor to negotiate these deals, nor has it made any attempt to participate in or oversee the negotiations between the mayor and individual corporations.

In the aftermath of the events of September 11, 2001, much of the city's economic development activity was focused on Lower Manhattan. At present, the city council is playing little or no role in this effort. The Lower Manhattan Development Corporation is a joint effort of the state and the city. The governor and the mayor both appointed members to the board of the corporation, but the city council has no formal representation on the board or direct input to the board. This has not stopped the city council from holding hearings on any number of economic development issues in Lower Manhattan in the wake of September 11. The new Council, elected in 2001, established a Select Committee on Lower Manhattan Redevelopment that monitors and holds hearings on the rebuilding of Lower Manhattan. Among the Lower Manhattan economic development issues the council has addressed are the overall vision for the redevelopment

of Ground Zero and the surrounding area, the rebuilding of transportation infrastructure, the role of federal aid in the redevelopment of lower Manhattan
including the use of Community Development Block Grant monies to aid small
business, the Federal Emergency Management Administration disaster loan program, the utilization of environmental designs in the rebuilding of Lower
Manhattan, and the possible movement of the U.S. Customs Service out of Lower
Manhattan. Since the council has little jurisdiction over much of the development of Lower Manhattan most of the hearings have been informational or oversight hearings. In terms of legislative output, as of 2006 the council had
produced no legislation directly relevant to the economic redevelopment of
Lower Manhattan, nor was there any legislation pending (Gotham Gazette–City
Government–City Laws). The council did pass one piece of legislation that
addressed street closings in lower Manhattan. The legislation mandated that the
city communicate more effectively with affected communities regarding long-
term street closings. The council has also held hearings on the health impacts of
those who participated in the cleanup of the World Trade Center site.

The City Council and Intergovernmental Relations

At the state and federal levels, the council's activities are hampered by a number
of factors. First, the mayor in his chief of state role is viewed as the official
spokesperson for the city. As a result, any council action directed at the state and
federal levels is secondary to the actions of the mayor. Second, both the state and
federal levels have their own legislative bodies with elected officials who represent the citizens of New York City.

The council does not have a long history or experience lobbying at the fed-
eral level. At this level, the council is much more likely to follow the mayor's lead.
Council members frequently communicate and cooperate with members of
Congress. They occasionally hold joint press conferences on the steps of City Hall
when they share a common perspective on an issue. In 1999, council member
Gifford Miller, along with Manhattan Borough President C. Virginia Fields and
Congresswoman Carolyn Maloney, held a press conference at which they called
for the building of the Second Avenue Subway. If the subway was going to be
built, federal monies would be needed, so Congresswoman Maloney's presence
signaled that the city had some support at the appropriate level of government
(New York City Council Press Conference 1999).

Federal elected officials occasionally testify at city council hearings. Public
appearances by federal elected officials with members of the city council are
often more symbolic than substantive. At the same time, support by local congresspersons and senators for local issues in need of federal support may be a
necessary, although not sufficient, condition for subsequent federal action. In
early 2002, the City Council Finance Committee held a joint hearing with the
Committees on Lower Manhattan Redevelopment and Federal, State Relations on

the role of federal aid in assisting the city out of its latest fiscal crisis. Senator Schumer and Congresspersons Maloney and Charles Rangel all testified (New York City Council Committee Finance 2002).

Members of the federal executive branch also testify at council hearings. When the city council was debating how to respond to the federal Environmental Protection Agency (EPA) mandate that the city's water be filtered, representatives of the EPA and the Army Corps of Engineers testified before the Council Committee on Environmental Protection on several occasions offering expert testimony on the meaning and implementation of the applicable mandates (New York City Council Committee Environmental Protection 1999). On occasion, the council will pass resolutions calling for federal action. The resolutions carry no weight, but are simply a request by the council that action be taken. In 2001, the council passed a resolution calling on the federal and state governments to cooperate in the removal of PCBs from the Hudson River. In the aftermath of the attack on the World Trade Center, the council passed resolutions calling on FEMA and the Department of Justice to give additional financial assistance to the New York City Police Department and calling on FEMA to lift its five million dollar cap on the community disaster loan program. Again, in many cases these actions are more symbolic than substantive, but they do serve to lend emphasis to an issue and may be a precursor to future action.

Given that the bond between the city and the state is much stronger and far more comprehensive than the city's relationship with the federal government, the council over time has placed more of its resources in lobbying at the state level. There was not much council activity at the state level prior to Peter Vallone's becoming speaker and prior to the abolition of the Board of Estimate. After he became council speaker, Vallone established a permanent presence in Albany with a full-time representative. In addition, Vallone made numerous trips to Albany, although not nearly as many as the mayor. In 1999, when the state was considering abolishing the commuter tax, both Vallone and the mayor went to Albany in an attempt to convince state legislators and the governor not to repeal the tax (Vallone 2002b).

City council members frequently run for state legislative office. In somewhat of a reversal, in 2001, four of the newly elected members of the council had previously served in the state legislature. Term limits may increase the number of city council members running for state office and, conversely, may also cause more state legislators to run for the city council, given the increasing number of council vacancies that will occur. If this takes places, there will be more city legislators with knowledge of the state political system and more state legislators with a knowledge of the city, further facilitating state-city relations in the legislative branch.

In addition to lobbying by the council speaker, the city council communicates with the state level through the use of resolutions and home rule messages. Similar to resolutions that the council sends to Congress or federal agencies, resolutions sent to the state level carry no official weight. They are simply requests by the council that specific action at the state level be taken. In 1999, the council passed a resolution calling on the state legislature "to pass a law that would require uniformed members of the NYPD to reside within the city" (Citizens Union 1999). They passed the resolution even though they knew that, given the power of the Patrolman's Benevolent Association at the state level, the resolution would never be enacted into law (Citizens Union 1999). In September 2002, the Council Committee on Aging held hearings on proposed resolutions asking the state to require more stringent staffing and reporting standards for nursing home and hospice employees. Among other requirements, the standards, if converted into law by the state legislature, would have required fingerprinting and criminal background checks on current and prospective employees in nursing homes and hospices (New York City Council Committee on Aging 2002).

Home rule messages are more formal resolutions asking the state to give the city the ability to act in an area where the city has no authority under the state's home rule provisions. The most significant use of the home rule message is in the area of taxation. Under the city charter, governed by the state's home rule provisions, the only tax the city can levy without state approval is the property (real estate) tax. For any other tax, the city needs state approval. Elected state officials do not want to be held responsible for raising the taxes of city residents. As a result, if the city wants to raise a tax over which they have no authority, the council and mayor will send the state legislature a home rule message asking it for the ability to raise the tax. If the state responds positively to the home rule message, it will pass enabling legislation allowing the city to raise or lower the tax within limits (Altman 2002).

The City Council and Racial/Ethnic Diversity

As the political system's institution of representative governance, the city council is influenced to a great extent by ethnic and racial relations. The ethnic and racial makeup of the council has changed significantly over time, giving minorities a larger role in the governance of the city's political system. The federal Voting Rights Act (chapter five) mandated that when governments engage in redistricting it be done in a nondiscriminatory manner. The act also established special review procedures for those units of state and local government that had a history of discrimination. Three of New York City's boroughs fall into this category. The 1989 charter revision expanded the number of seats on the city council from thirty-five to fifty-one in order to give minority representatives a better chance to win a seat on the council.

The redrawing of city council legislative district boundaries is directed by an appointed commission. The city charter mandates that the districting commission include fifteen members, seven appointed by the mayor, and eight appointed by the city council, with the majority party appointing five members and the minority party appointing three. The charter also mandates that the commission "shall have among its members . . . members of the racial and language minority groups in New York City which are protected by the United States Voting Rights Act of 1965, as amended, in proportion, as close as practicable, to their population in the city" (quoted in New York City Districting Commission 2002). In April 1990, the members of the city's districting commission that were appointed by the mayor and the council included seven Whites, four Blacks, three Hispanics, and one Asian American (Roberts 1990). As a result of the 1989 charter revision, there was an expectation that new council district lines would be drawn to increase the percentage of minority members on the council. Many hoped, if not assumed, that with the inclusion of sixteen new council districts, the percentage of minorities on the council would increase to at least one third. Throughout 1990 and 1991, the districting commission and its staff held numerous meetings with civic, religious, and ethnic groups as well as over two-dozen public hearings throughout the city. In preparation for the November 1991 council elections the commission and its staff were required to produce a new council district map by May 1991. In constructing council districts that would favor minority candidates, the commission used an informal rule that if a minority group made up 60 percent of the district's population, it would favor a minority candidate. The sixty percent rule was used because minority populations usually produce "fewer eligible voters and lower voter turnouts" (Lee 1991a). As a result, 60 percent is the minimum population needed to give a minority candidate a chance of winning. Prior to the 1991 redistricting, there were ten council districts (out of thirty-five) that had over a 60 percent minority population and these ten districts produced the council's nine minority members, six Blacks and three Hispanics (Lee 1991a). In addition to the charter regulation that the redistricting "ensure fair and effective representation of the racial and ethnic language minority groups," and the implicit mandate that the redistricting produce a greater percentage of minority council members, the charter mandated that the commission had to produce council districts whose population did not exceed 10 percent "of the average population for all districts" in order to guarantee within reason the concept of one person–one vote (New York City Districting Commission 2002). The commission was also mandated by the charter to "keep intact neighborhoods and communities with established ties of common interest and association, whether historical, racial, economic, ethnic, religious, or other" (quoted in New York City Districting Commission 2002).

With fifteen members on the commission, nine positive votes would be needed to approve a districting plan. In addition, any districting plan produced by the commission would have to be approved by the U.S. Department of Justice under the Voting Rights Act (Pear 1991d; Roberts 1991b).

One of the conflicts that plagued the districting commission was the interest on the part of some of the commissioners appointed by the city council to draw the new district lines in a way that would protect incumbent members of the council. In order to limit this conflict as much as possible, both Mayor Dinkins and Speaker Vallone were successful in getting the state legislature to approve a "one-time rule change to permit council candidates to run anywhere in their home borough" regardless of residence, with the understanding that they would move into their district if they won the election (*New York Times* 1991a). This was done not only to assuage the fears and gain the support of council incumbents, but also to limit the amount of gerrymandering taking place to keep individuals, either incumbents or challengers, out of a district (*New York Times* 1991a).

There was considerable conflict on the commission between those members appointed by the mayor and those appointed by the city council. The commission members appointed by the mayor believed that the council-appointed members were more interested in protecting incumbents than increasing the number of minorities. The eight commission members appointed by the council were successful in electing the chair, Frank Macchiarola, a political ally of Speaker Vallone. The conflict was exacerbated by the fact that some of the members of the commission appointed by Mayor Dinkins were associated with insurgent wings of the Democratic Party in Brooklyn and Queens. Some council incumbents feared that this group wanted to draw district lines that would not only help elect as many minorities to the council as possible but also unseat as many party regular incumbents as possible, even if they were minorities (Glaberson 1991). The mayor's appointees on the Districting Commission were supported by a coalition of minorities, White liberals, and some union leaders who were seeking a council that would be more responsive to the mayor's agenda as well as one that had a higher percentage of minorities (Lee 1991c; Purdum 1991a). At one point, Speaker Vallone described the districting conflict as a "fight between the legislative and executive branches" (Lee 1991c).

Another split on the commission was between Black and Hispanic interests. Hispanic leaders accused several Black members of the commission of pursuing an agenda that would produce more Black council districts at the expense of Hispanic council districts. Ezmeralda Simmons, a Black member of the commission, argued that the Blacks on the commission wanted to protect the interests of Blacks, not necessarily damage the interests of Hispanics. "I believe this is something inevitable when it comes down to dividing power. . . . There is no easy way of resolving it, particularly when people are losing power and others are gaining power and the question is who gets what when" (quoted in Gray 1991d).

In a split and highly divisive eleven to four vote, the districting commission released its plan in mid-May 1991. It contained seventeen districts where minorities comprised over 60 percent of the population and therefore would have a good chance of electing a Black or Hispanic representative. In addition, there were several districts where minorities made up a majority of the population but fell short of the 60 percent benchmark (Lee 1991d). Using a 50 percent majority criterion, the Commission created twelve districts with a Black majority, ten districts with a Hispanic majority, and five additional districts in which a combination of minority groups would comprise a majority (Roberts 1991a). There was a district in Greenwich Village where it would be possible for a gay candidate to win a seat on the council, something gay and lesbian groups had been lobbying for throughout the districting process (Lee 1991d). Asian Americans were not given a district where they comprised a majority of the population, but there was a district in Lower Manhattan where they comprised a plurality of the population (Lee 1991c).

Hispanic leaders opposed the plan, arguing that Hispanics made up at least 25 percent of the city's population but that there were only six districts where Hispanics had a 60 percent majority (Lee 1991b). They believed that Hispanics had been packed into a smaller number of districts resulting in fewer districts where Hispanics had a chance of electing a member of the council (Gray 1991b). In early June, the Puerto Rican Legal Defense Fund filed suit in federal court to stop the election process until the U.S. Justice Department certified the plan as nondiscriminatory. By law, the Justice Department had sixty days to approve the plan unless it requested additional information from the districting commission, in which case it would have more time.

When the U.S. Justice Department issued its initial review of the commission's districting plan, they agreed with the city's Hispanic leaders. Assistant Attorney General John Dunne stated that he was concerned that some districts were drawn in such a way as to dilute Hispanic voting strength and that in some other districts, Blacks had been given an opportunity to win council seats at the expense of Hispanics. Dunne explained that some districts were drawn in such a way as to give Hispanics a majority in one district but at the same time decrease their influence in neighboring districts (Roberts 1991b). Districting commission officials responded that Black majority districts were more easily created because Blacks tended to live in "discernible communities" while Hispanics were more "dispersed" throughout the city (Pear 1991a). In their response to concerns from both the Justice Department and the Hispanic community, the commissioners argued that in some of the districts singled out as being drawn in a way to dilute Hispanic voting strength in council elections, all the candidates who had filed petitions to run for the council were Hispanic, thus guaranteeing Hispanic members of the council from those districts (Pear 1991b).

Both the city's Hispanic leadership and the Justice Department cited a district encompassing Jackson Heights, Queens, as an example of Blacks gaining at the expense of Hispanics. In this district, Whites made up a plurality of the registered voters but Hispanics made up a majority of the district's population. Toward the end of the commission's districting process, the boundaries of this district had been shifted to include a housing project, Lefrak City. The inclusion of the twenty apartment buildings of Lefrak City decreased the percentage of Hispanic registered voters and Hispanic population. It also gave Black registered voters the plurality in the district and created a district with a Black incumbent councilperson, Helen Marshall, even though Hispanics still made up a majority of the district's population. Questioned by the Justice Department as to why Lefrak City was added to the district, a spokesperson for the commission responded that "the choice was whether to draw a district with a majority Hispanic population, but with blacks as the largest group in terms of registration or to draw a district with a larger Hispanic population but with non-Hispanic whites as the major voter influence" (Gray 1991a).

In response to complaints by Hispanic leaders that the district had been "stacked" to favor an African American candidate, Black incumbent council-woman Marshall replied, "I have represented the area for nine years, but lived here for thirty-three. . . . You can't win this district by being black, Hispanic, or white. You've got to be able to pick up black votes, Hispanic votes and white votes to win. . . . I don't want to see this as a black versus Hispanic fight" (quoted in Gray 1991a).

On July 19, 1991, the Justice Department informed the city that it could not approve the districting commission's plan because the city's Hispanic voters had been "consistently disfavored" in several of the districts it created (Pear 1991c). The Justice Department singled out two districts in Brooklyn where Hispanic voting strength had been highly concentrated. The claim was that in the district encompassing the Williamsburg section, Hispanics had been stacked at the expense of Hispanic voting strength in the neighboring district encompassing Bushwick and Cypress Hills (New York Times 1991b). From the perspective of the districting commission, the only way that the Hispanic voters in the district encompassing Bushwick and Cypress Hills could have been strengthened would have been by adding Ridgewood, Queens, to the district. The residents of Ridgewood, including its Hispanic residents, had been adamant about not becoming part of that district (Barbanel 1991). Given that all of the candidates who had filed petitions to run for the council seat in this district were Hispanic, some residents of the district questioned the logic of the Justice Department ruling (Ravo 1991). Despite these claims by the commission, many believed that the Williamsburg district had been stacked with Hispanic voters in order to protect incumbent Victor Robles (Gray 1991c). The Justice Department also identified the bi-borough district covering East Harlem and parts of the Bronx where boundary line changes had negatively affected Hispanic voting strength (New York Times 1991b). With both the mayor and the council speaker urging fast action to correct the plan in order not to delay the September primary, the districting commission scrambled to meet and agree on proposed corrections. Despite their differences over the districting process, both the mayor and the council speaker wanted the elections to take place on time.

Meeting over several days and nights in what was described as highly conflictual and sometimes raucous meetings, the districting commission produced a response to the Justice Department on July 26. The plan addressed the Justice Department's earlier critique. The percentage of Hispanic registered voters in the bi-borough East Harlem–South Bronx district was increased slightly by redrawing the boundary lines. Boundary lines were redrawn to create more equity in Hispanic voting strength between the district encompassing the Williamsburg section of Brooklyn and the district encompassing Cypress Hills and Bushwick. Lefrak City was removed from the district in Queens where Hispanics would now make up a larger percentage of registered voters and overall population (Lee 1991e). Black incumbent councilwoman Helen Marshall called the move "racial gerrymandering" (Lee 1991f). The Justice Department approved the revised plan the following day.

Most members of the coalition supporting Mayor Dinkins's vision of a new city council expressed disappointment with the approved plan but agreed to drop any subsequent challenge so that elections could take place (Daniels 1991). Black Congressman Major Owens of Brooklyn and union leader Dennis Rivera attempted to heal rifts between Black and Hispanic leaders over the districting process and results (Gray 1991d). Some Hispanic leaders, however, were still not satisfied with the plan and the Puerto Rican Legal Defense and Education Fund had a suit pending in federal court challenging the plan's legality and stopping the election process (Pear 1991d). In late July, a panel of federal judges approved the various changes to the city election law allowing the election process to move forward and the elections to take place despite challenges. Included in the election law changes was a one-time rule that candidates could run in any district in the city regardless of where they lived. Most thought that this rule would have little or no impact on the council races, given time and money constraints (Lee 1991g).

In the September 1991 Democratic primary, only one-fifth of the primaries had candidates of a different race or ethnicity competing against one another. To the extent that the commission and the Justice Department were seeking a balkanized city council where there was very little interethnic/racial competition, they appeared to have been successful (Roberts 1991c). Critiquing the result of the districting commission's efforts, Henry Stern, former member of the city council and President of Citizens Union, noted, "Race is now being made the principal characteristic, abetted by race based districting. . . . Multi-racial districts foster accommodation. Narrow based districts encourage candidates of racial polarization" (quoted in Roberts 1991c).

Similar to the comments of Henry Stern, there were many who argued that the city's districting process had served to separate the racial and ethnic groups in the city more than it served to bring them together. Countering that perspective were those who argued that in the past, minority interests had always been secondary to incumbent protection in the redistricting process; and for once, the two values were being given equal weight (Gottlieb 1991). In the primary, White candidates won in three of the districts that had been drawn to give minorities a better chance of gaining a council seat. A district that had been established in Greenwich Village to produce a gay candidate did so (Roberts 1991f). And a district in Upper Manhattan produced the council's first Dominican candidate, who won in November (McKinley 1991a). In addition, in only thirteen of the districts did incumbent Democratic council members face no competition in the September primary (*New York Times* 1991d). This is far fewer unopposed incumbents than was the case in 1993 or 1997, and was similar to the term-limits council primary of 2001 in which there were only seven districts where the incumbent had no opposition in the primary.

Attempts by the Dinkins coalition to craft a city council closer to the mayor's values, and attempts by insurgent Democratic Party organizations to take council seats away from the county organizations, met with little success. Only four of the Dinkins coalition candidates made it through the primary out of twenty-nine endorsed (Roberts 1991d; Roberts 1991e). With the exception of a few incumbents who retired and one very liberal incumbent who ran on the Lower East Side of Manhattan and lost to a Hispanic newcomer, all incumbents were returned to office. Democratic county organizations won twenty-three of twenty-six races in which they endorsed a candidate (Roberts 1991e). Both money and organization were responsible for the victory of the county organizations. Given the short time period that candidates had to raise money and campaign, indigenous party organizations had a distinct advantage. In addition, while the Dinkins coalition fell far short of its fundraising goal, Speaker Vallone's support was significant to moderate Democrats not only in campaign funds from his political action committee but also the approximately one hundred volunteers sent to work for candidates in close races (McKinley 1991b).

In the November 1991 elections, as a result of the redistricting and the addition of sixteen seats on the council, minority representation on the council went from 25 percent to over 40 percent. Blacks occupied twelve seats and Hispanics occupied nine seats (*New York Times* 1991e). In effect, two-thirds of the newly established seats had gone to minorities. One of the other big winners in the council redistricting was the Republican Party, which went from occupying one seat in the council to occupying six (Roberts 1991f).

Despite their numbers on the council, minorities as a group have yet to exert much influence on council structure or policy. Like other council members, most minority council members remain associated with their county party organization or insurgent organization as a means to get reelected and advance their careers. As seen in the votes for speaker in early 2002 and 2006, county party organization membership is a far more significant factor in the behavior of council members than race or ethnicity.

The Black and Hispanic Caucus of the City Council, comprising all the minority members, has attempted to pattern itself after similar organizations in Albany and Washington. Despite an occasional press conference, however, where they have denounced budget cuts or activities of the mayor, the caucus has not had major impact on council activities. In the mid-1990s, a spokesperson for the African-American Leadership Summit, an organization of civic, service, and neighborhood groups, criticized the caucus. "The Mayor is planning to lay off 8,000 workers from the Health and Hospitals Corporation, which serves the very people these council members represent in black and brown communities. But what are they going to do? They don't seem to have the constitution to stand up to the Mayor and Speaker Vallone" (quoted in Hicks 1996). Minority council members claim that they have been able to moderate the activities of the speaker and the mayor by applying pressure informally (Hicks 1996). Members of the caucus have pushed the city council, and occasionally the mayor, to address issues raised by the city's increasing racial and ethnic diversity and the social, economic, and political disadvantages suffered by many of these groups. These issues include the increased participation of minority-owned businesses in city contracts, the funding of immigrant support services, language services for non–English speaking parents of children in the city's school system, and environmental racism.

Conclusion: The City Council: From Silent Partner to Junior Partner

Most would agree that over the last fifteen years, the city council has evolved into a significant institution in the governance of New York City. The abolition of the Board of Estimate along with the leadership of Peter Vallone elevated the role that the council plays in policymaking relative to where it was in the early 1980s. Despite the council's recent elevation, few would claim, however, that the mayor and the council are equal partners in the city's governance. As chief executive, the mayor has vastly superior staff and resources to collect, process, and analyze information regarding city issues and problems, in addition to the chief executive's ability to mold policy as it is being implemented. As the chief of state, he commands public and media attention well beyond what the city council and its leadership can mobilize. The speaker's ability to maintain and control a working majority sufficient to override a mayoral veto is critical to the council's continued success in countering the mayor. A council that is highly factionalized would limit its ability to stand up to the mayor when the two institutions disagree.

One of the areas of city policy where the council is at a disadvantage relative to the mayor is economic development. With the exception of land use and zoning (and this is not an insignificant exception), the council does not play a major role in economic development policymaking. Most economic development policy and activities undertaken by the city are place oriented and the council has opted to play more of a representative than lawmaking role. As a result, whether the issue is a tax exemption for a corporation moving to Midtown, a BID in an outerborough community, or a new stadium, council members as representatives view economic development from the perspective of their districts and their constituents. Term limits may have added a short-term perspective to the council's view on economic development. Council members want benefits for their districts today because they will not be around in the future. Since this set of built-in constraints inhibits the council's ability to initiate economic development policy, they can better react to what the mayor proposes than initiate on their own.

The city council owes much of its current status and composition to the federal courts and the U.S. Department of Justice. The federal courts started the process that resulted in the abolition of the Board of Estimate, and the Department of Justice monitored the redistricting process upon which the current council is based. Mostly as a result of activity at the federal level, Blacks and Hispanics now make up over 40 percent of the council and in 2001, the council elected its first Asian American member. But the legacy of infighting among minority groups in the city and the overlay of loyalties to county party organizations inhibit the mobilization of minorities on the council as a powerful bloc of votes. While some view this disunity as a stumbling block to minorities achieving greater power in the city's political system, others view the disunity as simply one of the artifacts of representative/legislative government. Minority legislators, similar to all other legislators, seek to enhance their chances of getting reelected by serving their constituents and maintaining close ties to those organizations and interests who can enhance their chances of getting reelected. In the term-limit council elections of 2001, the Working Families Party and the Fresh Democracy Council mobilized candidates, but these groups all but disappeared from council deliberations less than a year after the election. Just as important, if the ability of the council to counter the mayor even as a junior partner is a function of the council speaker being able to mobilize the entire council behind him or her, any attempt to mobilize a subgroup of council members might enhance the status or influence of that group but could very well work to weaken the council overall.

9

The Municipal Bureaucracy

Bureaucrats and the Exercise of Discretion

The primary role of the city's executive branch is to implement the laws and programs created by the legislative branch in conjunction with the chief executive or responsibilities granted in the city charter. Since New York City is a unit of local government, some of the laws and programs being implemented or administered by its executive branch are created by the state legislature and governor. Bureaucrats whose function it is to implement and administer the law, and particularly those at the street level who interact with the public in the process of delivering a service, exercise considerable discretion in their implementation activities. Due to the choices that bureaucrats can make in the process of implementing the laws and programs of the city's political system, they can greatly influence the direction and shape as well as the success or failure of public policy. The concept of bureaucratic discretion has received considerable attention among those who study public administration and public policy because of its relationship to the issues of bureaucratic accountability and control. In democratic political systems, there is an expectation that important policy decisions will be made by elected officials who are accountable to the people. There is an additional concern that governmental power be applied in a "nondiscretionary manner so that the coercive powers of government cannot be exercised arbitrarily" or in a discriminatory way (Bryner 1987, 2).

The Roots of Bureaucratic Discretion

Bureaucrats have discretion because they are responsible for the implementation and administration of the laws and programs of the political system. The implementation function not only gives bureaucrats choices to make, it demands that they make choices. Classical theories of public administration were less concerned with the discretion that bureaucrats exercised as part of the implementation process because those theories suggested that the discretion was tied to how policy was implemented, not the ends of policy itself (Rourke 1984, 36). Toward the middle of the twentieth century, those who studied bureaucracy, as well as chief executives and legislators, woke up to the realization that the process of implementation gave bureaucrats a significant role not only in the means by which the policy would be implemented, but the ends of policy as well. The choices that bureaucrats make while implementing a law or program can influence the goals of the program or law even though those goals might have been articulated clearly by the legislature or chief executive earlier in the policymaking process. If anything, the second half of the twentieth century has seen an increased reliance on bureaucrats by the legislative branch and chief executive rather than a decreased role. As the functions of government expanded and became more complex, the political system became more dependent on specialists and experts for their implementation skills regardless of the influence they were being given over the ends of public policy. And while this could be viewed as a necessary evil within the scope of a democratic political system, others viewed the expansion of bureaucratic power as entirely functional.

The roots of bureaucratic discretion lay in legislation and in the city charter. The charter, as revised in 1989, lays out the jurisdictional responsibilities of most agencies in the executive branch of the city government. Since 1989, most changes in executive agency/departmental structure have been codified through charter amendments. Based on the jurisdictional authority described in the charter, the mayor and the city council, as part of the legislative process, determine which agency will administer pieces of legislation as they are formulated and signed into law. Legislation usually designates the agency or agencies responsible for making sure the law is carried out.

How much discretion an agency or department has in administering a program or law is partly a function of the specificity or amount of detail in the legislation or grant of jurisdiction. The more vague the legislation or granting of jurisdiction, the greater discretion bureaucrats have. Bureaucrats supply detail to legislation when it has not been supplied by the legislature. The charter mandates that the Department of Parks and Recreation "manage and care for all parks" and "maintain the beauty and utility of all parks" (New York City Charter Revision Commission, Chapter 21, Section 533). Given that there is no other legislation specifically addressing how the city's parks should be managed, the bureaucrats in the Department of Parks and Recreation who administer the city's parks have considerable discretion in responding to their mandate. The section of the city charter describing the function and jurisdiction of the Department of Parks and Recreation says nothing about active versus passive uses of the city's parks. It says nothing about whether an athletic field should be permitted to children over adults, baseball teams over soccer teams, or whether the field should be fenced off for a season to allow the grass to grow back. Nor is there a law that addresses these issues. Since there is no charter or legislative source of rules to be followed by the bureaucrats in the Department of Parks and Recreation, they are able to make the rules themselves. They will make these decisions because the legislature and the chief executive have ceded the power to make policy in this area to the bureaucrats in the Department of Parks and Recreation.

Why would elected officials give non-elected officials this much discretion/ power to make policy? First, in the case of park usage, the mayor and the city council believe that, for the most part, there are other issues that need attention more than who uses the city's parks and how they are used. As a result, they willingly cede their authority to make policy in this area to bureaucrats. Second, even if the mayor and council believed this to be an issue that merited more attention and even legislative action, there would be limits as to how far the mayor and council could go in crafting legislation that would manage the use of the parks. Legislation in this area could easily establish rules as to who uses the parks how and when, but such a law would deprive the city of any flexibility. For most aspects of city government, elected officials as generalists prefer not to micromanage the delivery of services. As a corollary to the first two points, some have argued that in order to achieve consensus on an expanding agenda, legislatures cannot spend too much time on any one issue. As a result, out of necessity the legislation they produce is general and creates a broad mandate for those who are responsible for implementing or administering the law (Bryner 1987, 5). Third, the mayor and city council view the bureaucrats in the Department of Parks and Recreation as experts. They were hired to work in the department because they have knowledge and training that enables them to make decisions regarding parks in the public interest. Compared to bureaucrats, legislators and chief executives are generalists who rarely spend an extended period of time discussing or learning about one issue or program. Bureaucrats, on the other hand, are specialists. Over time they gain experience and knowledge in making decisions regarding, in this case, how the parks should be used.

The New York City Police Department's Street Crimes Unit (SCU) offers another example of the exercise of bureaucratic discretion, but one that is far more controversial than the administration of athletic fields by the Parks Department. The function of the SCU was not only to apprehend criminals but also to deter crime. Created in the early 1970s, the SCU was a plainclothes unit that attempted to blend into New York City's street life, especially at night, in order to perform their role more effectively (Roane 1999). The unit became one of the cornerstones of the Giuliani administration's successful attempts to lower the city's crime rate. As a highly mobile unit of the NYPD, the Giuliani administration would send the SCU to areas of high crime where it would focus on searching for weapons (Kocieniewski 1999). At one point, the approximately one hundred officers in the unit were responsible for 20 percent of all arrests. In 1997, in part due to the unit's effectiveness, the Giuliani administration quadrupled the number of officers in the SCU. In the late 1990s, the four hundred SCU officers, comprising less than 2 percent of the city's police force, were responsible for almost 40 percent of the gun arrests in the city (Roane 1999). Yet despite the

SCU's success, they were the subject of complaints. Many minority leaders and some in the law enforcement community were concerned about the SCU's use of search and seizure techniques, especially when it was questionable whether the SCU officers had "reasonable suspicion" (Wilgoren 1999; Roane 1999). Under the U.S. Constitution, in order to obtain a search warrant, the police must convince a judge that they have sufficient cause to believe that criminal activity is taking place. Most street searches, however, take place without a warrant with the police exercising their own judgment and discretion regarding what is and what is not a constitutional search (Epstein and Walker 2001, 487). And although evidence obtained from illegal searches can be excluded at trial, the search itself or other police activity related to a search may have a negative impact on the individuals being stopped and searched, and on an entire community if these searches become routine. According to NYPD records, the SCU stopped and frisked 18,023 people in 1997 and 27,061 people in 1998. Further, the SCU made 9,546 arrests in that two-year period, meaning that a majority of those who were searched were never arrested. While some viewed these statistics as reasonable given the success the Giuliani administration had in lowering crime rates, civil rights and community leaders from minority neighborhoods, where the bulk of SCU activity took place, were highly critical of this use of discretionary power by the police (Kocieniewski 1999). Describing the impact of the SCU activities in his neighborhood, one Bronx community leader stated, "We're grateful for a lot of what the police have done to bring down crime and we realize most officers, like most residents of our community, are honest, hard working citizens. . . . But people are being stopped for no reason, thrown against a fence and searched. Their cars are stopped without probable cause. Sometimes there's vulgar language to people who are just minding their business. What some of the officers are doing is just creating an atmosphere of fear" (quoted in Kocieniewski 1999).

The exercise of bureaucratic discretion and its impact on public policy in a democratic political system raises two issues. First, what do bureaucrats do with the discretion that they are given? What kinds of choices do they make and what influences those choices? And second, assuming bureaucratic discretion exists throughout the executive branch and that bureaucrats have a significant impact on public policy, what tools do the elected officials, the mayor, and the council have to keep the power of the bureaucracy in check?

The Exercise of Bureaucratic Discretion

Given that bureaucrats have discretion and that the exercise of this discretion affects the direction as well as the success or failure of the policy being implemented, what influences bureaucratic decision making in the exercise of this discretion? Two related and very important influences upon bureaucratic decision making are training and experience. Training may be very formal. Both police recruits and child welfare caseworkers go through a formal training process that includes coursework as well as examinations. Formal training is one of the ways that a chief executive or his or her appointees can influence the exercise of bureaucratic discretion. In the aftermath of the highly publicized child abuse death of Elisa Izquierdo in 1995, caseworkers in the Child Welfare Administration (CWA) and others expressed the opinion that a lack of training might have been one reason caseworkers were not responding appropriately to cases of child abuse and neglect. Mayor Giuliani's reform of the city's child welfare agency included a significantly longer period of formal training for caseworkers. Training and recruitment were also raised as issues with regard to the NYPD's SCU in the aftermath of the shooting of Amadou Diallo. When the SCU was expanded in size in 1997, it was opposed by some in the NYPD. They believed that entry into the SCU would no longer be as selective as it had been, and the one-on-one training that took place would be diluted (Kocieniewski 1999). Prior to 1997, applicants to the SCU went through a screening process, with approximately half of the applicants being rejected. Due to the small number of SCU recruits, training took place in the field with experienced SCU officers mentoring recruits on a daily basis (Kocieniewski 1999). With its expansion in 1997, the screening process for recruits was abbreviated; and given that the size of the SCU was increased by almost a factor of four, it was no longer possible to pair each new recruit with a more experienced SCU officer. The four officers involved in the shooting of Amadou Diallo all joined the SCU after its expansion (Kocieniewski 1999). In the cases of the CWA and the NYPD's SCU, the lack of training was cited as an issue after a publicized breakdown in the performance of bureaucrats (i.e., caseworkers, police officers). In both cases, the lack of adequate or sufficient training was seen as giving bureaucrats too much discretion and not enough direction.

Closely related to the issue of training is experience. Although not as systematic nor comprehensive as formal training, experience can provide bureaucrats, through exposure to a range of situations, and through trial and error, with informal guidelines on the exercise of discretion. The role of experience in influencing the exercise of bureaucratic discretion suggests that if a choice made by bureaucrats in response to a problem is viewed by the bureaucrats as effective and acceptable, it will be employed the next time the problem or issue arises. Over time, experience tempers the exercise of bureaucratic discretion. Despite the discretion they have been granted, bureaucrats do not face each situation or dilemma with unlimited choices. In his study of executive branch decision making and the Cuban missile crisis, political scientist Graham Allison (1969) describes an organizational process model that views bureaucracies as bundles of routines with standard operating procedures that they have developed to respond to problems they encounter (Allison 1969, 698). These routines are developed through trial and error over time, and perfected because bureaucracies face similar if not identical problems and issues repeatedly. The fact that bureaucrats have a response that works for most of the problems they face makes their job that much easier. From a public perspective, the fact that bureaucrats have developed routines that successfully respond to problems enhances the view of the bureaucrat as a specialist or expert (Allison 1969, 700).

New York City's bureaucrats must develop and utilize routines that gain consensus. Bureaucrats serve multiple publics. Their immediate supervisors, the mayor, the city council, the public they serve, and the media all have an interest in their performance. All of these actors also have the ability in various ways to register their approval or disapproval of how bureaucrats are performing. As a result, they must develop routines that not only eradicate or resolve problems, they must also develop routines that do not anger their various publics. And when the publics disagree, bureaucrats must decide which actor to follow. In the case of the police, when the mayor and the police commissioner are in agreement, there may be little debate. Shortly after Mayor Giuliani took office, officers in the NYPD SCU reported being instructed to "become far more aggressive" (Kocieniewski 1999). In the mid-1990s, the effectiveness of the SCU in making arrests resulted in the mayor and the officials at the highest levels in the police department deciding to significantly expand the size of the unit. At the same time, leaders in many of the city's minority communities were complaining about the aggressive style of policing used by the SCU. Until the shooting of Amadou Diallo, this perspective was ignored outside those communities. Similarly, when the size of the SCU was expanded by Mayor Giuliani and Police Commissioner Safir, some police officials were concerned about the diluted screening process and training. This perspective was also ignored until the Diallo shooting.

Consensus can support the continuation of a bureaucratic routine even if it is ineffective. Throughout much of its recent history, the city's child welfare caseworkers utilized a routine that responded inconsistently to cases of abuse and neglect. At times, the routine was based on the fact that caseworker caseload was far too high, and at times the routine was constrained by the inadequate training that they received prior to being sent into the field. The fact that the child welfare system was performing poorly was known to many through the intermittent reports by advocates, state agencies, or nonprofit groups monitoring child welfare in the city. In the aftermath of Elisa Izquierdo's death in 1995, even the caseworkers articulated their awareness of the ineffectiveness of the routine developed to respond to cases of abuse. Yet the lack of attention that the child welfare system received from the mayor, the Commissioner of the Human Resources Administration, the city council, and other city officials prior to Elisa's death was an expression of tacit support for the operations of the city's child welfare system. The death of Elisa, and more important the media attention the death received, brought the child welfare system under greater public scrutiny. In addition, the fact that child welfare advocates sued the city in federal court a few weeks after Elisa's death forced the city to act.

The NYPD's SCU also employed routines. As previously stated, the primary goal of the SCU under Mayor Giuliani was to get guns off the streets. This meant that for an SCU officer on the street, the goal was to "spot and seize a handgun before a suspect can use it" (Kocieniewski 1999). Through training and experience, SCU officers, to be successful, learned how to "read the walk, mannerisms and subtle movements of someone carrying a concealed weapon" (Kocieniewski 1999). Describing the work of the SCU, a former police commander explained, "These officers have the normal stress of policing plus the additional stress of the unknown, because you're looking for the worst people in the worst neighborhoods during the worst hours.... Every time they go out they have to worry about acting legally correct, procedurally correct and safely, just so they can make it home in the morning" (quoted in Kocieniewski 1999). To accomplish their goal, the SCU officers were required to make numerous judgment calls. The shooting of Amadou Diallo by four members of the SCU raised the issue of how much racial profiling had become one of the routines used by the NYPD in its aggressive policing strategy. Racial profiling involves the consideration of race or ethnicity as a clue in criminal investigations or deterrence (Wilgoren 1999). Law enforcement experts argue that police work involves making quick judgments, and that skin color is a factor, among others, that police officers in the street must use to be effective (Wilgoren 1999). Former NYPD Commissioner William Bratton stated, "Whether they call it profiling or street smarts, awareness—whatever the names might be—profiling is essential" (quoted in Wilgoren 1999). A former NYPD officer added, "Cops work on an exception principle: they learn what's normal in a neighborhood, and things that are abnormal draw their attention; quite often that involves issues of race" (quoted in Wilgoren 1999).

At the time of the Diallo shooting those defending the practice of the SCU focused on the large number of arrests made by the unit. Minority leaders focused on the many more individuals, mostly minorities, who were stopped and frisked by the police, where the search found nothing. They viewed this practice as humiliating and abusive (Wilgoren 1999). Critics note that police cadets do receive training in racial and ethnic diversity and sensitivity but argue that it is doubtful that the training is robust enough to counteract the lessons they learn from their fellow officers once they leave the academy (Wilgoren 1999).

Those who supervise street level bureaucrats frequently attempt to formulate rules hoping they will evolve into or at least influence bureaucratic routines. Prior to Elisa Izquierdo's death, the Bronx office of the CWA was urging its caseworkers to close two cases for every new case they opened. Some members of the SCU reported being pressured to adhere to an unwritten quota system that they seize at least one gun a month, given the Giuliani administration's focus on crime statistics. One SCU officer, speaking anonymously, explained, "There are guys who are willing to toss anyone who's walking with his hands in his pockets.... We frisk 20, maybe 30 people a day. Are they all by the book? Of course not; it's safer and easier just to toss people. And if it's the 25th of the month and you haven't got your gun yet? Things can get a little desperate" (quoted in Kocieniewski 1999).

Elected Officials and the Bureaucracy

As elected officials, the mayor and the members of the city council are accountable to the citizens through the electoral process. Since bureaucrats are not elected, their accountability to the people only exists through the mayor's and the city council's ability to oversee, direct, and control the activities of the executive branch. Given the size of the city's executive branch, overseeing and directing its activities becomes quite a challenge. In addition, as just discussed, the mayor and council sometimes exacerbate the problem of controlling the bureaucracy by giving those who staff the executive branch considerable discretion in carrying out the missions of government.

Throughout much of the nineteenth century, the mayor's ability to control the bureaucracy was enhanced through the existence of an executive branch based on patronage and a political party hierarchy that rewarded loyalty and effort by party members with a government job. The bureaucrats who staffed the executive branch got their jobs because they were loyal members of the party in power. This party machine model maximized accountability to the mayor and the party leaders in two ways. First, those who received positions in the executive branch had already proven their loyalty through their membership and work in the party and therefore could be trusted to perform their functions in government according to the directions of the mayor/party leader. Second, since there was no set of rules that protected bureaucrats in their positions, anyone viewed as disloyal to the chief executive could be dismissed without any recourse. Of course, while this model maximized accountability to the chief executive, there were disadvantages. Those who staffed the executive branch received their positions primarily because of their membership in and loyalty to a political party, not because they had some level of expertise in the executive branch position to which they were appointed. As the functions of government became more complex, this model of recruitment compromised the ability of government to carry out functions such as public health, sanitation, and civil engineering. In addition, a model of executive branch recruitment that was based on political party loyalty meant that as mayoral administrations changed, there would be significant changes in the personnel staffing the executive branch. This interruption and lack of continuity also served to compromise the ability of the city government to carry out its functions and deliver services.

In response to the problems created by a patronage system, New York City was one of the first units of government to establish merit-based employment for public employees. This began in the city in the 1880s. In 1894, the New York State Constitution stated that municipal employees should be "appointed and promoted according to 'merit and fitness' determined in competitive examinations" (quoted in Benjamin 1995, 237). The growth of the civil service and merit-based employment in the city's executive branch marked the demise of the patronage model of executive branch recruitment, though vestiges of the model remained throughout the twentieth century. Under the civil service model, New York City's governmental bureaucracy was increasingly staffed by those who were hired based on a level of expertise or a set of qualifications. Further, to achieve and maintain a level of continuity and consistency in executive branch performance, the civil service system protected public employees from the whims of changing mayoral administrations. While incoming mayors could appoint commissioners and deputy commissioners to run the executive branch in his name, mayors could not replace the staff of an entire agency. The values that had been minimized by the patronage system such as expertise, stability, and continuity were maximized by the civil service merit model. Accountability, possibly the one positive value maximized by the patronage model, was sacrificed under the civil service model. Mayors could not fire and replace public employees hired under the civil service system at will, but only according to set procedures. Public employees could not be fired without a hearing and/or due process. They were protected from the whims of the chief executive, but at the same time they were detached from the immediate control of elected officials. As a result of the civil service reforms, bureaucrats were more competent and more expert, but it became more difficult for elected officials and particularly the mayor to control them. To the extent that increased bureaucratic discretion resulted in bureaucrats playing a greater role in the ends of public policy, the decreased ability to control bureaucratic behavior became a problem.

While the civil service reforms decreased elected officials' ability to control the municipal bureaucracy, it did not leave them powerless. Both the mayor and the city council have several instruments that can be employed to move the bureaucracy in a desired direction. By using the various instruments in tandem, the mayor and the city council have the ability to influence the overall direction of the executive branch and bureaucratic behavior more specifically.

Mayoral Oversight and Control of the Municipal Bureaucracy

Mayors have multiple tools to control the bureaucrats who staff the executive branch. These tools include the appointment of commissioners, the ability to reorganize agencies, budgetary controls, the construction and publication of the Mayor's Management Report, special investigations of individual agencies, contract negotiations with public employee unions, and the bully pulpit.

According to the public administration literature, one of the primary tools chief executives can use to control the bureaucracy is the power to appoint officials to administer the bureaucracy according to the executive's political philosophy and policy preferences (Meier 1993, 169). With a few exceptions, the city charter gives the mayor the power to appoint and remove the commissioners and administrators of most of the agencies that comprise the executive branch of the government (New York City Charter Revision Commission, Chapter 1, Section 6). Most of these appointments do not require confirmation by the city council. The commissioners and administrators serve as line officials in that they have the responsibility to administer an agency. The city charter also gives the mayor the ability to appoint deputy mayors to serve on his staff (New York City Charter Revision Commission, Chapter I, Section 6). Unlike the commissioners and other line officials who administer agencies or organizations in the city's executive branch, deputy mayors have no immediate administrative responsibilities for an agency or organization. Nevertheless, some mayors have organized their deputy mayors in a way that they are responsible for the activities of a functional grouping of agencies (e.g., economic development, health and human services) within the city's executive branch. Under those circumstances, commissioners and agency administrators report to the deputy mayor who has been given jurisdiction over their respective agency, rather than reporting directly to the mayor.

While the primary purpose of mayoral appointments of agency administrators might be to further the mayor's agenda in the implementation of public policy, the purposes of mayoral appointments to head executive branch agencies has expanded and evolved over time. Today, the mayoral appointments to head executive branch agencies serve at least two additional goals. First, some appointments reflect the coalition of party organizations and groups who helped the mayor get elected. Mayor Koch distinguished his administration from that of his predecessor, Abraham Beame, by arguing that while Beame ceded the appointment of city commissioners to the county Democratic party leaders who helped him get elected, Koch would only accept "recommendations" from the party (Koch 1985, 18). Despite this distinction, Mayor Koch appointed Anthony Ameruso, a close associate of Kings County leader Meade Esposito, as his transportation commissioner over the recommendations of his own transition team. The appointment of Ameruso along with the appointment of Jay Turoff as Commissioner of the Taxi and Limousine Commission was viewed by many as a quid pro quo to the Kings (Brooklyn) County Democratic Party leader for his support (Newfield and Barrett 1988, 15, 143–144). Mayor Giuliani's appointment of Fran Reiter as deputy mayor, Henry Stern as Commissioner of Parks and Recreation, and two of the sons of Liberal Party leader Ray Harding to high-level posts in the administration were partly in response to the Liberal Party's endorsement and support he received as a candidate (Chou 2000). Possibly offering a defense of his appointments, Mayor Giuliani wrote, "Patronage does not mean giving a job to someone who supported you politically. It means giving a job to someone only because he supported you politically. Of course I hired people who supported my campaigns. After all, the reason they did so was because they shared my beliefs—and I wanted my staff to carry out and believe in what I value. . . . But I did not hire people simply because they worked for my campaign or made a donation" (Giuliani 2002, 99).

Mayor Bloomberg, a long-time Democrat who became a Republican to run for mayor, and who won mostly through the use of his personal wealth, was much less beholden to any party or group than his predecessors. In fact, a month after he won the election, Mayor-elect Bloomberg's initial appointments of four deputy mayors, corporation counsel, and the leader of his transition team were all Democrats. Commenting on this fact, one Republican Party leader commented, "It was a pretty difficult campaign, and a lot of people extended themselves. . . . One way you extend yourself back is by appointing at least one Republican, that is how the book runs. I hope going forward he becomes more sensitive to that fact" (quoted in Steinhauer 2001).

Aside from appointing someone to run an executive branch agency in accordance with the mayor's philosophy, the second goal served by mayoral appointments is ethnic and racial representation. As discussed in chapter five, ethnic and minority groups have attached a great deal of significance to representation in the government. This applies not only to elected positions but to appointed positions as well. Leaders of prominent racial and ethnic groups expect a mayor to recognize their group's importance in the political composition of the city by appointing a member, or members, of their group to his administration. If the group has played a significant role in getting the mayor elected, then the expectation would be for multiple appointments. Although women's groups have not played as much of a role in the city's political system as have many ethnic and racial groups, if mayoral appointments neglected to include a significant number of women, the mayor would be open to criticism by these groups as well.

Despite the existence of other goals in making mayoral appointments, mayors still have the ability when necessary to appoint individuals to a position in their administration because they believe that these individuals will be effective in pursuing the mayor's agenda. They also have the ability to appoint someone because they believe that the individual will be a good administrator for that agency. Mayor Giuliani appointed Nicholas Scoppetta to head the newly formed Administration for Children's Services (ACS) not only because Scoppetta and Mayor Giuliani were friends, but also because the mayor thought Scoppetta had the requisite experience in city government and knowledge of the child welfare system to make him an effective administrator of that agency (Giuliani 2002, 302). Adrian Benepe, Mayor Bloomberg's appointee as Commissioner of the Department of Parks and Recreation, had served as an official in the department during the Koch, Dinkins, and Giuliani administrations. And Mayor Bloomberg's appointment to be Commissioner of Business Services, the department that oversees the operations of the city's business improvement districts (BIDs), was Robert Walsh. Unfamiliar with Walsh prior to his election, Bloomberg appointed him based on the recommendations of his transition team. Walsh, who had been Executive Director of the 14th Street–Union Square BID, was viewed as an effective executive and an energetic spokesperson for BIDs and the role of small businesses in the city.

A frequently cited concern about the use of mayoral appointments to control the bureaucracy is that some of the appointees to lead an agency and its bureaucrats get co-opted by the values of the agency they are sent to lead. That is, they cease to represent the interests and values of the chief executive in administering the agency and adopt the perspective of the career employees of the agency. In effect, they become a spokesperson or advocate for the programs being implemented by the agency they are leading. Since commissioners and agency administrators spend more time with their agencies than they do with the mayor, the probability of being co-opted increases over time. Henry Stern was Commissioner of the Department of Parks and Recreation for much of the Koch administration and was appointed by Mayor Giuliani to be Commissioner of Parks and Recreation again in 1994. On May 21, 1997, Commissioner Stern testified at a city council hearing on the mayor's fiscal year 1998 executive budget for the Department of Parks and Recreation. At issue was the transfer of fifty-five individuals out of the department, where they were serving as Parks Enforcement Patrol (PEP) officers, or urban park rangers. The Giuliani administration wanted these individuals' positions converted to traffic enforcement agents. Commissioner Stern opened the hearing with an approximately twenty-minute statement on the state of the parks department and the Giuliani administration's proposed budget for the department. In the middle of his statement, he addressed the Giuliani administration proposal to transfer the positions:

> A one and a half million dollar cut to our Urban Park Service including a 25 percent reduction of the Parks Enforcement Patrol. These are the PEP officers who are out in the field protecting the parks, protecting nature and the environment and making it possible for people to be safe in the parks. And the proposed reductions would, on a borough basis would reduce the force in the Bronx from thirty to twenty, by ten. The force in Brooklyn would be reduced by twelve from thirty-six to twenty-four. The force in Manhattan would be reduced by fourteen, from thirty-nine to twenty-five. Queens would go from thirty-two to twelve, and Staten Island from twenty-one to fourteen, a total of seven. Now that's fifty-five PEP and rangers lost. These people will not be fired. This is not a question of saving their jobs. They would become traffic enforcement agents. So the question of course is where they are most needed which is a judgment that has to be made by elected officials. And we think the PEP program has been effective in the past. (quoted from New York City Council 1997)

In his presentation, Commissioner Stern was telling members of the city council he believed that the PEP program was a valuable and effective program. He was also informing them how many PEP officers their boroughs would lose if the cut to the parks department budget went through. Finally, he was telling them that as elected officials, they had the ability to reverse the transfer of these individuals out of the department, something they already knew. And Stern did this without formally articulating a position on the cuts.

When Commissioner Stern finished his statement, members of the council asked him questions on the mayor's proposed budget for his department and on his statement. Councilwoman Joan McCabe, from Brooklyn, asked Commissioner Stern a series of questions regarding the PEP officers:

MCCABE: What is the rationale for that movement of personnel?

STERN: That question is properly addressed elsewhere.

MCCABE: Where?

STERN: OMB (the Mayor's Office of Management and Budget). I assume that the rationale is that these people are in some way ineffective or unnecessary or duplicative of the work the police officers who really should do the work in the parks. I assume it's based on some judgment that someone had made that they're not effective, which isn't the same as ours. I think people can differ on this question.

MCCABE: But commissioner, you would say that you are supportive of your agency's request to have these individual's transferred?

STERN: This has gone on for many years. Let me put it this way. This is not a request of our agency that the people be transferred out. This is not a Park's proposal. Is that what you are asking?

MCCABE: It's not a Parks' proposal you're telling me, right?

STERN: That's correct.

MCCABE: And you're supportive of the administration's position?

STERN: Of course I am. I am a member of the administration.

MCCABE: So if during budget negotiations, someone was to say we have *x* amount of dollars, should we put this towards the Urban Park Rangers and the PEP officers, the answer well we're going to say Commissioner Stern said he was supportive of the administration's proposal, so no? What do you want us to do Henry? You want them or not?

STERN: I think that the council understands the issues and will act appropriately.

MCCABE: It's good that we can understand what you've just said. I appreciate that. So we'll work our hardest to get them back for you. (quoted from New York City Council 1997)

As Mayor Giuliani's appointed Commissioner of the Department of Parks and Recreation, it would have been disloyal for Henry Stern to tell the council that he disagreed with the mayor's proposal to cut the PEP officers and convert them into traffic enforcement agents. As a spokesperson for the Department of Parks and Recreation, when pressed by the city council to give his opinion on the proposed transfer, Commissioner Stern made it clear that he believed that the positions should stay in the parks department. Note that he stated the administration's position but referred to the Department of Parks and Recreation's position as "ours." Commissioner Stern had been co-opted.

As illustrated in Commissioner Stern's testimony, another instrument that the mayor can use to control the bureaucracy is the budget. As chief executive, the mayor is responsible for constructing the budget for the executive branch and sending it to the city council for approval. Construction of the budget involves members of the mayor's immediate staff including deputy mayors and the Mayor's Office of Management and Budget; but it also involves the various agencies that make up the executive branch as well. In the early stages of the budgetary process, mayors inform their agencies how much more or less funding the agencies can expect for the upcoming fiscal year. In turn, the agencies inform the mayor what can be done with the additional funding, or what will not be done due to the decreased funding. Mayors can use the budgetary process to emphasize some areas of city policy and deemphasize others. At the time of Elisa Izquierdo's death, the Human Resources Administration (HRA), the agency that housed the CWA, was scheduled to be part of a 7.5 percent across-the-board budget cut to help the city balance the 1995 fiscal year budget (Myers 1995). In early 1996, when Mayor Giuliani pulled the CWA out of the HRA and established the Administration for Children's Services (ACS), not only was the new agency spared the budget cut, but it was given additional funds to hire more caseworkers and upgrade their training.

A frequent target of Mayor Giuliani's budget cuts was the city's school system. The mayor frequently claimed that due to inefficiencies in the operations of the central school board and bureaucracy, the school system could cut its budget significantly without having a negative effect on classroom activities. The mayor, however, lacked the control over the school system that he had over other agencies in the city's executive branch. As a result, school chancellors frequently countered the mayor's proposed budget cuts by arguing or threatening that the cuts would have an impact on classroom activities even though the mayor believed that the cuts would not have this impact.

Since budgets are formulated on an annual basis, they give the mayor a periodic and systematic opportunity to recast the direction of individual agencies or the entire executive branch. The Giuliani administration achieved considerable success in downsizing the executive branch. Much of the budget savings he achieved went to city agencies involved in public safety, and to tax cuts. In addition to the budget cuts, the mayor achieved minimal staff reductions throughout much of the bureaucracy through severance packages and early retirements. The total number of staff reduced was small because many of the positions cut from the health and social services agencies were added to the public safety agencies (Weikart 2001, 365–369).

The use of the budget can be a very effective way for a mayor to change policy direction within the executive branch as well as reward or punish those agencies that are deserving. There are, however, limits to the mayor's ability to use the budget in this way. As illustrated in the Department of Parks and Recreation example, the city council has the ability to give back what the mayor takes away. The mayor and council share budgetary authority, so the mayor can only use the budget to guide the executive branch to the extent that the council agrees with the mayor or is willing to compromise. In addition, because budget cuts are closely tied to issues of personnel, as in the cases of the city's child welfare system and the school system, mayors cannot always direct where the specific impact of the budget cut will be felt. If an agency decides to deal with a reduced budget through the attrition of its personnel force, the impact will be felt wherever the vacancies occur. The impact is similar if the mayor offers early retirement packages or buyouts. Once the offer is made, the mayor has no control over how many or from where the attrition will take place.

Another instrument a mayor can use to control the executive branch is the Mayor's Management Report (MMR). Mandated by the 1977 city charter revision, mayors must issue a preliminary management report in the early part of the year and a final report by September. It was first designed to examine the fiscal auditing of the city's agencies and programs. Over time, it has evolved into a document that tracks most of the executive branch agencies in terms of their ability to meet the goals and objectives established for them by the mayor (New York City Comptroller's Office 2002, 2). Despite the fact that the MMR offers the mayor and the public the ability to examine the performance of executive branch agencies, the document does have its limitations. As a public document, mayoral administrations have been tempted to use the report more as a public relations vehicle than a candid report on the operations of the executive branch. Mayor Giuliani was frequently criticized for using the MMR to show "how well the city was doing under his supervision" (Berkey-Gerard 2002; Pasanen 2002). In addition, a report by City Comptroller William Thompson in early 2002 found several structural flaws. First, many of the issues addressed in the narrative portion of the report are not documented in the section of the report that includes indicators of performance or activity. Second, some city agencies and mayoral staff agencies, such as the Office of Management and Budget (OMB), are not included in the report. Third, indicators are not always reported in a way that allows one to examine an agency's performance over time. Fourth, the comptroller's report noted that over time, the MMR had moved from output measures focusing on activity to more sophisticated performance-based outcome measures that attempted to gauge the impact of activity. The comptroller's report noted, however, that the use of better measures was very inconsistent across agencies and that some agencies were without measures of their key functions (New York City Comptroller's Office 2002). Mayor Bloomberg's first completed MMR, published in October 2002, was praised for including tables that allowed for comparisons over five years, comparing New York City to other large cities in some performance areas, and including an online database where one can look at indicators disaggregated by neighborhood. The report was also criticized, however, for eliminating many of the measures that had been used in the past (Pasanen 2002).

Mayors can also control the activities of the executive branch through reorganization. The organization of the city's executive branch in part reflects the priorities of the city in the implementation of public policy. Taking the CWA out of the larger HRA and renaming it served several purposes for Mayor Giuliani. First, on a symbolic level, it informed the public that the mayor was responding to a problem. Second, the establishment of the ACS as an independent agency allowed the Giuliani administration to treat caseworkers in ACS differently from caseworkers in HRA. To the extent that the operations of the city's child welfare system were being hampered by its existence in a much larger bureaucracy, this problem was solved as well. Giuliani said: "We needed a separate agency, so I could look at it directly. The founding of the ACS was a perfect example of how administrative structure makes a vital difference. The fact that it began life buried within HRA was a big mistake. That we planned to make it independent and give it stature and prestige and have it report directly to the mayor was critical. The point was to create an agency with a single purpose: to protect children at risk" (Giuliani 2002, 302). And third, the fact that the new Commissioner of ACS would report directly to the mayor allowed the Giuliani administration to find a high-profile and probably more capable leader for the new agency. According to Mayor Giuliani, "by giving ACS a 'seat at the table,' with its own budget and commissioner, I gave it the power—and responsibility—to fix its own problems" (Giuliani 2002, 315). Less than a year after the shooting of Amadou Diallo by members of the NYPD SCU, Police Commissioner Howard Safir announced that the SCU would be "broken up into eight separate units reporting to regional commanders" (Blair 1999). The reorganization was only one of several changes in the SCU implemented by Commissioner Safir and the Giuliani administration in response to the Diallo shooting and the criticism the administration received in the weeks and months that followed. Approximately a month after the shooting, Commissioner Safir announced that the overwhelmingly white SCU would replace fifty existing officers with minority recruits. In addition, Commissioner Safir stated that the SCU would no longer work in plainclothes (McFadden 1999).

As the ACS and SCU examples illustrate, some reorganizations take place in an attempt to improve the performance of an agency. Mayors also reorganize the executive branch in order to achieve efficiencies in order to streamline the operations of the executive branch. The most commonly used reorganization technique to achieve efficiencies is the merger. This usually involves two or more agencies who are performing similar or related functions. Similar to the establishment of new agencies as in the ACS case, mergers need the approval of the city council. To be given permanent status, they also require a charter revision. Mayor Giuliani's merger of the NYPD, the Transit Police, and the Housing Police not only achieved efficiencies in law enforcement but also eliminated the problems of interagency coordination issues in fighting crime. The Giuliani administration also merged all the construction divisions of executive branch agencies and created a new Department of Design and Construction that would serve all agencies in an attempt to save money (Giuliani 2002, 317). Late in his first year -as mayor, Michael Bloomberg proposed merging the city's Department of Corrections and the Department of Probation. The catalyst for the mayor's announcement was the resignation of the Commissioner of the Department of

Corrections, a holdover from the Giuliani administration, who was under investigation for abusing the power of his position (Polgreen 2002). The first step in the merger was the mayor's appointment of his Commissioner of the Department of Probation, Martin Horn, Commissioner of the Pennsylvania Department of Corrections for five years, to head the Department of Corrections as well. Horn would be commissioner of both departments. (Robin 2002). In his announcement regarding the pending merger of the two departments, Mayor Bloomberg expressed the expectation that there would be "efficiencies" realized by the merger due to the functional overlap of the two agencies (New York City Mayor's Office 2002).

Since the majority of the employees in the city's executive branch are members of unions, public employee unions play a role in mayoral attempts to oversee and control executive branch activities. In attempting to control the executive branch via public employee union relations, the mayor is constrained by the political clout public employees unions have both locally and in Albany. Public employee union political strength was at its peak in the early seventies. Several strikes in the late sixties demonstrated the power of public employees to bring the city to a halt. At that time, although over one hundred unions represented municipal employees, six unions represented a majority of the city's public workforce. Most of the unions, including the United Federation of Teachers, the Patrolman's Benevolent Association, the Uniformed Firefighters Association, the Uniformed Sanitationmen's Association, and the Transport Workers Union, represent workers along functional lines. The largest union, District Council 37 of the American Federation of State, County and Municipal Employees (AFSCME), represents employees in practically every agency within the city government. For the most part, each union represents a different type of municipal employee, so there is little competition or conflict over members. It also meant that each union's negotiation with the city was a separate activity (Brecher and Horton, 1993).

For the most part, contract negotiations between the city and unions address salary and benefit issues. On occasion, however, mayors have used collective bargaining as a means to achieve changes in the rules governing the behavior of public union members. In the 2005 contract negotiations with the United Federation of Teachers (UFT), the Bloomberg administration was able to increase the school day by ten minutes as well as eliminate some of the seniority rights of teachers (Herszenhorn 2005). In his dealings with public employee unions, the mayor has been helped by an inability of the unions to cooperate with each other. In the past, some public unions have reached an agreement to coordinate their bargaining with the city in order to gain better outcomes for their members. These agreements have rarely lasted past one round of bargaining (Greenhouse 1999; Greenhouse, 2001). Most recently, both the police and teachers' unions demanded wage increases in excess of other union demands in an attempt to catch up to suburban counterparts (Cardwell 2001).

On occasion, public employee unions have openly opposed many mayoral attempts to control the bureaucracy. As part of the city welfare reform program, Mayor Giuliani attempted to use the work requirement for welfare recipients to replace public employees. In response, public employee unions sued the Giuliani administration to stop the administration's use of Work Experience Program (WEP) workers to replace city employees, members of public employee unions, who were being laid off (McFadden 1998).

In some cases, it is the mayor's own investigations, or those of others in city government, that result in the mayor initiating changes in an executive branch agency. The mission of the city's Department of Investigation, an executive branch agency, is to investigate municipal employees and those who contract with the city if there is evidence of corruption or fraudulent practices. A second function of the agency is to study management practices inside city government and recommend to the mayor ways in which an agency's operations can be improved, particularly to minimize opportunities for criminal misconduct and waste (New York City Department of Investigation 2002). In September 2000, as a result of a joint investigation by the Manhattan District Attorney and the Department of Investigation, five employees in the city's Department of Buildings, including a deputy commissioner, were indicted for accepting gifts. The gifts were received from "expeditors," individuals hired by builders and contractors to guide them through the city's complicated and costly processes of obtaining multiple approvals during the construction of a building (Bumiller 2000). The Department of Buildings is responsible for issuing permits and monitoring residential and commercial construction throughout the city. According to many in the construction industry, the agency has never had a sufficient number of employees to handle its workload. The department only allows builders to renew four permits at a time, and some of the larger construction firms may have as many as one hundred permits that need renewal at any one time. So the builders hire expediters to wait in line at the Department of Buildings, get four permits renewed and then go to the back of the line to get four more renewed until all the necessary renewals have been obtained (Webber 2002). As a result of the indictments, Mayor Giuliani assembled a task force to conduct a comprehensive review of the operations of the Department of Buildings. The task force held public hearings in which many of those testifying, primarily representatives of the construction industry, argued that the Department of Buildings should be replaced with a public authority or nonprofit agency that would "receive dedicated funding from the current fee structure and be less encumbered by the city's bureaucratic process" (quoted in Hevesi 2000).

Mayor Giuliani's task force made its recommendations in April 2001. The recommendations included "streamlining the permitting process, instituting anti-corruption measures, and implementing technological innovations" (Webber 2002). In response to the recommendations, the Department of Buildings expanded its hours for permitting, allowed some permitting to be conducted through computer filings, and upgraded its website to include more information as well as the entire building code (Steinhauer 2002; Webber 2002). In spring 2001, Mayor Giuliani also moved part of the building inspection process to the Fire Department, transferring approximately forty employees with the longer term goal of moving much of the Department of Buildings inspection process, approximately four hundred employees, to the Fire Department. The city council, however, never approved the plan. And in the aftermath of September 11 and its impact on the fire department, Mayor Bloomberg decided to return the inspection function to the Department of Buildings (Steinhauer 2002).

The role of mayoral attention paid to an agency or to the bureaucracy should not be underestimated. As discussed in chapter seven, the mayor receives a great deal of media attention on a day-to-day basis. He can use that attention as a bully pulpit to inform the public, including bureaucrats in the executive branch, what he thinks of them, and what he wants them to do. In the aftermath of Elisa Izquierdo's death, Mayor Giuliani announced that the child welfare policy for the city would be the protection of children "first, last and always" (Firestone 1996). In the year following the mayor's statement, ACS caseworkers removed 25 percent more children from abusive families or families suspected of abuse, than they had in the previous year (Buettner 1997).

The city's Board of Education was a frequent target of Mayor Giuliani's criticism. Throughout much of his two terms in office, the mayor argued that the board should be abolished and the school system placed under mayoral control, similar to other line agencies in the city government. Though Mayor Giuliani never got the reforms he wanted during his administration, his comments and constant criticism did help pave the way for his successor, Michael Bloomberg, to convince the governor and state legislature to restructure the school system and place it under mayoral control. Moreover, through his constant criticism, Mayor Giuliani kept educational performance and the need for reform high on the public agenda. One commentator has noted that while it was Mayor Giuliani's "bulldog" style that enabled him to achieve the executive branch reforms that he did, it was the same style that inhibited his ability to negotiate and compromise with those groups whose cooperation was needed if further executive branch reform was going to take place (Weikart 2001, 377–378).

One way Mayor Giuliani tried to control the municipal bureaucracy was via privatization, although he was not very successful. The idea behind privatization was that greater efficiencies could be achieved for the delivery of public services if placed under the control of organizations that responded to competitive market pressures. In the area of education, Mayor Giuliani would have implemented a voucher program throughout the city school system had the city council, teachers' union, New York State Assembly, and private schools supported his efforts. The only privatization success he had in the education arena was the implementation of a privately funded private/parochial scholarship program for a small number of low-income students in poorly performing public schools. An attempt to get the Edison Corporation to take over six poorly performing public schools failed because the parents at those schools voted not to support the effort. In the area of health care, an attempt by the mayor to sell three city hospitals was stopped by the state courts through suits filed by the city council and health care advocates (Weikart 2001, 375). Despite these very visible failures, the Giuliani administration had a few successes in privatizing city government. It was able to sell almost half of the housing and much of the land the city had taken over since the 1960s as a result of property tax payment delinquency. In addition, Giuliani was able to increase the share of the city budget going to private contracts from almost 11 percent to over 13 percent. Much of this increase was in the area of social and homeless services (Weikart 2001, 375).

City Council Oversight and Control of the Bureaucracy

The city council has some of the same instruments to oversee and control the bureaucracy as does the mayor. Yet lacking all of the tools held by the mayor, and lacking the mayor's role as chief executive, the city council's ability to oversee and control the bureaucracy is not nearly as potent as the mayor's. Unlike the mayor's attempts to control the bureaucracy, city council examinations of the bureaucracy rarely result in immediate changes. Council members have the ability to discover and call attention to activities in the executive branch with which they disagree, but they lack the direct control to obtain an immediate response to their complaints. Nevertheless, the council has utilized every opportunity to collect information about and call attention to those aspects of the operation of the executive branch. Both the budget process and the issuance of the MMR offer the city council a periodic and comprehensive mechanism through which to examine the executive branch. Recently, the council has merged its hearings on the budget and on the preliminary MMR. This gives them one opportunity during the year to systematically review the activities of each executive branch agency.

During the normal budget cycle, the city council holds two sets of hearings on the budget, one in response to the mayor's preliminary budget in March and the other in response to the mayor's executive budget in May and June. During both sets of hearings, representatives from the executive branch agencies will testify before the council regarding the operations and needs of their respective agencies. Members of the council will use these hearings to find out about the operations of agencies, particularly as they relate to members' home districts and constituents. During Parks and Recreation Commissioner Stern's testimony on the fiscal year 1998 executive budget, a number of council members asked the commissioner questions regarding Parks Department activities in their districts. During his testimony, in addition to discussing the potential loss of Parks Enforcement Patrol officers, Commissioner Stern discussed a new initiative in which the parks department was placing computers in some of the recreation centers around the city. After his presentation, Commissioner Stern received a number of questions from council members regarding which recreation centers were receiving the computers as well as questions about when the computers would be in place. One member of the council, however, was critical of the Parks Department effort to install computers in recreation centers. She argued with the commissioner and his staff about whether computer education and literacy was an appropriate goal of the Parks Department and whether department resources should be utilized in this effort. The commissioner and his staff explained that the computers had been donated and that someone from a local university had donated their time to train recreation center workers to maintain the computers, resulting in very little expense for the department. One parks department staff member present at the hearings testified that many of the computers were being placed in recreation centers in low-income neighborhoods where both children and adults who did not own their own computers would have access. At the end of a brief debate, the member of the city council and Commissioner Stern and his staff agreed to disagree on this issue (New York City Council 1997). But this example illustrates the inquiry tool the council possesses.

While city council members can use the hearings on the budget to scrutinize the operations of the executive branch, representatives from executive branch agencies can use the hearings as a means to appeal to the council to restore funds that have been cut by the mayor. This appears to be what Commissioner Stern was doing in his testimony regarding Mayor Giuliani's proposal to transfer fifty-five PEP officers out of the department.

Agencies that serve politically powerful or articulate clientele can mobilize those clientele to lobby the city council or testify at city council hearings on their behalf. Public employee unions have been particularly involved in supporting budget requests of the agencies for whom their members work, as have those nonprofit organizations who contract with city agencies for the delivery of services. During the preliminary budget hearings for the fiscal year 2001 budget, a number of health care advocates testified before the Council Committee on Health in support of the budget for the Health and Hospitals Corporation (HHC). Advocates for the disabled testified to maintain funding for specialty services at Bellevue Hospital for those with chronic conditions. Others testifying argued that budget cuts would exacerbate an already existing nursing shortage as well as a shortage of supplies and equipment. A number of advocates for children testified that the Department of Health's asthma programs needed to be expanded, not reduced. Although the vast majority of groups testifying at the hearing were supportive of the programs being implemented by the HHC and the Department of Health, a few groups testifying were critical. The New York Public Interest Research Group (NYPIRG) testified against the Department of Health's program of pesticide use in the city, and a community group from the Riverdale section of the Bronx testified that the Department of Health needed a more "integrated" pest management program (New York City Council 2000).

The city council used to hold hearings dedicated to the MMR. This gave the council an additional means to examine the entire executive branch. During

Speaker Miller's tenure, MMR hearings were merged with preliminary budget hearings. In most, if not all, of those hearings the council and the agency/department representatives emphasized the budget, so the MMR as a means of council oversight of the executive branch was deemphasized.

Between budget hearings and the publication of the MMR, members of the city council have several opportunities a year to find out about the operations of executive branch agencies. Council committees, however, will hold hearings on selected aspects of agency activities throughout the year as the need or issue arises. Some of the issues—such as the city's response to domestic violence, the hate crimes task force, and housing for AIDS patients—focus on implementation activities involving multiple agencies and therefore could not be adequately addressed within a process that examines one agency at a time. In addition, some oversight hearings such as the hearing on safety at city pools and beaches, or the hearing on the proposed takeover of several failing city schools by the Edison Corporation, result from incidents or a series of incidents that raises public and city council awareness of a problem. Interest groups or clientele groups frequently have a role in the initiation of an oversight hearing. Social service delivery groups that were negatively affected by delays in payments from the HRA were active in the council hearing on contract payment delays. Groups forced to pay the Parks Department mandatory donations in exchange for the use of department facilities were instrumental in that oversight hearing.

As noted before, council oversight hearings rarely result in an immediate response by the agency or agencies being scrutinized. On some occasions, however, oversight hearings by council committees may result in proposed legislation to strengthen or modify a law and/or the way it is enforced. The Committee on Housing and Buildings proposed changes in parts of the city's housing code as a result of oversight hearings. And the Council Committee on Consumer Affairs has on occasion proposed new rules for the licensing, regulation, and enforcement of an industry after an oversight hearing on current enforcement.

Interest Groups and Bureaucratic Oversight

The role that interest groups play in monitoring the activities of the bureaucracy should not be overlooked. In the cases of both the SCU and the child welfare system, the initial pressure to change came from outside the executive or legislative branches of government. In the case of the SCU, the pressure came from leaders of minority communities. And in the case of the city's child welfare system, the pressure came from child welfare advocates. In the child welfare case, the suit filed by Marcia Lowery and Children's Rights Inc. shortly after Elisa's Izquierdo's death, seeking a federal court–appointed receiver for the city's child welfare system, played a major role in influencing Mayor Giuliani's changes in the child welfare bureaucracy. The fact that Lowery's group had been successful in getting court-appointed takeovers of child welfare systems in other jurisdictions added to its influence on the mayor.

Bureaucracies, especially those at the local level, serve clientele or interested publics. These clientele or interested publics pay attention to the activities of the bureaucracy because those activities affect them more than other citizens. In some cases, the clientele group is comprised of those who are the recipients of the service being delivered. In the case of the city's child welfare system, those children at risk for being abused or neglected make up the bulk of the system's clientele group. In other cases, as with the Department of Parks and Recreation, the clientele group is made up of the subgroup of citizens using the parks. The NYPD delivers a service that affects everyone. Some who live in high crime neighborhoods, however, may be more affected by police activities than others even though everyone receives the service being delivered.

Clientele groups differ in their degree of organization, and this has an impact on their ability to monitor and influence the bureaucracy delivering the service. Many clientele groups are organized, such as the youth sports organizations, because their use of the service being delivered necessitates a group or collectivity. Of course, not all individuals who use the parks require a group to do so. And many groups interested in the city's parks are comprised of people who use the parks as individuals. Based on their wealth and education, some clientele groups are more capable of organizing than others. Many community groups in minority neighborhoods on their own lack the affluence and organizing skills to monitor the activities of the NYPD and influence the behavior of the police. The alliance of these community groups with larger and more affluent civil rights and civil liberties groups has enhanced their ability to influence NYPD activities. The at-risk children who receive the services delivered by the ACS also lacked the wealth or education to organize. Despite this handicap, there are advocates for children who have the affluence and organizing skills and who represent those children in the child welfare system and in the larger political system. However, not all clientele groups who lack the affluence or skills to organize have surrogate representative groups similar to at-risk children.

The Bureaucracy as a Function of Intergovernmental Relations, Economic Development Needs, and Ethnic and Racial Relations

Intergovernmental Relations

The federal and state levels of government influence the operations of the municipal bureaucracy in two primary ways. First, through the issuance of mandates and the funding of public programs that are intergovernmental in scope, the federal and state levels of government affect the organization and operation of the executive branch. Second, because some of the municipal bureaucracy's long-standing activities are the result of intergovernmental programs, municipal bureaucrats have developed relationships with, and have been influenced by, bureaucrats at other levels of government.

As has been previously discussed, many of the programs implemented by the city are programs that originated at another level of government and are currently funded and/or mandated by that level of government. Without these funded programs or mandates, the city's municipal bureaucracy would be considerably smaller and entire agencies might not exist. Some of the largest programs implemented by the city, such as Medicaid and Temporary Assistance to Needy Families, are programs that have both a federal and state footprint. Many of the activities being undertaken by the ACS are mandated and partially funded by the state. The same can be said for the city's Department of Education. The city's Department of Homeless Services is as much a function of state court rulings as it is a function of city policies. For the most part, federal and state programs and mandates tell the city what must be done in a given program area. In some cases, they tell the city how these activities should be undertaken as well. The federal and state levels of government, however, rarely tell the city what organizational format the city must adopt in implementing intergovernmental funded or mandated programs.

The Division of Health Access and Improvement in the city Department of Health and Mental Hygiene is the office responsible for implementing Medicaid, Child Health Plus, and Family Health Plus. All of these programs are funded jointly by the state and federal levels of government along with the city. The primary role of this division is to determine eligibility for the programs it administers as well as oversee the city's portion of the state Medicaid managed care initiative started in the late 1990s (Kirk 2002, 183–184; New York City Department of Health and Mental Hygiene). Access to adequate health insurance has been a perennial problem for low-income New Yorkers, especially those who do not qualify for Medicaid. The state's implementation of Child Health Plus and the federal government's passage of the Child Health Insurance Program in the 1990s made significant progress in providing insurance coverage to children who fell just above the Medicaid eligibility threshold. The passage of welfare reform in 1996 separated eligibility for income assistance from eligibility for Medicaid, two programs whose eligibility had been fused for several decades. As a result, a large number of Medicaid-eligible families, either through their own ignorance or poor information given to them by welfare officials, thought they were no longer covered. By 2000, city officials estimated that there were over half a million individuals, many of them children, who were eligible for Medicaid, Child Health Plus, and Family Health Plus, but were not enrolled (New York City Mayor's Office of Health Insurance Access). In 2000, the mayor initiated a citywide outreach program, HealthStat. The stated role of HealthStat was to enroll as many uninsured New Yorkers in public health insurance programs for which they were eligible.

The mayor did not place operational responsibility for HealthStat in the Department of Health and Mental Hygiene's Division of Health Access and

Improvement, the agency that had administrative responsibility for Medicaid, Child Health Plus, and Family Health Plus. Instead, an office was created within the Office of the Mayor, the Office of Health Insurance Access, to run the program (New York City Mayor's Office of Health Insurance Access). This was done for at least three reasons. First, the location of a program in the mayor's office gives it visibility, prestige, and importance that it would not have if it were placed in a line agency. Second, the mayor's office determined that the agency with the responsibility for determining eligibility for public health insurance programs as well as dealing with Medicaid-managed care providers would probably not be the proper agency to conduct an outreach campaign for the programs. There is a potential conflict of interest between conducting outreach and determining eligibility. Further, the Division of Health Access and Improvement lacked the staff and/or expertise to conduct an outreach effort. Third and more important, by design, the HealthStat outreach campaign was being conducted by over twenty different city agencies and several private organizations. These additional agencies including the City Planning Commission, the New York City Housing Authority, and the Board (now Department) of Education were included to better identify and reach those individuals and families who were eligible but not enrolled (New York City Mayor's Office of Health Insurance Access). Given the number of agencies involved, the program is more effectively administered from the mayor's office than from a line agency. Officials speaking directly for the mayor have a much better opportunity to obtain cooperation from an agency than officials from the Division of Health Access and Improvement in the city Department of Health.

The second way that intergovernmental relations affect the operations of the municipal bureaucracy is through its impact on individual bureaucrats. In the late 1960s, Terry Sanford's work on American federalism discussed the bonds between bureaucrats at the federal, state, and local levels of government working on the same grant programs. Sanford labeled the concept "picket fence federalism" (Walker 1995, 26). According to Sanford, due to the proliferation of federal grant programs going to state and local governments, professional relationships had developed and grown between grant administrators at the federal level and state and local program specialists administering these grant programs. From Sanford's point of view, the existence of picket fence federalism was evidence that the intergovernmental grant system had strengthened the influence of program specialists on public policy at the expense of elected officials, who are program generalists. Grant monies and the requirements attached to them went from the federal level's program specialists to the state and local level's program specialist's. At times, elected officials were not even aware of what grants their own executive branch was applying for, let alone what was being done with the grant money once it was received. As a result, intergovernmental fiscal assistance programs were undermining the ability of elected officials to govern. The vertical pickets of the fence represented the relationships among program specialists at each level of government (Dilger 1986, 21).

In New York City's case there is sufficient evidence to conclude that the concept of the picket fence still exists. As developed by Sanford, the concept applied primarily to federal grant in aid programs. Expanding the concept to include mandates in addition to grant programs and programs that are only state-local in structure makes the concept as relevant today as it was in the seventies. The strong working relationship between New York City's executive branch and the federal bureaucracy is partly due to the many bureaucrats at both levels who share a similar perspective in wanting government programs, those based on mandates as well as grants, to work and expand. Throughout the history of federal–New York City relations the federal executive branch's picket-fence relationship with New York City's executive branch has been two-way. While the federal level promulgates grants and mandates that affect the city, New York City has frequently led the way in innovative program design and implementation. This occurred particularly in the housing and health policy areas where New York City programs frequently served as the parents of federal programs. Although the fiscal crisis compromised the city's leadership in some of these areas, it by no means eliminated the city's role as a policy innovator. The mere fact that the city was one of the first units of local government to contend with problems such as homelessness and AIDS made the city a model for other units of government, federal, state, and local, to follow or from which to learn.

As intergovernmental grant funding declined in the 1980s, mandates took on more importance as a tool of intergovernmental policy influence. Although the relationship built around a requirement to implement a mandate may not be as strong as that built on the receipt of money, it exists nonetheless. In addition, although Sanford developed the picket fence concept to apply to federal relations with state and local governments, the concept and the relationships it implies apply just as well to state-local relations. Similar to the city's relationship with the federal level, its relationship with New York State encompasses grant programs as well as mandates. State program administrators in Albany have many of the same relationships with their programmatic counterparts in New York City.

In developing the picket fence federalism concept, Terry Sanford's concern was that elected officials as program generalists were losing influence over their administrators/bureaucrats, the program specialists, in part because of the influence of program administrators from other levels of government. New York State's Office of Children and Family Services administers no fewer than six programs that fund various activities in the city's ACS. These programs include adoption assistance funds, child abuse and neglect prevention capacity building, child abuse and neglect investigations and determinations, and family preservation and reunification programs (New York State Legislative Commission on State-Local Relations 2001, 42–65). These programs fund some of the primary activities of ACS, and all of them come with requirements regarding performance by the unit of local government receiving the funding. Some of these programs are funded in part by the federal government, and the state office is merely acting as a conduit for the funding. The city lost some of this money due to its poor performance in investigating child abuse and neglect allegations in the mid-1990s. (Sexton 1996). At present, more than two thirds of the ACS budget comes from intergovernmental revenues (New York City Office of Management and Budget 2002, 138). Due to this fiscal dependence, the need for programmatic monitoring by the state, and the obvious functional overlap between the state Office of Children and Family Services and the ACS, there exists a frequent and routine level of interaction between officials in ACS and the state office.

Economic Development

The most significant link between the municipal bureaucracy and economic development concerns how the bureaucracy is organized to meet development strategies. The organization of the executive branch is a result of years of decisions by mayors and city councils as to how public policy should be implemented. Periodic reorganizations reflect decisions by elected officials that a new format for the implementation of policy is needed. In 1991, the Dinkins administration reorganized the economic development activities of the city's executive branch. The reorganization was formalized in a city charter revision the same year. Six different agencies were merged into two larger administrative units. The Office for Economic Development, Office of Business Development, and Office of Labor Services were merged to become the Department of Business Services. And the Public Development Corporation, the Financial Services Corporation, and much of the office of Ports and Trade were merged to become the Economic Development Corporation (New York City Mayor's Office of Operations 1991, 347). The purpose of the merger was to achieve "savings through administrative cuts without sacrificing the programs that serve the business community" and "to make it easier for firms to do business with the city" (New York City Mayor's Office of Operations 1991, Introductory Letter). At the time of the reorganization, the mayor's office projected that the mergers would save the city five million dollars over two years and reduce seventy-five staff positions (New York City Mayor's Office of Operations 1991, 346). Prior to this reorganization, the city Office of Economic Development, located in the Office of the Mayor, and established in 1977, coordinated the activities of some but not all of the agencies that were merged in 1991. The Office of Economic Development was run under the direction of a deputy mayor (New York City Mayor's Office of Operations 1989, 333).

The Economic Development Corporation (EDC) was established in 1991 as a not-for-profit corporation, in order to allow the agency to serve as a more flexible institution for funding economic development projects. Formally, the EDC is funded through a contract with the Department of Small Business Services. The most visible activities of the EDC are its development and/or funding of development projects for the city. Such projects include a minor league baseball stadium on Staten Island, the renovation of the Whitehall Staten Island Ferry Terminal, and the expansion of the Kaufman Astoria Studios in Queens. The EDC administers the Industrial Development Agency, which offers tax-exempt financing for manufacturing and other development projects. Related to this function, the EDC is involved in most of the firm-specific business retention and attraction deals entered into by the city. The EDC also manages the city's wholesale and retail food markets and participates in the management of the city's waterfront properties (Kirk 2002, 117).

The organizational structure of the city's economic development programs has not changed significantly since 1991. The Department of Business Services did change its name in 2002 to the Department of Small Business Services to better reflect its activities and focus. The most visible activities of the agency are the development and administration of BIDs, the administration of New York State's Empire Zone program, and the administration of commercial revitalization funding to nonprofit groups to improve communities through capital projects and real estate development. The department also helps New York City businesses participate in the city government procurement program with an emphasis on helping minority- and women-owned businesses (New York City Department of Business Services 2002). Early in his first term, Mayor Bloomberg abolished the city's Department of Employment. The department's programs were split between the Department of Small Business Services and the Department of Youth and Community Development. This was not only done to achieve efficiencies but also to connect employment and training programs with agencies who had better links to community economic development programs.

There are other agencies that play a significant role in the city's economic development policies that do not fall under either the EDC or the Department of Small Business Services. The most significant of these agencies is the City Planning Commission, which oversees the city's zoning and land use planning policies. Due to the complicated Uniform Land Use Review Process (ULURP) in which the mayor, city council, and public all play a role, it is important that this agency stands alone. The commission oversees a process (ULURP) in which those promoting specific economic development projects and those opposing them have a voice and a chance of having their position adopted. In the perennial debate between those who pursue economic development as a priority and those who oppose development, ULURP must be, or at least appear to be, neutral. Placing the City Planning Commission under the control of an agency whose purpose is to promote economic development would destroy that appearance of neutrality.

Agency leadership may at times be just as important as executive branch organization. Mayor Bloomberg's appointment of a former BID executive as commissioner of the Department of (Small) Business Services signaled to the BID community the mayor's desire to reinvigorate this economic development technique, contrary to the stance of the Giuliani administration, which had been hostile to BID development in its second term.

Racial and Ethnic Diversity

Racial and ethnic relations in New York City are closely linked to the municipal bureaucracy. Racial and ethnic groups gauge their relationship with and attachment to the political system through two facets of executive branch structure and function. First, just as ethnic and racial groups are concerned with representation in the city council or among the mayor's commissioners, they are also concerned with representation throughout the executive branch. Second, ethnic and racial groups are concerned that they be treated equally in the implementation of policy and delivery of services by the city's executive branch.

New York City has a long history of ethnic and racial group identification with the executive branch of government. Government employment in the city has always been a source of upward mobility for immigrant groups as well as recognition of the group's increased status in the political system and society. The unionization of many municipal jobs in the mid-twentieth century made city employment even more attractive due to increased benefits and job security as well as the increased political clout that unions gave group members. In addition, ethnic and racial group leaders have viewed increased government employment by their members as a way of making the implementation of public policy more sensitive to the needs of their group, although this may not always be the result. At the same time, however, it is only recently that the distribution of city government jobs has even come close to approximating the ethnic and racial composition of the city's population.

In the nineteenth century, the Democratic Party's (Tammany Hall) success in controlling the city government was due to its courting of the city's Irish Catholics, whose loyalty was paid for by municipal jobs (Binder and Reimers 1995, 71). By 1900, Irish New Yorkers held over one-third of the sixty thousand municipal jobs controlled via patronage. In the early twentieth century, the municipal government labor force showed the early signs of ethnic segregation, with Irish dominating the police and fire departments and Italians dominating the sanitation department (Binder and Reimers 1995, 141, 160). The victory of Fiorello La Guardia's fusion ticket over Tammany Hall opened up municipal employment to Jews, Italians, and to a lesser extent, Blacks, at the expense of Irish dominance (Binder and Reimers 1995, 184, 189). By the 1970s, Jews comprised 60 percent of public school teachers and Italians also began to find jobs as teachers and police officers while still dominating the sanitation department (Binder and Reimers, 1995, 203). In addition, throughout the 1970s, as a result of the civil rights movement and consequent government commitments to equal opportunity and affirmative action, Black representation in the city bureaucracy increased dramatically. Although the federal push for equal opportunity employment had the most significant impact on city government minority hiring, as early as the 1950s, mayors had issued orders about nondiscrimination in municipal hiring (Binder and Reimer 1995, 312). Minority representation, however, was not even across all agencies. Blacks were prominent in agencies devoted to health and welfare but still underrepresented in the police and fire departments as well as the schools (Binder and Reimer 1995, 215–216). In addition, the layoffs that occurred as a result of the fiscal crisis affected Black and Puerto Rican municipal workers disproportionately, under the informal principle of "last hired, first fired" (Binder and Reimer 1995, 250). Despite these problems, in the 1980s, one quarter of all jobs held by Black New Yorkers were with the city (Binder and Reimer 1995, 253).

The NYPD has been one of the focal points of minority group representation complaints. In 1999, a study concluded that the NYPD was the "least racially diverse" police force of the nation's ten largest cities. The study also found that "the lack of Black and Hispanic representation was most pronounced in the higher ranks" (Wilgoren and Cooper 1999). Whites comprised over 67 percent of the police force but only 43 percent of the population of the city. In addition, whites comprised 94 percent of all captains (Wilgoren and Cooper 1999). And among the 669 officers at the rank of captain or above, only 19 were Black males (Chivers 2001a). In 2000, 34 percent of the city's forty thousand police officers were Black, Hispanic, or Asian (Chivers 2000).

In 1995, the NYPD went through a routine audit by the city's Equal Employment Practices Commission. The commission's report, issued in 1997, highlighted the fact that the NYPD had been uncooperative in responding to its requests for information. The commission recommended that the NYPD examine whether its selection process was biased against minorities. Commissioner Safir agreed to conduct the study. In early 2001, however, the study had still not been done (Chivers 2001b). In early 1999, commenting on the fact that the NYPD did not take race into account in promotion or recruiting decisions, Police Commissioner Safir stated, "I'm going to select the most talented people" (Wilgoren and Cooper 1999). Critics compared the Giuliani years to the Dinkins and Koch years, when two minority police commissioners, Lee Brown and Ben Ward, made much greater efforts to diversify the NYPD (Wilgoren and Cooper 1999). Yet even their efforts resulted in little change in total minority composition in the department (Chivers 2001a).

Recently, the city has had greater success in attracting Hispanics to the force. In 1999, the city was 24 percent Hispanic and the NYPD was over 17 percent Hispanic (Wilgoren and Cooper 1999). In addition, the NYPD has had much greater success over the last decade in recruiting Black females than males (Chivers 2001a).

After the Louima and Diallo incidents, the NYPD responded with recruiting drives that attempted to attract more minorities. In 1999, the Giuliani administration launched a ten-million-dollar campaign to increase the number of non-Whites on the police force. The campaign included advertisements, "speakers, links to community groups and recruitment stations" (*New York Times* 1999). In 1998 and 1999, the police academy classes were only 11 percent Black and 20 percent Hispanic (*New York Times* 1999). These percentages improved in 2000–2001. The 2001 academy class was only 47.6 percent white and the proportion of white male officers dropped in 2000 from 61.4 percent to 58.6 percent (Chivers 2001b). Despite some successes, the NYPD is still unrepresentative of the city's ethnic and racial mix, particularly Black males. Numerous reasons have been cited for the limited success of the city's minority recruitment efforts. An editorial in the *New York Times* suggested that the NYPD's White majority "may reflect the historic tendency of some white families to encourage their young to go into police work, while others, mainly minority families, teach their children to cross the street to avoid the police altogether" (*New York Times* 1999). Other minority recruitment problems stem from NYPD internal issues. The department relies on civil service tests as its primary tool for promoting. Although many minorities take the exams, a much lower percentage score in the higher percentiles, decreasing the prospects of promotion. The tests have had a disparate impact on minorities, particularly Black males (Chivers 2001a). Minority officers inside the department also complained that they were being passed over for positions in the more prestigious units in the NYPD (Wilgoren and Cooper 1999). This further blocked their paths to promotion within the department. The fact that minorities fare poorly in departmental promotions is, in part, self-perpetuating. Some officers reported that having contacts in the NYPD hierarchy who would simply inform them that an opening existed was often extremely helpful. When there are so few minorities at the top of the hierarchy, minorities have less access to information necessary to advance within the department (Chivers 2001a).

Not only did racial and ethnic groups demand better representation in the service delivery bureaucracies, they also wanted, when possible, the service to cater to the needs or preferences of their group. As discussed above, some have argued that one of the necessary conditions to creating a bureaucracy that is sensitive to the needs of racial and ethnic minorities is to have a bureaucracy that is representative of these groups. Other have suggested that in order to make the bureaucracy more sensitive to the needs of racial and ethnic minorities, the operations of the agency should be decentralized to give the community control over agency decision making, which in turn may produce a bureaucracy that is more representative of those in the community. Even if it does not do this, however, community control over agency decision making should still result in service delivery that responds to the needs of those in the community, regardless of the ethnic and racial make-up of the bureaucrats delivering the service.

The most visible and possibly most volatile set of demands for community control came out of the Ocean Hill–Brownsville dispute over community control of the schools. With funding from the Ford Foundation and cooperation from the city's Board of Education, Ocean Hill–Brownsville was given the status of an experimental decentralized school district in 1967. Part of the experiment involved a parent-elected school board that was given control over the operations of the schools in the district, although the extent of the control was never articulated clearly by the city Board of Education. Almost immediately, conflict arose over who would control the staffing of the school—the elected parent board and their designated administrator, or the traditional procedures backed by the UFT (Freeman 2000, 218–221). The conflict involved labor and religious issues as much as racial differences (Rogers 1990, 151). And although the teaching staff retained by the parent board and their superintendent was still mostly White, the attempt by the community to remove White teachers who were deemed insensitive to community needs or uncooperative with the parent board placed the community in direct conflict with the teachers' union. The UFT countered the community's demand for school control with the equally legitimate demand that teachers be given due process before being removed from their positions. The stand-off between the union and the community, backed by the mayor and the central school board, resulted in several teacher strikes during 1967 and 1968.

The settlement, brokered by the state, initiated the evolution of elected decentralized community boards participating in school governance and administration (Freeman 2000, 221–225). The elected community school boards had some control over the staffing of elementary, junior high, and middle schools in the district, but little control over high schools or special education. The boards did have the power to hire a district superintendent and school administrators in the district below the high school level (Pecorella 1994, 102). The decentralization, along with increased minority hiring by the school system, over time, resulted in decreased demands by minorities for a more representative school system. Over their thirty-two year history, the community boards experienced several perennial problems that contributed to their demise (Rogers 1990, 152–155). Community boards were frequently the victim of mismanagement and corruption, resulting in intervention and more regulation from the chancellor or the central school board. In addition, the level of community participation in the community school boards was low from the outset. Average voter turnout for community school board elections never surpassed 10 percent and in some years was as low as 5. In the late 1980s, nearly one quarter of the individuals sitting on community school boards were employees of the school system, with the UFT playing a major role in school board elections (Pecorella 1994, 104). In 2002, as part of the Bloomberg-initiated school reform, the state passed legislation that stripped the local community school boards of most of their power and initiated a search for new forms of parental participation in the schools. Plans for the abolition and replacement of the boards were announced early in 2003. Each school would have a paid parent coordinator who would serve as a liaison between the parents and school officials. The coordinators are selected by groups including parents and school staff (Gootman 2003).

There are several different ways that the delivery of a service can be decentralized. Not all of them include or lead to community control. In New York City, many services including schools, the police department, the fire department, libraries, and parks are physically dispersed throughout the city. In a city the size of New York this is necessary for efficient and effective delivery of services.

It would be as inefficient and ineffective to run the NYPD from one central location without precincts as it would be to have one central library in the city with no branches. Yet, the mere physical dispersal of a service does not imply administrative decentralization unless those delivering the service have discretion to tailor the delivery to the specific populations within their geographic area. To the extent that dispersed bureaucratic service deliverers have this discretion, administrative decentralization exists (Hallman 1977, 113). All the services listed above are administratively decentralized but they all still receive considerable direction from the central bureaucratic headquarters as well. In addition, the presence of administrative decentralization, meaning that the physically dispersed bureaucrats have discretion, does not necessarily mean that the service being delivered will be sensitive to the needs of those in the community. All it means is that the physically dispersed bureaucrats making those decisions have the ability to mold the delivery of the service in that direction if they so choose. Political decentralization occurs when citizens or their elected community representatives directly control the physically dispersed bureaucracy (Hallman 1977, 114). This control could include budget, staffing, or both. If those delivering the service are accountable to the community and/or its representatives, then there is a high probability that the service being delivered will cater to community needs and tastes. This is what the communities of Ocean Hill–Brownsville sought and did not achieve.

In the wake of Ocean Hill–Brownsville, the Lindsay administration experimented with several types of decentralization designs spanning much of the executive branch. To some extent, the Lindsay administration viewed decentralization as not only an executive branch reorganization strategy, but also a way to build a political constituency for a mayor who had weak ties to political parties in the city. None of the decentralization strategies attempted by the Lindsay administration, however, ever achieved the mayor's administrative or political goals, nor did they approach or achieve a degree of community control that would have given neighborhoods and/or minority groups control over the services delivered. After the Ocean Hill–Brownsville debacle, Lindsay adopted a decentralization strategy that was far more administrative than political. Lindsay's Office of Neighborhood Government, established in 1971, created several experimental community planning districts, each with a district manager appointed by the mayor, which were authorized to coordinate the delivery of city services for the district. Participating agencies were required to designate personnel who would represent the agency at district meetings chaired by the manager. The manager would serve as the liaison between the citizens of the district and the agencies delivering services and coordinate the delivery of services across city agencies (Pecorella 1994, 107–108). The program failed because the district managers, although mayoral appointees, never had sufficient power to modify services being delivered by the line agencies. In addition, the line agencies delivering the services never decentralized to the point where their field representatives had the ability to modify services even if they wanted to comply with the district managers. All changes in service delivery still had to go through the central headquarters of each line agency, making it difficult to coordinate or modify service delivery at the community level (Pecorella 1994, 109). Abe Beame, charging that the Office of Neighborhood Government had misused funds, ended the experiment when he became mayor (Forman 2003).

The 1975 charter revision, in part mandated by the state, created the most recent iteration of decentralization: the community board. The city was divided into fifty-nine districts, each with its own community board. Boards would be comprised of members appointed by the borough presidents, with half the members nominated by the relevant member of the city council. The boards would participate in the land use and zoning process on an advisory basis, they would participate in the budget process, and they would address service delivery issues in their districts. They were staffed by a full-time district manager and staff hired by the board (Pecorella 1994, 128). Similar to the community planning boards under Mayor Lindsay's Office of Neighborhood Government, the primary focus of the district manager was to coordinate the delivery of services to the community. In support of the manager's coordination role, the 1975 charter revision mandated that the city make the executive branch agencies' service delivery districts coterminous with community board boundaries (Rogers 1990, 166). In addition line agencies were required to send local representatives to attend community district service cabinet meetings (Rogers 1990, 166–167). With few exceptions, this effort was unsuccessful. With regard to service delivery, boards have served in an "outreach and complaint handling" capacity but have had little substantive impact on tailoring service delivery to community needs or tastes (Rogers 1990, 172). Similar to the community planning districts under Mayor Lindsay, community boards lack the authority over the line agencies delivering the services.

There is evidence that minority membership on community boards has lagged behind their composition in the city's population and that some boards have been dominated by local party organizations (Pecorella 1994, 134–135). What is most significant though is that the boards have never had sufficient authority or played a meaningful enough role in community service delivery issues or city politics to make representation a significant issue. As previously noted, community board participation in ULURP is advisory, and there have been instances, as in the case of Donald Trump's Riverside South proposal, when the community board voted unanimously to oppose the project, yet it was approved at higher levels of the process. From a representative, or "not in my back yard" (NIMBY) perspective, community boards have served as mobilizing institutions for communities opposed to specific projects. In this capacity, they allow the community to formally articulate opposition. When this type of opposition is successful, developers or the city are forced to modify projects or negotiate with the community, sometimes through the board (Rogers 1990, 181). Most important, community board involvement in land use has been reactive. Boards "have not taken the initiative in land use planning" (Rogers 1990, 171). A 1990 city charter revision gave community boards the ability to construct their own advisory master plan that would be submitted to the City Planning Commission via the 197-a planning process. Few community boards have taken advantage of this charter provision (Forman 2003). In the mid-1990s, when the city council gave the community boards the ability to participate in land use planning for megastores, few community boards responded with a plan. With regard to the budget process, although community boards have at times played a role in the capital budget, their impact has been minimal. In fiscal years where there is a projected deficit, greater centralization in budget decision making usually results in community boards having even less influence (Rogers 1990, 173).

Part of the reason for the lack of effectiveness of community boards and the problems with administrative, let alone political, decentralization in the city has been the lack of support decentralization has received from mayors after Mayor Lindsay. Mayor Beame, who was in office during the 1975 city charter revision, was distracted by the fiscal crisis. Subsequent mayors never viewed decentralization as an important goal for their administrations. And as previously noted, to the extent that Mayors Koch, Dinkins, and Giuliani experienced their own fiscal problems, greater centralization rather than decentralization was the strategy of choice to gain greater control over the executive branch as a means to save money. Even during the years of the Giuliani administration, when the city enjoyed a degree of fiscal health not experienced in several decades, there was little interest on the administration's part in decentralizing the operations of the city's executive branch. The community board and community district office structure, already weak when Mayor Giuliani took office, languished under his administration. Furthermore, to the extent that the city's school system was decentralized through the empowerment of community school districts, Mayor Giuliani sought to dismantle this structure. Mayor Bloomberg was ultimately successful in centralizing educational policymaking by eliminating community boards. And although the attempt to make foster care services more neighborhood-based can be viewed as decentralization, the further privatization of social services was a primary goal in this effort as well (Weikart 2001, 373).

One of the lessons of Mayor Lindsay's decentralization attempts is that even if a chief executive favors greater decentralization, it is not clear whether it can be achieved. In order to decentralize power, one must centralize it first. Whether mayors have sufficient control over the bureaucracy to decentralize power to the community level has not yet been demonstrated. Those in the central bureaucracies will resist attempts to give up their discretion, and they have allies. As in the Ocean Hill–Brownsville conflict, unions also view administrative and certainly political decentralization as having a negative impact on their control. The abolition of the Board of Estimate, an institution that further centralized government, and its replacement with an expanded city council, also may have decreased the need for community boards in the city. A fifty-one-member council with expanded power and increased status elevates the role of each council member in their district. In their constituency service role, council members become service coordinators and ombudsmen as much, if not more, than the district managers and the staff of the community boards. Through their budgetary and oversight functions, the council members have far more influence over the executive branch than do the community boards. While decentralization would appear to be a necessary precondition to community control over service delivery, there is little evidence that decentralization in the past was successful. Moreover, there is little evidence at present that meaningful decentralization of the executive branch will be attempted in the near future. Minority and community groups are not demanding it and the current fiscal problems of the city suggest greater centralization.

Conclusion

New York City's executive branch is vast. It includes police officers, teachers, sanitation workers, urban park rangers, accountants, social workers, and physicians, among others. All of these individuals are bureaucrats. Given the vastness of the city's bureaucracy, it is difficult, if not impossible, to generalize about the positive or negative aspects of the bureaucracy as an institution other than to note that citizen interactions with the political system take place primarily through interaction with bureaucrats.

The role of the bureaucracy in New York City's political system creates dilemmas that all democratic political systems share. Bureaucrats are not elected officials yet they play a significant role in the implementation of public policy and consequently have an impact on the outcomes of public policy. The discretion that bureaucrats exercise in their implementation role gives them control over service delivery outcomes and makes them critical actors within the structures of government and the greater political system. In the extreme, not only can the exercise of bureaucratic discretion damage the political system's attempt to achieve service delivery equity, but it can also decrease the level of civil harmony and democratic accountability

The dilemma for democratic political systems is that bureaucrats are not accountable to the citizens through elections, as are other government officials. Elected officials, the mayor, and the city council, have a number of mechanisms at their disposal to achieve a degree of bureaucratic accountability. And there is anecdotal evidence that elected officials can move executive branch agencies in a desired direction using appointments, budgets, reorganizations, and other tools. The evidence, however, is insufficient to quell fears on the part of some who claim that the bureaucracy is simply too vast for a small group of elected officials to control. To those critics, elected officials have simply become one of a number of factors including clientele groups, unions, and executive branch officials at other levels of government, in addition to forces and processes from inside the agency itself that influence bureaucratic behavior. Moreover, executive branch agencies and the bureaucrats who staff them are not passive when others attempt to influence bureaucratic behavior. Rarely are all the factors that can influence bureaucratic behavior working together.

10

Conclusion

This final chapter will address three themes related to the governance of New York City. First, it will summarize the impact of the economic growth imperative, federal and state relations with the city, and racial and ethnic diversity on the governance of the city. Second, the prospect that forces, other than the three emphasized in this discussion, are influencing the governance of the city will be examined. And finally, the chapter will discuss the implications for the future of theory and theory-building in the broader study of urban politics.

Governing Gotham

Throughout this work, governance has been defined as three related activities undertaken by political systems: the maintenance of democratic accountability; the maintenance of civil harmony; and the delivery of public goods and services.

Democratic Accountability

Democratic accountability requires a set of accessible procedures linked to the key decision-making apparatus of the political system. It also requires that the citizenry be effectively represented in these procedures, ideally through elections, but also through appointments, dedicated representation structures, or more informal means that guarantee critical groups input into political systems' decision-making. Democratic accountability contributes to the legitimacy of the decisions made by the political system.

Given the importance of economic development to the political system, mayors as chief executives and as chiefs of state are held accountable for the city's economic performance. The mayor has certainly become the most significant actor in the city's promotion of economic growth, but many of his decisions are subject to an open, democratically accountable decision-making process. The promotion of economic development has become so important in the city's political system that these decisions are some of the most visible decisions made. As a result of this visibility, the processes by which the decisions are made have become almost as important as the decisions themselves. Democratically accountable procedures in economic development decisions have not always been present. Procedures such as the Uniform Land Use Review Process (ULRUP) are relatively recent amendments to the city's political system. These new procedures have resulted from a variety of influences including the civil rights movement, federally mandated citizen participation regulations dating back to the 1960s, and the slow but steady reform of the city's political system attached to the reemergence of reform politics after World War II.

There are still areas of economic development policy, such as firm-specific tax incentives, where the mayor and/or his or her appointees act with very little public scrutiny. Yet even those economic development decisions that are not the result of a transparent process are still receiving more public attention. As in the case of the Atlantic Yards, even without ULURP, communities and groups at the grassroots level can still influence economic development decisions.

Similar to economic growth promotion, the city's relationship with the federal and state governments produces influences that both encourage and retard the maintenance of democratic accountability. The state continues to play a major role in the city's promotion of economic growth. The Atlantic Yards decision, the redevelopment of the World Trade Center site, and the decision not to build the Olympic/Jets Stadium on Manhattan's Far West Side were all decisions controlled by the state. To the extent that major pieces of the city's economic development future are controlled in Albany and not through the city's political system, democratic accountability is not being served. This inhibition of democratic accountability also occurs whenever the state or federal level imposes a mandate on the city's political system. Regardless of the substance of the mandate, many of them laudable, intergovernmental unfunded mandates not only impose priorities of another level of government on the city, but they also force the city to move resources, dedicated through a democratically accountable budget process, to alternate, nondemocratically established priorities.

Of course, citizens of the city can also vote in state and national elections, thereby participating in those levels of government that create unfunded mandates. At these levels of government, however, the city's electorate is only one voice among many.

Through the Voting Rights Act, the federal government's influence on the city has produced one of the most significant positive impacts on the maintenance of democratic accountability. As previously discussed, the act adds an additional layer of checks on the city's election procedures, further ensuring that ethnic and racial minorities will receive equal representation in the city's political system. Racially and ethnically diverse societies produce greater demands for democratic accountability than more homogenous societies. Racially and ethnically diverse political systems experience a greater range of policy preferences necessitating better representation. In addition, descriptive representation not only becomes more of an issue in racially and ethnically diverse political systems, it is also more easily measured.

Although racial and ethnic diversity places demands on the city for greater democratic accountability, when racial and ethnic groups are well organized, as is sometimes the case in New York City, democratic accountability is more easily maintained. Identifiable and politically active leaders of racial and ethnic groups reassure group members that they are being represented inside the political system. These same leaders also inform the political system of the need to be more inclusive.

Civil Harmony

Civil disharmony occurs within a political system when groups challenge the legitimacy of the system or a decision in a way that is uncomfortable or disruptive to the system. Democratic political systems clearly have far less of a problem in maintaining civil harmony than those political systems that lack democratic procedures. Even democratic political systems, however, and especially those that are highly diverse, incur challenges to their civil harmony. These challenges arise due to flaws in democratic procedures or problems with the equitable delivery of services. Similar to the maintenance of democratic accountability, diversity creates challenges to civil harmony because of the strains heterogeneous political attitudes and views place on any set of democratic procedures or service delivery bureaucracies.

Demonstrations of civil disharmony are not limited to vocal or militant expressions of opposition to a decision. They could involve the amassing of resources in a continuous protracted effort to reverse a decision or reform the political system in a significant way. This might involve litigation and/or protest activity, but it could also involve nonlegal means of articulating a position.

The promotion of economic development affects civil harmony through demands that some neighborhoods bear the burdens of economic development projects or policies whose benefits accrue to the entire city. As in the case of the Atlantic Yards development, the Broadway Theater Air Rights initiative, or even the failed attempt at the Olympic/Jets Stadium on the Far West Side of Manhattan, communities are frequently opposed to economic development projects targeted for their neighborhoods. These projects exact costs on communities including disruption, environmental health issues, and the changing character of the neighborhood. If these communities and their citizens are excluded from the process by which the economic development decision is made, the legitimacy of the project/program is called further into question. These issues would also exist for those communities neglected by economic development but bearing the burden of economic growth through the placement of necessary infrastructure such as highways, bus depots, or waste transfer stations. The negative impacts of economic development do not fall equally across the city's neighborhoods.

The city's relationships with the federal and state levels of government affect civil harmony primarily through their impact on democratic accountability discussed above. For the most part, the impact is marginal. While intergovernmental mandates remove important decision making from the city's political system, those same mandates may service the interest of civil harmony by directing the city's political system to engage in more equitable service delivery activities or by creating more democratic procedures. In addition, when civil harmony declines, the state and federal levels may provide outlets where aggrieved groups and communities can seek redress from the negative impacts produced by the city's political system. This occurred when minority groups went to the federal level to seek reforms of discriminatory police practices.

Racial and ethnic diversity affect civil harmony most directly through the production of a diverse set of demands on the city's political system. The demands can be procedural, claiming greater representation within political decision-making bodies, or the demands can be substantive, such as a demand for a multilingual educational system or a police department more sensitive to cultural diversity. These demands challenge the political system because they may not only raise the cost of service delivery or the achievement of democratic accountability, but they may also challenge the ability of the political system to make good on these commitments.

Racial and ethnic diversity also challenges the maintenance of civil harmony through both the reality and perception of discrimination. Groups who have been victims of societal discrimination are acutely aware of both the process and substance of government activity and how it can further discrimination and disadvantage. Racial and ethnic group leadership plays a critical role. As discussed in chapter five, group members look to group leaders for an assessment of how the group is being treated by the political system. In the face of discriminatory treatment, group members will look to group leaders for guidance on how to react.

Delivery of Public Goods and Services

For most New York City citizens, expectations of local government performance are directly related to the delivery of public goods and services. Education, law enforcement traffic control, and public health are governmentally provided services that affect citizens on a daily basis. And in many cases, issues of democratic accountability or civil harmony initially arise as concerns about service delivery.

To the extent that economic growth produces a positive fiscal flow, it has a significant impact on the ability of the city to deliver services. Given constraints on other mechanisms to increase the tax base, economic growth remains the most politically palatable mechanism to maintain or enhance a positive fiscal flow. As noted above, economic growth may affect service delivery in other ways. Growth in some parts of the city will place demands for greater service delivery in those areas. To the extent that economic development takes place in advance of infrastructure improvements, it may place a strain on the city's service delivery apparatus.

The city's relationship with the federal and state levels of government affects its ability to deliver services. Financial aid from other levels of government, in areas such as education, housing and law enforcement, enhance the city's ability to deliver more and better services. In effect, fiscal assistance from the state and federal levels lowers the city's cost of delivering services in those funded areas. At the same time, however, federal and state mandates occasionally tell the city not only what services must be delivered but how they are to be delivered. State court cases in the early 1980s established that the city would have to provide homeless individuals and families with shelter. Subsequent court rulings mandated how the city should do this. The federal No Child Left Behind Act mandated a series of educational practices that the city would not have otherwise offered.

As previously noted, racial and ethnic diversity requires the city's service delivery bureaucracies to respond to a much wider variety of demands and/or be sensitive to the multicultural context within which city services are being delivered. The city's Department of Education concluded that in order to increase educational quality among its students, parents would have to be drawn into the educational process more than in the past. In order to do this, however, the department would have to communicate with the large number of parents for whom English is not the primary language. This requires homework assignments, report cards, school notices, and parent-teacher conferences to be sensitive to the language needs of the parents.

From the perspective of the racial or ethnic group, increasing diversity has heightened concerns about service delivery equity. Equal treatment by the service delivery bureaucracy, regardless of whether it is the police, the school system, or the public health authorities, has become a standard by which racial and ethnic groups assess their relationship with the political system, if not the overall quality of governance. At the extreme, these concerns have resulted in demands for community control of service delivery in order to better assure that service deliverers are more sensitive to the needs of the divergent communities.

The Forces that Affect New York City Governance

The central thesis of this work has been that the governance of New York City is influenced by three sets of forces: the need of the city to promote economic growth; the city's relationships with the state and federal governments; and the city's racial and ethnic diversity. Are there other forces that might affect the governance of the city as much, or are there forces that might, over time, become more important in their impact on the city? The three forces being featured in this work have not always had the impact on the governance of the city that they have at present. Prior to the Depression of the 1930s and possibly as recent as the 1950s, the federal government did not exert the type of influence on the city that it does today. The federal government's response to the civil rights movement and the urban crises of the 1950s and 1960s, as well as President Johnson's Great Society programs, established a relationship between the federal government and cities that did not exist before. Similarly, in the 1950s and 1960s, when the city was receiving a great deal of intergovernmental economic development funding, pressure on the city to promote economic growth, on its own, was not as great as it is today.

Two factors that have been mentioned as possible forces in influencing the governance of the city are terrorism and the mayor.

New York City and the Threat of Terrorism

The events of September 11, 2001, left an indelible mark on the city and its citizens. The impact can be measured in lives lost, jobs lost, businesses destroyed, as well as lost revenue to the city. In order to become one of the forces driving the governance of the city, however, the events of September 11 would have had to produce major concerns about future terrorist attacks. These concerns would have had to become such a significant dimension in life of the city that the process or substance of governance was affected. This has not happened. In the wake of the terrorist attacks, the city has reallocated the resources of its law enforcement, health, and emergency management bureaucracies in order to address the possibility of future terrorist attacks. In addition, the citizens of the city are certainly cognizant of the prospects of terrorist attacks in the future, not only because of the political system's reallocation of resources but also because the citizens are frequently reminded that the city's assets make it a target for future attacks.

The three factors featured in this work became major forces affecting the governance of the city over a long period of time, not just as the result of one event, no matter how catastrophic. In the case of each of the factors, it took several decades, or longer, to establish their prominence in the governance of the city. If New York City were to become the target of a number of terrorist attacks over a period of years, it is certainly possible that the fears of the citizens and security concerns of the political system might begin to affect the governance of the city in a significant way.

The concerns about terrorism have not reached the level of significance in affecting the governance of the city equivalent to the three factors discussed in this work. In many ways the events of September 11, 2001, and their aftermath reinforced the significance of race and ethnicity, intergovernmental relations, and the promotion of economic growth in the governance of the city. In the aftermath of September 11, the city became focused on retaining businesses in lower Manhattan as the city began to rebuild. The events of September 11 certainly also underscored the city's continued dependence on the state and federal levels of government. And finally, to a lesser extent, the events of September 11 certainly had ethnic overtones not only in terms of who perpetrated the attack but also in the attack's impact on various groups and neighborhoods across the city.

The Mayor

The mayor is clearly the most influential actor in the city's political system. As discussed in chapter seven, his formal and informal roles, as well as the resources accompanying these roles, give him a scope of influence across the political system equaled by no other actor or institution. More than any other actor, the mayor has discretion to move the city's political system in a desired direction. Mayor Giuliani's emphasis on addressing the city's crime problem and Mayor Bloomberg's programs to promote the building of affordable housing across the city are both examples of the exercise of this discretion. Can the mayor, using his discretion, have an impact on the governance of the city equal to the forces being featured in this study? The answer to this question may very well be "it all depends."

How much discretion a mayor has to pursue his agenda is, in part, a function of forces and events not always under the mayor's control; those forces are discussed in this volume. Mayors Giuliani and Bloomberg were able to take advantage of periods of fiscal health and political stability in the city, especially during their second terms, that allowed them the freedom to pursue their agendas. Mayors Dinkins, Beame, and certainly Koch in his first term had to respond to other forces and did not have this freedom.

The forces discussed in this volume both distract and constrain mayoral behavior. There may be periods of time in which these forces are less pressing, giving the mayor greater ability to pursue his agenda. There are clearly other periods in which the mayor must deal with these forces to the exclusion of his agenda. Most important, however, in their pursuit of their agendas, mayors are constrained by the need to promote economic growth, federal and state government influences, and racial and ethnic diversity. Mayor Giuliani's anti-crime programs were in part designed to make the city more attractive for economic development. The aggressive policing tactics practiced by the police department under Mayor Giuliani were ultimately constrained not only by the response of minority groups in the city but also by the response of the federal government. Federal funding allowed the Giuliani administration to expand the police department as part of its anti-crime campaign, but in the years that followed minority group leaders and the federal government were involved in checking the aggressive tactics employed by the police. Similarly, Mayor Bloomberg's housing policies are tempered not only by the need to promote economic growth but also by support from the federal and state levels.

Given the position they occupy in the political system, mayors have some leeway and discretion in choosing which issues to pursue. In their pursuit, however, mayors are constrained by the need to promote economic growth, intergovernmental relations, and the demands of racially and ethnically diverse society.

Governing Gotham and the Future of Urban Politics Theory

This examination of New York City politics has not attempted to address the role that theory plays in the study of urban politics. The approach taken in this work does, however, have implications both for prior efforts to develop theoretical perspectives on urban politics as well as future attempts.

Over the last five decades, a number of contending approaches to understanding urban political systems have emerged. These contending approaches attempt to describe a context and to some extent a process within which the governance of urban political systems takes place. While these approaches have certainly advanced understanding of urban governance, they nevertheless lack a perspective that draws attention to the economic, social, and intergovernmental contexts within which the governance of urban political systems takes place.

Among those contending perspectives, pluralism has received a great deal of attention, although much of it critical. Pluralism views interests and the organization of interests as the central element in understanding politics. What makes pluralism controversial is its perspective on the distribution of political power. Pluralists argue that power has its roots in a number of different societal activities, the accumulation of wealth and social status being only two. While pluralists do not claim that all citizens have equal political power, they do claim that all citizens have some political power in a system of dispersed inequalities (Dahl 1961). In addition, they argue that the political system is open and accessible to all, allowing any individual or group to use or not use the power they have. As a result, the political process that pluralists describe is a relatively fair one where those who choose to use their political power compete with each other for the benefits allocated by the political system.

Pluralism was critiqued for creating an inaccurate view of the urban political system. While pluralists touted the neutrality or fairness of the rules under which group political competition took place, critics argued that the same dispersed inequalities that the pluralists recognized had, over time, created an imbalance in the rules under which group competition takes place. These conditions created an unfair political process structured in a way that excluded some from competition and biased the process further in favor of some privileged interests. From the perspective of this study, the problem with pluralism is not only that it ignored biases in the arrayed interests influencing the governance of urban political systems, but also that it failed to recognized the overall structure of these interests. The focus of this work has been, in part, to apply structure to the array of interests affecting the governance of New York City.

The primary criticism of pluralism, as it was applied to urban political systems, was that it failed to account for the primacy of economic development interests in the governance of those systems. Pluralism viewed economic development interests as just another set of groups in the competitive political process. This criticism was responsible for the creation of several new approaches that emphasized the impact of economic development interests on urban governance. Two of these approaches were the growth machine and the regime theory approaches.

The growth machine perspective, developed by Logan and Molotch (1996), is based on the assumption that cities contain a group, or groups, of elites, who because of the nature of their business, are tied to the city. Local realtors, banks, utilities, newspapers, labor unions and others do not have unrestricted freedom to move their capital nationally or globally as economic conditions dictate. These rentiers, as Logan and Molotch label them, have parochial capital, which cannot be moved easily. As a result, their orientation is to the local economic environment and to receive the most out of their investment in the city in which they are located. They do this by attracting mobile capital of nonlocal investors (Harding 1995, 42). In order to accomplish this, a positive business climate must be created. According to Logan and Molotch (1996), the local growth machine and its allies have sufficient power to successfully pursue their goals. In addition, they attempt to gain broader public support for economic growth by espousing it as a goal whose achievement will benefit all (Harding 1995, 42). The growth machine perspective is unclear on the role that local government officials play. Some have noted, however, that in the United States, where local governments must raise a greater share of their own revenue, local government officials are likely to share the same goals as members of the growth machine. In addition, local government control over land use policy and zoning in the United States makes growth machine–local government relations a necessity (Jonas and Wilson 1999, 14).

Similar to the diversity of economic development interests in New York City, Logan and Molotch (1996) recognize that while all members of the growth machine may favor economic growth, they may differ on how best to achieve it. Logan and Molotch do not consider cleavages in the growth machine a threat to its existence as long as all members maintain the belief in growth as the primary goal (Logan and Molotch 1996, 302). At the same time, however, there is much about the governance of urban political systems that the growth machine perspective fails to address. While growth machine–local government relations is necessary, what about the relationship of the growth machine to the state and federal levels of government? Is the growth machine active in Albany and Washington, realizing the impact that these levels can have on economic development? How much of a role does the growth machine play in issues not directly related to economic development such as school reform, police brutality, or environmental racism? How would the growth machine deal with issues of service delivery inequities in communities of color?

Regime theory appears to offer more breadth than the growth machine in understanding the urban political milieu while still focusing on urban economic development. Regime theory views the economic development interest–government relationship as an informal set of relationships between public and private actors that evolves out of mutual dependence and necessity. According to regime theory, to govern effectively, elected officials must coalesce with other types of societal actors (Stone 1989, 227). Government officials recognize that a successful state, and their continued tenure in it, requires positive economic performance by those who have capital. They also realize that, left alone, those with capital will make some investment decisions, but that optimal investment performance on the part of the managers of capital will not occur without state initiative. Public officials must create an environment within which private investors will have confidence enough to take investment risks. In addition, officials must offer potential investors positive inducements to take risks (Elkin 1985). For their part, the holders of capital need a supportive environment for investment as well as inducements to invest in order to maximize their profits (Stone 1992).

The "regime" in regime theory is the set of relationships that results from the mutual dependence of the two groups of actors, as well as the process by which the relationships evolve. Relations among actors in a regime exist in a network where cooperation and mutual support define the interactions among the actors more than hierarchy or bargaining (Stoker 1995, 59). Unlike approaches to the study of urban politics that focus on one group's dominance of the political system, regime theory posits that urban societies are too complex for any one group to gain control. "Regimes bridge the divide between popular control of government and private control of economic resources. Beyond the inclusion of local government and businesses, participants may vary, including neighborhood organizations, or organizations representing middle class African-Americans" (Mossberger and Stoker 2001, 813). As a result, although regime theory emphasizes the political system's relationship with those who hold capital, the regime may also include minority groups.

Regime theory offers analysts of urban politics greater structure than pluralism in attempting to understand relationship among actors. Yet the structure is not well articulated and is also incomplete. Can a set of structural relationships encompassing a regime be found in every urban political system at any point in time? The transition from the Koch administration to the Dinkins administration is a case in point. Did the Dinkins administration represent a new regime, a continuation of the Koch regime, or no regime? Assuming the Dinkins administration represented the victory of one coalition of interests over another and therefore a new regime, how would regime theorists explain the fact that midway through Mayor Dinkins's term he was pursuing many of the same economic development strategies as his predecessor? Finally, given the extent to which the state and federal levels of government influence major governance decision in New York City, how does regime theory account for these intergovernmental impacts?

Approaches such as the growth machine and regime theory adjusted for pluralism's failures to recognize the imperative that urban political systems promote economic growth and the imbalance of interests that this imperative creates. Moreover, these approaches evolved at a time when federal aid to cities was declining and urban political systems were being pressed to find new ways of raising revenue on their own. As a result, even greater attention was paid to approaches emphasizing local government economic development activities. In explaining the governance of urban political systems, however, the growth machine and regime theory emphasize the importance of economic growth at the expense of other critical aspects of urban governance. This creates problems for those who want to examine a greater range of urban policies or programs or explore the workings of the entire political system.

There is more to urban governance than economic growth. Regime theory, the growth machine, and other similarly situated approaches can explain the Bloomberg administration's pursuit of the Olympic/Jets Stadium or the Nets Arena as part of the imperative faced by cities to promote economic growth. They cannot, however, explain why one project failed and the other succeeded. The approaches also cannot explain the role that the state level played in either decision. And while regime theory recognizes the role that minority coalitions might play in regime governance, it does not treat the role of racial and ethnic diversity in urban governance with sufficient breadth or depth.

This work has been based, in part, on the premise that these approaches do not offer a comprehensive perspective on the governance of urban political systems. At the same time, this analysis has no desire to return to earlier approaches that have already been critiqued and discarded. The lack of structure offered by pluralism is simply too loose a framework to provide an adequate explanation of urban governance. The critique of pluralism offered by approaches such as the growth machine and regime theory is correct; yet they too have their shortcomings in focusing solely on one of the sets of interests that constrain urban governance. Studying New York City politics offers one an opportunity to examine the full array of factors that constrain urban governance. To the extent to which these factors reoccur or become routinized in the mindset of those governing, they create a context within which political systems operate and governance takes place.

REFERENCES

CHAPTER I   INTRODUCTION

Bagli, Charles V. 2002. West side plan envisions Jets and Olympics. *New York Times*, May 1.

———. 2003. Grand plan in Brooklyn for Nets' arena. *New York Times*, December 1.

———. 2004. Report suggests forgetting about stadium on west side. *New York Times*, July 20.

———. 2005a. Deal is signed for Nets arena in Brooklyn. *New York Times*, March 4.

———. 2005b. Pataki agrees to delay vote on stadium for 2nd time. *New York Times*, May 24.

———. 2005c. Hurdle cleared, west side stadium backers turn to Albany. *New York Times*, June 3.

Bagli Charles V., and Michael Cooper. 2005. Olympic bid hurt as New York fails in west side stadium. *New York Times*, June 7.

Bondy, Filip. 1990. Apples of our eye: city sets sights on 2012 Olympics. *New York Daily News*, March 2.

Cardwell, Diane. 2001. Bloomberg adds six to his team. *New York Times*, December 29.

———. 2005. Instant skyline added to Brooklyn arena plan. *New York Times*, July 5.

Cohen, Michael, et al. 1972. A garbage can model of organization choice. *Administrative Science Quarterly* 17:1–25.

Colford, Paul D. 2005. MTA on track for Nets green-lights Ratner sports complex. *New York Daily News*, September 15.

Confessore, Nicholas, 2005a. Miller backs $3.5 billion plan for Brooklyn sports complex. *New York Times*, June 5.

———. 2005b. To build arena, developer first builds bridges. *New York Times*, October 14.

———. 2005c. From huge project a mighty anger grows. *New York Times*, October 20.

Cooper, Michael, and Charles A. Bagli. 2005. Board vote on stadium is still in doubt. *New York Times*, June 2.

Dahl, Robert. 1961. *Who governs?* New Haven: Yale University Press.

Easton, David. 1965. *A framework for political analysis*. Englewood Cliffs, NJ: Prentice-Hall.

Farrell, Bill. 2003. Boro courting the Nets beep says 500M stadium focus of talks with owners. *New York Daily News*, July 24.

Giuliani, Rudolph. 1997. Mayor Giuliani town hall meeting—Queens. The Crosswalks Network: New York City Department of Information Technology and Telecommunications, June 25.

Green, Penelope. 2005. Battling developer's mammoth plans. *New York Times*, February 27.

Hemel, Daniel. 2005. Private memo guarantees Ratner space. *New York Sun*, August 18.

Herbert, Bob. 2005. Bloomberg's billionaire boondoggle. *New York Times*, May 19.

Kolben, Deborah. 2005. Ratner touts Net gains to nabe. *New York Daily News*, June 28.

Lund, Leonard. 1984. Factors in corporate location decisions. In *Crisis and Constraint in Municipal Finance*, ed. James Carr, 267–288. New Brunswick, NJ: Center for Urban Policy Research.

Martin, Joanne. 1982. A garbage can model of the research process. In *Judgment Calls in Research*, ed. Joseph McGrath et al., 17–40. Beverly Hills: Sage Publications.

McNickle, Chris. 2001. (panelist) A mayor for the new millennium. New-York Historical Society. New York City, The Crosswalks Network, New York City Department of Information Technology and Telecommunications, October 10.

Muschamp, Herbert. 2003. Courtside seats to an urban garden. *New York Times*, December 11.

New York City Comptroller's Office. 2002. One year later: the fiscal impact of 9/11 on New York City. William Thompson, Comptroller, September 4.

New York City Council Press Conference. 2005. Atlantic Yards oversight announcement with members of the council Brooklyn delegation. The Crosswalks Network, New York City Department of Information Technology and Telecommunications, April 12.

New York City Department of City Planning. 1990. Uniform land use review procedure.

New York City Independent Budget Office. 2005. The long-term costs and benefits of the New York Sports and Convention Center (Background Paper), February.

New York City Mayors Office (News and Press Releases). 2005. News from the Blue Room: Mayor Michael Bloomberg, Forest City Ratner CEO and President Bruce Ratner and civic leaders sign community benefits agreement, June 27. www.nyc.gov.

New York City Office of Management and Budget. 2001. Monthly report on current economic conditions. Adam Barsky, Director, Office of Management and Budget, August 31.

New York Times. 2005a. Sharpton support plan for west side stadium, March 23.

———. 2005b. West side stadium figures, June 7.

Nielsen, Rachel. 2006. "Public" board shapes city in private Albany huddles. *City Limits Weekly*, October 30.

O'Keefe, Michael, and Luke Cyphers. 2002. Political games: Doctoroff make play in city sports plans. *New York Daily News*, January 13.

Pulley, Brett. 1995. East Harlem supermarket is approved. *New York Times*, April 28.

Rutenberg, Jim. 2005. Metro Briefing New York: Manhattan: small business aid for stadium. *New York Times*, February 15.

Rutenberg, Jim, and Michael Brick. 2005. Unlike stadium on west side, arena is still a go. *New York Times*, June 9.

Saul, Michael. 2002a. Mike sacks stadium plan. *New York Daily News*, January 11.

———. 2002b. Mike carries torch for new stadium. *New York Daily News*, October 13.

Stone, Clarence. 1989. *Regime politics: governing Atlanta*. Lawrence: University of Kansas Press.

Stout, David, and Charles A. Bagli. 2005. West side stadium plan clears hurdle as lawsuit is dismissed. *New York Times*, June 2.

Tiebout, Charles. 1956. A pure theory of local expenditures. *Journal of Political Economy* 64: 416–424.

Zimmerman, Joseph. 1992. *Contemporary American Federalism*. New York: Praeger.

Zinser, Lynn, and Michael Cooper. 2005. 2012 bid survives as Mets commit to stadium deal. *New York Times*, June 13.

CHAPTER 2   THE ECONOMIC DEVELOPMENT IMPERATIVE

Alliance for Downtown New York. Lower Manhattan Economic Revitalization Plan—1997 (short summary). www.downtownny.com.

———. 1997. Information Technology District. www.downtownny.com.

———. Rebuilding Updates. www.downtownny.com/rebuilding_index.asp (accessed November 2003).

Angotti, Tom. 2003. Greenpoint/Williamsburg zoning changes. *Gotham Gazette*, July 7. www.gothamgazette.com/article/landuse/200030728/12/474.

———. 2004. Rezoning proposals squeeze out affordable housing from both ends. *Gotham Gazette*, October 10. www.gothamgazette.com/article/landuse/20041007/12/1140.

———. 2005. Zoning instead of planning in Williamsburg and Greenpoint. *Gotham Gazette*, May 17. www.gothamgazette.com/article/landuse/2005–05–17.

Bagli, Charles, 1997a. Anglo-Dutch firm ING seeks tax breaks to remain. *New York Times*, January 30.

———. 1997b. S & P reportedly wants tax breaks for staying in NYC. *New York Times*, March 27.

———. 1997c. ING Barings deal ties tax breaks to job growth. *New York Times*, April 7.

———. 1997d. NY-NJ battle heats up over Standard & Poor's. *New York Times*, April 19.

———. 1999. Office tower said to get tax breaks. *New York Times*, June 6.

Bellush, Jewell. 1990. Clusters of power. In *Urban politics New York style*, ed. Jewell Bellush and Dick Netzer, 296–338. Armonk, NY: M. E. Sharpe.

Candaele, Kerry, and Sean Wilentz. 1995. Labor. In *The encyclopedia of New York City*, ed. Kenneth Jackson, 646. New Haven: Yale University Press.

Cardwell, Diane. 2002a. More cafes may sprout on sidewalks. *New York Times*. July 18.

———. 2002b. City council is urged to act quickly on proposed new regulations for sidewalk café permits. *New York Times*. December 13.

———. 2004. Panel approves plan by Ikea to open store in Red Hook. *New York Times*, October 6.

———. 2005a. Brooklyn rezoning plan assailed. *New York Times*, January 15.

———. 2005b. Red Hook resident group sues to block an Ikea store. *New York Times*, February 11.

———. 2005c. Council threatens to block plan to rezone in Brooklyn. *New York Times*, April 5.

———. 2005d. City is backing makeover for decaying Brooklyn waterfront. *New York Times*, May 3.

Center for an Urban Future. 2001. Payoffs for layoffs. www.nycfuture.org/econdev/0211payoffs.htm (accessed 2001).

Cooper, Cynthia. 1998. Initiative to save theaters may drive out artists (letter to the editor). *New York Times*, January 15.

Cooper, Michael. 2004. Little job creation is found in audits of tax break zones. *New York Times*, March 10.

Drennan, Matthew. 1991. The decline and rise of the New York economy. In *Dual city: restructuring New York*, ed. John Mollenkopf and Manuel Castells, 25–42. New York: Russell Sage Foundation.

Dunlap, David. 1998a. Theater air rights plan awaits reviews. *New York Times*, January 25.

———. 1998b. Manhattan lawmakers resist theater plan. *New York Times*, April 17.

———. 1998c. Theater zoning plan attracts some high-profile supporters. *New York Times*, May 7.

Dwyer, Jim. 1999. Need a handout? Be a corporation. *New York Daily News*, January 24.

Empire State Development, 1997a, We've changed. www.empire.state.ny.us/changes.html.

———. 1997b. International. www.empire.state.ny.us/intl.html.

———. 1998. New York State Economic Development Zones Program (fact sheets). www.empire.state.ny.us/ (accessed 1998).

Ferguson, Sarah. 2005. Hipsters defend Brooklyn: NYC pols want a Williamsburg gold coast. Cool kids and neighborhood vets say no. *Village Voice*, April 3.

Giuliani, Rudolph. 1997. Mayor Giuliani Press Conference. The Crosswalks Network, New York City Department of Information Technology and Telecommunications, July 7.

Gold, Joyce. 1996. SoHo. In *The encyclopedia of New York City*, ed. Kenneth Jackson, 1088. New Haven, CT: Yale University Press.

Gonzalez, David. 1999. For Red Hook, pierside brawl with City Hall. *New York Times*, January 16.

Good Jobs New York. 2001. Press Release-February 13. www.ctj.org/itep/gjny/valentines.htm.

———. 2002. Reconstruction Watch. February. www.reconstructionwatch.net (accessed February 8, 2003).

———. 2006. New York's Biggest Retention Deals Sorted by Size. www.goodjobsny.org/deals (accessed 2006).

Group of 35. 2001. Preparing for the future: A commercial development strategy for New York City. http://urban.nyu/g35/html (accessed June 25, 2001).

Halbfinger, David. 1998. A shopping center plan that local merchants back. *New York Times*, February 4.

Hernandez, Raymond. 1996. Audit questions benefits of economic development zones. *New York Times*, August 8.

Herszenhorn, David M. 2000. Giuliani to propose tax cuts in effort to help business. *New York Times*, January 13.

Hevesi, Dennis. 1998. Providing places to work, places to live. *New York Times*, August 16.

Johnson, Kirk. 1996. Where a zoning law fails, seeds of a New York revival. *New York Times*, April 21.

Kantor, Paul, and Dennis Judd. 1992. *Enduring tensions in urban politics*. New York: Macmillan.

Kivelson, Adrienne. 1991. *What makes New York City run?* New York: The League of Women Voters.

Kwartler, Michael. 1996. Zoning. In *The encyclopedia of New York City*, ed. Kenneth Jackson, 1288. New Haven, CT: Yale University Press.

Lankevich, George, and Howard Furer. 1984. *A brief history of New York*. Port Washington, NY: Associated Faculty Press.

Levy, Clifford. 1996. NYC business districts barred from taking out loans. *New York Times*, September 14.

Lueck, Thomas. 1992. Messinger is criticized for supporting plan by Trump. *New York Times*, August 28.

———. 1994a. New York is vengeful in the face of a 'raid' by Connecticut. *New York Times*, October 11.

———. 1994b. Business districts grow at price of accountability. *New York Times*, November 20.

———. 1998. Giuliani's edict extends city council control over business improvement districts. *New York Times*, April 5.

Lyman, Rick. 1997. Analysis: Broadway zoning plan faces many questions. *New York Times*, December 31.

Lynam, Elizabeth. 1999. The unlevel playing field, or why discretionary tax breaks are a bad idea. *The Gotham Gazette*. www.gothamgazette.com/iotw/taxbreaks/doc1.html (accessed November 8, 1999).

McCarthy, Kevin. 2001. Lobbying. *Gotham Gazette*, May 21. http://gothamgazette.com/ iotw/lobbying/ (accessed: March 31, 2003).

New York City Comptroller's Office–Bureau of Management Audit. 1997. Audit report on the administration of job retention agreements by the Economic Development Corporation (MH96–183A), August 14.

New York City Council. 1995. *Cities within cities: business improvement districts and the emergence of the micropolis*. Staff Report to the Finance Committee, November 8.

New York City Council Committee on Land Use (Subcommittee on Landmarks, Public Siting and Maritime Uses). 1998. Public hearing. The Crosswalks Network. New York City Department of Information Technology and Telecommunications, June 1.

New York City Department of City Planning. 1993. *Plan for lower Manhattan.*

New York City Department of Finance. N.d. New York City Introduces the New Commercial Expansion Program.

————. 1996. Industrial and commercial incentive program: preliminary application and instructions.

————. Office of Tax Policy. 2001. Annual report on tax expenditures: fiscal year 2001.

————. Office of Tax Policy. 2002. Annual report on tax expenditures: fiscal year 2002.

New York City Department of Small Business Services. 2006. Business improvement districts. www.nyc.gov/html/bid/html (accessed February 24, 2006).

New York City Economic Development Corporation. 2003. ICIP-industrial and commercial incentive program. www.newyorkbiz.com/Business_Incentives/Tax_Benefits/Tax_Benefits_a.html (accessed February 5, 2003).

New York City Economic Development Corporation. 2003. Lower Manhattan economic revitalization plan. www.newyorkbiz.com/Business_Incentives/Tax_Benefits?Tax_Benefits_d.html.

New York City Independent Budget Office. 2001, June. Full disclosure? Assessing city reporting on business retention deals.

New York City Mayor's Office. 1993. Revisions to sidewalk café approval process. http://nyc.gov/html/misc/html/café.html (accessed January 31, 2003).

New York City Mayor's Office. 2003. Mayor Michael R. Bloomberg names Staten Island growth management task force (Press Release-PR 208–03). July 22.

New York City Office of Management and Budget 2001. Monthly Report on current economic conditions. August 31.

New York State Comptroller–Press Office. 2004a. Reports Find poor oversight, mixed job growth results in three New York City empire zones. March 16.

New York State Comptroller. 2004b. News from the office of the New York State Comptroller–Alan Hevesi. Testimony of New York State Comptroller Alan G. Hevesi on Empire Zone Program Reform. (Before the Assembly Standing Committee on Ways and Means, Assembly Standing Committee on Economic Development, Job Creation, Commerce and Industry, Assembly Committee on Corporation, Authorities and Commissions, and Assembly Standing Committee on Labor. Press Office. April 26. www.osc.state.ny.us/press/releases/apr04/empzonetestimony.htm.

New York State Comptroller's Office-Division of Management Audit. 1995. Department of Economic Development, economic development zone program, report 95-S-78.

New York State Empire Zones. 2002a. Empire zones program. www.nylovesbiz.com/Tax_and Financial_Incentives/Empire_Zones/default.asp (accessed February 8, 2003).

New York State Empire Zones. 2002b. Description of benefits. www.nylovesbiz.com/Tax_and_Financial_Incentives/Empire_Zones/descriptions_benefits.asp (accessed February 8, 2003).

New York Times. 1992. Riverside South: still questions (editorial), August 13.

————. 1998. The last peep show for smutland in Times Square, June 4.

————. 2001. Luring business with dinner and a show, October 20.

Newman, Andy. 1999. Judge annuls rule allowing sale of air rights by theaters. New York Times, July 1.

Oser, Alan. 1997. New residential space arrives in lower Manhattan. New York Times, August 3.

Pristin, Terry. 2001. Improvement districts balk at city plan for new fee. New York Times, February 4.

————. 2002a. For improvement districts, restored alliance with city. New York Times, February 18.

————. 2002b. Mayor envisions a bigger role for 44 improvement districts. New York Times, May 15.

Prokesch, Steven. 1992. Panel clears Trump plan on west side. New York Times, October 27.

Rohde, David. 1997. Banks make discovery in South Bronx. New York Times, April 16.

Sassen, Saskia. 1991. The global city. Princeton, NJ: Princeton University Press.

———. 1997. Cities, foreign policy, and the global economy. In *The city and the world: New York's global future*, ed. Margaret Crahan and Alberto Vourvoulias. 171–187. New York City: Council on Foreign Relations Press.

Savitch, H. V. 1988. *Post industrial cities: politics and planning in New York, Paris, and London.* Princeton, NJ: Princeton University Press.

Schumer, Charles E. 2001. Group of 35 Report finds New York City's long-term economic growth is limited by severe lack of available office space (press release), June 11. www.senate.gove/~schumer/html/group_of_35_report_finds_new_y.html.

Scott, Janny. 2005. In a still growing city, some neighborhoods say slow down. *New York Times,* October 10.

Smith, Michael Peter, Rand Ready, and Dennis Judd. 1992. Capital flight, tax incentives and the marginalization of American states and localities. In *Enduring tensions in urban politics*, ed. Paul Kantor and Dennis Judd, 532–544. New York: Macmillan.

Son, Hugh. 2004. Revise plan spares college panel alters downtown rezoning. *New York Daily News.* May 12.

———. 2005. Judge axes Ikea foes' suit. *New York Daily News*, June 30.

Sternberg, Ernest. 1993. *Rethinking state and local economic development strategies.* Albany: The Nelson A. Rockefeller Institute of Government.

Stohr, Kate. 2002. Unions and the new workplace. *Gotham Gazette.* June 17. www. gothamgazette.com/iotw/unions/ (accessed December 12, 2002).

Toy, Vivian. 1996. New York judge delays enforcement of sex shop law. *New York Times.* October 25.

United States Department of Commerce, Bureau of Economic Analysis, Regional economic information system. 2002. www.bea.doc.gov/bea/regional/reis/ (accessed February 2, 2003).

Walsh, Robert. 2002. BIDS. (Power Point presentation at ATCM Conference, London, UK.) New York City Department of Business Services. October 15.

Weiss, Marc. 1995. Real Estate Board of New York. In *The encyclopedia of New York City*, ed. Kenneth Jackson, 990. New Haven: Yale University Press.

Wyatt, Edward. 2001. Committee leader says victims' memorial will be main priority. *New York Times*, November 30.

CHAPTER 3   THE STATE AND THE CITY

Bailey, Robert. 1984. *The crisis regime: the New York City financial crisis.* Albany: State University of New York Press.

Benjamin, Gerald. 1988. The political relationship. In *The two New Yorks: state-city relations in the changing federal system*, ed. Gerald Benjamin and Charles Brecher, 107–150. New York: Russell Sage Foundation.

Berg, Bruce, and Paul Kantor. 1996. New York: the politics of conflict and avoidance. In *Regional politics: American in a post-city age*, ed. H. V. Savitch and Ronald Vogel, 25–50. Thousand Oaks, CA: Sage Publications.

Blau, Joel. 1992. *The visible poor: homelessness in America.* New York: Oxford University Press.

Bloomberg, Michael. 2003. Testimony by Mayor Michael Bloomberg before the joint legislative fiscal committees (of the New York State Legislature). Albany, New York, February 3. http://home.nyc.gov/cgi/bin/misc/pfprinter=cgi?action=print&sitename=OM (accessed February 5, 2003).

Blum, Barbara, and Susan Blank. 1988. Mental health and mental retardation. In *The two New Yorks: state-city relations in the changing federal system*, ed. Gerald Benjamin and Charles Brecher, 383–419. New York: Russell Sage Foundation.

Cooper, Michael. 2003a. Mr. Bloomberg goes to Albany, hat in hand, and gets shrug. *New York Times*, February 4.

———. 2003b. Bloomberg says disagreements with Pataki will stay private. *New York Times*, February 5.

Dillon, John F. 1911. *Commentaries on the laws of municipal Corporations*, 5th ed. Boston: Little, Brown.

Dionne, E. J. Jr. 1982. Financing method for schools ruled valid in New York. *New York Times*, June 24.

Doig, James. 1995. Port Authority of New York and New Jersey. In *The encyclopedia of New York City*, ed. Kenneth Jackson, 925. New Haven: Yale University Press.

Dye, Thomas. 1991. *Politics in states and communities*. 7th ed. Englewood Cliffs, NJ: Prentice-Hall.

Finder, Alan. 1986. Financial control board loses most of its control. *New York Times*, June 30.

———. 1992. Dinkins aide seeks to loosen rules on homeless. *New York Times*, December 4.

Fisher, Ian. 1993. New York fined again on homeless. *New York Times*, August 5.

———. 1995. Port Authority has long favored New Jersey, Pataki says. *New York Times*, August 31.

Gold, Steven D. 1983. *State and local fiscal relations in the early 1980s*. Washington, DC: Urban Institute.

Goodnough, Abby, 1999a. Giuliani and Vallone see a budget tangle if the commuter tax ends. *New York Times*, May 15.

———. 1999b. Big challenge on allocating school funds. *New York Times*, October 12.

———. 1999c. Trial begins in suit challenging New York State's formula for school funds. *New York Times*, October 13.

———. 2000. News analysis: the paradox of the school aid rules. *New York Times*, December 19.

Goodwin, Michael. 1982. Costs to shelter homeless in city climbing sharply. *New York Times*, October 2.

Green, Cynthia, and Paul Moore. 1988. Public finance. In *The two New Yorks: state-city relations in the changing federal system*, ed. Gerald Benjamin and Charles Brecher, 211–242. New York: Russell Sage Foundation.

Gruson, Lindsey. 1982. City asks judge to alter agreement on the homeless. *New York Times*, October 6.

Guttfreund, Owen. 1995. Urban development corporation. In *The encyclopedia of New York City*, ed. Kenneth Jackson, 1218–1219. New Haven, CT: Yale University Press.

Haberman, Clyde. 2003. Smiling all the way to a deficit. *New York Times*, February 4.

Hakim, Danny, and Jennifer Median. 2006. Deal in Albany on budget gives new school aid. *New York Times*, March 29.

Hallman, Howard W. 1977. *Small and large together: governing the metropolis*. Beverly Hills: Sage Publications.

Henderson, Keith. 1994. Other governments: the public authorities. In *Governing New York State*, ed. Jeffrey Stonecash et al., 211–224. Albany: State University of New York Press.

Herszenhorn, David M. 1999. Giuliani and McCall fight repeal of commuter tax. *New York Times*, May 17.

———. 2006. New York court cuts aid sought by city schools. *New York Times*, November 21.

Kolbert, Elizabeth. 1991. Albany, squeezed, puts pressure on local governments. *New York Times*, March 31.

Leone, Richard C. 2002. The Port Authority role in the World Trade Center. *New York Times*, August 6.

Levy, Clifford, 1997a. Ending standoff, Giuliani agrees to allow state audits. *New York Times*, April 12.

———. 1997b. Giuliani's tax cut plan faces GOP opposition in Albany. *New York Times*, May 19.

——. 1999. New York governor moves to eliminate New York City commuter tax. *New York Times*, May 13.

Medina, Jennifer. 2006a. Albany school aid logjam persists despite a surplus. *New York Times*, January 16.

——. 2006b. Judges once again order more money for city schools. *New York Times*, March 24.

——. 2006c. With a little bark, but no bite. *New York Times*, March 25.

Miller, Gifford. 2003. State of the city address. New York City. February 2. www.gothamgazette.com/print273 (accessed February 5, 2003).

Musselwhite, James. 1988. A comparative view. In *The two New Yorks: State-city relations in the changing federal system*, ed. Gerald Benjamin and Charles Brecher, 211–242. New York: Russell Sage Foundation.

Myers, Steven Lee. 1995. City shortfall even worse than forecast. *New York Times*, June 9.

Nagourney, Adam. 1997. Analysis: McCall opts for being Democrat as well as comptroller. *New York Times*, April 3.

New York City Comptroller's Office. 1969–1970, 1970–1971, 1971–1972, 1972–1973, 1973–1974, 1974–1975, 1975–1976, 1977, 1980, 1986, 1989, 1990, 1994, 2001, 2002, 2003, 2004, 2005. *Comprehensive Annual Financial Report of the Comptroller*.

New York City Council. 2003. City council stated meeting minutes. *Gotham Gazette*, May 28. www.gothamgazette.com/article/20030528/203/1282.

New York City Department of City Planning. 1995. A Critical analysis of the role of the Port Authority of New York and New Jersey.

New York City Department of Citywide Administrative Services. 1996. *The 1996–1997 green book*.

New York State Comptroller's Office. 1995. New York City transit and the New York City police department fare evasion on the New York City subways. www.osc.state.ny.us/divisions/management/audits/9596/95s121.htm.

——. 1996a. New York City Department of Sanitation follow-up review of recycling program: better controls and increased commitment are needed to ensure its success. www.osc.state.ny.us/divisions/management/audit/9596/a1596.htm.

——. 1996b. New York City Health and Hospitals Corporation second follow-up review of planning for disasters. www.osc.state.ny.us/divisions/management/audits/9596/a1295.htm.

New York State Financial Control Board. 1997. Financial Control Board Meeting. The Crosswalks Network, New York City Department of Information Technology and Telecommunications. July 19.

New York State Financial Control Board. 2006. Mission statement. www.fcb.state.ny.us (accessed March 11, 2006).

New York Times. 1997a. Deadbeats in Albany (editorial), March 15.

——. 1997b. Let Mr. McCall's auditor in (editorial), April 7.

——. 1999. Legislature ends a tax in a hurry, May 18.

——. 2001. Excerpts from judge's ruling on school financing, January 11.

——. 2003. Excerpts: court ruling on financing of city schools, June 27.

Nix, Crystal. 1986. Housing family in a shelter cost city $70,000 a year. *New York Times*, March 7.

Perez-Pena, Richard. 1997a. Pataki and legislative leaders reach budget accord. *New York Times*, July 30.

——. 1997b. Albany to let New York City raise debt ceiling. *New York Times*, February 12.

——. 2002. Court reverses finance ruling on city schools. *New York Times*, June 26.

Perez-Pena, Richard, and Abby Goodnough. 2001a. Court ruling on state's school financing may force city to pay more. *New York Times*, January 12.

———. 2001b. Pataki is ready to file appeal on school aid. *New York Times*, January 17.

Peterson, Paul. 1995. *The price of federalism*. Washington, DC: Brookings Institution Press.

Rahimi, Shadi. 2005. State disputes order to spend $5.6 billion on city schools. *New York Times*, October 12.

Robertson, Wyndham. 1975. Going broke the New York way. *Fortune*, August.

Rothstein, Richard. 2001. News analysis: The unforeseen costs of raising academic standards. *New York Times*, January 11.

Ruby, Mark. 1975. New York's near d-day. *Newsweek*, October 27.

Sayre, Wallace, and Herbert Kaufman. 1965 *Governing New York City*. New York: W. W. Norton.

Shefter, Martin. 1988. *Political crisis/fiscal crisis: the collapse and revival of New York City*. New York: Basic Books.

Steinhauer, Jennifer. 1997. In New York, tax free clothing and confusion. *New York Times*, January 14.

———. 2003. Pataki's plan raises city's Medicaid bill. *New York Times*, January 31.

Tobier, Emanuel. 1989. The homeless. In *Setting municipal priorities, 1990*, ed. Charles Brecher and Raymond Horton, 307–338. New York: New York University Press.

Tobier, Emanuel, and Barbara Gordon Espejo. 1988. Housing. In *The two New Yorks: state-city relations in the changing federal system*, ed. Gerald Benjamin and Charles Brecher, 445–478. New York: Russell Sage Foundation.

Toy, Vivian. 1997. Judge rules NYC must surrender records to state comptroller. *New York Times*, October 11.

United States Congressional Budget Office. 1975. *New York City's fiscal problem: its origins, potential repercussions, and some alternative policy responses*.

Verhovek, Sam Howe. 1990. School aid battle threatens accord on Albany budget. *New York Times*, March 31.

Winter, Greg. 2002. Decent education, figured in dollars. *New York Times*, October 2.

Wolff, Jessica, and Joseph Wardenski. 2003. The school funding victory. *Gotham Gazette*. June 6. www.gothamgazette.com/article/education/20030627/6/438.

Worth, Robert F. 2003. City to support suit seeking more state aid for schools. *New York Times*, January 18.

Wyatt, Edward. 2001. In school aid blame game, fingers also point back at city. *New York Times*, February 15.

Zernike, Kate. 2001. What New York schools get in aid often has little connection to needs. *New York Times*, February 14.

CHAPTER 4   THE FEDERAL GOVERNMENT AND THE CITY

Anderson, Martin. 1964. *The federal bulldozer: a critical analysis of urban renewal*. Cambridge, MA: MIT Press.

Bagli, Charles V. 2002. Federal funds will keep 14 companies downtown. *New York Times*, April 27.

Baker, Al. 2003. Pataki approves city water plant. *New York Times*, July 23.

———. 2006. U.S. will help city pursue cases against gun dealers. *New York Times*, May 27.

Barstow, David. 2001. Guarding against dark side of disaster relief. *New York Times*, September 22.

Beck, Bertram. 1969. Organizing community action. In *Governing the city: challenges and options for New York*, ed. Robert Connery and Demetrios Caraley, 162–178. *The Proceedings of the Academy of Political Science*. Volume 29, Number 4. New York: The Academy of Political Science.

Becker, Elizabeth. 2001a. Cities seek millions in crisis aid. *New York Times*, October 25.

————. 2001b. Ridge deflects pleas to help the cities pay security costs. *New York Times*, October 26.

Brinkley, Joel. 2002. Mayors seek payback of spending on security. *New York Times*, January 24.

Brooke, James. 1985. Koch assails cuts in federal budget. *New York Times*, February 10.

Bumiller, Elisabeth. 1997. Harlem renewal chief takes Wall St. standards uptown. *New York Times*, March 28.

Clarke, Kenneth, and Jeannette Hopkins. 1968. *A relevant war against poverty*. New York: Harper and Row.

Clymer, Adam. 2001. Schumer and Mrs. Clinton want F.B.I. to share facts. *New York Times*, November 1.

Cooper, Michael. 2002. City seeks to close gap by using disaster aid. *New York Times*, May 29.

Criscitello, Douglas. 1997. Testimony of Douglas Criscitello, Director, New York City Independent Budget Office On Implementation of the Federal Personal Responsibility and Work Opportunity Reconciliation Act of 1996 in New York State, Before the New York State Assembly Standing Committee on Ways and Means. Albany, New York, January 23. www.ibo.nyc.ny.us.

Donovan, John. 1967. *The politics of poverty*. Indianapolis: Bobbs Merrill.

Farkas, Suzanne. 1971. *Urban lobbying*. New York: New York University Press.

Firestone, David. 1995. Giuliani criticizes a U.S. crackdown on illegal aliens. *New York Times*, August 23.

————. 1996. NYC mayor to sue over U.S. welfare provision on aliens. *New York Times*, September 12.

————. 1997a. Praising workfare, Giuliani finds campaign theme. *New York Times*, March 20.

————. 1997b. In pact on workfare, little change is provided. *New York Times*, August 9.

Flanagan, Richard. 1997. The Housing Act of 1954: The sea change in national urban policy. *Urban Affairs Review* 33, no. 2, 265–286.

Fossett, James. 1984. The politics of dependence: federal aid to big cities. In *The changing politics of federal grants*, ed. Lawrence Brown, James Fossett, and Kenneth Palmer, 108–163. Washington, DC: The Brookings Institution.

Fried, Joseph P. 2002. Returnees to lower Manhattan will be exempt from tax on aid. *New York Times*, October 8.

Friedan, Bernard. 1966. Policies for rebuilding. In *Urban renewal: the record and the controversy*, ed. James Q. Wilson, 585–623. Cambridge, MA: MIT Press.

Greenstone, J. David, and Paul Peterson. 1973. *Race and authority in urban politics*. New York: Russell Sage Foundation.

Gruson, Lindsey. 1987. End of federal revenue sharing creating financial crises in many cities. *New York Times*, January 31.

Herbers, John. 1969. President adds to mayor's power in urban aid plan. *New York Times*, April 29.

————. 1970. Rebuilding plans of cities reduced by Nixon's curbs. *New York Times*, March 1.

————. 1973. U.S. commitment to renew cities is in doubt under new program. *New York Times*, January 29.

Hernandez, Raymond. 2001a. Bush opposes more aid now for New York. *New York Times*, October 18.

————. 2001b. Seeking a united voice on Capitol Hill. *New York Times*, November 5.

————. 2004a. New York struggles with a weaker voice in congress. *New York Times*, March 6.

————. 2004b. House rejects extra security aid to high risk cities. *New York Times*, June 19.

Holsendolph, Ernest. 1981. Reagan plan stirring fear of mass transit cutbacks. *New York Times*, April 9.

————. 1983. New law on trucks will permit big rigs on more U.S. roads. *New York Times*, December 24.

Hu, Winnie. 2004. Mayor scolds security chief on U.S. funds to protect city. *New York Times*, June 5.

Jackson, Kenneth. 1995. *The encyclopedia of New York City*. New Haven, CT: Yale University Press.

Johnston, David. 1994. Experts doubt effectiveness of the newly enacted crime bill. *New York Times*, September 14.

Kettl, Donald. 1980. *Managing community development in the new federalism*. New York: Praeger.

Kihss, Peter. 1968. Badillo calls city poverty unit's action divisive. *New York Times*, January 24.

Koch, Edward I. 1980. The mandate millstone. *The Public Interest* 61, 42–57.

Kovach, Bill. 1973. Mayors oppose Nixon fund plan. *New York Times*, June 21.

Lewis, Neil. 1994. President foresees safer U.S. *New York Times*, August 27.

Liebschutz, Sarah. 1991. *Bargaining under federalism: contemporary New York*. Albany: State University of New York Press.

Liebschutz, Sarah, and Irene Lerner. 1987. New York. In *Reagan and the states*, ed. Richard Nathan and Fred Doolittle, 169–207. Princeton, NJ: Princeton University Press.

Lizza, Ryan. 2004. Bush to New York: here's your $20 million—now drop dead. *New York Magazine*, June 14.

Lueck, Thomas. 1998. Largest business for Harlem improvement zone. *New York Times*, April 28.

Madden, Richard. 1970. 10 mayors united to seek U.S. help. *New York Times*, March 4.

———. 1984. Order on trucks by U.S. defied by Connecticut. *New York Times*, May 20.

Mastro, Randy. 1998. *New York City 1998 federal program*. New York City Washington Office.

McIntire, Mike. 2004. City expects 50% less in federal aid for security. *New York Times*, May 18.

McKinley, James. 1992. Clinton gets a letter from Dinkins. *New York Times*, November 6.

Morehouse, Ward III. 1980. Koch sees Reagan as net gain for New York. *Christian Science Monitor*, December 2.

Moss, Mitchell. 1995. Empty promises for Harlem (letter to the editor). *New York Times*, April 15.

Nathan, Richard, and Charles Adams. 1977. *Revenue sharing: the second round*. Washington, DC: Brookings Press.

Nathan, Richard, and Fred Doolittle. 1983. *The consequences of cuts: the effects of the Reagan domestic program on state and local governments*. Princeton, NJ: Princeton Urban and Regional Research Center.

New York City Comptroller's Office. 2002. One year later: the financial impact of 9/11 on New York City. September 4.

New York City Department of Finance. N.d. New York City introduces the new commercial expansion program.

New York City Independent Budget Office. 1998a. New York City's use of Community Development Block Grant funds. www.ibo.nyc.ny.us/budgfax.

———. 1998b. Fiscal impact of the new welfare law on New York City. www.ibo.nyc.ny.us.

———. 2003. Inside the budget. Number 117. World Trade Center assistance aid received, aid to come. July 31.

New York City Mayor's Office–Press Office. 1996. Mayor Giuliani announces city has filed suit to challenge federal welfare and immigration laws. (Release #511–96), May 11. www.ci.nyc.ny.us/html/om/html/96/sp511–96.html.

New York State Governor's Office–Press Office. 1998. Governor Pataki commits $3 million to Harlem USA. (Press release), July 27. www.nylovesbiz.com/Press/1998/harlrel.htm.

New York Times. 1996. Giuliani sues U.S. over welfare law, October 12.

———. 2001a. Federal help for New York City (editorial), October 11.

———. 2001b. Johnnie Cochrane in deep water (editorial), November 20.

———. 2002. Threats to be shared with city and state. *New York Times*, March 7.

O'Neil, Hugh, and Megan Sheehan. 1995. The impact of new federal budget priorities on America's cities. Taub Research Center. New York University. www.nyu.edu/urban/research

Pear, Robert. 2002. Bush administration approves $700 million grant to help rebuild lower Manhattan. *New York Times*, February 3.

Perez-Pena, Richard. 2002. U.S. agrees to give 4.5 billion to link subway and PATH hub at Trade Center. *New York Times*, August 10.

Peterson, Paul, Barry Rabe, and Kenneth Wong. 1986. *When federalism works*. Washington, DC: The Brookings Institution.

Plunz, Richard. 1990. *A history of housing in New York*. New York: Columbia University Press.

Pristin, Terry. 2001. Harlem development program not much help, critics and officials say. *New York Times*, June 29.

Purnick, Joyce. 1986. Koch persuades group of mayors to emphasize anti-drug efforts. *New York Times*, December 1.

Randall, Ronald. 1986. Changing conceptions of federal urban policy from LBJ to Reagan. Paper presented at the annual meeting of the American Political Science Association, Washington, DC.

Rashbaum, William K. 2002. Kelly seeking federal money for city police. *New York Times*, November 11.

Rich, Michael. 1982. Hitting the target: the distributional impacts of the Urban Development Action Grant Program. *Urban Affairs Quarterly* 17:3, 268–301.

Riposa, Gerry. 1996. From enterprise zone to empowerment zone. *American Behavioral Scientist* 39:5, 536–551.

Roberts, Steven. 1967a. Three areas will share funds. *New York Times*, November 12.

———. 1967b. Communities get model cities veto. *New York Times*, November 11.

———. 1967c. Mayor charges U.S. scrimps on city aid. *New York Times*, September 8.

Salwen, Peter. 1989. *Upper west side story*. New York: Abbeville Press.

Savitch, H. V. 1999. *Urban policy and the exterior city*. New York: Pergamon Press.

Shipler, David. 1971. Lindsay defends model cities aid. *New York Times*, January 12.

Shipp, E. R. 2006. Jobs will keep Harlem hopping. *New York Daily News*, March 26.

Smith, John, and John Klemanski. 1990. *The urban politics dictionary*. Santa Barbara, CA: ABC-CLIO.

Stanfield, Rochelle. 1978. Death of countercyclical aid means cities may go hungry. *National Journal*, November 11.

Steinhauer, Jennifer. 2001a. Bloomberg asks for aid in Washington pilgrimage. *New York Times*, November 10.

———. 2001b. Bloomberg is changing strategies on U.S. aid. *New York Times*, December 18.

Steinhauer, Jennifer, and David Chen. 2001. Mayor urges U.S. to improve its exchange of information. *New York Times*, October 30.

Swarns, Rachel. 1997. Analysis: Giuliani's grade on welfare reform—incomplete. *New York Times*, October 29.

Treaster, Joseph B. 1994. Local reaction to the crime bill: delight with some doubts. *New York Times*, September 14.

U.S. Advisory Commission on Intergovernmental Relations. 1977. Community development: the workings of a federal-local block grant. A-57.

U.S. Congressional Budget Office. 1980. Community Development Block Grants: reauthorization issues.

U.S. Department of Housing and Urban Development. 1998. New York/Bronx County empowerment zone. www.ezec.gov/ezec/NY/ny.html.

Upper Manhattan Empowerment Zone. 2001. The Upper Manhattan Empowerment Zone annual report 2001.

Van Horn, Carl. 1979. *Policy implementation and the federal system*. Lexington, MA: Lexington Books.

Wakin, Daniel. 2001. E.P.A. will not make city build expensive water filtration plant. *New York Times*, July 24.

Washnis, George. 1974. *Community development strategies: case studies of model cities*. New York: Praeger Publishers.

Wehman, Jerry. 1981. UDAG: targeting urban economic development. *Political Science Quarterly* 96:2, 189–207.

Wyatt, Edward. 2002. Washington approves grants to entice people to lower Manhattan. *New York Times*, June 8.

———. 2004. As New York fumes, Wyoming says it, too, needs anti-terror funds. *New York Times*, June 1.

Wyatt, Edward, et al. 2002. After 9/11, a torrent of money and anger. *New York Times*, December 30.

CHAPTER 5   RACIAL AND ETHNIC DIVERSITY

Allen, Mike. 1998. City council panel seeks to suspend parking rules for yet another holiday. *New York Times*, April 8.

Asian Americans for Equality. 2005. Congressional testimony for Community Development Block Grant (CDBG) funds in New York City. 216.147.28.223.pgs.hilite_090605.html (accessed July 10, 2006).

———. N.d.a. AAFE History: 1st Decade 216.147.28.223.pgs.history_first.html (accessed July 10, 2006).

———. N.d.b. AFE History: 2nd Decade 216.147.28.223.pgs.history_second.html (accessed July 10, 2006).

———. N.d.c. AAFE History, 3rd Decade 216.147.28.223.pgs.history_third.html (accessed July 10, 2006).

Associated Press. 1997, November 5. Results of Exit Polling Conducted for the Associated Press by Voter News Service in Tuesday's New York City Mayoral Election. WFUV Newsdesk.

Association of Community Organizations for Reform Now (ACORN)–New York Acorn Schools Office. 1997. Secret apartheid: a report on racial discrimination against Black and Latino parents and children in the New York City public schools.

Association of Community Organizations for Reform Now (ACORN). 1999. ACORN's 25 year history. www.acorn.org/ACORN_25_history.html.

Barry, Dan and Marjorie Connelly. 1999. Most New Yorkers see police bias, poll finds. *New York Times*, March 16.

Barry, Dan. 1996. New York schools chief overreached by ousting Bronx board, U.S. rules. *New York Times*, November 17.

———. 1997. Officer charged in torture in Brooklyn station house. *New York Times*, August 14.

———. 1998. Giuliani and Dinkins: A war of words still rages. *New York Times*, April 4.

———. 1999. Giuliani softens tone in Diallo case. *New York Times*, March 24.

Benjamin, Gerald, and Frank Mauro. 1989. The reemergence of municipal reform. In *Restructuring the new city government: the reemergence of municipal reform*, ed. Gerald Benjamin and Frank Mauro, 1–15. New York: The Academy of Political Science.

Berger, Cheryl Melissa, and Fox Chapel. 1998. End environmental racism (letter to the editor). *Pittsburgh Post Gazette*, March 16.

Bernstein, Nina. 1995. Advocates for young sue New York City. *New York Times*, December 14.

Blair, Jayson. 1999. Street crimes unit will be split into 8 pieces. *The New York Times*, October 16.

Bode, Nicole. 2004. Parents divided over councils panels replace local school boards. *Daily News*, January 2.

Bowen, William, et al. 1995. Toward environmental justice: spatial equity in Ohio and Cleveland. *Annals of the Association of American Geographers* 85:4, 641–663.

Bratton, William, J. 1999. Dispelling New York's latest fear. *New York Times*, February 28.

Brick, Michael. 2005. Brooklyn arena plan calls for many subsidized units. *New York Times*, May 20.

Bruni, Frank. 1997. Sharpton's political future may be at stake when he testifies about his past. *New York Times*, December 2.

Bumiller, Elisabeth. 1998. Public lives: labor movement's latest 800-pound gorilla. *New York Times*, January 8.

Calderone, Joe. 1998. Asthma death link soars—lung diseases connected to 500 cases a year in city. *New York Daily News*, November 8.

Calderone, Joe, et al. 1998. The South Bronx—asthma's battleground. *New York Daily News*, February 22.

Cooper, Michael. 1999. State investigating complaints of bias against New York City police. *New York Times*, March 18.

———. 2003. Mayor honors vow to Sharpton who returns the disfavor. *New York Times*, January 21.

Dao, James. 1999. Immigrant diversity shows traditional political climb. *New York Times*, December 28.

Dugger, Celia. 1996. Some old timers in Queens could do without its Asians. *New York Times*, March 31.

Egbert, Bill, and Joe Calderone. 1998. Asthma bout nearly fatal for 9 year old. *New York Daily News*, March 25.

Filkins, Dexter, and Adam Nagourney. 2001. Sharpton endorses Ferrer in mayoral race. *New York Times*, August 28.

Firestone, David. 1995. Major ethnic changes under way. *New York Times*, March 29.

———. 1998. Public lives: ACORN organizer knows the value of tenacity. *New York Times*, January 16.

Flanders, Stephanie. 2001. Fewer children are hospitalized for asthma since 1997 city effort. *New York Times*, August 6.

Flynn, Kevin. 1996a. Cardinal presides as Black leaders and police begin talks. *New York Times*, March 6.

———. 1999b. State cites racial inequality in New York police searches. *New York Times*, December 1.

———. 1999c. Police poll finds strong support from Blacks and Hispanics. *New York Times*, December 11.

Foner, Nancy. 1987. Introduction: new immigrants and changing patterns in New York City. In *New immigrants in New York*, ed. Nancy Foner, 1–34. New York: Columbia University Press.

———. 2001. Introduction: new immigrants in a new New York. In *New immigrants in New York*, ed. Nancy Foner, 1–31. Rev. ed. New York: Columbia University Press.

Forman, Seth. 2002. One city, one standard. *Gotham Gazette*. www.gothamgazette.com/commentary/85.forman.shtml (accessed December 12, 2002).

Fried, Joseph. 1997. NYC school board settles suit by Muslims on holiday displays. *New York Times*, June 14.

Glazer, Nathan, and Daniel P. Moynihan. 1970. *Beyond the melting pot: the Negroes, Puerto Ricans, Jews, Italians, and Irish of New York City*. 2nd ed. Cambridge, MA: M.I.T. Press.

Gonzalez, David. 1996. In Brooklyn, these foes say injustice isn't blind. *New York Times*, May 11.

Goodnough, Abby. 2002. Justice Department allows a shift in school powers. *New York Times*, September 4.

Gottlieb, Martin, and Dean Baquet. 1991. Street wise impresario: Sharpton calls the tunes and players take their cues. *New York Times*, December 19.

Greenhouse, Linda. 1996. Court hears voting rights argument. *New York Times*, December 10.

Greenhouse, Steven. 1997. The odd couple that did the heavy lifting on Pataki's Medicaid deal. *New York Times*, July 16.

———. 2002a. Union boss says even Democrats can err. *New York Times*, January 20.

———. 2002b. Outspoken from youth: Roger Ernest Toussaint. *New York Times*, December 13.

———. 2005. Tough stance, tougher fines: union leader is in a corner. *New York Times*, December 22.

Herbert, Bob. 1999. Beyond the Diallo case. *New York Times*, April 4.

Hernandez, Raymond. 1997. Pataki signs bill changing congressional district lines. *New York Times*, August 29.

Hicks, Jonathan. 1995. Mayor woos Hispanic voters as their support drops sharply. *New York Times*, June 12.

———. 1996. Sharpton's candidacy has Democratic leaders stewing over strategy. *New York Times*, September 23.

———. 1997a. Hispanic congresswoman gets show of support in Albany. *New York Times*, March 9.

———. 1997b. Winning isn't everything: Sharpton eyes multiple prizes. *New York Times*, March 14.

———. 1999. The protesters: varied coalition plans its next step in pressuring the police. *New York Times*, March 28.

Holloway, Lynette. 1996. Justice Dept. reverses itself and approves plan for school district takeover. *New York Times*, December 10.

Holmes, Steven A. 1999. New York City faces a study of police acts. *New York Times*, March 6.

Horowitz, Craig. 1994. The Sharpton generation: how Al Sharpton and a band of insurgents are making a grab for power in the post Dinkins era. *New York Magazine*, April 4.

Kantrowitz, Nathan. 1995. Population. In *The encyclopedia of New York City*, ed. Kenneth Jackson, 920–923. New Haven, CT: Yale University Press.

Kasinitz, Philip. 1992. *Caribbean New York*. Ithaca, NY: Cornell University Press.

Kassel, Richard, and Katherine Kennedy. 1996. Asthma and air (letter to the editor). *The New York Times*, October 7.

Kocieniewski, David. 1997. NYC police chief dismisses officer in death of man in choke hold. *New York Times*, February 22.

———. 1999. Police unit creates fear of unchecked aggression. *New York Times*, February 15.

Kraly, Ellen Percy, and Ines Miyares. 2001. Immigration to New York: policy, population and patterns. In *New immigrants in New York* ed. Nancy Foner, 33–79. Rev. ed. New York: Columbia University Press.

Krauss, Clifford. 1996. Amnesty International says NYC police abuse rights of suspects. *New York Times*, June 26.

Lee, Felicia. 1991. Panel approves plan for New York's council seats. *The New York Times*, July 26.

———. 1997. Black parents teach kids how to cope with police bias. *New York Times*, October 23.

Levy, Clifford. 1997. U.S. court voids N.Y. congressional district drawn for Hispanics. *New York Times*, February 27.

Lii, Jane. 1998. Chinatown leaders negotiate using New Year firecrackers. *New York Times*, January 24.

Lin, Jan. 1998. *Reconstructing Chinatown*. Minneapolis: University of Minnesota Press.

Lowery, Mark. 1990. The Black minister: still on the battlefront. *New York Newsday*, November 18.

Lueck, Thomas J. 2000. Environmentalists assail plan to add diesel buses. *New York Times*, January 2.

Maher, Timothy. 1998. Environmental oppression: who is targeted for toxic exposure? *Journal of Black Studies* 28:3, 357–367.

McFadden, Robert D. 1999. Police division in Diallo death is overhauled. *New York Times*, March 27.

McNickle, Chris. 2001. A mayor for the new millennium (panel discussion). New-York Historical Society. The Crosswalks Network, New York City Department of Information Technology and Telecommunications, October 10.

Mollenkopf, John. 1997. New York: The great anomaly. In *Racial politics in American cities*, ed. Rufus Browning et al., 95–116. New York: Longman.

Nagourney, Adam. 1999. Diallo protest buffs image for Sharpton. *New York Times*, March 29.

———. 2001. Squirming in Sharpton's embrace: fidgeting without it. *New York Times*, October 5.

New York City Council Department of Sanitation and Solid Waste Management. 2006. Hearing on mayor's solid waste management plan. The Crosswalks Network, New York City Department of Information Technology and Telecommunications. June 26.

New York City Department of City Planning. 1992. *Demographic profiles*.

———. 1996. *The newest New Yorkers, 1990–1994*. (DCP# 96–19). December.

———. 1999. *The newest New Yorkers, 1995–1996*. (DCP# 99–08). September.

———. 2002. Demographic Profiles–New York City. www.nyc.gov/html/dcp/html/cenus/popdiv.html.

New York City Department of Health—Community Health Works. 1999. *Asthma facts*.

New York City Department of Health—Community Health Works. 2001. What is the "Public Health" approach to asthma? *Asthma initiative info*. New York City Childhood Asthma Initiative. Winter.

New York City Department of Health—Community Health Works. 2002 From the Director—Lorna Davis. *Asthma initiative info*. New York City Asthma Initiative. Fall.

New York City Mayor's Office—Press Office. 1997a. Mayor Giuliani salutes the 50th anniversary of Pakistan's independence. (Press Release). August 19.

———. 1997b. Mayor Giuliani proclaims "German American friendship week" (Press Release). September 15.

———. 1997c. Mayor Giuliani joins celebration of Deepavali, The Indian festival of lights. (Press Release). October 5.

———. 1997d. Mayor Giuliani proclaims "Bronx Dominican parade week" (Press Release). July 7.

———. 1997e. Mayor Giuliani hosts reception celebrating the completion of the reading of the Talmud. (Press Release). September 24.

———. 1998a. Mayor Giuliani delivers proclamation declaring Sunday, February 1st, 1998, "Hellenic letters and arts day" (Press Release). February 1.

———. 1998b. Mayor Giuliani proclaims Puerto Rico week in New York City. (Press Release). June 9.

New York Times. 1990. Asthma deaths are found to rise steadily in U.S. October 3.

———. 1997a. A portrait of New York City voters, November 9.

———. 1997b. The primary surprise (editorial), September 11.

Pear, Robert. 1991a. Citing race bias, U.S. vetoes 2 states' redistricting. *New York Times*, July 5.

———. 1991b. U.S. rejects New York plan for city council districts; finds Hispanic voters hurt. *The New York Times*, July 20.

Pecorella, Robert. 1994. *Community power in a postreform city: politics in New York City*. Armonk, NY: M. E. Sharpe.

Pierre-Pierre, Gary. 1993. A slow boil in the melting pot: Bensonhurst resists Russians. *New York Times*, August 8.

———. 1997a. For NYC Haitians, it's a generational struggle. *New York Times*, September 24.

———. 1997b. New York Haitians sensing betrayal in a land of refuge. *New York Times*, August 18.

———. 1998. Striving to muster political clout for Haitians. *New York Times*, March 16.

Puerto Rican Legal Defense and Education Fund. 2006. Voting rights reauthorization www.prldef.org/Civil/votingrights/latinovotingrights.htm (accessed July 10, 2006).

Rappaport, Shelly. 2002, November. Beyond bilingual education: meeting the needs of English language learners in the New York City public schools. A report of the Puerto Rican Legal Defense and Education Fund.

Roberts, Sam. 1991. Reshaping of New York City hits Black-Hispanic alliance. *New York Times*, July 28.

———. 1993. For race and ethnicity, shifts in roles in politics. *New York Times*, October 18.

Robinson, Gregg. 1995. Al Sharpton. In *The encyclopedia of New York City*, ed. Kenneth Jackson, 1064. New Haven, CT: Yale University Press.

Sachs, Susan. 1999. The newcomers: from a babel of tongues, a neighborhood. *New York Times*, December 26.

Salins, Peter. 1997. *Assimilation, American style*. New York: Basic Books.

Scott, Janny. 2001. Rethinking segregation beyond black and white. *New York Times*, July 29.

Sengupta, Somini. 1998. Programs for gifted favor whites study says. *New York Times*, June 18.

Sleeper, Jim. 1992. Rigging the vote by race. *Wall Street Journal*, August 4.

Steinberg, Jacques. 1997. Power shift in New York City schools gets federal approval. *New York Times*, April 2.

Stewart, Barbara. 2000. Complaint says 3 neighborhoods bear brunt of city garbage. *New York Times*, July 25.

Stolberg, Cheryl. 1999. Poor fighting baffling surge in asthma. *New York Times*, October 18.

Swarns, Rachel. 1998. Finding common ground on protection of children. *New York Times*, December 6.

U.S. Department of Justice–Civil Rights Division, Voting Section. 2000, Introduction to Federal Voting Rights laws—the Voting Rights Act of 1965. February 11. http://www.usdoj.gov/crt/voting/intro/intro_b.htm (accessed November 4, 2002).

Van Gelder, Lawrence. 1997. Federal inquiry sought in death of teen. *New York Times*, July 3.

Wakin, Daniel. 2001. Breathless. *New York Times*, May 13.

Waldinger, Roger. 1995. From Ellis Island to LAX: immigrant prospects in the American city. Taub Research Center, New York University. http://www.nyu.edu/urban/research/immigration/immigration.html.

Weiser, Benjamin. 1998. U.S. prosecutors widen probe of police brutality. *New York Times*, July 3.

———. 1999. Lawsuit seeks to curb street crimes unit, alleging racially biased searches. *New York Times*, March 9.

Weisskopf, Michael. 1992. EPA study addressed 'environmental racism.' *The Washington Post*, January 19.

White, Andrew. 2000. Ethnic politics and the changing face of New York. *Gotham Gazette*, August 7. http://www.gothamgazette.com/iotw.ethnic/ (accessed December 12, 2002).

Wilgoren, Jodi. 1999. After Diallo shooting, new focus on hiring city residents for police. *New York Times*, February 28.

Wilgoren, Jodi, and Michael Cooper. 1999. New York's police rank among the most racially imbalanced in U.S. *New York Times*, March 8.

Wright, Richard, and Mark Ellis. 2001. Immigrants, the native born, and the changing division of labor in New York City. In *New immigrants in New York*, ed. Nancy Foner, 81–111. Rev. ed. New York: Columbia University Press.

Youngblood, Johnny Ray. 1999. In search of minority officers. *New York Times*, April 20.

CHAPTER 6   POLITICAL PARTIES IN NEW YORK CITY GOVERNANCE

Barrett, Wayne. 2000. *Rudy!* New York: Basic Books.

Benjamin, Gerald. 1988. The political relationship. In *The two New Yorks: state-city relations in the federal system*, ed. Gerald Benjamin and Charles Brecher, 107–150. New York: Russell Sage Foundation.

Brecher, Charles, and Raymond Horton. 1993. *Power failure: New York politics and policy since 1960.* New York: Oxford University Press.

Browne, Arthur, Dan Collins, and Michael Goodwin. 1985. *I, Koch.* New York: Dodd, Mead.

Cardwell, Diane. 2001. Liberal party gives Hevesi its backing. *New York Times*, June 3.

———. 2002. New council feeling its way, faces a test. *New York Times*, April 8.

Chou, Jerome. 2000. Third (and 4th and 5th) parties . . . *Gotham Gazette*, April 24. www.gothamgazette.com/iotw/indyparties/index.shtml.

Cooper, Michael. 2003a. Mayor dueling with governor on solutions to shortfall. *New York Times*, January 28.

———. 2003b. Mayor Bloomberg gets little help from Governor Pataki. *New York Times*, January 30.

Costikyan, Edward. 1966. *Behind closed doors: politics in the public interest.* New York: Harcourt, Brace & World.

Dao, James. 1993. For Giuliani, big job in Albany: separating friends from foes. *New York Times*, November 8.

Freeman, Joshua. 2000. *Working class New York.* New York: The New Press.

Giuliani, Rudolph. 1998. Mayor Giuliani's Daily Press Conference. The Crosswalks Network, New York City Department of Information Technology and Telecommunications. February 3.

———. 1999a. Mayor Giuliani's Daily Press Conference. The Crosswalks Network, New York City Department of Information Technology and Telecommunications, August 12.

———. 1999b. Mayor Giuliani's Daily Press Conference. The Crosswalks Network, New York City Department of Information Technology and Telecommunications, August 10.

———. 1999c. Mayor Giuliani's Daily Press Conference. The Crosswalks Network, New York City Department of Information Technology and Telecommunications, January 13.

———. 1999d. Mayor Speech before the Manhattan Institute for Policy Research Luncheon. The Crosswalks Network, New York City Department of Information Technology and Telecommunications, May 22.

Goodnough, Abby. 1998. Unions and local groups join to form a new political party. *New York Times*, July 7.

Isserman, Maurice. 1995. American Labor Party. In *The encyclopedia of New York City*, ed. Kenneth Jackson, 29–30. New Haven, CT: Yale University Press.

Koch, Edward. 1985. *Politics.* New York: Simon and Schuster.

———. 1984. *Mayor: an autobiography.* New York: Simon and Schuster.

Koch, Edward (with Daniel Paisner). 1992. *Citizen Koch: an autobiography.* New York: St. Martin's Press.

Kolbert, Elizabeth. 1998. Liberal Party has one ideal—survival. *New York Times*, May 14.

Lawson, Kay. 1997. *The human polity.* Boston: Houghton Mifflin.

Lentz, Philip. 2001. Campaign update: at the first turn . . . *Gotham Gazette: Searchlight on Campaign 2001: Mayor*, April 25. www.gothamgazette.com.

Liff, Bob. 2001. The nod of the bosses. *Gotham Gazette: Searchlight on Campaign 2001*, April 25. www.gothamgazette.com.

Ludington, Charles. 1995. Liberal Party. In *The encyclopedia of New York City*, ed. Kenneth Jackson, 667. New Haven, CT: Yale University Press.

McCarthy, Robert J. 1998. New political party with labor roots may provide primary edge for Vallone. *Buffalo News*, July 10.

Mollenkopf, John. 1992. *A phoenix in the ashes: the rise and fall of the Koch coalition in New York City politics.* Princeton, NJ: Princeton University Press.

Nagourney, Adam. 2001. Political memo: Liberal Party has problem after Giuliani. *New York Times,* April 24.

New York Times. 1984. Excerpts from text of the state of the city address given by Mayor Koch. January 10.

———. 1996. Victory in a war of attrition (editorial), October 15.

———. 1997a. A party for hire (editorial), February 27.

———. 1997b. A bad bill on police (editorial), July 2.

Pleven, Liam. 1998. Statewide campaigns: a report on races in New York/left wing aims to take flight/liberal lines hoping for more influence. *Newsday,* October 19.

Purdum, Todd. 1994. Mayor's endorsement of Cuomo reflects political interests. *New York Times,* October 25.

Sack, Kevin. 1995. Giuliani is hopeful after going to Albany. *New York Times,* May 24.

Sargent, Greg. 2003. Mayor's team: we got stiffed in Pataki deal. *New York Observer,* January 23.

Spitzer, Robert. 1994. Third parties in New York State. In *Governing New York State,* ed. Jeff Stonecash, John Kenneth White and Peter Colby, 103–118. Albany: State University of New York Press

CHAPTER 7   THE CHARTER, THE MAYOR, AND THE OTHER GUYS

Adrian, Charles, and Michael. 1991. *State and local politics.* Chicago: Nelson-Hall.

Arian, Asher, et al. 1991. *Changing New York City politics.* New York: Routledge.

Bagli, Charles V. 1997. Companies get second helping of tax breaks. *New York Times,* October 17.

———. 2001. Some see Giuliani as right for an emergency, but wrong for rebuilding. *New York Times,* October 7.

Baker, Al, and Jennifer Steinhauer. 2003. Pataki approves city water plant. *New York Times,* July 23.

Barry, Dan. 1999. News analysis: a killing widens racial divide for Giuliani. *New York Times,* February 11.

Barstow, David. 2000. Brooklyn Museum is cautious, as Giuliani looks to November. *New York Times,* March 29.

Benjamin, Gerald. 1995. Charter. In *The encyclopedia of New York City,* ed. Kenneth Jackson, 208. New Haven, CT: Yale University Press.

Berger, Stephen. 1991. Stoning the wrong goliath. *Newsday,* May 2.

Berkowitz, Harry. 1989. Breaks for the boroughs; Dinkins' incentives won't favor Manhattan. *Newsday,* December 15.

Blumenthal, Ralph. 1990. New year, new mayor, new hopes. *New York Times,* January 1.

Bumiller, Elisabeth. 2000. Final year, final ambitions. *New York Times,* December 31.

———. 2001. Mayor says decency panel progress made. *New York Times,* March 2.

Calderone, Joe. 1992. He's mayor cool! even critics praise Dinkins for ensuring city kept calm. *Newsday,* May 4.

Cardwell, Diane. 2002. Betsy Gotbaum, the advocate, struggles to reach her public. *New York Times,* December 2.

Carroll, Maurice. 1994. Green says office has three roles. *Newsday,* January 2.

Conason, Joe. 1995. Police mayor in FIRE city. *The Nation,* December 18.

Cottman, Michael. 1995. About the mayor; Rudy's invisible constituents. *Newsday,* January 10.

Deutsch, Claudia. 1993. Mastercard and midtown: city hall wins in New York. *New York Times,* June 11.

Dugas, Christine. 1992. Is the city world class? *Newsday*, August 3.

Dutt, Jill. 1990. Securities tax slammed; Dinkins says levy on trades would cripple local economy. *Newsday*, September 8.

Dwyer, Jim. 1993. They're set to run, win, self destruct. *Newsday*, June 28.

Eaton, Leslie (with Julian Barnes). 1998. Wall Street gloom has New York tense. *New York Times*, October 12.

Eaton, Leslie. 2001. Wall Street may be spoiler for New York's economy. *New York Times*, August 14.

Finder, Alan. 1989a. Presidents of boroughs: vestigial or vibrant. *New York Times*, May 10.

——. 1989b. Coalition opposing charter revision starts its campaign. *New York Times*, September 28.

——. 1989c. Redefining comptroller, council head. *New York Times*, October 21.

——. 1989d. The 1989 elections: charter. *New York Times*, November 8.

——. 1989e. New York charter revision approved by Justice Department. *New York Times*, December 14.

——. 1992. Dinkins, respected by foes, seeks to pacify friends. *New York Times*, July 25.

——. 1993a. Dinkins says Albany's budget threatens his. *New York Times*, April 15.

——. 1993b. Dinkins' budget proposal to show worst case cuts. *New York Times*, April 27.

——. 1993c. Dinkins campaign strategy; show them who's the mayor. *New York Times*, May 30.

——. 1993d. Dinkins plans more cuts to fill $280 million gap. *New York Times*, June 4.

——. 1993e. Dinkins and council face fiscal maw's 300 million sharp teeth. *New York Times*, June 6.

Flynn, Kevin. 1990. Mayor: the other guys blinked: Dinkins says he lured leaders into calling for more cops. *Newsday*, September 15.

Flynn, Kevin, and Rex Smith. 1990. Dinkins says he'll put 6000 more cops on beat; Cuomo vows to back new taxes in city. *Newsday*, September 12.

Gasparino, Charles, and Manuel Perez-Rivas. 1995. Lowered bond rating is BBB blow to city, Rudy. *Newsday*, July 11.

Giuliani, Rudolph. 1997. The entrepreneurial city. Speech before the Manhattan Institute, New York City. The Crosswalks Network, New York City Department of Information Technology and Telecommunications, December 3.

Giuliani, Rudolph (with Ken Kurson). 2002. *Leadership*. New York: Talk Miramax Books.

Goldman, John J. 1990. Dinkins offers $1.8 billion 'battle plan' against fear. *Los Angeles Times*, October 3.

Goodnough, Abby. 1999. Former head of charter panel attacks Giuliani's latest plan. *New York Times*, July 1.

——. 2002. Deal would give New York's mayor school authority. *New York Times*, June 7.

Goodwin, Michael. 1982. Sovern will head city charter unit. *New York Times*, April 9.

Gootman, Elissa. 2004a. Schedule set for replacing school boards. *New York Times*, January 15.

——. 2004b. Favoritism raised in Snapple deal. *New York Times*, March 19.

Guttenplan, D. D. 1989. New York's 106th mayor; a victory that defied the odds and old guard. *Newsday*, November 8.

Haberman, Clyde. 1981. News analysis: who cured fiscal crisis in the city? *New York Times*, March 7.

Hammack, David. 1998. Presentation at New York Law School 100th Anniversary of the New York City Charter Celebration. The New York Law School, The Crosswalks Network, New York City Department of Information Technology and Telecommunications, January 22.

Herbert, Bob. 1998. One man feud. *New York Times*, June 28.

——. 2001a. The right answer. *New York Times*, September 20.

——. 2001b. Rudy's no exit strategy. *New York Times*, October 1.

Herszenhorn, David. 2003a. Chancellor gives old school districts a role. *New York Times*, May 22.

————. 2003b. City comptroller raises questions on deal to put Snapple products in schools. *New York Times*, October 9.

Hicks, Jonathan. 1993a. Green sees consumers as his base of support. *New York Times*, September 11.

————. 1993b. 6 candidates contend for a chance to define the retitled position of public advocate. *New York Times*, September 12.

————. 1994. Advocate Green gives public an inside look at new job. *New York Times*, January 3.

Johnson, Kirk. 1997. Wall Street providing fewer jobs but more money to New York. *New York Times*, October 29.

King, Wayne. 1991. The federal budget: New York: Dinkins and other officials assail Bush's budget over spending cuts. *New York Times*, February 6.

Kivelson, Adrienne. 1990. *What makes New York City run?* New York: The League of Women Voters of the City of New York.

Kolbert, Elizabeth. 1990. Where's Cuomo? he called for more police but finds Dinkins' tax plan hard to swallow. *New York Times*, October 6.

Lane, Eric. 1998. Presentation at New York Law School 100th Anniversary of the New York Charter Celebration. New York Law School. The Crosswalks Network, New York City Department of Information Technology and Telecommunications, January 22.

Levy, Clifford. 1996a. Comptroller versus the chief, the sequel. *New York Times*, September 23.

————. 1996b. Wall St. profits may give New York city a surplus but deficits loom. *New York Times*, December 11.

Liff, Bob. 1992. Dinkins warned of risky business. *Newsday*, December 23.

————. 1993. Hopeful Mr. Dinkins goes to Washington. *Newsday*, March 11.

Lipper, Kenneth. 1989. What needs to be done? *New York Times*, December 31.

Lipton, Eric. 2000a. Comptroller predicts big shortfalls and cutbacks in mayor's 4-year budget. *New York Times*, February 24.

————. 2000b. Hevesi quietly drops 10 month fight to block welfare to work contracts. *New York Times*, December 2.

Lueck, Thomas. 1987. Stock impact feared grave in New York. *New York Times*, October 29.

————. 1989. Assessing New York's charter change. *New York Times*, September 3.

————. 1995. Giuliani plan puts health care jobs at risk. *New York Times*, February 18.

————. 2000. New pharmacy laws are sought for the posting of drug prices. *New York Times*, August 6.

Marinaccio, Paul. 1990. Mayor woos Atlanta firms. *Newsday*, April 17.

Martin, Douglas. 1998a. Water settlement may not settle much. *New York Times*, May 21.

————. 1998b. Pledge of a water plant won't end a long battle. *New York Times*, May 24.

Mauro, Frank, and Gerald Benjamin, eds. 1989. *Restructuring the New York City government: The reemergence of municipal reform.* New York: Academy of Political Science.

McKinley, James C. Jr. 1991a. Control board assails Dinkins 4-year fiscal plan. *New York Times*, December 19.

————. 1991b. Dinkins plans to spur city economy. *New York Times*, December 31.

————. 1993. Financing of $31.4 billion budget presented by Dinkins is criticized. *New York Times*, May 4.

Mitchell, Allison. 1994a. Giuliani demands new spending cuts from all agencies. *New York Times*, July 26.

————. 1994b. In New York City's budget fight, comptroller chooses sides: both. *New York Times*, December 10.

Mollenkopf, John Hull. 1994. *Phoenix in the ashes: the rise and fall of the Koch coalition in New York City politics.* Princeton, NJ: Princeton University Press.

Moreno, Sylvia. 1992. Dinkins fiscal plan provokes concern. *Newsday*, January 6.

Mouat, Lucia. 1993. Dinkins faces service cuts to big apple. *Christian Science Monitor*, May 14.

Newsday. 1993. A needless office; but Green would bring it talent. October 29.

———. 1994. Ought to be a bestseller. July 29.

New York City Charter. 2004. New York City Charter Revision Commission. www.nyc.gov/htm/charter/html/home/home.shtml.

New York City Comptroller's Office. 2002a. One year later: the fiscal impact of 9/11 on New York City. September 4.

New York City Comptroller's Office. 2002b. www.comptroller.nyc.gov/bottom.asp (accessed November 22, 2002).

New York City Comptroller's Office. 2002c. Audits. www.comptroller.nyc.gov.bureaus/audit/current.asp (accessed November 22, 2002).

New York City's Comptroller's Office. 2004. 911: three years later–securing the federal pledge. August.

New York Times. 1989. An unpresident for the city council, May 12.

———. 1990. Mr. Dinkins' orphan crime program (editorial), November 16.

———. 1992. The region: Q & A: Barry Sullivan; new deputy mayor, a banker outlines his business plan, March 29.

———. 1998. Arming the public advocate (editorial), November 10.

———. 2001. Mayor of the moment (editorial), September 14.

Pelissero, John et al. 2000. Does political incorporation matter? The impact of minority mayors over time. *Urban Affairs Review* (September), 84–91.

Perez-Pena, Richard. 2001. Court blocks a water plant in Bronx park. *New York Times*, February 9.

Perez-Rivas, Manuel. 1994. Ex-mayors assail public advocate cuts. *Newsday*, June 3.

Peterson, Helen. 2004. Bottleneck broken, Snapple deal's a go. *New York Daily News*, July 30.

Pohlman, Marcus D. 1993. *Governing the postindustrial city.* New York: Longman.

Powell, Michael, and Sylvia Moreno. 1992. What's in it for us? Officials counting the days till they count Clinton aid. *Newsday*, November 5.

Preston, Jennifer. 1991a. Dinkins proposes furloughs to close a $465M budget gap. *Newsday*, April 18.

———. 1991b. The good, bad and ugly: mayor gets mixed reviews in midst of budget problems. *New York Times*, November 24.

Purdum, Todd. 1989a. Politicians scrambling to decide who won. *New York Times*, March 23.

———. 1989b. 3 borough leaders seek strategy to save board. *New York Times*, March 28.

———. 1989c. Panel finishes plan to revise New York City's government. *New York Times*, August 3.

———. 1990a. A familiar budget: much of spending plan from Dinkins is reminiscent of the Koch approach. *New York Times*, February 2.

———. 1990b. Dinkins to seek new payroll tax to pay for hiring more officers. *New York Times*, October 1.

———. 1990c. Dinkins stands by troubled tax proposal for police. *New York Times*, November 15.

———. 1990d. Dinkins in accord on financing plan for hiring. *New York Times*, December 6.

———. 1991. Dinkins woos Rohatyn's aid on budget gap. *New York Times*, November 7.

———. 1993. Buttoned up. *New York Times*, September 12.

Purnick, Joyce. 1987. City's mood dips from the celebratory to the cautionary. *New York Times*, December 13.

———. 2001. In a crisis, the Giuliani we wanted. *New York Times*, September 13.

Revkin, Andrew C. 1997. EPA seeks to fine New York City over proposed clean water plant. *New York Times*, March 4.

Roberts, Sam. 1991. Mayor Dinkins: every day a test. *New York Times*, April 7.

Rohde, David. 1998. Pressed by U.S., Giuliani agrees to build a plant to filter water. *New York Times*, May 20.

Sack, Kevin. 1991. Political memo: Cuomo sends Dinkins smoky fiscal signal. *New York Times*, April 22.

Sanger, David. 1997. New York has different way to deal with Swiss bank. *New York Times*, August 25.

Saul, Michael. 2003. Bloomberg budget buoys city bonds. *New York Daily News,* May 28.

Schwarz, Frederick A. O. 1998. Presentation at New York Law School 100th Anniversary of the New York Charter Celebration. The Crosswalks Network, New York City Department of Information Technology and Telecommunications. January 22.

Serant, Claire. 1999. Pols have eyes on the prize: Boro pres wanna bes already getting their ducks in a row. *New York Daily News*, February 21.

Siegel, Fred. 1999. Rudy awakening. *The New Republic*, April 19.

Sirica, Jack. 1992. Dinkins pleads for urban plan. *Newsday*, December 10.

Steinhauer, Jennifer. 2001a. In crisis, Giuliani's popularity overflows city. *New York Times*, September 20.

———. 2001b. From political shadows to center stage, Giuliani stays in character. *New York Times*, September 26.

———. 2001c. Citing comments on attack, Giuliani rejects Saudi's gift. *New York Times*, October 12.

———. 2002. Bloomberg is increasing city lobbying in Washington. *New York Times*, January 29.

Tierney, John. 2001. Is New York big enough for Giuliani and a new mayor. *New York Times*, September 21.

Tomasky, Michael. 1993. Identity politics in New York City. *The Nation*, June 21.

Traub, James. 2001. Giuliani internalized. *New York Times*, February 11.

Waldman, Amy. 2001. Despite ruling, E.P.A. insists that city must filter water. *New York Times*, February 10.

Walsh, Elsa. 1990. Dinkins: drug war funds inadequate; 'that's what they always say,' Bennett responds to mayors. *Washington Post*, April 25.

CHAPTER 8   THE CITY COUNCIL

Altman, Gary. 2002. Politics vs. good government: the Albany question. Panel presentation by Peter Vallone at Fordham University, New York City, October 8.

Barbanel, Josh. 1986a. A surprise coalition throws council selections into doubt. *New York Times*, January 1.

———. 1986b. Council is split over choosing majority chief. *New York Times*, January 8.

———. 1991. U.S. ruling reopens feuds on New York council map. *New York Times*, July 21.

Barbour, Christine, and Gerald Wright. 2001. *Keeping the republic: power and citizenship in American politics*. New York: Houghton Mifflin.

Barry, Dan. 2001. A sea change ahead in the city council. *New York Times*, February 18.

Bellush, Jewel, and Dick Netzer, eds.. 1990. *Urban politics: New York style*. M. E. Sharpe: Armonk, NY.

Boorstin, Robert. 1986. Dryfoos named to be chairman of a committee. *New York Times*, January 23.

Bunch, William. 1993. 2 terms and yer out; measure may curb career politicians. *Newsday*, November 3.

Bunch, William, and Jessie Mangaliman. 1993. Term limits, SI secession: call to arms. *Newsday*, November 4.

Cardwell, Diane. 2001. As he leaves, Vallone scorns calls for change. *New York Times*, December 24.

———. 2002a. New council members dive in, with a caucus to change some rules. *New York Times*, January 3.

———. 2002b. A candidate for speaker gains support. *New York Times*, January 7.

———. 2002c. Miller doles out power to a clamoring council. *New York Times*, January 15.

———. 2002d. Council speaker planned to cut stipend for himself and others. *New York Times*, January 16.

Chester, Lenore. 2002. Rules changes: some better, some worse, some just as bad. *Searchlight on the City Council* (Citizens Union), 13:1, 9.

Citizens Union. 1997. *Searchlight on the City Council*, 8:5

———. 1998. *Searchlight on the City Council*, 9:6.

———. 1999. *Searchlight on the City Council*, 10:4, 2.

———. 2000a. *Searchlight on the City Council*, 11:3, 2.

———. 2000b. The big turnover.

———. 2002a. *Searchlight on the City Council*, 13:1, 11.

———. 2002b. *Searchlight on the City Council*, 13:3–4.

Collins, Gail. 1993. Your chance to kick out the rascals. *Newsday*, October 24.

Cooper, Michael. 2002. Upper east side councilman has speaker's job all but won. *New York Times*, January 8.

Daley, Suzanne. 1986. Vocal and aggressive Vallone redefines role. *New York Times*, August 16.

Daniels, Lee A. 1991. Districting foe, in new tactic, backs elections. *New York Times*, July 29.

Davidson, Roger, and Walter J. Oleszek. 2002. *Congress and its members*. Washington, DC: Congressional Quarterly Books.

Eichenthal, David. 1990. The other elected officials. In *Urban politics: New York style*, ed. Jewel Bellush and Dick Netzer, 86–106. Armonk, NY: M. E. Sharpe.

Eristoff, Andrew. 2001. Show up. *Searchlight on the City Council* (Citizens Union), 12:6, 3–5.

Finder, Alan. 1988. City council wakes up but still lags. *New York Times*, January 29.

Glaberson, William. 1991. Old feuds tangle new city council as deadline nears. *New York Times*, April 28.

Gotham Gazette, City government–city laws (gothamgazette.com/city/vote_records.php).

Gotham Gazette, Searchlight on the City Council. 2002. 2002 salaries and stipends for the city council.

Gottlieb, Martin. 1991. New York's democratic experiment. *New York Times*, September 15.

Gray, Jeffrey. 1991a. Council district 21 creates angry Hispanic majority. *New York Times*, July 19.

———. 1991b. Panel members differ on districting ruling. *New York Times*, July 22.

———. 1991c. Creating new council districts: minority concerns vs. incumbency. *New York Times*, July 23.

———. 1991d. New prize in districting tug of war. *New York Times*, August 5.

Hicks, Jonathan. 1994. Council chief wheels and deals, and New York's budget is passed. *New York Times*, June 24.

———. 1995a. Council creates police monitor, but Giuliani plans to ignore vote. *New York Times*, January 20.

———. 1995b. Mayor takes council to court on independent police panel. *New York Times*, April 19.

———. 1995c. Judge invalidates creation of police corruption panel. *New York Times*, June 29.

———. 1995d. The council and how it really works. *New York Times*, November 26.

———. 1996. This caucus seeks a place at the table. *New York Times*, May 19.

———. 2001a. Races for council reveal shifts in demographics of city politics. *New York Times*, August 6.

——. 2001b. The 2001 elections: the city council election of mayor will affect speaker vote. *New York Times*, November 8.

——. 2001c. City council transformed by term limits. *New York Times*, November 11.

——. 2001d. Lively battle to be speaker bursts out of back room. *New York Times*, December 6.

——. 2002. An alliance builder: Alan Gifford Miller. *New York Times*, January 8.

Holloway, Lynette. 1997a. New York council offers plan to give more control on sites for superstores. *New York Times*, May 29.

——. 1997b. Few NYC community boards meet deadline on superstore. *New York Times*, July 6.

Hu, Winnie. 2006a. Council ready to fill the job of speaker. *New York Times*, January 3.

——. 2006b. New council speaker is set for her first test, filling committee leadership positions. *New York Times*, January 18.

Jacobs, Andrew. 1996. The war of nerves downtown; or how a councilwomen, Kathryn Freed works a district rocked by change (Enemies? She has plenty). *New York Times*, July 17.

Kivelson, Adrienne. 1991. *What makes New York City run?* New York: The League of Women Voters of New York City.

Lauder, Ronald. 1993. New York needs term limits for city council and top posts (letter to the editor). *New York Times*, September 4.

Lee, Felicia. 1991a. Minority districts for council added in New York plan. *New York Times*, May 2.

——. 1991b. District map for council changes little. *New York Times*, May 17.

——. 1991c. Dinkins coalition fights for council. *New York Times*, June 3.

——. 1991d. Plan for new city council passes in praise and anger. *New York Times*, June 4.

——. 1991e. Panel approves plan for New York's council seats. *New York Times*, July 26.

——. 1991f. Candidates say new districting creates disorder. *New York Times*, July 30.

——. 1991g. Judges clear way for new election. *New York Times*, July 31.

Liff, Bob. 1993. Beginning of the end? Referendum would limit terms to 8 years. *Newsday*, October 29.

——. 1994. The dealmaker; long Astoria's favorite son, Council Speaker Vallone is now the most influential Democrat in city politics. *Newsday*, March 6.

Lipton, Eric. 2000. Cordial talks yield accord on city budget. *New York Times*, June 6.

——. 2001. The annual cut-and-restore budget game begins. *New York Times*, January 31.

Lueck, Thomas. 1993. Term limits, an ad campaign says two terms are enough. *New York Times*, October 26.

McKinley, James C. 1991a. Primary day: new voices to mold power balance in the new city council. *New York Times*, September 13.

——. 1991b. Money talked in race, but so did volunteers. *New York Times*, September 15.

Mitchell, Alison. 1994a. In New York City's budget fight, comptroller chooses sides: both. *New York Times*, December 10.

——. 1994b. Judge voids disputed cuts of mayor and council. *New York Times*, December 22.

Muzzio, Douglas, and Tim Tompkins. 1989. On the size of the city council: finding the mean. In *Restructuring the New York City government: the reemergence of municipal reform*, ed. Frank Mauro and Gerald Benjamin, 83–96. New York: Academy of Political Science.

Myers, Steven Lee. 1994a. Giuliani and council still at odds on budget. *New York Times*, December 7.

——. 1994b. Giuliani sued by city council in a budget test. *New York Times*, December 8.

Newsday. 1993. Its snake oil: on Nov. 2, say no to term limits (editorial). October 27.

New York City Charter Revision Commission. 2004. New York City Charter. www.nyc.gov/html/charter/html/home/home.shtml.

New York City Council. 2002a. Council member profiles. www.council.ny.ny.us/committees/details.cfm? (accessed November 4, 2002).

New York City Council. 2002b. Committees. www.council.ny.ny.us/committees/details.cfm? (accessed November 4, 2002).

New York City Council. 2002c. Budget process. www.council.nyc.ny.us/index.cfm? page= process (accessed November 4, 2002).

New York City Council Committee on Aging. 2002. Hearing on resolutions on nursing home and senior citizen institution employee hiring. The Crosswalks Network, New York City Department of Information Technology and Telecommunications, September 17.

New York City Council Committee Economic Development. 2002. Oversight hearing on tax incentives to companies thinking of leaving the city. The Crosswalks Network, New York City Department of Information Technology and Telecommunications, June 11.

New York City Council Committee on Environmental Protection. 1999. Watershed permit program. The Crosswalks Network, New York City Department of Information Technology and Telecommunications, April 15.

New York City Council Committee on Finance. 2002, February. NYC fiscal crisis—role of federal aid. The Crosswalks Network, New York City Department of Information Technology and Telecommunications, February 11.

New York City Council Press Conference. 1999. 2nd Avenue subway campaign. The Crosswalks Network, New York City Department of Information Technology and Telecommunications, September 8.

New York City Department of Citywide Administrative Services. 1996. *The 1996–97 green book: official directory of the City of New York.*

New York City Department of General Services. 1985. *The green book—1985–86: the official directory of the City of New York.*

New York City Districting Commission. Chapter 2-A Districting Commission (City Charter). www.nyc.gov/html/nydc/html/charter.html (accessed November 4, 2002).

New York Times. 1991a. Run now move later, April 7.

———. 1991b. Excerpts from U.S. letter rejecting districting plan, July 20.

———. 1991c. Voting vengeance (editorial), July 30.

———. 1991d. Results in primary races for New York City Council, September 14.

———. 1991e. Results of city council and judiciary races in New York City, November 6.

———. 1994. Time for a budget truce, November 26.

Onishi, Norimitsu. 1998. Giuliani sues to block police board. *New York Times,* March 26.

Pear, Robert. 1991a. Problems arise in New York map. *New York Times,* July 18.

———. 1991b. Council map makers argue it mirrors New York mosaic. *New York Times,* July 19.

———. 1991c. U.S. rejects New York plan for city council districts; finds Hispanic voters hurt. *New York Times,* July 20.

———. 1991d. New York's plan wins U.S. backing. *New York Times,* July 27.

Pristin, Terry. 1999. Superstores find room in New York. *New York Times,* December 20.

Purdum, Todd. 1991a. More than a long hallway keeps Dinkins and Vallone apart. *New York Times,* May 23.

———. 1991b. At the budget wall: mayor still holds sway: tenuous compromise shows Dinkins power. *New York Times,* July 1.

Purnick, Joyce. 1985. After 24 years on city council, finance chief says he'll step down. *New York Times,* April 15.

Ravo, Nick. 1991. Candidates fault ruling on districts. *New York Times,* July 21.

Roberts, Sam. 1990. Now it's the law, but new charter still riles Koch. *New York Times,* April 23.

———. 1991a. As population grows, Hispanic power lags. *New York Times,* July 18.

———. 1991b. The legal mosaic and political art of council maps. *New York Times,* July 22.

———. 1991c. In some council contests, it's still us against them. *New York Times,* September 2.

———. 1991d. Primary day: council's new era takes shape in New York vote. *New York Times,* September 13.

———. 1991e. After the voting: council tallies assure diversity under the old guard. *New York Times*, September 14.

———. 1991f. The ins and outs: GOP chances in council races. *New York Times*, October 21.

———. 1993a. Metro matters: term limits have support of people out of office. *New York Times*, June 21.

———. 1993b. Bid to limit terms can be on ballot in New York City. *New York City*, October 20.

Ruiz, Albor. 2001. A new school kid on the bloc. *New York Daily News*, December 17.

———. 2002. Council rookies boast fresh ideas. *New York Daily News*, January 7.

Steinhauer, Jennifer. 2003. Council chief punishes 3 for voting no on raising tax. *New York Times*, February 13.

Vallone, Peter. 2002a. Balance of power and principles (lecture at Fordham University—Government and Politics in New York City). September 10.

———. 2002b. Politics vs. good government: the Albany question (lecture at Fordham University—Government and Politics in New York City. October 8.

CHAPTER 9   THE MUNICIPAL BUREAUCRACY

Allison, Graham. 1969. Conceptual models and the Cuban missile crisis. *American Political Science Review*, 63:3, 689–718.

Benjamin, Gerald. 1995. Civil service. In *The encyclopedia of New York City*, ed. Kenneth Jackson, 237. New Haven, CT: Yale University Press.

Berkey-Gerard, Mark. 2002. Guide to Mayor's Management Report. *Gotham Gazette*, October 7. www.gothamgazette.com/iotw/mayorsreport/.

Binder, Frederick, and David Reimers. 1995. *All the nations under heaven*. New York: Columbia University Press.

Blair, Jayson. 1999. Street crimes unit will be split into 8 pieces. *New York Times*, October 16.

Bryner, Barry. 1987. *Bureaucratic discretion: law and policy in federal regulatory agencies*. New York: Pergamon Press.

Buettner, Russ. 1997. Foster kids glut system surge worst since crack heyday. *New York Times*, May 12.

Bumiller, Elisabeth. 2000. Giuliani plans to overhaul buildings unit. *New York Times*, September 29.

Cardwell, Diane. 2001. Contract deal for workers in uniform. *New York Times*, July 28.

Chivers, C. J. 2000. Poaching adds new hurdle to police recruiting efforts. *New York Times*, April 6.

———. 2001a. For black officers, diversity has its limits. *New York Times*, April 2.

———. 2001b. Alienation is a partner for black officers. *New York Times*, April 3.

Chou, Jerome. 2000. Third (and 4th and 5th) parties . . . *Gotham Gazette*, April 24. www.gothamgazette.com/iotw/indyparties/index.shtml.

Dilger, Jay. 1986. The expansion and centralization of American government functions. In *American intergovernmental relations today: perspectives and controversies*, ed. Jay Dilger, 5–29. Englewood Cliffs, NJ: Prentice-Hall.

Epstein, Lee, and Thomas Walker. 2001. *Constitutional law for a changing America*. Washington, DC: Congressional Quarterly Press.

Firestone, David. 1996. Giuliani is forming a new city agency on child welfare. *New York Times*, January 12.

Forman, Seth. Community boards. *Gotham Gazette*. www.gothamgazette.com/lessons/boards. shtml (accessed January 21, 2003).

Freeman, Joshua. 2000. *Working class New York*. New York: The New Press.

Gootman, Elissa. 2003. 1200 parents prepare to take on role as paid liaisons in schools. *New York Times*, August 21.

Giuliani, Rudolph. 2002. *Leadership*. New York: Talk Miramax Books.

Greenhouse, Steven. 1999. Unions find their voice at city hall. *New York Times,* May 13.

———. 2001. Uniformed workers faulted for reducing demands. *New York Times*, January 3.

Hallman, Howard. 1977. *Small and large together: governing the metropolis*. Beverly Hills: Sage Publications.

Herszehorn, David M. 2005. Push is nearing shove in teacher contract talks. *New York Times*, September 26.

Hevesi, Dennis. 2000. Takeover of agency for buildings is proposed. *New York Times*, December 1.

Kirk, Krishna, ed.. 2002. *The 2002–03 green book: official directory of the city of New York*. New York: New York City Department of Citywide Administration Services.

Koch, Edward. 1985. *Politics*. New York: Simon and Schuster.

Kocieniewski, David. 1999. Police unit creates fear of unchecked aggression. *New York Times*, February 15.

McFadden, Robert D. 1998. In shift, union chief assails workfare as slavery. *New York Times*, April 19.

———. 1999. The Diallo shooting: the overview: elite police unit in Diallo death is overhauled. *New York Times*, March 27.

Meier, Kenneth. 1993. *Politics and the bureaucracy*. 3rd ed. Pacific Grove, CA: Brooks/Cole.

Myers, Steven Lee. 1995. Child welfare agency offers plan to cut budget. *New York Times*, December 7.

Newfeld, Jack, and Wayne Barrett. 1988. *City for sale*. New York: Harper and Row.

New York City Charter Revision Commission. New York City Charter. www.nyc.gov/html/charter/html/home/home.shtml.

New York City Comptroller's Office. 2002. How are we doing? Enhancing accountability through the mayor's management report. February.

New York City Council. 1997. Executive Budget Hearing—Department of Parks and Recreation. The Crosswalks Network, New York City Department of Information Technology and Telecommunications, May 21.

———. 2000. Preliminary Budget Hearing—Committee on Health. The Crosswalks Network, New York City Department of Information Technology and Telecommunications, March 9.

New York City Department of Business Services. 2002. Strategic plan. (Abridged). October 29.

New York City Department of Health and Mental Hygiene. Health care access and improvement. www.nyc.gov/html/doh/html/hca/hca.html (accessed January 4, 2003).

New York City Department of Investigation. About DOI. www.nyc.gov/html/doi/html/about-doi.html (accessed December 30, 2002).

New York City Mayor's Office. 2002. Mayor's press conference. The Crosswalks Network, New York City Department of Information Technology and Telecommunications. December 26.

New York City Mayor's Office of Health Insurance Access. HealthStat. www.nyc.gov.html/hia/html/healthstat.html (accessed January 4, 2003).

New York City Mayor's Office of Operations. 1989. Mayor's management report. September 17.

———. 1991. Mayor's management report. September 17.

———. 1997. Mayor's management report—Fiscal Year 1997, Volume 1, Agency Narratives.

New York City Office of Management and Budget. 2002. City of New York executive budget fiscal year 2003—message of the mayor. April 17.

New York State Legislative Commission on State-Local Relations. 2001. *Catalog of state and federal program's aiding New York's local governments*.

New York Times. 1999. To reflect the city they serve (editorial), March 13.

Pasanen, Glenn. 2002. Editing out the facts. *Gotham Gazette*, October 2. www.gothamgazette.com/iotw/mayorsreport/doct1.shtml.

Pecorella, Robert. 1994. *Community power in a postreform city: politics in New York City.* Armonk, NY: M. E. Sharpe.

Polgreen, Lydia. 2002. A widening inquiry tarnished Giuliani's jail legacy. *New York Times*, December 3.

Roane, Kit. 1999. Elite force quells crime, but at a cost, critics say. *New York Times*, February 6.

Robin, Joshua. 2002. Mayor names new corrections chief. *Newsday*, December 26.

Rogers, David. 1990. Community control and decentralization. In *Urban politics: New York style* ed. Jewell Bellush and Dick Netzer, 143–187. Armonk, NY: M. E. Sharpe.

Rourke, Francis. 1984. *Bureaucracy, politics, and public policy.* 3rd ed. Boston: Little, Brown.

Sexton, Joe. 1996. State faults agency's inaction in overseeing foster children. *New York Times*, March 23.

Steinhauer, Jennifer. 2001. Bloomberg appointments trouble some GOP leaders. *New York Times*, December 13.

———. 2002. Bloomberg moves away from shift of inspectors. *New York Times*, February 22.

Walker, Jack. 1995. *The rebirth of federalism: slouching towards Washington.* New Jersey: Chatham House.

Webber, Rebecca. 2002. Department of Buildings. *Gotham Gazette*, February 8. www.gothamgazette.com/iotw/construction/.

Weikart, Lynn. 2001. The Giuliani administration and the new public management in New York City. *Urban Affairs Review* 36:3, 359–381.

Wilgoren, Jodi. 1999. Police profiling debate. *New York Times*, April 9.

Wilgoren, Jodi, and Michael Cooper. 1999. New York's police rank among most racially imbalanced in U.S. *New York Times*, March 8.

CHAPTER 10   CONCLUSION

Dahl, Robert. 1961. *Who governs?* New Haven, CT: Yale University Press.

Elkin, Stephen. 1985. *The democratic state.* Lawrence: University of Kansas Press.

Harding, Alan. 1995. Elite theory and growth machines. In *Theories of urban politics*, ed. David Judge et al. 35–53. London: Sage Publications.

Jonas, Andrew, and David Wilson. 1999. The city as growth machine: critical reflections two decades later. In *The urban growth machine: critical perspectives two decades later*, ed. Andrew Jonas and David Wilson, 3–20. Albany: State University of New York Press.

Logan, John, and Harvey Molotch. 1996. The city as growth machine. In *Readings in urban theory*, ed. Susan Fainstein and Scott Campbell, 291–337. Cambridge, MA: Blackwell.

Mossberger, Karen, and Gerry Stoker. 2001. The evolution of urban regime theory: the challenge of conceptualization. *Urban Affairs Review* 36 (July), 810–835.

Stoker, Gerry. 1995. Regime theory and urban politics. In *Theories of urban politics*, ed. David Judge et al. 55–71. London: Sage Publications.

Stone, Clarence. 1989. *Regime politics: governing Atlanta.* Lawrence: University of Kansas Press.

Index

ABOUT THE AUTHOR

BRUCE F. BERG is an associate professor of political science at Fordham University. He has published articles and book chapters on the delivery of health care to the elderly, interest group behavior, bureaucratic politics, program evaluation, and politics in the New York City metropolitan area. He has lived on the Upper West Side of Manhattan for the last thirty years.